RUNNING WITH REINDEER

RUNNING WITH REINDEER

Encounters in Russian Lapland

Roger Took

Westview
PRESS

A Member of the Perseus Books Group

Copyright © 2004 by Roger Took

Published in the United States of America by Westview Press, A Member of the Perseus
Books Group, 5500 Central Avenue, Boulder, Colorado 80301–2877, and in the United
Kingdom by Westview Press, 12 Hid's Copse Road, Cumnor Hill, Oxford OX2 9JJ.

Find us on the world wide web at www.westviewpress.com

Westview Press books are available at special discounts for bulk purchases in the United
States by corporations, institutions, and other organizations. For more information, please
contact the Special Markets Department at the Perseus Books Group, 11 Cambridge
Center, Cambridge, MA 02142, or call (617) 252–5298, (800) 255-1514 or email
j.mccrary@perseusbooks.com.

A Cataloging-in-Publication data record for this book is available
from the Library of Congress.
ISBN 0–8133–4210-4

First published in 2003 by John Murray (Publishers) Ltd,
50 Albemarle Street, London W1S 4BD

The paper used in this publication meets the requirements of the American National
Standard for Permanence of Paper for Printed Library Materials Z39.48–1984.

Typeface used in this text: Bembo

10 9 8 7 6 5 4 3 2 1

For my wife, Patricia Anne Cleary

And in memory of
Edward Rae of Birkenhead, explorer of Russian Lapland, 1879

Contents

Illustrations

Grateful acknowledgement is made to the following photographers and institutions for their kind permission to reproduce photographic material: Yulian Konstantinov, 7, 11; Vladimir Kuznetsov, 8, 12, 27; The London Library, 2–4; Aleksandr Raube, 30; Ivan Vdovin, 10, 29; Museum for the History of the Exploration of the Russian European North, Apatity, 19–22; Regional Museum, Murmansk, 9, 13–17; 23–25 (photos: Yevgeny Khaldey).

Photograph 5 is from Henry Pearson, *Three summers among the birds of Russian Lapland*, London: Porter, 1904; 6 is from Alexander Engelhardt, *A Russian province of the North*, London: Constable, 1899.

Photographs 1, 18, 26, 28 and 31 were taken by the author.

The elk motif at section openings is reproduced from a petroglyph at Lake Kanozero dating from 2,000–1,000 BC.

The Territory of Russian Lapland – Look for the Potato

Russian Lapland sits in the far north-west corner of the Russian Federation. It is still part of the old Soviet empire, yet its geography, its human history and its position on the world map of warfare and trade have produced divided cultures, confused identities and, not least, an assortment of names.

Historically the area contains the easternmost territories of the Lapps, or Saami, the ancient local people whose ancestral lands straddle much of northern Fennoscandia – that is, northern Sweden, Norway, Finland and the far north-west of Russia. During the Middle Ages, when Novgorod held sway, this part of Lapland – Sameland, or Sapme, as the Saami call it – was known to Novgorod fur-traders and fishermen as Tre, Ter, or Tersky Navolok, to Norsemen as Biarmia or Bjarmeland, and to most Westerners as Lappia or Lapland. Following Muscovy's overthrow of Novgorod in the fifteenth century and its colonization of the north-west, the territory became 'Russian', and was known internationally thereafter as 'Russian Lapland', a name that lasted until the twentieth century. However, with the Soviet Union's development of the region, followed by forced immigration and the demise of the indigenous Saami themselves, the name was officially dropped.

Russian Lapland today is largely contained within the boundaries of modern Murmansk *Oblast*, or Murmansk Region, an area measuring approximately 400 kilometres from north to south, 500 kilometres east to west. The oblast is also often referred to erroneously as the Kola Peninsula, so called after the prominent potato shape which protrudes towards the east and amounts to sixty per cent of Murmansk Region's 145,000 square kilometres.

Described over the centuries by some outsiders as bleak and

inhospitable, the region and its geography are deceptive. Most of the oblast lies north of the Arctic Circle, but benefits from the Gulf Stream and enjoys a generally cool climate without extremes of temperature. The warm season, which lasts from early June to mid-October and includes midsummer 'white nights' of non-stop sunshine, is unpredictable but generally 'comfortable', with July temperatures ranging between 8 and 14 degrees Celsius. The cold season, which can bring heavy snowfall at any time between October and mid-May and can occasionally produce temperatures of minus 35 degrees, has an average January temperature of minus 12 to 15 degrees in the interior and a mere minus 8 on the littoral. The notorious 'polar nights' of midwinter, when the sun hides below the horizon for nearly two months, bring little more than pale gloom at midday, yet even at this time of the year the cold may be crisp and invigorating.

Almost the entire region's terrain can be described as open undulating tundra in the north, changing to taiga – boreal forest and bog – in the south. A dividing line in this respect can be drawn approximately diagonally from the north-west to the south-east. The mountain ranges are relatively small, with few peaks above 1,000 metres high; more typically, the undulating tundra uplands rise to around 300 metres above sea level. There are thousands of lakes and rivers, and for this reason the whole area is sometimes presumed to be predominantly wetland and bog, but these features amount only to about six per cent of the region. Far more common are the dry, open spaces of the lichen-covered tundra or the firm, open floor of the taiga forest with the ground-cover rich in mosses, berries and mushrooms.

In modern times Russian Lapland is perhaps best known for the large port of Murmansk which played a prominent role in both World Wars, as well as for the natural harbours of the Barents Sea coast which since the Cold War have been home to a formidable, if fated, nuclear-powered fleet. Infamous among ecologists are the two large nickel-smelting plants at Monchegorsk and Nikel in the Region's west, which have damaged thousands of square kilometres of tundra and taiga and sent noxious airborne emissions into neighbouring Scandinavia. In contrast to this, most of the region – and in particular the roadless east – preserves one of Europe's last and largest wilderness areas where rivers teem with salmon, and birds of prey raise healthy broods of young.

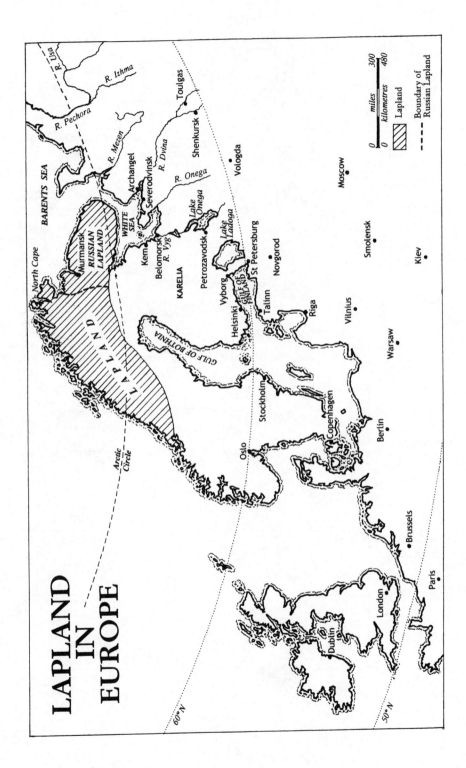

LAPLAND IN EUROPE

R. Usa

R. Izhma

R. Pechora

R. Mezen

Toulgas

R. Dvina

Shenkursk

Archangel

Severodvinsk

R. Onega

Vologda

BARENTS SEA

WHITE SEA

Lake Onega

Murmansk

RUSSIAN LAPLAND

Kem

Belomorsk

R. Vyg

Lake Ladoga

Moscow

North Cape

KARELIA

Petrozavodsk

St Petersburg

Smolensk

Vyborg

Novgorod

L A P L A N D

FINLAND

Helsinki

Tallinn

Riga

Kiev

GULF OF FINLAND

Vilnius

GULF OF BOTHNIA

Warsaw

Arctic Circle

Stockholm

Oslo

Copenhagen

Berlin

Brussels

Paris

London

Dublin

60°N

50°N

miles 300
kilometres 480
0

Lapland

Boundary of
Russian Lapland

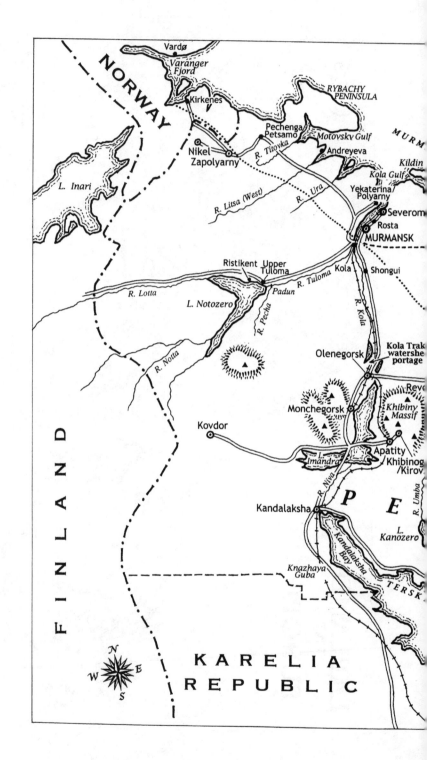

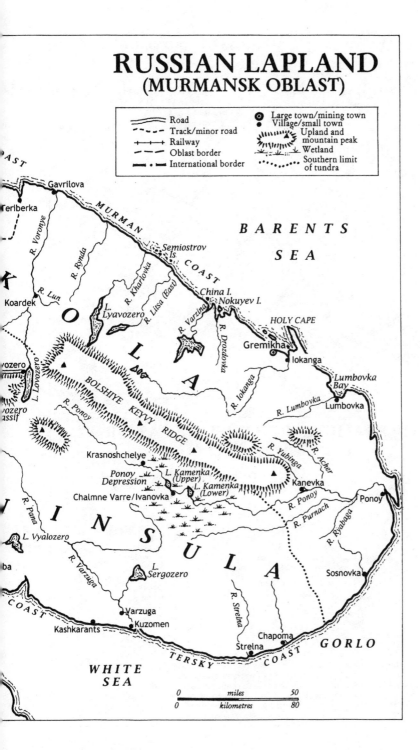

RUSSIAN LAPLAND
(MURMANSK OBLAST)

Road
Track/minor road
Railway
Oblast border
International border

Large town/mining town
Village/small town
Upland and mountain peak
Wetland
Southern limit of tundra

AST

Gavrilova

Teriberka

MURMAN

BARENTS

SEA

R. Voronye

R. Rynda

Semiostrov Is.

COAST

R. Lun

Koardek

L. Lyavozero

R. Kharlovka

R. Litsa (East)

China I.

Nokuyev I.

R. Varzina

HOLY CAPE

ozero

R. Drozdovka

Gremikha

Iokanga

K

O

L

A

R. Iokanga

Lumbovka Bay

L. Lovozero

BOLSHIYE KEYVY RIDGE

R. Lumbovka

Lumbovka

ozero
assif

R. Ponoy

Krasnoshchelye

R. Yubinga

R. Acher

Ponoy Depression

L. Kamenka (Upper)

L. Kamenka (Lower)

Kanevka

Chalmne Varre/Ivanovka

Ponoy

J

I

N

S

U

L

A

R. Pana

R. Ponoy

R. Purnach

R. Ryabaga

L. Vyalozero

ba

R. Varzuga

L. Sergozero

Sosnovka

R. Strelna

Varzuga

Kuzomen

Kashkarants

Chapoma

GORLO

Strelna

COAST

TERSKY

COAST

WHITE
SEA

| 0 | miles | 50 |
| 0 | kilometres | 80 |

MEDIEVAL TRADE ROUTES FROM NOVGOROD

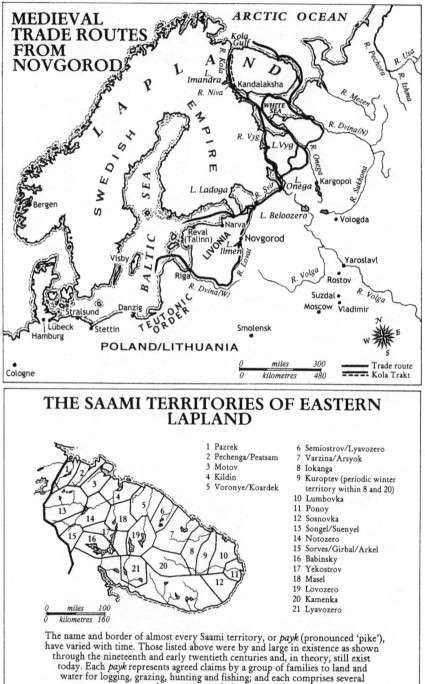

THE SAAMI TERRITORIES OF EASTERN LAPLAND

1 Pazrek
2 Pechenga/Peatsam
3 Motov
4 Kildin
5 Voronye/Koardek
6 Semiostrov/Lyavozero
7 Varzina/Arsyok
8 Iokanga
9 Kuroptev (periodic winter territory within 8 and 20)
10 Lumbovka
11 Ponoy
12 Sosnovka
13 Songel/Suenyel
14 Notozero
15 Sorves/Girbal/Arkel
16 Babinsky
17 Yekostrov
18 Masel
19 Lovozero
20 Kamenka
21 Lyavozero

The name and border of almost every Saami territory, or *payk* (pronounced 'pike'),
have varied with time. Those listed above were by and large in existence as shown
through the nineteenth and early twentieth centuries and, in theory, still exist
today. Each *payk* represents agreed claims by a group of families to land and
water for logging, grazing, hunting and fishing; and each comprises several
seasonal encampments (*seit, seyt,* or *siit*)

I

ENGLISHMAN ABROAD

Herders

THE REINDEER TEAMS were working well. The dogs ran with us, now alongside the sledges, now tearing away into the forest after ptarmigan, barking excitedly. Vokan moved in crisp Bruegelesque profile against the snow, jet-black on dazzling white under a crystal sky; Norka had stopped to roll, snatching a mouthful of snow before shaking herself and rushing on. For long periods there was little sound apart from Sasha's gentle exhortations to the three draught bulls, the hypnotic swish of the sledge runners and the clicking of tendons. We were trying a recruit at the number three position. The young buck was proving slow to learn; by pulling a little more weight he could avoid catching his fetlocks against the front of the sledge. To my suggestion that he adjust the harness, Sasha grunted:

'He'll get the idea in a day or two, stop fretting.'

'What happens if he doesn't learn?'

'I just kill him; meat's important too.'

Sensing my discomfort Sasha drew the team up and shortened the harness to keep the buck further forward.

We were on our way to herd 1. The other sledge was driven by Afanasy, the head of the reindeer-herding brigade – the *brigadir*.

'We have to bring some of the deer into the corral,' he had explained before we left the village. 'We'll join the duty crew in the forest and take a look at the herd there first.'

'We expect to find them somewhere here.' Sasha pointed to a spot on my map. His facility with my map always surprised me. His family didn't own or use maps. I never saw a herder use a map.

We had travelled the better part of the day almost without stopping and I was rigid with cold even in my deerskins. When Sasha signalled that we were getting near our campsite for the night, I was eager to

3

be off the sledge and active. Within a kilometre we turned towards some low hills. Soon, ahead of us, standing among old pine trees in an open part of the forest but sheltered by a ridge, was a large conical frame of spruce poles that identified the place as a regular campsite. Herders favoured this one in particular for its copious lichen and the spring that flowed throughout the winter.

The unharnessed reindeer shook themselves, then Sasha and Afanasy roped them and walked them further into the forest towards the lichen pastures. As each animal was tethered to its tree it burrowed and scooped vigorously with its large front hooves, sending snow flying in all directions, searching for a succulent supper one metre down.

We unloaded the rolls of canvas from the sledge and I watched the two men open the large sheets and throw them up on to the spruce frame, pushing them into position with the long reindeer-driving poles and securing the guy ropes to the trees. They were adept; even after a few years it still took me several efforts at throwing and prodding the heavy canvases on to the frame before I got them just right. At Sasha's suggestion I collected fresh spruce branches and spread them on the snow to start a floor for the *kuvaksa*, the herders' tent. A few blackened rocks, retrieved from under the snow, made a ring for our fire, and the lateral wooden rod which was ready-lashed in position between the poles would be the crane for our cauldron and kettle. Over the spruce branches Afanasy threw several reindeer skins, I fetched my rucksack and sleeping bag, and the place began to look like home.

A pile of split logs had been left at the site, stacked in the traditional manner for the next incumbents; this left me the easy task of collecting birch bark and kindling wood while Afanasy and Sasha prepared food. The fire crackled and hissed into life, catching first on the resin of the birch bark and then consuming the dry pine twigs and the dead juniper branches, sending rich smoke billowing around the conical canvas walls and filling the *kuvaksa* before being drawn up through the small hole at the apex. Sasha was peeling potatoes. I sliced some cheese and sausage. Afanasy cut reindeer meat into small pieces which he then pushed on to whittled green birch skewers. These he stood upright in front of the fire ready for the birch logs to give off heat. Sasha went outside to check the sledges, the reindeer and the dogs.

'Roll us one of those,' said Afanasy, seeing me get out my tobacco pouch. My hand-rolled cigarettes were always popular, and I was pleased to have something to offer. During my early days in Russian Lapland, when my command of Russian was particularly limited, the cigarettes were so good at stimulating conversations with strangers that I called them 'icebreakers'.

With darkness the temperature outside fell swiftly to minus 20 Celsius but we had staked a refuge within our poled fortress. Although the wall that separated the outside air from the radiating warmth of the fire was only millimetres thick it enclosed a comfortably habitable space: the *kuvaksa* was a warm island in a cold sea. The dented black kettle and the heavy iron cauldron of boiling potatoes hung steaming from the crane. We smoked and waited in silence, feeding the fire with birch logs, turning the standing skewers as the meat coloured.

After supper – modest by herder standards – the *brigadir* and Sasha reverted to smoking strong Belomor cigarettes, their knees drawn up to their chins as they stared into the fire, talking spasmodically to each other, now in Russian, now in Saami.

'*Rodzher*,' said Sasha, turning to me and grinning broadly, 'didn't I see you putting some vodka into your rucksack before we left the village?'

In the morning Sasha and Afanasy were up before me. When I awoke they were relighting the fire, filling the *kuvaksa* with smoke. I stayed down in my bag until it cleared and the air warmed. I wasn't anxious to be up and out.

After breakfast we waited for the duty crew to arrive. We heard the barking dogs from a distance well before the sledges were within sight. As the three teams of reindeer appeared at the edge of the forest I heard the familiar short guttural sounds of the drivers urging them through the drifted snow and then, as they came on, the farts and grunts of the deer themselves, excited at their arrival. Leaving the deer near ours among the trees to dig down to the lichen, the herders – I counted a dozen – walked over to exchange greetings with Sasha and the *brigadir*, shaking hands with them but introducing themselves to me from a distance with characteristic reticence. The men stood discussing tactics, smoking, stamping their feet, hugging their chests for warmth.

'We expect to locate the deer fairly easily this morning,' Sasha explained to me afterwards, 'and then we'll try to bring some of them into the corral. We'll travel by sledge at first and then switch to skis.' I was dubious about my skiing competence but he assured me I was not required to do anything. I had only to stay by the corral.

After we had drunk tea all five teams departed in convoy. Within the hour we had caught sight of a few reindeer grazing among sparse small pines and spruces. Then the remainder of the herd, remarkably well camouflaged, appeared in the forest on the rising hill beyond: hundreds of them, maybe a thousand. Our presence alerted them and they moved slowly away.

From this point *Brigadir* Afanasy and eight men were to move carefully ahead and skirt the herd at a distance on skis; Sasha and the others would take me with them to the corral. I watched Afanasy as he put on his skis and took off his heavy deerskin *malitsa* for the hot work ahead. Alongside the young crew, who had been out in the forest base camp for four weeks and now looked rough, he cut a fine figure – the classic reindeer herdsman. His woollen *sovik* (smock) was of superior quality, the hood and hem trimmed with the soft, grey-brown pelage of a calf. At the waist his smock bloused over the indispensable *tazma,* a broad leather belt decorated with brass medallions and small antler pendants, from which a large sheath-knife hung low on the left side.

The skiers moved off and disappeared among the trees. We turned north, with the dogs tied on at the back.

Corralling is a delicate manoeuvre at any time, especially if there are only a few herdsmen available to press from behind or appear at the sides at the last moment. The deer must feel settled and confident about the route they are taking. One hesitation from the leading animals and the rest of the herd take fright and retreat into the forest in panic.

Our wooden corral formed a circle of about sixty metres in diameter with two long converging fences that acted as a funnel. Considered more of a liability than an asset, I was instructed to stay hidden. I found shelter behind a small hut and waited. Sasha had done some explaining before leaving me on my own.

'We complete most of the corralling and local slaughtering by

January. After that we herd thousands of animals the long distance to the slaughterhouse at Lovozero. Later in the season, like now, we sometimes need to bring in part of the remaining herd if we notice disease or have to do some castration, or need more meat for ourselves. Don't be disappointed if we don't manage to bring them in. Sometimes they get nervous and just won't move on.'

After two long cold hours I was woken from my daydreaming by the deep clonk-clonk of a bell, very faint for a long time, then louder and nearer. It seemed an age before the first deer emerged from the trees. From my hiding-place in the cabin I saw the *brigadir* leading one of the large bulls. Behind him was another reindeer, a bell hanging from his neck, a grand beast with a deep chest and near-full set of antlers – a metre long and with copious branches, in spite of the season – his head high, scenting suspiciously. He was the real leader, the one the others would trust and follow. Behind him came the first wave of the animal flood: black, white, and many shades of dun, grey and brown, at first gradually, in small groups, then a throng of undulating fur, loping, trotting, some of the animals throwing their heads nervously, the calves close to their mothers. As they came into the lead fences the air was shaking with the presence of snorting, grunting animals. I shivered with suppressed excitement. It was an astonishing, unforgettable sight. A primordial ritual.

The herd approached the inner corral. Moving on through the opening, they broke into a trot, then a canter, circling the perimeter, forming a dense cloud of snow, obscuring the *brigadir* and the small team left standing in the middle.

Everything happened in a flurry. Sasha worked close to the *brigadir* amongst the swirling beasts, one moment hidden from sight, the next in apparently mortal combat with the unfortunate deer that had been identified, lassoed and brought down.

Old-style castration – occasionally still practised – is invariably done by mouth: one man pins the deer to the ground, sitting on the neck and holding the head or antlers, while his companion kneels at the other end, forcing the hind legs apart, taking one testicle at a time firmly in the mouth and biting. The testicles come free in the scrotum like large plums and the whole operation, which is said to be hygienic – for the reindeer – is completed by simply massaging the pouch. Today's emasculator looked like a pair of long-handled pincers. The unfortunate victims put up a valiant struggle but then just got up, shook themselves and trotted away to join their friends.

Twenty or more deer were caught, either by hand or lasso, for reasons not all clear to me, and three of the captives were slaughtered by Afanasy. As the first animal was held firm I had not noticed the knife being drawn; it was only the abruptness with which it went down that caused me to notice that it had been dealt a swift stab in the neck and had fallen unconscious. The herdsman made a further plunge into the heart, twisting the blade several times, leaving it in the flesh for a while in order to ensure that the blood drained into the chest cavity.

The corral was opened, the herd released. Free to pour through the fence, the deer jostled frantically to return to liberty and lichen. The thunder of the hooves and the wild grunting died as the last animals disappeared into the trees. Only the dead animals remained where they had fallen. Sasha and the *brigadir* walked over to where I was standing outside the fence with members of the crew.

'He's learning about reindeer,' said Sasha, explaining my presence to the others, tossing his head at me and grinning gold. It was not in his nature to be sarcastic but I wasn't certain.

They shoot reindeer, don't they?

THE HERDERS joked and smoked, leaning on the picket fences, coiling their hide lassos or idly sharpening their knives (they were always bringing out small sharpening stones from a pocket deep inside their bulky *malitsy*). I understood little of what they were saying. Whenever they got together as a group or put their feet round the fire I could still barely follow the conversation, whether it was in Russian, Saami or Komi.

If the herders were curious about my presence among them, I hardly understood myself what I was doing in the north-west corner of Russia in the first place. I still don't fully understand. I dislike the cold, I can't cope with bogs, and, like the reindeer, I abhor mosquitoes.

My wife Pat liked to say that I went for the fishing. But that's not the whole story and, as it turned out, I was there more during the months when the rivers were frozen. I'd read an article by Steinar Wikan, a Norwegian conservationist: 'The region is probably the largest area of uninterrupted natural landscape in Europe,' he wrote. 'I call it Europe's last wilderness.' I was hooked. And I wanted to see Russia while it was changing.

How does one 'see Russia?' I asked myself. With a country so large, where does one start? I didn't want to go to Moscow (the wrong kind of wilderness), and I didn't want to go to St Petersburg (too much European culture). Like the British admirals staging punitive raids during the Crimean conflict of 1854–56, I picked on Russian Lapland: it was near home, probably easy to get to, not too large, not too cold, not too hot. It also had few roads, and therefore might be sufficiently exotic for a first-time visitor to Russia. It seemed as good a place as any for an adventure. And I was cartographically bewitched from the start: I liked its potato shape.

I rushed there before I could learn anything that might change my mind.

*

One of my best investments prior to departure was a crash course of one-to-one lessons in Russian from Dmitry Nikolayevich, a talented linguist who used to run his own department at Moscow State University and had just moved to London. Sensing the urgency of my requirements, Dmitry worked me hard and did a fine job. But in one sense he wasn't the person I needed. He was soon asking me questions about my planned adventure, and during our second week he could no longer contain his concern.

'Listen, Roger. You've done well with your Russian but you're heading for a region where nobody speaks English and probably not everybody speaks Russian. You insist on travelling alone, you know nobody on the Kola Peninsula, and you don't even know anyone in all Russia. You've found little practical information about the region and you've only got large-scale US aeronautical maps. I see no roads, I see thousands of square kilometres of bog, I see empty tundra with no settlements – the little huts marked on the map mean nothing – and your map indicates only winter trails which will be useless during the summer months.

'You're travelling by the single-line railway from St Petersburg to Murmansk and your train won't have an armed guard. There's been trouble everywhere with gunmen on the line stopping trains.* As you probably know, many of the prisoners who were released from the *gulag* in the north following the amnesties have now settled there. You've no idea what you could be walking into, especially in remote country. I sincerely advise you to reconsider this journey.'

Dmitry was not the only Russian with whom I had difficulty discussing my intended journey. A number of chance acquaintances in London had advised me against the expedition on grounds of physical danger, and on the telephone to my prospective in-transit hosts in St Petersburg I received further negative responses.

'We can't be held responsible for your physical safety if you leave for the north,' I was reminded at the end of every conversation.

---

* Even Aleksandr Solzhenitsyn was not immune. On his return from exile in 1994, his train was boarded by armed thieves between Vladivostok and Moscow, in spite of the presence of television cameras.

In the early 1990s the new criminal bosses were still fighting their turf wars in Russia, and the hardship and turmoil caused by Gaidar's economic policies had created a volatile society where resentment was often directed at Westerners, who were deemed partly responsible for Russia's demise. I was told that I could expect to be set upon for my cash, and in the open country I could well be shot at. A lone foreigner travelling in the middle of nowhere could be presumed to be carrying dollars, and who was to know where or how, in the vast taiga and tundra or along fast-flowing rivers, I might meet my end? The thought of having to carry a firearm did not appeal to me. Even under the abnormal circumstances of the time it felt excessive, but certain Russians whom I consulted said there was no alternative if I were to be sure of my physical safety.

I was put in touch with a pair who owned premises under railway arches in South London. Here, I was assured, I could learn all I needed to know about killing people before they could kill me. The unnerving procedure of contacting my would-be instructors and then making my way at night through the unfamiliar and intimidating hinterland of railway arches and lockups was enough almost to put an end to the whole enterprise but, finding myself in capable hands, I was soon enrolled in the fraternity to whom gun-ownership is an inalienable right. I was passed to Mike, an ex-SAS man in his thirties. First I learned how to avoid police, organized criminals and petty thieves. Then came the hardware. I learned how to fire, strip and reassemble a 9-mm semi-automatic, how to judge ammunition quality ('it's more than likely you'll be offered deficient or recycled shells'), and how to carry a gun unobtrusively about my person.

Mike constantly reminded me that my gun was 'not for waving or pointing'; it was for killing a human being outright, preferably with one shot to the heart. The only time I was to draw the gun was to shoot and kill; about that there must be no confusion.

My heart sank further. The whole exercise seemed to be removing me far away from the kind of adventure I had originally envisaged.

*

Arriving in St Petersburg I had the onerous task of coping at first hand with my 'visa hosts' Roman and Larisa, a depressive Russian couple in their forties who had fallen on hard times and, probably as a result, looked a lot older. Roman, as I had suspected from my telephone conversations, had a grovelling respect for authority and bureaucracy, and at the visa office he had been asked a 'string of very difficult questions' about me.

Once I had settled in, Roman and Larisa set about the task of weakening my resolve with vigour. They had made enquiries about Murmansk Region, they said, and learned that I would not be allowed to travel around on my own. Did I know I was going to a closed military zone? There were almost no roads outside the concentrated string of mining towns. How would I travel? Where and with whom would I live? The people were quite 'wild' and 'primitive'. And had I heard about the amnesty for prison convicts in the region? (I never managed to get any reliable information on the subject.) Was I aware of the amount of theft on trains in Russia and that there would be no armed guard on the train from St Petersburg? They considered it quite out of the question, anyway, that I would be able to travel without a better command of spoken Russian (this point worried me).

Light relief came during my last two Russian lessons with Larisa. Her attitude had changed. She seemed resigned to my journey and had prepared a repertoire of what she called 'essential vocabulary and colloquialisms for travelling in the country'. She made sure that I knew how to give an account of myself when arriving at remote settlements, that I knew the names of the berries, mushrooms, trees and animals that I would commonly encounter, and finally she told me about the protocol of the *banya*, the village steam baths: the bowls, the *veniki* (birch twigs), the back-rubbing towels, and so on. I was relieved to see that these particular lessons brought on a happier, nostalgic mood in my teacher as she recalled better times in the company of her parents at the family dacha.

Before I left London, close friends had been politely suggesting that I might have become unnecessarily concerned with the survival aspects of my adventure. I had confidently dismissed such observations, basing my precautions on an instructive book by Frith Maier, an American woman with long and *recent* trekking experience of remote Russia and Central Asia. I had accordingly equipped myself with a full complement of military combat fatigues and a second-hand pair of Soviet Army leather jackboots. However, by the time I was making my way on a hot evening in late May through the picturesque centre of historic St Petersburg, carrying a large rucksack disguised with bespoke soiling and a holdall sewn into a malodorous sack taken from my stable in Ireland, to join the orderly and polite Russian families boarding the sleeper train to the north, I felt self-conscious, if not absurd.

My first Russian train journey was sociable and homely. The adult passengers had soon changed into comfortable clothing and were shuffling to and fro in slippers as if in the intimacy of their apartments. Everyone seemed to carry more food than luggage, whereas I carried more luggage than food. My carriage, which steadily assumed a character of its own, was fussed over by a woman attendant, a *provodnitsa*, who distributed bedding and ensured that everyone had a plentiful supply of tea from the urn at the end of the corridor. As we drew out of St Petersburg she was taking great care that passengers in each compartment were well matched, shuffling individuals or whole families until she was satisfied. Having been allocated a compartment together with a sullen family who were travelling with an unhappy, restless boxer dog, I also benefited from her attentions and was settled into a compartment with one other passenger, a naval officer in his early thirties headed for Murmansk.

'I've had to leave my wife and small son in St Petersburg,' said my neighbour, introducing himself as Aleksandr Melnikov. 'I won't see them for a year.'

He was on his way to the far north-east of the Kola Peninsula, to Gremikha, one of the strategic submarine bases of the Northern Fleet. 'I'm a designer. I design everything for the ships, except the ships themselves,' he explained.

Aleksandr was copiously supplied with food which had been lovingly prepared and packed by his wife. On seeing my paltry provisions, he insisted on my sharing his. I was lucky to be engaged in conversation with this amiable man who spoke clear, simple, slow Russian for my benefit, sharing beer and cigarettes, discussing the merits of Manchester United and Chelsea, his own team Spartak, British soccer hooliganism (of world renown), and the relative merits of rugby and ice hockey.

13

The journey was occasionally broken by long stops at the major railway stations. Most passengers, including myself, disembarked for a smoke and some leg-stretching. I took the opportunity to practise my Russian phrases on the local population who were selling produce and salt-fish or simply passing time on the platforms. On one of these occasions I was asked to explain my attire.

'Why are you wearing Russian Army boots? And why do you dress like a soldier anyway? It doesn't look ... well ... friendly.'

It was unlikely I would come to harm on the train journey. Our *provodnitsa*, whom I now knew as Olga Vasilyevna, kept a watching brief over Aleksandr and me as if we were her only charges. She implied, however, that in her ten-year stint on the railway – she had taken the job when her husband left home – she had never felt so concerned about a newcomer to the region. She found my intentions of exploration vague to the point of irresponsibility, but by now I was recognizing the irksome, though well-intentioned, Russian reluctance to allow a foreigner to travel anywhere unaccompanied. I tried to reassure her.

'Well, if you get into any sort of trouble you must make your way to my home in Kola town. It's very near Murmansk. Here's my address.'

A seamless forest of birch and pine, with occasional views of rivers and lakeside hamlets, continued for much of the two-day, two-night journey. Instead of finding it tedious – there is, after all, a limit to the pleasure or interest to be had from watching more than a thousand kilometres of forest pass the window – I found it reassuring. I was at last entering the Russia that I wanted to see and which had been so long in coming. The last phase of the journey ran parallel to the White Sea coast and through the Karelian town of Kem.

Shortly after passing out of Karelia, we crossed the Arctic Circle and drank toasts: to Aleksandr's wife and son, to Olga Vasilyevna's grandchildren, and to my Lapland adventure that lay ahead. When we pulled into the town of Kandalaksha, at the north-western corner of the White Sea, we had arrived in Russian Lapland proper.

A pioneer port

THE BUS INTO Murmansk was almost empty. The tall, thin ticket-collector – a kindly but exhausted-looking woman – came for the fare, asked me extra for my baggage, ambled to the driver's booth, exchanged a desultory word, and then slumped into her own seat. With the diesel engine beneath the floor at the back roaring in the lower ratios, the bus rattled ahead, using the full breadth of the empty road to negotiate the potholes.

After a few kilometres we took on board a single passenger, a man who had been standing at a decayed concrete shelter. I absent-mindedly watched him offer his veteran's card, and resumed my scrutiny of the bus interior. The ticket-collector's area was separated by vertical and horizontal handrails, its shabby but amply upholstered seat raised on a dais. On the floor to the side of the seat was a bucket filled with grey wood ash, to provide extra comfort during the winter rotas, during the long polar nights when the subzero air temperature sent the mist rolling off the warm waters of the Kola Gulf and across the port, icing the quayside gantries, the ship superstructures and the overhead railway cables, searing the windows of the Murmansk Shipping Company and the Fish Port offices. Each time, after that first journey along the eastern shore of the Kola Gulf, whenever I looked down at the year-round-ice-free Gulf Stream tidal waters – a cocktail of warm salt from the Barents Sea and bog-tinted sweetness from the interior – my imagination was activated. At first this must have been because I too had been brought up in a port – the port of Dover – that had played an important role in the twentieth century but which was now in decline; in the years that followed, it was because my historical awareness was fused with ambivalence.

That first approach to Murmansk was on a warm early June weekend when the afternoon sun was blazing and the Gulf waters almost invited one to swim. The bus came out of a long bend through birch trees, all of which were in new leaf, and drew up at the next stop where a large crowd of people surged towards the bus, bringing the dormant ticket-collector to her feet. Within moments the doors had admitted what seemed like a substantial proportion of the port's population.

I looked out over a cemetery wall on the left and open ground on the right. Spread over several acres, cheek by jowl in all directions, were gravestones. Many of these stood within iron railing enclosures, where countless family groups had today thrown colourful cloths over the permanent tables and set them with provisions for their graveside sojourn. It was *Svyataya Troitsa*, Holy Trinity. Some people were still unloading baskets of sausage, salt-fish, salads, loaves of bread and bottles of beer and vodka, but many were at the postprandial stage or already packed and ready for the fifteen-kilometre journey home. With a *babushka* almost in my lap I offered my seat and stood up to squeeze among the old and young who were trying to stay in contact with their baskets and boxes, patiently awaiting departure and exchanging good-natured banter. When the bus finally lurched forward I was thrust among the bosoms of the people whom I had come such a long way to see.

Arriving at the bus terminal and being ignorant about Murmansk, I sought solace at the town's flagship hotel, the Arktika, a bland sixteen-storey building designed and built by Finns in the 1970s. It dominated the central Five Corners Square where it was complemented by an ugly three-storey shopping centre and a tall building in the Soviet neo-brutalist style. Determined not to be intimidated by three surly leather-jacketed men standing inside the hotel entrance – they were exactly as I had imagined new-style Russian hoods would look – I crossed the bleak and empty lobby towards the reception desk. Before I arrived at the desk, however, I was distracted by the English conversation between a young, smartly dressed Russian woman and an elderly oriental man in a dark suit. She was helping him to plan his visit.

'I want open sea, the Arctic Ocean. I want aboriginal people.

Aboriginal people,' he was intoning, mantra-like. The man, who styled himself simply as Mr Soo, had been in town for two days but already had travel ambitions not dissimilar to my own; we were both interested in experiencing the coasts and the interior. Although she said she was in the middle of exams, the young woman, whose name was Olga, promised to help. She and I decided to keep in touch and parted company.

On learning that the Arktika hotel wished to charge me a foreigner's premium of 80 per cent on what seemed an exorbitant starting price for a room, I made for the alternative across the square, the brutalist Meridian Hotel (not to be confused with the international group of Meridien hotels). Passing through the double doors I found myself in a large low lobby that had the atmosphere of an underground car park and where more men in suits and leather jackets loured from the corners. These men, I was later reliably informed, were minders for the main rivals to the mob based at the Arktika. The reception desk, which I had difficulty identifying in the gloom, was managed by a woman who generously agreed to process my request for a room. Murmansk being a major port, I could hardly have been the first foreigner to have stayed there during the new era, but if she wanted to make a newcomer to Russia like myself feel nervous and unloved she knew how to do it. My status appeared to be in question. She shuffled papers in the back office, returned to examine my documents, telephoned colleagues for advice and spoke with the Visa and Residency Office. As I waited, I listened to the hotel entrance doors slamming, and flinched each time they crashed. The same doors were still slamming four years later.

More of the same was to come; when I stepped from the lift I was received by the duty lady, the *dezhurnaya*. This matron was responsible for the management of the floor, and monitored all comings and goings from a large desk with an old-technology telephone switchboard, placed at the end of a long corridor. She interrogated me briefly, showed me to my room, and asked me to be sure that I inform her of my intended movements. I soon understood why: the hotel was a stronghold of officers and sailors from the Northern Fleet and its visitors. If I had ever been inclined to do so, I could not have found a better place to acquaint myself with the activities of that most secretive and lethal protagonist of the former Cold War.

My first and overwhelming impression of Murmansk was its size; I was hardly prepared for its scale and spread. At the beginning of the century the town did not exist. After the Great War and the construction in 1916 of the railway from St Petersburg it was still no more than an untidy agglomeration of log cabins, huts and slums by the waterside with a socially diverse and disenchanted population of port and railway workers from all over the Russian Empire, the majority of whom had remained by default. By the end of the 1970s it was a city of almost 400,000 inhabitants, the largest town within the Arctic Circle, and a classic example of the Soviet Union's colonization of the Russian North.

As a first-time visitor to Russia, and like many Westerners before me, I was incredulous when confronted with the ubiquitous and deadening hand of Soviet architecture. A world superpower, which at one time could boast the most sophisticated nuclear-powered fleet on and under the seas, seemed to have given scant attention to the homes and offices in which the people of its cherished northern port were to live and work. The predominant visible heritage of the Soviet Union's seventy-year presence on the shores of the historic Kola Gulf consisted of ranks of five- and nine-storey concrete apartment blocks, all of which appeared to be in the late stages of their useful life. The older and smaller of these gauche and unnatural forms, built well after the Second World War largely by unskilled labourers – many of whom came from the region's prison camps – surrounded the port and occupied the lower levels. As Murmansk flourished and its population burgeoned, the larger, nine-storey, pre-fabricated versions marched up the higher ground. Most of these now closely resembled rusty metal filing cabinets, their ubiquity and uniformity only occasionally relieved by the dour pediments and ill-proportioned columns of stuccoed governmental and administrative buildings around the centre of town.

Arriving at the northern heights, I stood beneath the Second World War memorial, a giant concrete sculpture of a Soviet infantry-man gazing west towards the tundra battle-lines 80 kilometres away where the Germans' surprise invasion of 1941 was halted and

famously held until repelled in 1944. From here I was able to comprehend the size of the Gulf and the scale of the port operation.
Twenty kilometres away down the Gulf and towards the open sea was
the Northern Fleet's large closed-town headquarters of Severomorsk.
This was out of sight, but my panorama included much of the naval
docks of Rosta and the Murmansk Shipping Company's base for its
nuclear-powered icebreakers, as well as the cargo quays, the ship-
repair yards, the fish port and the oil terminal. A few vessels of
varying sizes were moving up and down the Gulf or lying at anchor.

From this vantage-point it was possible to understand the allure of
Murmansk to the hundreds of thousands of Soviet citizens who had
flocked north in the 1960s and 1970s, not just for work but also for
the coveted Arctic premium, the so-called *polyarki*, that would earn
them up to 100 per cent on top of the normal wage. Murmansk had
been earmarked for maximum investment, and its citizens were
promised good living conditions, long holidays and early retirement.
It was a boom town. For those who had been compelled throughout
the Stalin years to remain in their native village and to work for the
local collective, it had offered an escape with prospects. To younger
people the port had sounded an ideal place to raise a family and accu-
mulate a small fortune before returning south to retire.

By the 1960s Murmansk was teeming with ships. The fish industry
was flourishing, the strategically and economically important
Northern Sea Route, with Murmansk as its western terminus, had
been allocated top priority investment, and cargoes were at peak
levels. Concurrently also the Northern Fleet and its well-financed
bases were burgeoning, with naval personnel, their families and the
ancillary services all providing an additional layer to the flourishing
economy of arguably the richest town of the Russian North.*

One morning on a later occasion I received a message from an
acquaintance telling me that he had found a senior mariner to 'talk to
me about life at sea on the Soviet trawlers in the good days'. Using

---

* The population of the whole of Murmansk Oblast grew rapidly during the first two decades of
Communism, from well under 30,000 in 1920 to 290,000 in 1939. By 1989 it had reached 1,147,000. Of
this latter total probably 380,000 (including families) were associated with defence, the Northern Fleet
alone accounting for up to 130,000. The population of Murmansk port town alone reached 440,000 in
1989 before declining to about 360,000 in 2001.

his apartment for the interview, I prepared a handsome meal and laid on vodka in expectation of a long evening's listening to a rough-and-tough sea-salt with a repertoire of tales from the deep, but the person who rang the door bell was a sleek, athletic, well-groomed man in his forties with a whiff of quality eau-de-cologne.

Viktor had seen the last of the good times with the Murmansk fishing fleet. As a union representative he had enjoyed frequent contact with his foreign counterparts and seemed amply qualified to tell me all I could ever want to know about the world's former major player in the fish industry. He declined my food and drink, talked non-stop and, with well-turned phrases, recited his life story for nearly three hours. Naval salt ran in his family's blood, and his father had been a submariner, but Viktor himself had not been tempted to aim for a naval commission. Setting his sights on more profitable work, he had entered the USSR State Fisheries Marine Institute in Murmansk. In the 1970s it was prestigious and highly competitive; all the big managers had studied or lectured there at one time or another. When he eventually signed up with the fishing fleet as a graduate from the institute, he reckoned he was 'at the top of the heap'.

As well as the thousands of small trawlers working locally in the White Sea and the Barents there were usually at least 200 large fishery ships based at Murmansk. These stayed at sea for years and sailed long distances between the Atlantic and the Pacific, processing millions of tonnes of fish from their own fleet as well as catches from the ships of other countries, British trawlers included. Crew were flown to the ships and back. Viktor had worked on the processing side in one of the large vessels, the ones that came to be called factory ships, which had refrigerated hulls holding up to 5,000 tonnes of filleted fish. When the factory ships were full they were directed to an unloading point. This could have been at Murmansk itself or at one of the Soviet Union's fish stations in Peru, Chile or Morocco. Murmansk had the best processing plants – 'even superior to Norway's' – employing thousands of Murmanchaners and paying them handsomely.

Viktor explained the demise of the Soviet fleets. 'When perestroika came we had already been suffering from severe quota limits. The quotas affected everyone internationally in the 1980s but on our scale they were devastating. The other major problem was the lack of investment in new ships; most of our vessels were designed in the 1940s, built in the 1960s, rotting by the 1980s, and hopelessly out-of-date and uncompetitive by the 1990s. With planning and patience the fleets might have survived all this. But the so-called liberated economy resulted everywhere in the wholesale "redistribution" of property, almost before anyone knew what was happening. Well-financed business partnerships had unimagined opportunities to take over different branches of the fish industry, political bosses and people in the right positions at the right time made a killing, and our world-wide systems fragmented to where they are now. *Sovrybflot*, for example, the former central organizer for the whole of the northern-based fish industry, controlled some 500 vessels. Although its would-be successor *Sevryb* – Northern Fisheries – is a completely different animal, it neither owns nor controls a single ship. Whole fleets have sailed away into offshore bank accounts.

'Today, small fishing cooperatives are trying to do everything on their own. Most of them won't survive. Two friends of mine recently bought a dying cooperative with two small boats and four men. They're out there now in the Barents Sea fishing for cod, trailing five-kilometre lines with baited hooks. It's a technique that was used by the very first Slavs who fished up here hundreds of years ago.'

For the cultured or professional classes arriving from the south in the boom years Murmansk was not always the place of their dreams. 'I met my husband on a summer holiday in the Crimea in 1956,' said Lyudmila Ilinichna, a petite, quiet-spoken widow in her sixties who later became my landlady. 'My husband was an ear-nose-and-throat specialist who was born here and was working for the Northern Fleet at the time. In 1957 we got married and he whisked me away from Leningrad with the promise of a good life and a good income. Well . . . arriving at the naval base of Polyarny, near Murmansk, was a shock.' I pictured Murmansk of the 1950s, with its large multi-ethnic immigrant population, as a rough-and-tumble town, typical of pioneer ports throughout the world, with drunken fights on pay-days.

'No,' Lyudmila Ilinichna replied, 'it was a "clean" town. It felt European for a start, and wasn't a rough place like Vladivostok. The immigrant labourers were honest hard-working people, and there was little crime or serious friction in spite of the fact that for a long time there was a shortage of apartments, with everyone crammed like sardines into substandard temporary wooden homes with communal outside toilets and water from a standing pipe, or from a well in winter ... There was building mess everywhere but that was all part of the pervasive optimism. Most of us felt we were part of a larger enterprise. The state had a way of making us feel we were a privileged community in Murmansk and important to the national economy.'

Mikhail Mikhaylovich, who had immigrated from the Ukraine in the early 1960s and was now returning home to his roots, painted a different picture, not of Murmansk but of nearby Zapolyarny, which was then a new town mining nickel.

'It was an enormous relief to have the opportunity to escape from our village in the Ukraine but there was a lot of competition in the post-Stalin years for the better places. What I found when I got to Zapolyarny was worse than I expected. The town was sited on the bleak tundra not far from the coast. It was a lawless place, full of chancers. Many of the people that moved there had been long-term prisoners in labour camps and knew how to operate every racket under the sun. They seemed to have come from a different planet. I wouldn't have survived there if I hadn't become tough and learned a few tricks myself.'

Others came for more personal reasons. In the early 1970s young Galina Aleksandrovna was working as an intern at a hospital in Sudak, a Soviet Black Sea resort in the Crimea. She became friendly with a family from Murmansk that spent their summer holidays there, and in 1972 decided to move north. I could hardly believe the reason.

'I was keen to get married and raise a family and there weren't many suitable men in the Crimea – they were mostly Tatars or, worse, Armenians – but I had heard that Murmansk was a great place for work and ideal for meeting young men. There were men everywhere, I was told. Thousands worked in the fish industry or on the ships and there were endless numbers of bachelors in the navy and the army.

'I liked Murmansk from the start. It was an energetic, optimistic place. Everything seemed to be going for it. I got work at the Regional Hospital, made friends and, yes, there were masses of gorgeous young men. I got married in 1978. It was just unfortunate that I ended up with a Lapp who was an alcoholic. We parted soon after I gave birth to my twin girls, Lena and Tanya.'

Sitting in Galina's kitchen on the seventh floor of her apartment building in the northern part of town, I looked out at the rows of nine-storey buildings all around. She described to me how these buildings started going up everywhere in the late 1970s. 'They were a great improvement on the old three- and five-storey *khrushchevki*, we thought they were grand, just what was needed.' Her home, which she also shared with her mother, was immaculate and well-decorated. The sitting room had a balcony from where she was able to watch her two girls walking to and from school across the open ground between the buildings.

During the 1970s and even through the 1980s Murmansk benefited from the better aspects of Soviet planning and the centralized economy. The Gulf was full of shipping waiting for quay space, the fishing fleet was bringing home a vast harvest for value-added processing, and in its heyday the fishing industry formed 80 per cent of the industrial production of Murmansk town (the world market value of exports from the whole oblast before the collapse of the Soviet Union was valued at US$1–2,000 million, a large figure when compared to, say, Latvia's entire total export market of $25 million). But in the early 1990s, when I first saw Murmansk port, it was uncannily quiet, half full, a shadow of what must have been its former dynamic self. The fish industry had all but collapsed, the processing plants were closed, and much of the fleet was already using Norwegian ports for offloading and repair, benefiting from superior facilities and avoiding the excessive taxes and stifling bureaucracy at home. Immediately below the heights where I was standing, only the quays for apatite ore and coal were in use. Long stacks of anthracite, freighted by rail from elsewhere in Russia, were waiting to be loaded on to colliers that would make the onward journey to Siberia. Sailing behind the nuclear-fuelled icebreakers of the Murmansk Shipping Company, Russian ships with reinforced hulls would carry the vital fuel to the eastern communities where winters were beyond the reach of the Gulf Stream and temperatures consistently fell to minus 40 degrees. Eastbound coal-freighting was one of Murmansk's important domestic roles but it was not an income-generating activity for anyone except the Murmansk Shipping Company, which was fully exploiting its now-commercial monopoly of the Northern Sea Route. Only the apatite concentrate, an essential ingredient of phosphate fertilizers, had the potential of earning foreign currency.

'Murmansk used to be, above all, a fishing port,' Galina Aleksandrovna said. 'And whenever there were westerlies the lower town smelled strongly of fish. Nowadays you rarely smell anything.'

Olga, my first Murmansk acquaintance, offered to walk me around the town centre one evening. Since it was a festival weekend and the weather was warm, people were out for a stroll. I began to notice the more pleasing aspects of the dull city centre: there were trees everywhere, and these were now coming into leaf; the city's central Lenin Prospekt with its rendered and painted five-storey buildings of the 1930s and 1950s, the so-called *stalinki*, had a broad-brush character of its own; there was an almost complete absence of commercial advertising; and there was always the occasional view into the hills or across the Gulf.

Olga was about to graduate from a teacher training college. She was more self-assured than her years would warrant but I surmised that it was her training at Intourist, where she was working part-time and currently guiding Taiwanese war veterans, that produced the unhesitating and dogmatic replies to each of my questions, whatever the topic.

From my observations so far, all shopping in Murmansk presented difficulties. I had few needs, nor was I expecting to find anything I would want, apart from food, among the uniformly poor-quality offerings, but it was difficult to know what each shop was selling; with almost no unaccompanied visitors or foreigners in Murmansk, perhaps there was little practical justification for it to be otherwise. There were large shop windows along Lenin Prospekt but the displays were arbitrary and rarely gave any indication of what might be inside. There were almost no shop signs at all – a situation that continued up until the late 1990s – and above each entrance there was little more than a wall plaque that might read *Magazin 39*, giving hours of opening and the break-hour. A visitor to Murmansk would have to go through every door to be any the wiser. Bread shop, pharmacy, book shop, dental clinic, all looked the same.

Almost the only queues I encountered were at the Murmansk railway station where there was great demand for tickets to the Black Sea for the traditional family holiday. In the shops, however, now that there was plenty of produce on offer, the renowned old-style queues no longer existed. Only occasionally did I encounter shelves which were bare but for dry biscuits in polythene bags or an oversupply of second-rate Russian sweets. This was always due to a temporary cash-flow crisis within the larger Russian economy when importers, unwilling to be caught out by the roller-coaster exchange rates, had simply stopped buying.

As a first-time shopper in the early post-perestroika days, I found the purchasing procedure confusing. In the large food halls shoppers placed their orders at the various counters where they were given handwritten chits to take to the cashier's desk. This was often a raised, glass-fronted dais in the centre of the hall operated by an over-bearing matron. The receipted chits were then taken back to each counter in turn, the chit was examined, its edge torn by the sales person, and the items were handed over. It all required advance planning and a good list, a reconnaissance to locate the goods – not necessarily at the counter you expected – and an ability to judge which people at each counter were ordering or collecting. Like most systems it had its good points but I was a slow learner. The abacus was popular with old and young shop assistants alike and many traders used both abacus and calculator, adopting the now international practice of thrusting the calculator screen into the face of a foreigner. In the rough and tumble of the open-air markets I found this a boon. However, I never became accustomed to the enormous rouble sums before 1997. I had to look closely at the zeros on the banknotes – Russians do not use comma separators – and always had difficulty understanding large numbers when spoken in Russian.

I was beginning to feel at home at the Meridian; it had the comfortable institutional ambience of the old YMCA hostels. The stress of the unknown and the failure to realize my plans for the interior had weighed heavily on me for some time, but the comfort of the run-down hotel's small homely buffet and the feeling of comradeship emanating from the sailors and seamen who shuffled up and down the corridors in casual clothes and floppy sandals now made me almost reluctant to think about moving off into the wilderness. My room was clean, dry and warm. The shower and lavatory worked, there was plenty of hot water, an ample clothes cupboard, a chest of drawers, a vitrine containing plates, cutlery and glasses, a family-size fridge and a very large Soviet television which absorbed me for hours with its voiced-over output of Hollywood's worst offerings. I had also begun to establish daily personal routines, including setting up a clothes-line on the flat roof outside my window.

The Meridian's matron-invigilators continued to monitor my activities. A sneak view of the residents' log for my floor, which was unusually exposed on the desk one evening, showed day-pages neatly ruled and columned in pencil and completed in ink in elegant Cyrillic handwriting.

Took Roger Florian (foreigner)	*out*	*1020*
	in	*1415*
	out	*2000*
	in	*2330*

In time this intrusive supervision had the effect of dissipating my nervous tension and much of the insecurity that I had suffered since my arrival. It was as if, while under the wing of a *dezhurnaya*, I would be out of harm's way.

My new sense of security, however, was not altogether justified. Late one night I was sitting on the edge of my bed in my socks and underpants, checking personal documents and sorting my dollars which were in bulky quantities of small denomination notes and which I counted obsessively every day. The door, which was locked, crashed open. In a split second a large man was standing over me menacingly, his fist curled around a piece of metal or rubber. I was taken completely by surprise and was at a hopeless disadvantage – any items useful for personal protection were on the other side of the room – but shock and fear catapulted me to my feet and I heard myself shouting in surprisingly competent Russian, demanding to know who the intruder was and what he wanted. Thereupon the bear abruptly turned, left the room and ran down the corridor. I pursued him with my curses and was brought up short by two bewildered *dezhurnyye* who had been away from their post and had been sent flying when they turned the corner into the long corridor and collided with my would-be assailant.

Although I was already beginning to understand the Russian manner of completely ignoring strangers, the naval men at the Meridian seemed excessively uneasy with me; the Arktika hotel on the other side of the main square was, I concluded, the acceptable location for foreigners, not the Meridian. The old Soviet caution was still evident, and I suspected they were anyway frequently reminded on leaving ship of the importance of security with regard to the Northern Fleet's capability and activities. I was only once addressed by a naval officer. I was taking the lift down when the doors opened at the third floor to admit the broad hulk of a man in his forties, a warrant-officer type whom I had noticed before. In a stentorian voice and in Russian, half-way between a military order and a greeting, he barked: 'I am Viktor Ivanovich. I am pleased to make your acquaintance.' He then made a smart about-turn as if on a parade ground, and stood waiting for the lift doors to open at the lobby.

Olga's father was an electrical engineer on one of the Murmansk fishing fleet trawlers. His ship was in dock and he was at home on his own.

'My sister Natasha and my mother have gone south for a holiday, and my father's expecting you,' Olga said out of the blue with her habitual self-assurance.

For our three-kilometre journey to the southern suburb Olga and I took a taxi, one of the many old privately-owned Ladas that could be flagged down. Our destination was an unimpressive area with more than its fair share of Soviet architectural ugliness, and the entrance porch to the nine-storey apartment block was no more or less inviting or terrifying to a newcomer than all the others I had seen. The lift worked, but the staircase, which smelled of urine, was decayed, vandalized, dirty and covered with graffiti. Not until I was ushered over the threshold could I relax, feeling from that point I was enveloped by the emotional warmth of a Russian home.

Olga's father, Sergey Korytov, greeted me cordially and embraced his daughter, complaining good-naturedly that he had not seen enough of her since her wedding. Korytov was in his forties, gentle-mannered, trimly built with healthy brown hair, and, in a modest way, stylish, wearing a Western denim shirt and red braces with his jeans. We got on famously and I liked his direct manner. I was ushered to the kitchen table where the two of us consumed a bache-lor meal of sausages, eggs and spring onions, washed down with a few vodka toasts. My host, his dictionary at the ready, was eager to test his English on me. Taking the opportunity for hot water, still available in her father's district but shut down in hers for the summer, Olga went to the bathroom to wash her hair.

The kitchen, a complicated accumulation of disparate and ill-matched parts and accessories that seemed to have established them-selves naturally over time and according to availability rather than by plan, was very different from its designed, anodyne, space-saving equivalent prevalent in the West. The bathroom, which I used after supper, was, for a first-time foreigner, just as complicated as the kitchen. I had yet to become accustomed to the arrangement and adjustment of taps and to move effectively in these restricted spaces dominated by washing lines, bowls, electrical apparatus and storage shelves holding siege-capacity reserves of washing powder, lavatory paper, soap and toiletries. My clumsy movements during showering resulted in the mixer tap gouging a deep wound in the small of my back, bringing infection and pain for the next six months.

The sitting room was dominated by a *stenka*, a large glass-fronted bookcase of the kind I found in most Russian apartments, and also featured a long settee, a divan bed, a low table and a television. The furniture was of poor manufacture and mean design. Reading my thoughts, Olga had an explanation. 'This was all there was to buy in the 1970s when my father arrived here,' she said.

All in all, the apartment appeared modest and, to most Western eyes, would seem small for a family with two children. Was this the lifestyle that Korytov had envisaged for his future when he moved here in the 1970s, attracted north, like others from throughout the Soviet Union, by the Arctic wage premium? If this home, apartment block and district were typically for the well-paid privileged workers of the north, how was the rest of Russia living? I looked out of the apartment down on to the nearby two-storey maternity clinic, a modest, run-down building next to a children's playground that seemed little different from the rest of the surrounding wasteland. Husbands and relatives were walking up and down outside waiting for the appearance of mothers at the window. Hygiene regulations were strict, I was told; mothers were allowed no visitors at any time, and all conversations had to be shouted to and from the upstairs windows. Whether this was standard practice in Russia or something peculiar to Murmansk I didn't know, but it seemed to me that the well-paid and privileged Arctic workers of Murmansk were hardly enjoying the high level of healthcare that they might have been led to expect.

As time went on and I visited more northern urban homes I found most of them shabby, meanly furnished, often messy, and almost always 'under repair'. On a later occasion I was offered the explanation that most people who immigrated to Murmansk for the money felt, consciously or subconsciously, that they were there temporarily, and that was why they neglected their homes.

The next morning Korytov had to report to his ship and offered to take me with him. After we left home in his old Lada we stopped at a garage shed about a kilometre away. This was not unlike a small freight container with a gabled tin roof. It sat, together with hundreds of other similar structures, in a large hole in the ground, probably a former quarry. I had seen these sheds elsewhere around Murmansk; they provided valuable storage space for large families in small apartments, and sometimes accommodated hundreds of kilograms of potatoes as well as workbenches and clothes-cupboards, but when I first saw one of these 'container cities' and saw smoke coming from several of the sheds I thought it likely that they were used as homes.

Out of town we stopped at a petrol station. Its kind was absolutely standard in the days before the arrival of modern filling stations in Murmansk but it has remained vivid in my memory. This one, as most of them, stood on rough waste ground. The pump attendant and his controls were housed in a small building of grey concrete bricks that was so heavily reinforced that it could have sustained heavy machine-gun fire. The notice, wrought calligraphically in steel and planted on top of the building, said simply *Benzin*. The dark, rusted pumps were accessed by going to the control building, shouting the order through a small grille – usually placed somewhere around waist height – and paying the money. Although the areas in which such petrol stations stood made me feel unsafe and nervous in those early days, I irrationally missed these oddities when they all finally disappeared towards the end of the decade to make way for the large, brightly lit shopping-mall filling stations constructed by Norway's Statoil and other major oil companies.

The car took us down to the port levels where we rattled along a rough road parallel to the railway. Heavy lorries came towards us on both sides of the road, swerving to avoid potholes. We parked and then walked across the rail tracks between freight wagons loaded with nickel matte. The port security took some persuading to admit a foreigner but we succeeded. Walking through several docks, all with lines of gantry cranes but mostly empty, we came to a line of six large trawlers, including Korytov's ship. Its huge, rusted hull and superstructure much in need of paint evoked the decades of sea journeys that it had made in search of fish, in all seasons and in all weathers, working the notoriously temperamental seas of the North Cape and on to the Atlantic and Pacific. Access was up a perilous ladder that ran at forty-five degrees to the vertical and consisted of small wooden steps hung between two rope handrails like a suspension bridge. We went to the ship's bridge. It was quite unlike anything I had seen for real or in the movies: forty years old, large-scale, patched, repaired and much repainted, but clean, polished, ready for service and, to my mind, unmistakably Soviet.

We moved through the ship, up and down gantry steps and through bulkheads with the ship humming all around us, and emerged at the stern. Here, exposed to the cold onshore wind from the west, we looked down on to the vast open hatch into which fish were offloaded at sea from satellite ships for processing. From there we went down to the hall which at sea would house dozens of men working at the filleting tables, at speed and in all weather. I was reminded of the international antagonism generated by the voracious Soviet and other nationality 'factory fleets' when they first began to plough the sea floor. The size of the operation had been enormous: in 1984 one trawler alone, the Murmansk-based *Marshal Yerumenko*, recorded a catch of 21,000 tonnes.

A year later Korytov's ship was impounded at a North American port. The crew were stranded for nine months while the owners were pursued by creditors in several countries.

Aware that I was becoming physically and psychologically ensconced in Murmansk, I anxiously reminded myself of my objectives, and planned somehow to leave town within a few days in spite of the consistent opposition to my travelling anywhere, particularly on my own. I was determined to find a way to explore the interior. The town's so-called Folklore Museum did much to persuade me that travel through Russian Lapland, however problematic and arduous, would have its rewards. The museum had, in fact, so absorbed my attention on my initial visits that I generated suspicion among the janitors, women of the same calibre as the hotel *dezhurnyye* and all aged over fifty: I was a foreigner, not part of a group, I appeared to have no friends and acquaintances, I was always getting too close to the exhibits, and I read every label several times.

The process of readmission to the museum was always scrupulously conducted. On one occasion I transgressed – it had happened that nobody was around to check my ticket – and a lengthy altercation ensued. The janitors fell into two camps. One was for having me taken to the Director's office on grounds of suspicion, the other affected civic pride that their museum had given a foreigner such pleasure. (The woman in charge of the overstaffed lobby even suggested giving me unlimited free admission.) With the issue unresolved and under discussion in the lobby I was sent on my way to trudge around the museum – with the roubles still in my pocket – friendless and under close observation.

During my first weeks in Murmansk I spent many hours visiting and revisiting the displays, from the geology cabinets and the wildlife rooms to the historical models, the old photographs, and the section on the Great Patriotic War. The more it was made clear to me that the Bolsheviks had built a great port, a large pioneer community, a string of important mining towns, and won a war, the more apparent it became that they had all but eradicated Russian Lapland. Somewhere beyond the museum, I persuaded myself, there remained something of the pre-Soviet past. Among the flora and fauna of 'Europe's last wilderness' history must surely be there for the taking.

2

IN SEARCH OF ABORIGINALS

First Lapps

'YOU CAN'T go into the tundra, there are no roads,' all my acquaintances had said. 'Anyway, most of the region is closed to you, and you'd be picked up and treated like a spy. As for the Lapps – or Saami, as they call them now – they're history. The few you do find are usually drunk.'

It was only later that I realized how very little Murmanchaners knew or cared about the wider region in which they lived. They worked hard in a hostile climate for nine months of the year and dreamed of warm summer holidays on the shores of the Black Sea lasting from May to August.

As for myself, I was dreaming of finding indigenous people in the wilderness.

'We can't give you permission to travel into the country,' I was told by a smartly uniformed lieutenant in the Visa and Residency Office, whose authoritarian but correct manner was well matched by her emphatic and precise application of dark red lipstick. 'The whole of the north is closed. Why don't you go to one of the new fishing camps for foreigners? We hear the facilities are luxurious.'

My resolve to see something of the wilderness that I knew must exist beyond the towns and mining centres strung between Kandalaksha and Murmansk was strengthened by a lucky purchase. Hitherto I had been making do with US Air Force aeronautical charts which were on a scale of 1:1 million and gave me no idea of terrain, marking only a few rivers and the major contours. In a hunting and fishing-tackle shop in Murmansk, however, I found what had evaded me in London and St Petersburg. I was able to purchase, at risible cost, twenty-eight superb, recently updated, fully contoured 1:200,000 scale maps of Murmansk Oblast (Murmansk Region) imported illegally from former Soviet Union countries.

A casual conversation with a Finn in Murmansk gave me further hope. 'If you can get yourself to the town of Lovozero you'll be able to find some Saami people. They could take you by boat across the lake there and you could connect with one of the rivers that would carry you into the interior. There's also a museum at Lovozero where you can learn more about the Saami.' It was the very first positive response I had received to my questions about 'aboriginal people' – or about anything at all. From a foreigner, of course.

The modern main road south out of Murmansk had a small but constant flow of fuming trucks and cars, some of which seemed unlikely to reach destinations beyond the oblast. There was the occasional green Ural motorbicycle with sidecar, whose classic design evoked the pioneer era of rally driving, and at the roadside vendors sat on chairs or in old Lada cars, offering salmon and animal skins for sale.

Once the bus to Olenegorsk, my first stop on the way to Lovozero, had left the outskirts of Murmansk, the road continued through monotonous forest tundra of pine, spruce and birch. Three hours later the town of Olenegorsk, established in the Soviet era for mining and processing iron ore, appeared ahead of us, announcing itself by its works buildings, mountainous slagheaps and extensive tailing ponds. The bus deposited me near the railway station amongst a jungle of sidings and overhead power cables. Olenegorsk, even before one entered the town, seemed grim.

At the bus stop I hitched a lift from a man who had heard my imperfect Russian at one of the nearby kiosks, and I was soon on my way east to Lovozero. My driver, a Finn, was not only in talkative mood but during the course of a two-hour journey provided me with the perfect introduction to my Lappish adventures. He told me he travelled regularly from Finland to Lovozero, driving vanloads of food and gifts to Saami friends and relations there. 'These are hard times for most people but particularly hard for the Saami,' he said. My driver was a large, extrovert man in his forties, with a Nordic face and unruly tufts of pale brown hair, far removed from what I imagined a Lapp to look like. He was a type that I had met in other European countries. He shouted over the noise of the engine and frequently roared with laughter; his ebullient manner could have belonged to a scout leader or holiday camp manager. His large van had had much of its interior of bunks and kitchen cupboards removed to make room for dozens of cartons and sacks piled to the roof. I could smell smoked meat and soap powder, according to the direction of the draught.

My driver adjusted himself more comfortably into his seat. 'Saami now live away from the old territories. We no longer follow the traditional country way of life. The Saami in this part of Lapland "died" once they had all been forcibly moved to Lovozero. It's difficult for foreigners to understand that – and when I say foreigners I include Russians – because the general opinion is that history has moved on and native people should adapt to changed circumstances like everyone else.

'Some of the Saami in Lovozero are related to the Saami of my region in Finland. Even today, perhaps even more so since Gorbachev, Saami don't think about national borders as most people do. We've been living for thousands of years from the west to the east of Fennoscandia – that's Sweden, Norway, Finland and this part of Russia – so for me to be bringing provisions and household stuff all the way from Finland to families and friends in Lovozero seems in a sense natural.

'From the Middle Ages we Saami had to submit to Danes, Swedes, Norwegians and Russians. We paid tribute and taxes to whoever claimed to have been granted authority over us. Then in the nineteenth and twentieth centuries we were finally separated by national borders because governments didn't like our migration traditions. But we're still one nation, although we speak different dialects – sometimes incomprehensible to each other – and I like to think we can all still look to one another in rough times. Saami from Russia are now beginning to come to the Scandinavian countries.'

On the road to Lovozero we passed convoys of troops on manoeuvre, with lines of trucks and army personnel carriers parked off the road or near openings to the forest. We passed the turning to Vysoky, a strategically important air base on an area of high ground above a lake. Built into the side of the hill, I learned later, were vast underground hangars for fighters and jumbo-size Ruslan transports. Further east we passed the gates of the Protoki rocket base, a dingy collection of grey barracks surrounded by a high fence. Its entry gate had a small notice with the disingenuous title of Centre for the Observation of Cosmological Objects but a few kilometres further east, on higher open ground overlooked by an assortment of radar dishes and antennae, were the silos. (It was from one of these that a rocket was nearly launched in 1995 when Soviet coastal radar errone-ously identified Norwegian meteorological hardware as an enemy missile.)

The Second World War wrought dreadful destruction on the Saami in the west of Murmansk Oblast, near the Norwegian and Finnish borders. Here in the east, on the Kola Peninsula itself, it was not until later, with the military upgrade of the Cold War and the building of the Northern Fleet harbours from the 1960s onwards, that the Saami suffered a final and decisive blow and were moved away from the coast or prevented from living freely on their own lands. As fate would have it, the military activity coincided with a national drive to form larger collectives. The 1960s–70s were years of despair for those families forced to live in the modern town of Lovozero.

When Lovozero appeared in the distance I was surprised to see what looked like just another small modern Russian town. Since we were now moving closer to the geographical centre of the Peninsula, I had expected something different. As the road left the forest, we found ourselves on open ground overlooking an expansive plain and a small town of Soviet-style concrete buildings and five-storey apart-ment blocks not unlike those in Murmansk. Only a large lake beyond the town and a snow-clad mountain range on our right towards the south-east suggested wild country.

As we rolled into Lovozero a few people recognized my driver and waved with a smile; everybody else walking the roads looked gloomy. Lovozero was not a place to make one's heart leap. But here, hurrying to catch up with someone walking away from the road, my new acquaintance abandoned me.

From where I stood, looking up and down the empty road that ran straight through to the end of the town, Lovozero now appeared smaller; only the concrete architecture prevented me from thinking of it still as a village. At the counter of a shop inside an ill-shod build-ing constructed from grey cement bricks, bearing the misleadingly evocative name TUNDRA in large letters high along its front, I sought advice. An elderly woman, weighed down with two large net bags, offered to direct me and led me from the shop, helpfully shouting instructions and advice. I was shown to a hostel consisting of ten rooms either side of a corridor on the ground floor of a modest building. The 'administrator', who spoke to me in the manner of a disciplinarian headmistress, told me I was the first Englishman to stay. 'Finns, Swedes, Norwegians, Germans, yes. But no English.' What do the visitors do when they come to Lovozero, I asked.

'They come to buy reindeer meat. Every year in the past there were big markets and gatherings; now we have a new modern slaughterhouse ... Ah, your visa and passport.'

While she dealt with the documentation I looked around me. The hotel interior was austere but clean. I had the impression nobody else was staying. Beyond the desk a *babushka*, the administrator's mother, sat in a curtained area in front of a television. The volume was turned up high but she seemed not to be watching.

'The herdsmen from outlying villages now bring some of their deer here for slaughter locally,' the administrator continued helpfully. 'People from the villages also bring salmon, mushrooms and berries. We go out in the summer months ourselves, too.' To my surprise she then rattled off, quite unprompted, a list of berries and the better known mushrooms.

I asked how people got to and from the remote villages of the Peninsula's interior. Surely they didn't all travel by reindeer? 'Well, there may be a helicopter tomorrow going to Krasnoshchelye or Kanevka – the herding villages. It's been a two-week wait this time because there's absolutely no clean fuel at the moment. Some people are getting very impatient. Go to the airport and you might just be lucky.' At first I thought she was talking about the airport at Murmansk until she told me, in a slightly offended tone, that she was talking about their own – *'nash'* – at Lovozero.

After two days of alternating my waiting periods in the airstrip building with visits to the museum – a programme determined by the airport's weather forecast and the meteorologist's alchemical flight predictions – I learned that there would be no helicopter to the interior for the foreseeable future. I strolled restlessly around the town, looking for history and thinking about Lapps and wilderness, while trying to ignore the prefabricated architecture. My visits to the museum revealed that archaeologists had unearthed evidence of neolithic habitation near the modern town. Little was known of these prehistoric people but, in the light of this and what I had learned from my driver, I reflected that a visitor to Lake Lovozero at any time during the last one thousand years was likely to have found a community of a few Saami families of similar origin living near to where the town stood now. Adopting this information as my *leitmotiv* I wandered absent-mindedly eastwards and followed the small River Virma out of the centre. Along the banks I found colourful boat huts, working sheds and some older wooden houses with well-tended gardens, but few signs of activity and no friendly greetings.

Comprehensively studied by anthropologists, the ethnic origins of the Saami are wonderfully elusive. Long acknowledged as Fennoscandia's native people, living within ancestral homelands, with their own history and culture, and having developed their own branch of the Finno-Ugric group of languages, they represent, like the Basques, one of the few old enclaves of European local races. Certain scholars, led by the late Swede K.B. Wiklund, have claimed that the Saami survived even the Ice Age by retreating to the North Cape, where they benefited from the warmer air of the Gulf Stream.

The pan-Saami population living today within the modern frontiers of Norway, Sweden, Finland and Russia is hard to appraise or calculate, and its size varies wildly according to the criteria used. The maximum total number is most likely between 60,000 and 80,000, with Norway claiming 40,000, Sweden 20,000, Finland 6,000, and Russia no more than 3,000.*

Originally forming the majority in all these regions, the Saami are now very much the minority except in certain areas of Norwegian Finnmark and Finnish Lapland. The Russian Saami – the easternmost Saami – have an even lower demographic profile: in 1990 they amounted to less than 1 per cent of the 1 million, predominantly urban population of Murmansk Oblast, though a small number of Russian Saami and their descendants also live in St Petersburg.

---

* Conservative commentators, taking a more purist view of blood-lines, have recently put the total as low as 50,000, with Murmansk Oblast holding 2,000.

For 2,000 years and possibly for twice as long, the eastern Saami lived off their rich and extensive lands. Originally a hunting, trapping and fishing people, only later did they engage in breeding and working small herds of reindeer. In time, reindeer husbandry developed the Saami's distinctive life cycle, involving the migration of family groups between seasonal camps (*seity*) located within a traditionally assigned territory (*payk*).

In winter the Saami would live inland near lakes and forests, hunting bear, elk, deer and game, and trapping fox, wolverine, squirrel, ermine and marten for clothes and tradeable pelts. In early spring most families ran with reindeer to the coast where, in the summer months, they caught and trapped salmon and other anadromous fish running upriver from the sea. In the autumn deer and man returned inland, the Saami fishing the lakes en route and gathering mushrooms and vitamin-rich berries in great quantities to last the long polar winter.

'Far beyond the Germanic tribes live the Fenni,' wrote Tacitus in his *Germania* of AD 98, using one of several ancient names by which foreigners described the Saami. 'They have no possessions and live completely wild. They have neither arms, horses nor houses ... they are clad in skins ... they do not cultivate the land but eat what they find growing wild. Their beds are the bare ground ... Their only protection against wild beasts and the weather is a primitive hut made of twigs. They have no iron, but tip their arrows with bone. Thus armed they go hunting, and the women hunt with the men, taking their share of the kill.'

Around AD 1200 the Dane Saxo Grammaticus, writing of the natives' trapping and hunting skills, called their land Lappia, and from about that time increasing reference was made to Lapps, Lappia, and Lapland. The Lapps themselves spoke of Sam or Samer (we ourselves), and called their country variously Sapme, Sameatnam, or Sameland (our land). Russians still often refer to them derogatorily as *lopari* or *lop*, but during recent decades the Lapps have increasingly been addressed more correctly as Saami.

Returning from my solitary meanders along Lovozero's river and still looking for conversation, I stopped at the garden fence of a modest wooden house. A small woman in her sixties with a round, elfin face, wearing a white scarf tied at the back of her head and a gardening apron over a full, floral skirt, was working on her potato patch. She seemed pleased to have an excuse for a respite and responded cheerfully to my greeting – the first person to do so all day – though her daughter regarded me with suspicion from the safety of the porch. Desperate by this stage for first-hand information, I declared my intentions directly. To my surprise we fell easily into conversation – it was as if she were used to being asked about the Saami – and, having struggled gallantly to understand my foreign turn of phrase, and realizing also that I already knew something about recent Saami history and the reason for Lovozero's expansion, she sensed the real purpose of my questioning and went straight to the nub.

'Well, for a start my name is Kseniya Petrovna, and I'm Saami. But I'm not from Lovozero. We were moved here in the sixties. We used to live on the River Voronye about sixty kilometres downstream from Lake Lovozero, at Koardek, and quite separate from the Lovozero Saami.'

I asked what the place on the river had been like. Was it a large village with stone and cement houses, or was it a temporary seasonal camp? Life there must have been very different from life at Lovozero, I said, pointing out the cement apartment buildings. This seemed to tax her thought processes, as if she didn't know where to start, or what to select for my benefit.

'The Voronye Saami consisted of about thirty families. Koardek was our main settlement. It was a short way up the River Lun, a small tributary of the Voronye, and sheltered between some low hills. All of us had good wooden houses there, small but comfortable, and nice and warm in winter. The Dmitriyevs and the Fefelovs had the best houses and sheds, I suppose. Our house was just two large rooms and a long porch.

'There wasn't much forest around Koardek but we had good pastures and hay meadows along the river banks for the cattle and sheep … and plenty of fish in the river, of course. In April or early May, before the snow melted, my father used to take us north with the reindeer as they moved towards the coast after calving. We used to go by sledge to the estuary at Gavrilovo on the Barents coast, or to the River Rynda, and that's where some of our families spent the summers, living in cabins or under canvas, or in a *vezha* – that's our traditional small cabin, covered with bark and turf. Some of the men fished for salmon but my father, who was a herder, usually kept an eye on the reindeer along the coast.

'It was a great life for a young girl. I used to help with the salmon traps but I also went with my father to the reindeer once I was about twelve, and I knew how to work a pack reindeer from a very early age.

'In winter my friends and I used to make money catching ptarmigan and selling them in the village. There were always hundreds of them in the woods nearby and we were very good at setting and baiting the traps.'

In spite of an idyllic childhood, Kseniya's family history was not a happy one. Her grandfather was implicated in the Saami protests of the late 1920s and early 1930s led by the Russian activist Vasily Alymov and, like Alymov, was executed in 1939 by the NKVD. Many Saami were shot or sent to distant labour camps at that time, their families disgraced and their reindeer or cattle confiscated.

'And then in the 1960s all of us at Koardek were ordered off the land. Almost without warning we were forced to live here in Lovozero. Why? Because they wanted to build a reservoir and a hydroelectric plant.'

Electricity was indeed needed but, as Kseniya explained, the authorities had anyway decided that all the Saami everywhere should be 'settled centrally' to form large collectives. Soviet planning was unable to accommodate the fact that the Saami lived remotely and migrated seasonally, running with reindeer, hunting everywhere, and setting up camp at different fishing places.

In the 1960s the small village of Lovozero expanded rapidly as Saami were forcibly removed from their territories. Kseniya described how her neighbour Antonina Maksimovna left Koardek to go to school in Lovozero in September 1963 but, like all the children from the Voronye *seit* at Koardek that year, she never saw her own home or her own things again.

'For the Voronye children of Antonina's generation – that is, people who are in their forties today – everything happened at the same time, around the age of twelve or thirteen. Some children not only lost their homes but, once they had started their education at the Lovozero *internat* [boarding school], they were forced to speak Russian, and only Russian. The indoctrination was so effective that, when they joined their families in the holidays, the children were embarrassed by their parents' insistence on using their own language.'

Kseniya told me how the Saami language had in effect been killed off for almost forty years, but she was not altogether despondent.

'Many of us are beginning to use the language again and, although the teenagers rarely put a sentence together, I get very exited when I hear my little grandchildren and others of their age using both Russian and Saami at the same time.

'Perhaps we're in for a better life now that the old order has gone. And it's our first big chance to speak up for almost seventy years.' As she delivered this well-rounded affirmation of her people's future, she moved back from the fence and braced herself upright, shoulders back, with her spade in both hands.

'I must get on with my gardening. Come back and talk any time. I presume you've come for the festival on Sunday?'

On Sunday the flight to Krasnoshchelye had still not materialized so I followed others along the track out of town. The festival, which was held among pine trees on the sandy shore of a small lake about two kilometres from the town, had the atmosphere of a large family picnic. Most women wore traditional Saami dress of the kind I had seen in the Lovozero museum: long cotton or silk floral skirts or pinafores in brilliant scarlet, pink or blue, with equally bright-patterned blouses under short jackets. Their hats – low, cylindrical *shamshury* with the top bent forward over the forehead like a peak – were richly beaded, and held in place with silk headscarves.

I walked through the trees, treading on sand and soft mosses, wandering from stall to stall piled with reindeer-skin products: thigh-boots, full-length one-piece *malitsy*, bags and patchwork pouches decorated with beadwork, carved birchwood cups, engraved horn pendants, and lassos plaited from hide. Older reindeer herdsmen were competing nearby with similar lassos. Youths in blue trousers, stripped to the waist, were participating in the annual wrestling contest. Seeing many of the older men wearing the ubiquitous Russian green combat fatigues and most of the Saami boys in Western baseball hats, I asked one of the women why there were no men dressed traditionally for the occasion, but she could find no answer for me other than a shrug of the shoulders.

When the woods had filled with families from Lovozero – the majority in everyday Russian clothes – an accordionist gathered together a dozen women dressed uniformly in tall red headdresses, short red jackets over white blouses, and full long skirts, all trimmed with gold brocade. They began to sing. Some of the songs were punctuated with calls and shouts, some were full of harmonies strange to my ears, others sounded typically Russian.

'It's a fairly new idea, this festival,' said a woman standing beside me. 'The Lovozero Administration wasn't at all happy at first about our having a gathering. You like the singing? Wait till you see the Norwegians who've come from Kautokeino.'

Within half an hour the Norwegians appeared, all dressed in fine navy blue serge, the men in smocks and leggings, the women in dresses, their garments smartly trimmed and piped with red and yellow. In comparison with their Lovozero partners, they exuded health and happiness.

'They've just arrived by bus from the border,' said my neighbour. 'It's the first time we've been officially allowed to meet and perform together.'

The Norwegian Saami performed with flair. Young girls, also dressed in blue, their bonnets trimmed with the fine white fur of deer calves, danced a piece in imitation of birds: flying, swooping, calling, 'displaying', filling the air with a joyful sound. Two young male dancers then held the stage, one wearing reindeer antlers, the other lightly beating a small shallow drum of skin decorated with hieroglyphs.

Coming away from the performance area I bought a *shashlyk* of reindeer meat from a food stall, and was told 'the football' was about to start. Thinking at first that this was simply the men's response to Saami cultural revivalism, I soon learned that it was indeed 'Saami football'.

A short way through the wood on a piece of open ground, covered in moss, heather and cloudberry, a small playing area had been marked out with sticks at the four corners and the two goals. Two teams of six women had removed their hats, skirt-aprons, jackets and shawls and were kicking a large, lightweight ball of reindeer skin. The ball, I learned later, was stuffed with reindeer hair.

With mock officialdom and much whistle-blowing, the male

referee reminded the boisterous teams of the rules, and started the game by throwing the ball into the air. The women engaged with immediate and alarming ferocity. Long skirts, some of which were tucked into knickers, neither slowed the pace nor restricted legs. Feet flew dangerously. The goalkeepers, who apparently qualified for no protective ruling whatsoever, were roughly handled. In the nail-biting, closing seconds of the no-holds-barred contest, with honour hanging in the balance, one of the keepers was subjected to a brutal onslaught by the team more determined to squeeze a result from the level score. After two further games played by women, the men took the field. But the male version of Saami football, played in jeans, trainers and branded tracksuits, had none of the panache shown by the women, all of whom had collapsed at the touchline in a muck sweat and were now shrieking with laughter.

During the festival I was introduced to a woman who was said to be an important political figure in the Russian Saami community. Nina Yeliseyevna Afanaseva was in her early forties, small and compact in build. At her home next day she greeted me formally but answered my questions with warm enthusiasm and with an economy and pre-cision that revealed a formal academic training. She had been actively involved in the Saami movement ever since she went to Leningrad as an undergraduate in the 1970s. She had been present at the first-ever conference of Russian Saami in Murmansk in September 1989, and had been elected joint vice-president of the newly formed Association of Kola Saami, the first independent formal grouping of Russian Saami since the Revolution. 'When Saami from four nations gathered in the main square of Murmansk in 1989 for our first dem-onstration,' Nina Yeliseyevna told me, 'there was opposition from the authorities, and there has been antagonism towards the Association ever since. Even today our registration is still under threat.'

I asked about the reservoir that Kseniya Petrovna had mentioned during our meeting over the garden fence, the reservoir that had pro-vided an excuse to forcibly settle and collectivize the Voronye Saami families at Lovozero.

'The Voronye reservoir – the Serebryansky as it's now called – gen-erates electricity for the naval bases. A large area had to be flooded. When they flooded the River Alta in Norway in 1979, the Saami protest movement over there was so well organized that, although the protest failed, it was a milestone of international importance in the establishment of our minority rights. In Russia we're still not as well organized. Politically the Kola Saami still lag behind, and we're so much fewer in number.'

In 1992 the Russian Saami were admitted to the Nordic Saami Council by their Norwegian, Finnish and Swedish cousins and they still hoped for their own Saami parliament in Russia, however far off that might seem. However, as a result of life under Soviet rule, Nina Yeliseyevna's people still barely existed in a formal sense.

The Russian Duma's Constitution of 1993 included provisions for indigenous peoples, guaranteeing rights according to 'universally recognized principles and standards of international law' and recognizing rights to land and natural resources within traditional territories. Even so, lacking measures for political or legal implementation, the rights of the Saami have largely been ignored by Russians with political and administrative power in Moscow and Murmansk.

Old Saami places

SERGEY GANUSEVICH moved ahead of me, edging confidently along a narrow shelf, hugging the rockface with his arms spread wide. As I watched, his front foot slipped and then his whole body slowly but irretrievably fell away from the vertical. I froze to the spot, wondering, in the few seconds that passed, how I was going to carry or drag him across several kilometres of bog back to the river and the boat.

As luck would have it, a ledge about six metres below us held Sergey from plunging further and into the treetops. To my relief, he sat upright almost as soon as he had landed, and looked up at me with a wave and a smile.

'That was lucky,' he said as he clambered back up. 'For a moment I thought I was going the whole way. After all these years of climbing the same rocks I get overconfident. Stupid of me not to go down on the rope.'

Sergey seemed more concerned about me than himself and, to my surprise, he managed within a few minutes to calm me and my nerves and to coax me further along the narrow shelf to the point where it broadened and extended back under the overhanging rockface, allowing me room to crawl.

When I arrived on my hands and knees at the falcons' scrape nest I soon forgot that we were a hundred metres above the ground. In front of me on the floor of the ledge were four balls of white fluff. At first they looked as insignificant as dandelion heads until I made out the tiny eyes and beaks of fledglings, born two days earlier, huddling close to each other for warmth in the absence of their mother. The sand scrape seemed a poor place for newly-born creatures: no moss or small twigs provided warmth and comfort, the ledge would offer little protection from gales or heavy rain, and it seemed to me that a fox or a stoat would have no difficulty in taking the young.

The female peregrine had been circling as we climbed from the forest below, calling in alarm as it swooped and banked at speed past our heads. Sergey carefully examined each young bird in turn and tenderly rearranged them into the intimate group just as he had found them. He then pulled out a notebook and pencil from his breast pocket.

As he scribbled, the falcon circled and fretted.

'We'll move away now,' he said. 'It's not good to leave them at this age without their mother for more than forty minutes.'

I had met Sergey while waiting one warm evening at the Lovozero airstrip. Now, two weeks later, we were at the heart of the Kola Peninsula interior. From our vantage-point on the cliff face next to the falcon's nest, we had a bird's-eye view of the open terrain before us. Nearest to the foot of the cliffs were about two kilometres of raised bog with occasional small patches of dry land and spruce trees; this then changed to the paler green of wet bog and marshes, punctuated with dozens of pools and small lakes. In the middle distance a line of trees marked the winding course of a river. In the far distance the marsh and bog gave way again to higher ground of pine forest, with ridges and cliffs of bare granite like the one that we had just climbed.

In these lowlands, created by glacial erosion, the River Ponoy, the Peninsula's principal lateral waterway, delays its eastward course to the White Sea and disperses into a 2,000-square-kilometre area of lakes, bogs and myriad meandering streams. Unpolluted, undisturbed by man, home to plentiful populations of small mammals, fish and birds, the Ponoy Depression has remained, according to Sergey, one of Europe's most pristine ecosystems. Its rich biodiversity, combined with minimal human disturbance, has created *inter alia* one of the world's outstanding breeding grounds for birds of prey. To Sergey it was 'Europe's last wilderness'. He told me it had taught him more about old Russian Lapland and the Saami than anything else.

Sergey Ganusevich had been familiar with that part of the Peninsula since his undergraduate days at Moscow University in the 1970s. Since then, first as a researcher with the Russian Institute of

Nature Conservation and Reserves, and later as a senior curator at the Moscow Zoo, he had devoted every spring and summer holiday to the birds and wildlife of the Ponoy Depression wetlands. His chief interest was the raptor population – eagles, osprey, hawks, buzzards and falcons – most of which migrate to Lapland in the early spring to breed, returning to Southern Europe and Central Asia for the winter. Sergey knew each pair of peregrine falcons within his own survey area. Few ornithologists could claim to have monitored wilderness breeding grounds so consistently and over such a long period.

Raptor populations are at the top of the food chain and prime biological monitors of the world's environments. During the 1950s peregrine falcons notoriously approached extinction, predominantly on account of the pesticide DDT. During the 1970s and 1980s sea eagles also suffered dramatically. It took a long time for the affected populations of birds of prey to recover, but by the early 1990s Sergey began to notice a steady improvement in breeding success, and in summer 2001 he was to find a peregrine nest with five fledglings on the Peninsula, probably the first successfully hatched clutch of such size in Russia.

When I had met Sergey Ganusevich at the Lovozero airstrip we had both been waiting several days for the flight to the interior, and were both beginning to have doubts about getting away at all. As we sat outside the small airport building, smoking and swatting mosquitoes, Sergey had talked in fluent English about his work. He covered his survey area on foot and by boat for about two months every summer.

'What about the mosquitoes?' I asked, impatient to return to the protection of the airstrip building.

'The mosquitoes? They're always at their worst while I'm here. I've learned to live with them.'

For his expedition Sergey had brought a large trunk of provisions. 'In the years since perestroika, food supplies have become unpredictable. It's the same with petrol now. When I first came here in the 1970s there was no shortage of fuel; a small aeroplane went to Krasnoshchelye in the interior every day at a cost of about seven roubles, something most people could afford. That used to be one of the easier parts of the journey. Now it looks as if we shall have to walk there!'

I explained my own situation to Sergey. I told him I was a new-comer to the region and to all things Russian, that I had no overall plan or clear idea of where I was going, and up until a few days earlier had not even owned any useful maps. Everyone opposed my travel plans, I said, but I still wanted to explore the wilderness, get a feel for the taiga and the tundra, and travel the rivers. Most important of all, I wanted to see where and how the Saami had lived until recently. I told Sergey I was ready to go anywhere. I had a rucksack full of clothes and equipment, a tent, some dry food, two litres of vodka, a spoon, a cup, a saucepan and plenty of tobacco.

By the time we heard that a helicopter was on its way from Murmansk, Sergey had offered to take me with him. We would pick up his boat and engine at Krasnoshchelye, a small village on the Ponoy, and then head downstream to the wetlands of the Ponoy Depression. Showing me on the map some of the places where he planned to inspect eagle and falcon nests, he remarked proprietori-ally: 'When you're with me you'll see the remote places. Only when you're actually there can you fully understand how the Saami used to live and how they thought – and still think – about their land. Many of the inland Saami territories are difficult to get to, and I warn you that newcomers find the going tough. You'd never be able to explore it for yourself. You'll see.'

*

I didn't notice the small tributary until Sergey swung the boat to star-board, revealing the opening in the tall sedge grass that had lined the banks of the Ponoy for the last hour of our river journey. When we had motored away from the village of Krasnoshchelye earlier in the day the river was a hundred metres wide, surging smoothly and steadily through the forest. Once it had emerged into open lowland, it mysteriously diminished, dispersing into backwaters and ponds, filling old river beds, seeping away into marshes and bogs. Only far ahead at the south-eastern corner of the wetlands would I see it revert to its full size.

Sergey confirmed that the territories that we were entering had been occupied continuously up until the 1960s. Then everyone was moved to Krasnoshchelye or to towns like Lovozero. The immediate area had been known for centuries as Kamenka because of the rocks in the main shallow lakes. The lake we were going to now was called Verkhnekamenskoye, or Upper Stony Lake, and Sergey was going to show me one of the old Saami settlements there.

The tributary twisted confusingly, narrowing in places to a few metres. Birch trees and willow bushes enclosed us, forming a low canopy that frequently required me to duck below the gunwales. Sergey swerved the boat past fallen trees, keeping the engine's propeller turning fast enough to avoid snagging the bushes and grasses below the water. Wigeon, mallard and wood sandpiper, flushed from their nests, fled from us as we crashed upstream through the bushes. The trees gave way once again to open landscape, the lake came into sight and, as we approached it by a network of narrow winding channels through the sedge marsh, Sergey slowed the engine for us to row. Standing up in the boat I could see across a broad stretch of marsh and water.

When the Saami first lived in eastern Fennoscandia they probably inhabited only the northern coasts, benefiting from the warmth of the Gulf Stream, fishing in the estuaries and hunting seal, whale and walrus. Then they started to explore inland, travelling to the forests and the taiga to hunt, to fish lakes like the one we were entering, and to catch small herds of reindeer for their own use or for meat. From that time most adopted a transhumant lifestyle, migrating between their inland winter homes and their summer camps on the coasts or in the hills where the breezes kept the mosquitoes down. Over the last thousand years the Saami had actually preferred low inland country. 'You could say they became a bog and forest people,' remarked Sergey.

Ahead of us on the far bank of the lake was a large wooden cabin. Two men were moving around nearby, and smoke from a fire at the side of the cabin was rising straight up into the still, blue sky. Two wooden boats were drawn up on to the muddy bank and, as we rowed slowly across the shallow water, I could make out barrels, nets, fish-drying frames, and some small sheds. The two men came down to the water's edge as we arrived. Both were wearing thick, dirty cotton jackets and trousers, rubber thigh waders folded down below the knee, and hoods which came down on to their shoulders, the small circular openings exposing their faces from eyebrow to lower lip. As we stepped out of the boat I understood the significance of their headdress: mosquitoes assaulted us in their thousands, probing our clothing and dulling my senses with their noise and number.

The two men recognized Sergey and greeted us quietly. The balaclava hoods made it difficult to distinguish features or to guess their age. (During my first summer, people wearing protective clothing invariably appeared to me older than they were, and sometimes even looked rather threatening.) The older man, introduced to me as Grigory, was probably in his fifties; his companion Ivan was in his thirties. As they talked they constantly flicked and picked at each other's faces where the mosquitoes were working busily amongst beard stubble and grime.

Invited inside to 'drink tea', we walked towards the cabin. In the porch a bucket of smouldering wood chippings had been placed so as to allow the draught to carry the smoke in through the inner door. The interior consisted of one high-ceilinged, smoke-blackened room about five by six metres, with windows on three sides. Inside the door and to the right stood an unlit free-standing iron stove piled with black pots and kettles, its pipe going up through the roof. In the other corners there were large solid wooden benches built against the walls, doubling as seats and beds. On each bench there was a mattress and down-filled roll which had been pushed into the corner behind a mosquito net suspended from the ceiling. Under two of the windows were tables covered with old oilcloth where the remains of meals were scattered amongst knives, spoons and enamel mugs. The place was unkempt, rough-and-ready, much of it put together without care, but I reminded myself that a fishing cabin was not to be compared with a home. With the thick smoke almost down to the floor I could hardly keep my eyes open.

'Sit down,' said Grigory. 'The mosquitoes will go soon and then we'll ease up on the smoke.' To my surprise the predators did steadily sink in their thousands to the floor.

Sergey and I laid out some of the food which we had brought with us: fresh bread from the Krasnoshchelye bakery, cheese and salami sausage from Lovozero, some cloves of garlic, and a box of lump sugar. Ivan brought a large kettle in from the outside fire and added boiling water to the cold black tea which I had poured from the smaller *zavarnik* (brewing teapot) sitting on the stove. The tea was welcome even if flavoured with mosquitoes.

Ivan, who had now removed his hood, revealed sharp and striking features with piercing dark eyes under a boyish mop of black hair. Grigory, the older man, kept his hood on – and even added a black beret – but what I saw of his grey-bristled rotund face was of a calm gentleness. Both men were from Krasnoshchelye, members of the fishing collective. The two of them netted the lake for a few weeks at about this time every year, salting and barrelling the catch for distribution in the village or for sale in Lovozero. The lake was rich in pike, perch, bream and whitefish. The whitefish, which Russians call *sig* and find second only to salmon, were drying on free-standing frames outside, and dozens of pike heads, intended for dog food, had been threaded and hung against the wall outside.

As we smoked and talked I asked about the old Saami settlement nearby – the *seit* – and Grigory told me how to find it. It was 'only a few kilometres away. You can't miss it.' That evening, as Sergey went in search of the first of his eagle nests, I walked, as directed, across the marsh behind the cabin. A raking sun in the clear night sky gave the landscape a warm glow that had been missing earlier in the day. Over my head bright yellow-wagtails and a pair of plovers were worrying about their young which were recently out of the nest and on the ground ahead of me. As I walked, the bog rosemary exuded a resinous perfume when crushed underfoot, and everywhere was thick with flowering cloudberry, the large succulent berry much sought after by Saami, Russians and Scandinavians alike.

Finding the *seit* was not as simple as I had been led to believe; I should have suspected the remark 'You can't miss it'. The 'path' evaded me, and after a kilometre of bog everything looked the same. Using my map and compass I thought I could not have gone wrong, but the forest ridge that I walked yielded nothing: no signs of building foundations and no sight of open ground. This was a pathetic start to my explorations, and after crossing another raised bog which seemed even more densely populated with mosquitoes and to have more than its share of black holes, I was beginning to care little whether I found the old settlement or not. Working my way along a second ridge, however, I walked out of the forest and across a few acres of open ground. The south-facing slope was clear of trees, dry and grassy like a pasture, and patched decoratively with willow herb, labrador tea, chervil, wild onion, and the small blossoms of purple saxifrage. I had found the Saami's Upper Kamenka *seit*.

The slope was open to the south but sheltered from fierce prevailing northerlies by the surrounding forest. From where I stood I could see a large part of the territory in which the Saami of this place would have fished, hunted and minded winter herds of reindeer. The sun behind me in the north-west highlighted the Upper Kamenka Lake and the River Ponoy, and then picked out the bluffs and rocky outcrops rising above the wooded high ground in the distance. Their names on my map – a mixture of Russian and Saami – sounded evocative: Bear Mountain, Belfry Hills, Bride's Hill, Groom's Hill, Old Man's Mountain, Perch Mountain, Boat Mountain. The names of some of the smaller lakes and rivers still ended with the Saami word *yavr* and *iok* and had not been changed to the Russian *ozero* and *reka*. I lay back in the warm grass, smoked and dozed.

I almost forgot to look for the standing stones. At the top of the slope, set back into the trees, they were not immediately visible against the sun. The twenty or thirty concentric slabs of dark grey sandstone, stacked to about two metres high and tapering at the top, looked so similar to dozens I had seen on walks elsewhere in the world that I wondered just how old they really were.

Kavray stones, usually sited at settlements or regular camping places, were, as I learned later, venerated in the Saami animistic tradition as spiritual elder-brother surrogates to whom homage was paid. These lapidary idols, according to the Russian anthropologist Charnolussky who was in Russian Lapland in the 1920s, 'obeyed higher gods and were regularly consulted in matters of health and family affairs.' They were also said to have given man the wolf (to cull the reindeer) and the dog (to keep him company). Unaware on the present occasion of their spiritual significance and function, I gave them scant attention.

As I strolled further through the grasses and herbs I encountered evidence of past buildings and earthworks, the foundations of houses and cabins, and the remains of wooden bases to barns, but I found it difficult to recreate in my mind the atmosphere and bustle of a whole community.

Later that night in the cabin at the lake, when I voiced this failure of imagination on my part, Grigory remarked that at an inland *seit* it was usually the mid-winter weeks that were the most active and sociable, not the summer. In summer it was quiet, he said. Most people were away fishing or running with reindeer. In winter more people were at home enjoying time with their families or with their neighbours. The winter was ideal for visiting and socializing because everyone was less busy working; and when people travelled from one *seit* to the other it was easier by sledge over the snow than over the bog in summer.

'And each community had a *serpat*, a hall for meetings, games and dances,' Grigory added. 'The hall was always popular.'

Some Saami families travelled great distances in the winter, and for much of the pre-revolutionary past the Kamenka's main winter *seit* had flourished as the geographical centre of the Peninsula. It was a natural crossroads for traffic between Lovozero to the west and Ponoy to the east, between Iokanga on the Barents coast in the north and Varzuga on the White Sea to the south. Now only a few fishermen passed up and down the Ponoy, and in winter a few men would come by snowmobile from Krasnoshchelye to shoot game and hunt deer and elk.

Sergey and I awoke the next day to see Ivan and Grigory returning home across the calm lake water with the morning's catch. And then, after a meal, it was time to move on. We rowed away from the cabin as the two men sat at the edge of the lake, gutting and salting fish, and filling the small barrels which had been standing in the water during the dry warm weather.

'We're heading for Lodochnaya, the Boat Mountain,' said Sergey. It was a peregrine falcon nesting site, the first of many on Sergey's annual survey.

Sergey worked the boat through the maze of small lakes and connecting waterways. Then, leaving the boat at a bank, we prepared for the difficult walk that lay between ourselves and the hills ahead. Loading our smaller rucksacks with a few rations and ornithological equipment, and drawing our thigh boots up to their full height, we stepped on to the springy surface of a raised bog. Following in Sergey's tracks I made each reluctant step as an act of faith, pretending, as the soft vegetable matter broke beneath my feet, that all that was required was self-confidence and calm. But each time I felt my boot breaking through the fragile floor, my immediate reaction was to make the next stride as quickly as possible. This exacerbated the situation: my hurried step was too strong and I found myself falling up to my thighs and then sinking further up to my chest. With waders full of water and the immediate broken bog surface hardly strong enough to hold me as I drew myself out, I felt I would never last the distance.

Sergey, who was already finding me wanting in a number of things both on water and on land, showed little patience. 'Slowly, slowly. Don't hurry, man,' he called from a distance. 'Just walk like me and you'll be all right. You won't drown.' Feeling and looking like the Green Man who came out of the bog, I walked, balanced, bobbed up and down, and hovered or rested on the stronger raised tufts, peering into the black treacle all around me, waiting for my next plunge. Faith and prayer had little effect, and when I reached the firm higher ground, I pleaded with Sergey not to take us back the same way. 'Sorry, no alternative,' he replied without commiseration. 'You'll find it easier going back, and by the end of the month I guarantee you'll be walking on water.'

We walked on into pine forest where the lichen lay like a thick, seamless, silver-green carpet, so soft that I could have hung my wet socks and boots round my neck and walked barefoot.

'Recently more deer have been staying in these hills during the summer instead of moving north to the tundra,' observed my companion.

'Well, the lichen here looks good, doesn't it,' I said. Sergey turned and looked at me with an expression that I was now learning to read quite fluently.

'No, Roger. Deer don't eat lichen in summer. Once the snow has melted it gets dry and crisp and unpalatable. They eat grass, foliage and mushrooms.'

We walked on, skirting the steep cliffs of Lodochnaya. At intervals Sergey shouted and clapped his hands to flush nesting peregrine from the rocky ledges. Emerging into an open part of the forest, he stopped me and pointed ahead: on the side of the hill was a large rock of triangular profile, apparently balancing on a much smaller circular stone.

'That's one of the stones around here that the Saami consider sacred. You'll see others. They're just a result of glacial movement, of course, but when seen from certain angles they look impressive, and the Saami have long venerated them. Now walk ahead of me and you'll see something else. Keep looking at the outline of the hill.' After a hundred metres the side of the rock face was transmogrified into the profile of a male human head with a long flat forehead, large nose and deep chin.

'*Starik* he's called. And just beyond you'll see his companion *Starukha*. Old man and old woman. The place is often known as *Praudedki* [a respectful diminutive for ancestors]. Below them is a place that Saami traditionally venerate but also fear.'

In an open area at the foot of the cliffs a group of rocks stood in isolation on a low knoll. They were smooth, as if artificially shaped, and arranged almost like large altars and thrones. Saami used to come to places like these to pray to their gods. There are thousands of them throughout Lapland. The more public locations, near settlements or regular camp sites, were used for communal worship or supplication. The more secluded places, like this one, were often sacrificial sites, and usually distinguished by a curious and awe-inspiring natural rock feature called a *seid*, like the one Sergey had pointed out. At the sacrificial sites the Saami would bring reindeer to kill, drinking the blood, eating a small part of the flesh, smearing the rocks, and placing entrails on the 'altars', but leaving most of the carcass to be scavenged by wild animals or birds. Sometimes they placed deerskins on the ground and laid out the bones as if to indicate that the animals were sleeping. The belief at these reindeer-related rituals was that the gods would 'return' the animals healthy and in even greater numbers, and also protect future herds from excessive harassment by wolves and bears.

'There used to be a Saami ground-maze here too,' said Sergey. 'Maybe there still is, somewhere under the lichen.' He was referring to one of the many ground-level circles laid out by the Saami, called a *labirint*: a simple concentric arrangement of small smooth stones, the outer circle measuring between eight and fifteen metres in diameter. Some of the oldest have been confidently dated by archaeologists to the Mesolithic and Iron Ages, but their function has never been entirely clear. Charnolussky the anthropologist, who reported stone circles here at Lodochnaya in 1927 – they were almost hidden under moss and no longer in use, but still intact – wrote that in earlier times the Saami's shaman would jump in and out of the concentric circles, chanting, appeasing gods and indulging in fortune-telling and prophecy. Most frequently he was asked to pronounce on fishing, the weather, the health of reindeer herds, or a family's future.

Sergey shouted from a short distance, beckoning me to join him. I found him crouched over the carcass of a reindeer. Nearby were the remains of three other adult deer and one calf. They had been dead for probably two or three months and still gave off a slight odour of putrefaction when I bent over them.

'Now, Sergey. So where's the shaman?' I joked.

Sergey looked concerned. 'I've seen dead deer around here before. It's impossible to tell if they've been shot, but I can tell they haven't died naturally, and I doubt they've been killed by wolves or bears. Perhaps they were diseased, although then I wouldn't expect to find them in the open part of the forest. It's curious.' It *was* uncanny.

As we walked around the headland to the north side of the hill, a female peregrine falcon flew away from one of the ledges high above us. Sergey spotted the tell-tale excreta on a rock below the nest and we started to climb. When, forty minutes later, I watched Sergey fall from the nesting ledge, I began to imagine that we might have imposed too boldly on a sacred place. Sergey sat upright, looked back up at me and waved with a smile.

And he was right about the return journey across the bog. I walked on water and filled my waders only once.

When Sergey Ganusevich showed me the wildlife of the Kamenka territory, what had seemed to me at first an inhospitable, intimidating and untraversable, mosquito-infested wetland where lakes were rocky and shallow and waterways went round in circles or suddenly ran dry, was revealed to me as a remarkably rich ecosystem where man had lived for millennia in harmony with nature.

Sergey showed me white-tailed sea eagles' nests. Over the years he had ringed several dozen young birds in the nest. This particular year the spring had come earlier than usual and his approaches to the nests were proving difficult. At the foot of one tall pine he briefed me before he climbed the tree. 'This young bird looks active and may try to fly out, so put yourself at the bottom of the hill and divert it from landing in the bog. If it does end up in the wet, get to it as quickly as possible. When you get to it, make sure you hold the claws and keep your face away from its beak. And Roger, try not to fall in. Please.'

Sergey scaled the trunk of the twenty-metre tree in moments but at the top he had difficulty moving round on to the nest, a bulky tangle of sticks, enlarged over the years by the returning birds. As I reached the edge of the bog I looked up to see the young eagle flying away from Sergey's grasp, descending out of control through the trees. To my relief the bird decided against the soft-landing option.

By the time I had climbed back up the hill, Sergey had reached the bird, gathered the confused and blinking juvenile to his chest and had started back to his equipment near the foot of the tree. Meanwhile, the female parent, having returned to the nest and found her off-spring gone, was circling above us, complaining, and giving us a good view of her two-metre wing span. I watched as Sergey firmly and proficiently measured the legs and the wings of the young bird, and applied large colour rings to both ankles with a tool like a large staple gun, and then placed it in a canvas bag and weighed it with a small spring scale. None of this handling appeared to alarm the creature, which behaved throughout with calm, bemused resignation.

The coloured ring fixed loosely on each leg seemed very large on the young bird, and I wondered how both parent and daughter were going to respond to the sudden and unexpected appearance of this jewellery. Sergey assured me the effects were benign. With the bird in the bag Sergey and I walked back to the base of the tree.

Later that week we found a dead three-year-old sea eagle which Sergey had ringed at two months. Sergey remembered its every detail and statistic. Taking blood, tissue and feathers for analysis in Moscow, he guessed that the bird had consumed contaminated fish during the winter and had not survived the migration.

'There's no other reason for birds to die here. The region is rich in food, there are fish in the lakes and rivers, and plenty of small mammals.'

On several occasions I watched peregrine stooping – their vertical dives are said to reach 300 kilometres per hour. Each time I felt a twinge of pity for the victim but experienced an atavistic thrill from watching the precision of the mid-air kill, and even imagined having my own bird and mews at home to cull the growing population of Chelsea's feral pigeons.

When Peter the Great's father Tsar Aleksis Mikhaylovich created a fashionable craze for falconry throughout the Russian Empire, there was great demand for the eyas, the fledgling falcon taken from the nest. In Russian Lapland, hundreds of peregrine, gyr, merlin and goshawk were trapped annually to satisfy the market, and the trade was highly profitable for the Saami who were intimately familiar with the breeding grounds.

'Around the Black Sea and the Aral Sea today,' said Sergey, 'Russians train goshawk in as little as three days to catch quail. Each autumn the quail migrate in thousands. The slaughter must be an incredible sight.'

At the end of our time together, when Sergey was due to return to Moscow, he delivered me back to the Upper Kamenka Lake where I was to wait for a fisherman to take me further down the Ponoy. I expressed my gratitude to Sergey that he had shared so much of his knowledge, but four weeks with him had exposed my inferior field skills and tested our friendship. Sergey knew everything there was to know about living in the wild and had little patience with my short-comings. He could make a fire in moments during a rainstorm, and I was invariably scolded for using the wrong wood or for taking too long. I considered myself an experienced boatman but he could barely tolerate my rowing technique. A man who kept the contents of his rucksack to a laudable minimum, he scorned much of my equipment, my clothing, and the time I spent organizing my excessive inventory.

Sergey could see with his naked eye almost as much as I could with my binoculars. He was so alert to everything around him that he gave the impression of being in competition with the falcons and with nature itself, as well as with me. On occasions, when he was fully absorbed in his work, his features, which were already aquiline, seemed well on the way to metamorphosis.

Our relationship reached its nadir when I accidentally threw away our entire holding of *spirt*. This top-grade pure alcohol, which Sergey brought from Moscow and always carried with him, was a regular comfort at the end of a hard day's work. Sergey would mix one part *spirt* with two parts water, creating an excellent vodka substitute which we sometimes flavoured lightly with orange powder.

We anticipated the evening ritual with relish. One morning I had suggested I decant the remaining *spirt* into my strong aluminium water bottle which I never used. In the evening Sergey acted on my idea, but without telling me. Returning to the fireside after a short stroll along the river I picked up my water bottle from among our provisions and emptied it. As the last drops reached the ground I felt a sting on my finger where I had a small fresh cut. I had to take several deep breaths before facing Sergey with the news that the remainder of our expedition would be teetotal. The news was received in stony silence, and my every error thereafter – of which there seemed curiously to be an increasing number – was greeted with silent resignation and a long-suffering sigh.

Sergey had also become irritated by my obsessive struggles with mosquitoes, forgetting that he had lived with them every summer for almost two decades. One evening when he had finished telling me about the few ornithological colleagues who had enthusiastically accompanied him on expeditions to the Peninsula – but 'all of them only once' – I asked mischievously why none of them had ever returned for further joint fieldwork. 'It's the mosquitoes, Roger. They couldn't stand the mosquitoes.' I chuckled.

On the river

THE BOATMAN who arrived at the Upper Kamenka Lake where Sergey had left me was called Ilya. I never learned his family name or his patronymic. We agreed a reasonable fee in US dollars for him to take me down the river as far as the village of Kanevka and show me some old Saami places on the way, but on the evening of our departure, as I helped him load the fuel tanks and the spare motor, he was ill at ease, reticent to the point of discourtesy, as if he didn't want me in the boat at all.

Once under way I took a closer look at the man. He was, I supposed, in his forties. He had a round sallow-skinned face with straight black hair that usually fell over his forehead in a fringe. His dark almond eyes constantly flashed from side to side, busily alert, rather like his bustling, energetic gait which, I noticed earlier, was delivered by a pair of short, bandy legs. He was wearing a grey serge *sovik*, a smock-like garment, with the hood down. Around the *sovik* was a broad leather belt studded with brass ornaments and hung with small talismanic items and a large sheathed knife. His thick woollen trousers were worn inside rubber waders folded down below the knee. For the next hour he gripped the tiller without shifting his seat, looking well ahead as if searching the banks for wildlife, never once returning my curious gaze from where I sat at the bow.

As we rejoined the main river Ilya opened the throttle and we motored at speed. Irritated after a time by the noise of the engine and feeling cold from the wind, I buried myself beneath a canvas tarpaulin on the floor of the boat. Whenever I poked my head above the gunwales my face was whipped by insects and hatches of sedge, olive and duckfly, some of which finished deep inside my ears. How Ilya sat up at the stern so resolutely I couldn't imagine.

There was so much that I wanted to ask him – he was, after all, my first Russian Saami travel companion – but our exchanges across the length of the boat were unproductive. He had never before spoken to a foreigner, and I spoke limited Russian. He found conversation difficult and tiresome. He was shouting to me now but I couldn't hear or understand and I returned to the warmth of the canvas.

At about midnight the engine slowed and I sat up. In the dim light of the cloudy evening, through occasional gaps in the tall bankside bushes and grasses, I could make out an area of higher open ground in the distance where some half-dozen log cabins and barns were spread out across a broad slope of rocks and grass that ran gently from the edge of a forest down to the water. Near one of the log cabins a tall thin pole was flying a ragged flag with the horizontal white-blue-red colours of the new Russian Federation. It seemed to signal occupation and, as we approached the muddy shore, there were signs of recent activity where a wooden boat was drawn up. We had arrived at Chalmne Varre.

As we touched land I began my usual desperate struggle with mosquitoes. The insouciant Ilya calmly pulled the hood of his *sovik* over his head and started the short walk up the slope towards the cabin with the flag mast.

'*Kapitan! Kapitan!*' he bellowed as we walked.

The cabin was small but from the outside gave the appearance of being a home rather than a working hut. Some split pine logs, whose yellow ends had shone even when seen at a distance from the river, were neatly stacked next to an outside stove. Kettles, pans and bowls were laid out on a rough-hewn table supported by logs. Running from the flagpole to the cabin there was a full clothes-line. Reindeer skins had been nailed for curing on to the outside north and east walls. Tools and clothing hung neatly in the porch.

An invisible voice acknowledged our arrival. Once inside we were greeted with voluminous guffaws from a man in blue underpants sitting smoking at a table between two small windows in the far wall. Built against one of the side-walls and under a mosquito net was the Kapitan's bed, and along the same wall a second bench-bed. The cabin walls were decorated with a formal portrait of Leonid Brezhnev and a large collection of pages from magazines, almost all of which emphasized female anatomy. The small wood-burning stove was alight. Having suffered from the cold windrush on our journey to Chalmne Varre, I was thawed by the pleasant warmth that filled the cabin.

'I haven't had a visitor for weeks, and it's John the Baptist Day already,' said our host in his cups, brandishing one of two empty vodka bottles. The fish soup that he offered looked unpalatable and unhygienic but, in response to my gift of salami, cheese and a further bottle of vodka, he insisted on frying us some freshly caught pike.

'St John the Baptist Day has been and gone,' replied Ilya, pretending to snatch away the vodka. 'Anyway, I'm sure you've got plenty of your own brew.'

Ilya and the Kapitan joked and bantered as old friends. Since I was the first foreign visitor to the cabin, they both raised their voices to a shout when speaking to me – to 'help me understand the Russian' – but when Ilya and I started to eat our meal, the Kapitan retired to the far corner of the room where he squatted and smoked in silence, staring at me intently.

The Kapitan – Nikolay – had a small muscular body and was in his early fifties, though he looked older and ravaged, probably from an excess of impure vodka or *spirt*. His stubble was dark and heavy but his head had been recently shaven. This, together with his nakedness and the dark eyes constantly probing me from his squatting position, cast him as the wild backwoodsman: reserved and courteous in the company of a stranger, yet observant and alert. 'Kapitan' seemed an inappropriate sobriquet for this hermit.

On the second morning of our visit, when Nikolay had sobered up and felt he knew me better, he warmed to my curiosity about his family history and about Chalmne Varre. The son of a Saami father and Russian mother, he had started his working life as a reindeer herder. When he was a child, Chalmne Varre had been a thriving place with its own reindeer herds and a fishing collective, comprising a mixed community of about 350 people, but in the 1960s the villagers were forced to move out. It was the time of 'rationalization', as they called it: the reindeer were to be gathered into one large collective centred on Krasnoshchelye, a hundred kilometres upriver.

'We had no option but to move away from Chalmne Varre,' explained Nikolay. 'There were no supplies, and no medic or veterinary assistance. They even introduced restrictions on hunting. That was absurd when you consider that ten years later, in the seventies, the Gospromkhoz [state collective] started flying marksmen around in winter in helicopters to shoot deer and elk from the air. Hundreds and thousands of animals were killed that way, or wounded and lost. Those few years of slaughter almost annihilated our elk population.'

When his family eventually moved to Krasnoshchelye, Nikolay married a Saami girl and fathered two children, but he failed to adapt to collective life or to the new-fangled ideas of reindeer management promoted by the Party cadres at the time. In his thirties he took to drink and became violent, prone to persistent cadging and then to stealing. He had changed. He wasn't himself any longer. Life being intolerable for him in Krasnoshchelye, he left his family to return to his birthplace in the summer of 1976.

Nikolay filled our cups and stood at the window staring out across the river.

'My family didn't live in this small cabin. We had a larger house with a living room, a kitchen, a spacious *seni* [unheated entrance room] and a good loft. When we left Chalmne Varre in 1964 we dismantled our home, numbered each log, loaded the logs on to barges and rowed them up the river to Krasnoshchelye where the house was rebuilt. My old mother lives there now, but my father has died. I'm sure my sister Lyudmila would be happy to show it to you. I still go there occasionally. I'm very fond of it. Mother has kept it just as it was.' He went back to the corner for sugar, stirring in five spoonfuls.

'I survive well enough here, I'm good at fishing and hunting – well, good enough for my own needs. Fishermen come regularly from Krasnoshchelye and bring me a few essentials like bread, butter, oil and cigarettes. A few of my salmon ensure a good supply of vodka and *spirit* in return.'

In the afternoon Nikolay offered to show me round outside.

'It must be hard for you to imagine how this empty place used to be, with me now the only inhabitant. The other three cabins are occasionally slept in by fishermen from Krasnoshchelye. The far building over there is an old cattle shed where I sometimes keep the sheep that I tend. That earns me about half a dollar a month, the only cash I earn. The grass here is good for grazing, quite different from the tough sedge grass on the marsh. The small hut is a bath-house which still works. That's the well near it, over there with the railings.'

We climbed a narrow path that passed between granite boulders and up into the pine woods, and then across a grass clearing of several acres.

'We had good cattle and sheep, and through there in the other clearing we used to grow all the vegetables we needed: potatoes, two kinds of cabbage, turnips, beet, radishes, carrots … really healthy vegetables … and more than enough for the whole village.'

At the edge of the vegetable field Nikolay pointed out the cemetery. Most of the graves were dilapidated or overgrown but the wooden railings of his grandfather's grave were in good condition and the Orthodox cross was still upright, with the lower diagonal arm in place. Nikolay then led me further into the woods where he showed me another grave, overgrown but open, exposing the rotten remains of a small wooden coffin which looked like a Saami boat sledge. 'It belonged to a Saami child, I believe,' he said cryptically, walking away, leaving me to wonder what had happened to the corpse.

'Take a look at that view. The river's full of fish, there's game in the forest, good lichen for reindeer in winter, a few elk here and there for my needs. And there's duck everywhere. I sometimes wonder if the wildlife isn't grateful to the Party for clearing all the humans off these lands.'

I quoted the report of a Tsarist government official who had visited the region and some of the Saami settlements: 'Only a cock and three hens could live in those places,' he had written.

Nikolay laughed. 'A cock might be useful. With three hens I'd want for nothing!' He chortled at his own joke for the rest of the day.

We continued on to the well, filled a bucket of cold, crystal-clear water and walked back to the cabin. From across the marsh I heard for the first time the small, famously elusive jack snipe, with its call that is uncannily similar to the sound of galloping horses. For supper Nikolay fried us the liver of an elk that he had shot in the forest close to the cemetery in late spring. It was a delicacy worthy of its reputation.

I didn't see much of Nikolay that evening or the next day. When he got out of his bed the following morning he was incoherent from drink. I worried about his nets being neglected and the catch wasted, so I rowed his old wooden boat across the river and into the small adjacent lakes and streams where I had helped him set his nets the day before. Fighting mosquitoes, I hauled in pike, grayling, perch and bream by the bucketful and took them back to the bank below the cabin where I cleaned and salted them. As I walked up to the cabin and slopped the fish innards into the dog bowls, the door opened and Nikolay staggered towards the earth closet cabin. He insisted that I shouldn't have bothered with the fish-cleaning but was evidently pleased that I had. He lurched on past me but, with a much abused stomach to contend with, he failed to reach his destination, and I had to perform an unsightly rescue operation of the kind usually reserved for one's closest friends or family.

When I had first arrived, Nikolay had offered to walk me along the river bank and show me some ancient rock drawings nearby. Going out without him that night but remembering his directions, I searched the water's edge under the warm midnight sun and found the two large flat, smooth, pale brown rocks, each measuring about three metres square. Broadly etched into the fine-grained surface were dozens of small stick-figures of men and reindeer. I had already walked past the rocks in the middle of that same day and noticed nothing, but the raking midnight light from the north now animated each image. (Looking at other similar rock drawings during mid-summer some years later, I noticed again how in the noonday sun they were almost invisible, while the light at one o'clock in the morning revealed them in optimum conditions.)

The Saami gave this immediate stretch of the Ponoy the name Chalmne Varre, 'Sparkling Eyes of the Forest'. It was not a place where the Saami had lived for long – Nikolay's village was founded in the 1930s – but it was an ideal place for catching wild reindeer. During the autumn, when the herds migrated from the northern tundra to the protection of the forests further south, thousands of them crossed the River Ponoy, and still do so, near this point. The Saami would lie in wait for the returning summer herd, ready with lassos to catch the healthy bulls and calves, or with spears to throw from the bank and from boats to kill for meat. Chalmne Varre's role in the Kamenka Saami's seasonal cycle had been recorded in stone. Even though the imagery was limited to stylized frontal human figures and reindeer in profile, the rock drawings had an urgency that I could associate with lying in wait for a herd. I learnt later that these petro-glyphs were reliably considered to be over two thousand years old.

Ilya, who had been away setting his own nets since our arrival at Chalmne Varre, decided it was time for us to leave. Our evening easterly route, which followed a tortuous passage through a network of Ponoy tributaries and watercourses, was impossible to follow on the map. Ilya was either unable or reluctant to show me our precise position, but simply said 'Nizhnekamenka', which I took to mean that we were on our way to the Lower Stony Lake, another former *seit* of the Kamenka Saami, like the one I had visited at the Upper Stony Lake four weeks earlier.

When we entered the open waters of the lake I understood how it had come by its name: even in July, with plenty of water in the system, it was a treacherous, rocky stretch and, for a stranger, probably unnavigable. Ilya, who appeared to know the hazards intimately, motored the whole width of the lake very slowly.

The night sky was cloudy and dull, the warm windless air humid and close. Ahead of us on the banks of the lake I could make out human shapes moving amongst the scrub and small trees that lined the shore. As we came closer I saw a large tarred boat drawn up, several sets of nets hanging along the bushes, and countless barrels of different sizes in and out of the water. Two young men walked past us as we beached our boat but gave us no welcome; a man working on his boat engine also said nothing. Sitting on a long log, bending over a large metal tub of fish, there was a slow-moving shape of barely human appearance. It wore a blue beret over a mosquito hood, and a much-weathered quilted cotton jacket wrapped around with several layers of ragged material. Large grey felt *valenki* pushed out from the torso like stumps from a stuffed effigy. As we walked along the bank it briefly raised its head to reveal the features of an old man with black and expressionless eyes set deep beneath bushy eyebrows, the face a mass of grey stubble, planted with the soggy butt of a cigarette. His hands, with which he was lifting a large pike out of a tub by his side, were hugely swollen, with the index and major fingers of his left hand bound together with a blood-stained rag. On his knees there was a large board which he was using to gut the fish on, throwing innards on to the muddy ground around him which was already littered with malodorous fish parts. He continued his work without returning my greeting.

Everywhere there were fish, large and small, silver to green, lying in buckets and tubs, gutted and ungutted. Two boys, standing in the water wearing thigh boots, were washing and sorting; two others were salting. Ilya addressed a few remarks to a couple more men who were hurriedly closing the tops of the barrels with canvas and rope, and pointed to me as if to explain my presence. Without raising their heads they answered briefly in language I could not follow.

Ilya did not answer my questions – perhaps he couldn't understand them – but he saw my wide-eyed curiosity. He led me through the bushes and we emerged on to higher and drier sandy ground overlooking the lake. The open stretch of grass and heather continued up to a rocky bluff with pine trees above. Near us there was a tall pyramidal wigwam structure which Ilya identified to me monosyllabically as a *chum*. The apex was about four metres from the ground, and the conical frame of poles had been wrapped around with several sheets of brown canvas. Beckoning me to follow, Ilya drew back the large flap and ushered me in proprietorially, closing the flap again swiftly against mosquitoes. There was plenty of room to stand. On the ground there was bedding for about five people. Reindeer skins had been laid down over a floor-covering of spruce branches and sods of turf. Cups, pans and scraps of food were scattered among the bedding and clothing, and a fire ringed by stones in the middle of the floor was smouldering gently, sending smoke out through the opening in the roof. A blackened kettle and an iron cauldron hung from a wooden crane. Attached to a strut of wood high up was the head of an enormous pike that must originally have weighed as much as a small boy. As my eyes adjusted to the gloom I noticed two sleeping shapes beneath bedrolls and mosquito netting.

Outside, near the *chum* and built into the side of the slope, was a small hut that Ilya described to me as 'a traditional Saami *vezha*'. It had a square base of horizontal logs to a height of one metre and from there its four sides, made from planking, sloped up towards an apex. It was like a wooden, square version of the *chum* tent. The roof was covered with birch bark and thick sods of grass and heather, with a few branches on top. The door, which was set above the ground, opened out and slightly upwards. When Ilya pulled it open it let out a tongue of smoke and when I stepped over the threshold, the air pinched my nostrils and momentarily stopped me in my tracks. Closing the door behind me and stooping under the sloping roof-planks, I was disoriented by the dark and the smoke and the over-powering odours, not immediately noticing the four men sitting on the ground around the fire in the middle. Following Ilya's example I sat down, pushed myself between the men without remark, settled on the comfortable animal skins, and waited for my eyes to adjust. The fire, which was circled by small rocks and now down to the embers, had been quite large but I could see no way through the roof for smoke to go out or air to come in. As in the *chum*, a large black cauldron was hanging on a chain, and pots and pans, bowls, spoons, aluminium plates and tin mugs lay everywhere. There were some bedrolls piled against the walls.

The men stared at the embers, then at me, then back at the embers – all in silence. I saw little beyond their hoods and jackets except dark narrow eyes, stubbled faces, and thick soiled hands. The figures seemed small and, in the half light, almost indistinguishable from each other. In time a desultory, low-toned exchange of grunts circulated the group. Nobody addressed a word to me, nor did Ilya introduce me. I felt uneasy but not surprised.

As we all left the *vezha* and the men walked away towards the lake, Ilya told me that they were not convinced by my reasons for wanting to see the lake and the old encampment. As far as they knew, no other foreigner at that time had made the journey. And having heard so much about the foreign and Russian businessmen who were everywhere 'after Gorbachev', some suspected I had a financial interest in the area. Others said that I might be only a naturalist or a historian, but when I returned to Murmansk I would almost certainly say the wrong things to the regional administration about their fishing.

Ilya walked me around the open ground where the old *seit* had been, and then up the hill through the grass and heather to the foot of the cliffs. This was once a large summer place for the Saami, similar to the one I had seen near the Upper Kamenka Lake. Both dry terrains, with their panoramic views of the territory, were topographically alike, and had a similar resonance.

We took a narrow path to an old well amongst dwarf birches. It was protected by a large, carpentered wooden cover. Raising the small access lid, I looked down at the clear water and at the stones carefully set as a lining to the upper part of the well, and then used the clean tin scoop to refresh myself with a mouthful of cool water.

The Kamenka Saami territory, or *payk*, which comprised four *seity*, was one of the oldest on the Peninsula, probably in continual occupation for one and a half thousand years, ever since the north coast families began to move inland after the reindeer. It was also from here that some of the larger, richer families like the Matryokhin – still in existence today – had spread further east during the last two or three hundred years, taking their reindeer herds to Lumbovka on the east coast. The old Kamenka families had been replaced on the lakeside today by only a residual seasonal presence of mixed-race fishermen living single and rough, but the well was an abiding link with the original families who had lived and prospered there up until only thirty years earlier, herding, fishing, hunting and trapping, and caring for their homes.

We returned to the shore and walked among the boats, nets and barrels. The fishermen exchanged sporadic remarks, not always in Russian. Ilya explained something to some of the men and, indicating that I had their approval, invited me to take a photograph, but I felt uneasy and declined. The photograph would tell me nothing about how I saw these wild, wrapped people, or how they felt about me. Everything seemed removed, dreamlike and bleak ... the grey dawn light ... the mysterious reticent men ... the fish, the smell ... the mosquitoes.

'The hill straight ahead of us in the distance is called Trofim because that's where a Saami family of that name used to live,' explained my boatman. 'Its original Saami name is Seidpakhk, meaning Sacred Cliff.' Ilya turned off the engine and took the oars. Our course towards the south-east outlet of the Lower Kamenka lake passed over rocks visible just beneath the surface of the water. We then entered long narrow channels that twisted through sedge marsh and beds of large water lilies. Watching two cranes pacing with their characteristically slow-motion emphasis across the marsh, I was reminded of my own deliberate and ill-fated steps across the bogs en route to Sergey's peregrines and eagles. Dragonfly darted and hovered everywhere. A week ago they had been single-winged; now they were magnificent,

large double-winged species. The Arctic terns, those seasonal indicators which are the last of all Russian Lapland's migrant birds to arrive
and the first to leave, swooped and screeched in the pellucid morning
light. A few weeks earlier they had been in South Africa, 17,000 kilometres away.

We were about to rejoin the Ponoy, whose long, slow, multitudi-
nous diversions through the Depression wetlands were now recon-
verging into one main course and drawing us on. The channel
widened, straightened, settled, and then produced a surging current
that carried us ahead and out into the full-bodied river.

Trofim Hill was near the water. Ilya steered the boat into the
willow undergrowth of the bank and led me through the birches.
Within a few minutes we were walking below cliffs of a kind I now
associated with peregrine falcon. Ilya had lagged behind; he was
waiting for me to catch sight of something which then dramatically
appeared on the mountain above me. Looking as if it were momentarily airborne or hovering, a vast oval-shaped rock was precariously
balanced at the very edge of the cliff face.

'It's a *seid*, another sacred stone, but larger than the one you saw at
Lodochnaya. Let's climb.' We scrambled up the face pursued by the
bloodthirsty hordes and, emerging at the north-east end of the ridge,
found ourselves on the peak, standing next to the large rock. Glacial
activity millions of years ago had carved it into a smooth-surfaced
upright oval bowl and then planted it on the ridge.

Ilya explained to me that this rock was considered by Saami the most
important *seid* in the wider regon: it confirmed the powers of the
shaman, or *noaïd*, as he is called in eastern Lapland. A *seid* usually
related to a particular place where people lived or hunted, others
offered protection to travellers, but this one was seen as having wider
associations and was probably never used for sacrifice and supplication.
It was even said to have other mountain homes, and had also been seen
at Kolokolnaya Mountain – Belfry Mountain – to the west. That was
why it was also known as the Flying Stone. Further erosion underneath the rock, which must have weighed over a hundred tonnes,
meant that it was now raised on a very small stone base. This made it
look balletic but unstable. Ilya told me that parties of Christians led by
their priests had come in the past from as far as Varzuga intent on top-
pling the rock, hoping to undermine the influence of the *noaïd*.

'They came several times but never succeeded. The last time they came, which was in the 1870s, they were caught in a snowstorm on the way home and they all died.'

According to Ilya there was a stream which rose from a spring just below us and ran into a pool with a curiously circular motion before running off again and disappearing underground. There was a saying that 'while the stream flows the Saami will live on'. Ilya and others had looked several times for the stream but had never been able to find it.

We motored away from Trofim. At every turn in the river, duck flew from us, and otter and muskrat went swimming or scurrying into the banks. The ruffs were too engaged in their extravagantly vain, strutting display to pay us any attention. I dozed under the tarpaulin. We had not slept or eaten a full meal for a day and two nights. I didn't understand how Ilya stayed awake. He was still sitting high in the stern, eyes fixed ahead, though now clutching a canvas around him against the east wind.

'Now you work. I sleep,' said Ilya in the evening, smiling for the first time since we had met. 'Two hours. Catch me a salmon.'

Fatigue had got the better of him. Pointing to the nearby water as a good place for fishing, he banked the boat, took my tarpaulins, and in a trice had buried himself beneath them with not even his head showing.

Almost the entire 200 kilometres of the River Ponoy from Krasnoshchelye to this point had been flat, even where the current was fast. Below us was the first stretch of broken shallow water. It was big and fast-running, requiring difficult wading and long casts, but it looked promising for fishing with the fly and I was thrilled to be up to my waist in the water of Russian Lapland's longest river, famed for centuries for its run of salmon. Moreover, I had no idea where I would find myself the next day and how I would live once Ilya had put me out of the boat downstream at Kanevka. It seemed advisable to have a salmon in my rucksack, whether for barter or survival.

Although I had fished successfully with wet and dry fly on the lakes and slow-run streams near Chalmne Varre, I had not until then been on good salmon water. To my disappointment no salmon came to my fly in the rapids, but in the backwaters I caught a hard-fighting pike of about three kilograms and a grayling with a skin of sparkling silver. I could salt both fish and they would keep for days.

Since leaving Krasnoshchelye I had seen no other people travelling the Ponoy, but on the evening of the next day an old aluminium boat similar to ours – known universally in Russia as a *kazanka* – appeared ahead of us travelling upriver and carrying two men, a boy and a dog. The men hailed Ilya and cut their engine. We circled to face upstream and then went alongside. Ilya and the men talked and smoked, holding the boats together as we drifted. Ilya did not include me in the conversation; once again I was not even sure what language they were speaking. What I did understand was that we would all stop and have a meal on the river bank, and that Ilya had offered 'my' fish.

For our resting place we selected a stretch of dry ground which had come into view on the inner curve of a long bend as we drifted downstream. Under birch trees, surrounded by dwarf juniper, there was a conical framework of bare poles – a smaller version of the *chum* tent I had seen at Lower Kamenka, without the canvas – and an old sunken fireplace beside which some bark and kindling wood had been stacked.

We gathered more dry wood and built a generous fire, the sort that Russians call a Pioneers' fire, which we stood over to warm ourselves before settling. The process of stamping feet and swinging arms helped to thaw the ice with the new acquaintances. They were from Krasnoshchelye; they had been away from home for several days, netting the main river for salmon and sea-trout, and catching coarse species in the still water.

Following Ilya's suggestion that we make *ukha* (fish soup) I was about to gut the pike when he came to the water's edge and took the fish from me, drawing his own knife from its sheath. 'If we're going to make real *ukha*, I'll show you how to prepare the pike. Don't throw away the best ingredients. Look,' he said, slitting the pike's belly. 'Throw away the gills, the bladder and these bits but keep the rest and clean the inside of the stomach ... like this. The head, fins, tail and insides give the *ukha* the fat, the flavour, and all the goodness; the flesh is just for the appetite.'

We put all the fish into a large blackened saucepan which was then filled with water. From an inner pocket under his *sovik* Ilya pulled out a paper packet and tipped in some unidentifiable herbs and peppercorns. The boy filled a kettle and brought it to the fire. One of the other men had chopped a long stout branch of green birch which he stabbed into the ground near the fire and positioned over the now quieter flames. Rocks placed over and under the branch at its base made it firm enough to support the weight of pan and kettle together. As if drawing on the lower reaches of English humour, Russians call such a stick a *uanker*.

The Krasnoshchelye men poured vodka. 'You know the difference between *ukha* and fish soup?' asked one of them, addressing me for the first time. Throwing back the first shot, he answered his own question: 'Vodka.'

Even in spite of the persistent unmentionables it was an idyllic spot. The sun had appeared and was now warming the air. The glow of the fire and the sight of the suspended kettle and soup pan, as well as a large piece of salted salmon lying within reach on a piece of thick brown paper, melded with the sensations of vodka and cheered me after the isolation of Ilya's boat. We shared our food, drank two bottles, consumed all the delicious nourishing soup and the salmon, and the dog got the bones. Conversation was sporadic but even Ilya began to address me. I must have fallen fast asleep listening to the men talk.

I was awoken by the barking dog and the open throttle of a boat engine. My head jerked up from between my drawn-up knees. The Krasnoshchelye boat was moving away from the bank and heading upstream, with the boy sitting on the bows and the barking dog running the length of the boat. I looked back to the trees to see that Ilya had thrown our large tarpaulins around the tent poles and was securing the last sheet with a string stretched from a tree. Inside the tent I could see smoke. He had transferred the embers of the outside fire to the tent, brought my rucksack from the boat, and put down spruce branches and deerskins on the floor.

'I think it's time you got some real sleep. You haven't had any for a long time. The smoke will chase the mosquitoes out in a few minutes. Anyway you should sleep well after the vodka. You drink like a Russian.'

I remembered little until Ilya woke me from a deep sleep in our own boat to tell me that within half an hour we should be at

Kanevka. I paid him and thanked him. I asked about Kanevka but he replied that he didn't really know the village. I would have to find my own way, he said.

Half an hour later, as we took a long bend in the river, my destination came into sight.

A country hotel

M Y FIRST AND LASTING IMPRESSION of Kanevka was of children playing on the grass bank and swimming in the river under a hot sun. After the long boat ride, the indifference of my fellow-traveller, and my anxiety about where I was going, it was a euphoric picture. The village, which straddled a tributary on the Ponoy's left bank, consisted of about thirty modest wooden homes with sheds and barns. These were spread widely across a smooth grass-and-sand slope that ran down to the water. From west to east the village stretched for half a kilometre, and faced due south across 300 metres of the Ponoy towards more forest.

'There's a *gostinitsa*, Roger,' Ilya had reassured me before turning for home.

The word *gostinitsa* can mean anything from a grand hotel to a small establishment, but when Ilya pointed up the hill to a dilapidated log cabin I was uncertain what to expect. The nearer I approached, the less promising it appeared. Next to the porch, which had lost some of its steps, a man was standing facing me, relieving himself into the open air. He greeted me as I passed him, still pissing as he turned.

The smell was bad, and the litter and debris in the porch was its complement. I inspected my new home with mounting misgiving. Inside the porch was a small vestibule with a table and a gas ring which was fed by a cylinder. There was evidence of some basic cooking. Next to the table was an *umyvalnik* – a small bucket-like vessel for water, attached to the wall – above a grimy basin with a draining bucket below. The main body of the cabin comprised two large rooms, each containing four beds, one of which was not in use but had blankets. My acquaintance from the porch was standing behind me, adjusting his dress and urging me on.

I went to the empty bed half expecting a rival claimant. The bed-springs had sagged to the floor but it was a bed, a starting-point in a strange place. I busied myself with unpacking, and was surprised to find a wardrobe with one shelf and some coat-hangers. I cleared crumbs and litter off the table next to the bed and laid out my usual things: notebook and pens, maps and compass, knife and washing bag.

On one of the other beds in the room lay a good-looking fair-haired young man in an inebriated state. He had been babbling incessantly from the moment I appeared, introducing himself as Kolya and asking incoherent questions. On another bed, sitting in shirt-sleeves, propped up against the wall, regarding me suspiciously but saying nothing, was a clean-shaven and clean-shirted young man, apparently sober. I ignored him and continued to settle in. Several roughly-dressed men came and immediately left, surprised at the presence of a stranger but without addressing a word to me.

I needed to wash but the house hardly seemed the best place for personal ablutions. It was a warm day and the river apparently at a temperature for swimming, so I made my way down to the bank and selected a private spot 200 metres upriver for my first swim. The water was about eighteen degrees Celsius and comfortably refreshing. Relief overcame me. Discarding my worries about the next stage of the journey, I wallowed in the Ponoy waters, drifted downstream and walked back in the sun. I shaved, washed some clothes, sat on a log, sunbathed, wrote a few notes, and returned to my new home feeling optimistic.

As I re-entered the room I now understood the role of the sadly beautiful blond Kolya; my earlier arrival had interrupted some recreational activity. One of the men, also drunk, was kneeling by Kolya's bed, holding him by the head, imploring him to drink up – *Vypyem, vypyem!* – pouring vodka into his mouth and almost choking him. The clean-shirted but now trouserless man undressed Kolya and indulged in calm deliberate union, his rhythmic grunts of pleasure mingling weirdly with Kolya's gurgling incantations. There seemed to be an understanding that I was to be ignored, so I kept to my corner. The prostrate Kolya appeared to lapse into semi-consciousness as others lay on the bed and pleasured themselves in predictable ways – some with aggression, others with tenderness and alcoholic tearfulness. Nobody once addressed me and I fell asleep, lying on my bed fully clothed.

I awoke to a different picture. At the foot of my bed, looking down at me as I propped myself up on my elbow, was a six-person delegation.

'We can't allow you to stay here,' said one of the delegates, addressing me formally. 'Go with this person to his home and you can live there.' He gestured to a short man in his thirties with dark hair and a moustache. Volodya stepped forward.

I suggested to my visitors that I had already settled in. I had organized and cleaned part of the room, arranged my own belongings satisfactorily, and my washing was drying on a line outside the cabin. I was already home. But the delegation was insistent. There seemed little choice, therefore, but to place my future in the hands of my designated host. I persuaded myself that Volodya had an honest, kind face – whatever that might mean – I let him help me pack, and then followed him meekly outside, saying goodbye to the heedless Kolya, still recumbent but now abandoned. Volodya, carrying my large rucksack as if it were no heavier than a bag of socks, strode off at a quick pace along the grassy track towards the tributary river and its bridge. This was a primitive, plank gangway suspended on two wire cables. I wobbled and swayed my way towards the far bank. Two-thirds of the way across I looked back to see one of the men from the 'hotel' attempting to follow. I admired his ambition. He made three attempts at the start of the bridge, trying to get both feet on to the planks and his arms over the handrail cable, but the bridge's flexibility was defeating him – doubtless his world was spinning and his stomach churning. What was the urgency? I wondered. Was he making for home or for the next source of *spirt*? Sagging at the knees but staying upright, he pulled himself as far as the middle of the span but at that point, unable to cope with the increasing movement of the bridge, he lurched and collapsed in a cringed foetal position. Above the sound of the rapids I heard his loud groan, uttered probably out of surprise and relief that he had fallen just where the old and patched side-netting was still sound. He rose to his hands and knees but when he fell and rolled back into the mesh, he toppled beyond the edge and hung there over the water, held by the net like an exhausted fish.

Volodya, who had moved well ahead, was now impatiently gesticulating to me to leave the drunk where he was.

Unlike the western end of the village which we had left, where the houses, the hotel and the barns were set randomly and picturesquely on the slope among pine trees, most of the houses on the flatter ground at Volodya's end had been set symmetrically on either side of a broad straight swathe of grass. A group of children, some of whom I had seen the day before running excitedly in and out of the river, were playing in a large improvised sand pit in the middle of the highway, and a herd of sheep, fussed over by an elderly couple, was moving slowly towards me, greedily cropping the fresh grass at its edges. The houses on either side seemed in fair condition: no building was derelict, none was leaning at an angle – the hotel's detached earth closet had been an extreme example of that genre – and some had neat, well-tended gardens bordered with spruce picket fences and boasting healthy crops of potatoes, radishes, carrots and blackcurrants.

We arrived at a wooden house. In its garden was a small one-roomed log cabin and a fenced vegetable patch; beyond the house was a range of low sheds where the ground was strewn with boat paraphernalia, engine parts and fuel drums. As we opened the garden gate I was distracted first by a tame grey reindeer which had rushed to welcome Volodya but caught her antlers in my jacket, and then by a commotion and racket around the porch of the main house.

'*Khvatit! Khvatit! Schas domoy!*' 'That's enough now! You're coming home!'

Four people had tumbled out of the house and on to the porch. A young woman who was shouting these words – with a few expletives for emphasis – appeared to be pulling on one of the men. The two others were either holding him up or pulling him back; I couldn't decide which. Being the stronger party, the woman moved the group to the top of the porch steps from where they all rolled down into the garden. Much embarrassed on my account and apparently surprised to find his house in disarray, Volodya dropped my rucksack and leapt into the fray. Once the skirmishers had untangled themselves, he firmly ejected the whole lot towards the back of the garden, past the sheds and out through a side gate, yelling at them to get out and stay out.

Volodya led me up the porch steps and into the *seni*, the entrance room, where I left my bags and boots, and then showed me through a padded door into the kitchen. There, at the table, as if nothing untoward had happened, stood a diminutive elderly woman in a *sarafan* and colourful apron, a headscarf tied at the back of her neck. Volodya introduced her as his mother. Matryona Alekseyevna Zakharova greeted me quietly and almost deferentially, but she had the air of one who ran a tight ship.

The other person in the kitchen was Volodya's elder brother Aleksey. 'I saw you arriving by boat and going to the *gostinitsa*,' he said with an enormous grin, showing a handsome set of gold teeth. 'I said we couldn't have you staying there. I know what goes on in that place. Anyway, I felt embarrassed that nobody had welcomed you properly. Now you can stay with us. You've got your own cabin but you'll be eating with us here.'

As they discussed the details of my stay, changing from Russian to a different language, I took in my surroundings. Built into the inside wall of the kitchen was a large stove heating a diverse collection of saucepans and frying pans containing meat, fish and soup. Along the other wall a dresser, busy with crockery, reached to the ceiling. Underneath the window, which looked out on to the back garden and the sheds, was a small table. A television and ghettoblaster in the corner were playing concurrently with the sound turned low. Above a wall bench inside the door, a line of indoor clothing hung underneath a curtained shelf with hats and caps stacked along the top. At my feet a small, pale brown dog of indeterminate breed responded to my attentions by wagging her tail and rolling over on to her back, assuring me enthusiastically in a squeaky voice that I would be completely at home with the Zakharov family.

Just inside the padded entrance door from the *seni* there was a narrow curtained compartment with an enamelled tin wall-basin. I went through the curtains, looked in the mirror for the first time for two months at my heavily bearded face, and then used a long-handled pan to take water from a metal urn and fill the *umyvalnik* above the basin. With my cupped hands I pushed up the small piston at the base, releasing enough water to soap and rinse my face and hands.

Coming out of the washing area I peered into two of the other rooms. The nearest was little more than a cupboard, barely wide enough for its curtained bed. Then I put my head around the door of a small, tidy sitting room. There were divan beds in two of the corners, and a comfortable chair in front of a large television, a video recorder and piles of videotapes. On the floor there were modern, floral-pattern rugs; on the walls a large picture rug, several framed landscape reproductions and some old portrait photographs. The room came as something of a surprise after the interior of the Ponoy wetland cabins and the décor of the village hotel.

When Volodya called me back to the kitchen I had my first good look at the two men. With overjacket and fur hat removed, and his hair newly brushed, Volodya struck me immediately as handsome. He had a well-shaped head with a strong forehead and jaw, deep-set brown eyes, healthy black hair and a trimmed moustache. His body, which I had had a chance to study as I walked behind him across the village, was small, compact and well balanced. His moustache had initially complemented my impression of him as serious and severe, but as he now talked, with his boyish mop of hair regularly falling forward over his forehead and his mouth occasionally creasing into a grin, I swiftly warmed to him and, I believed, he to me.

His brother Aleksey was somewhat shy. He had proudly addressed me about his role in my 'rescue' from the hotel but thereafter he remained silent, smiling modestly and avoiding my gaze by lowering his eyes. He looked not just older but more worn than his brother. His chestnut-brown hair was also drawn across his forehead in the schoolboy manner, but it was dishevelled and never looked as if it enjoyed regular attention. He had none of the groomed, almost suave, appearance and manner of his younger brother, and this impression was encouraged by his thick beard stubble and poor teeth. His eyes, when I could see them, were markedly narrower than Volodya's, and he shared that feature – together with his overall slightly smaller proportions – with his mother, making both of them seem from a different branch of Volodya's race, a race of which I was anyway still uncertain. I assumed the family was Saami.

During an ample meal of vegetable soup followed by salted salmon, reindeer stew, boiled potatoes, tomato salad and sweet tea, Matryona Alekseyevna reached back into the dresser cupboard behind her and produced a bottle of vodka in honour of my arrival.

Volodya was teetotal and Aleksey abstained but we all offered toasts, clinking glasses and teacups. Matryona sipped at the *ryumka*, screwed her face up as if it were medicine, and quickly reverted to the tea which she poured into a saucer and drank though a half sugarlump held between her teeth. After refilling my glass twice, she reached back and replaced the bottle in its hiding-place, turning to me with a forefinger at her lips.

'My other brother,' explained Volodya sternly but not without embarrassment. This, perhaps, explained the commotion on the porch at my arrival.

I was contemplating my luck at finding myself in such pleasurable company when Volodya announced that he was about to go fishing. He had been moving off three hours earlier, he said, when Aleksey had alerted him to the 'appalling situation at the hotel' and urged him to make up a delegation.

Volodya's main livelihood during the summer months was fishing for salmon. Most days he was on the river. After the meal and without time even to unpack, I gathered my flyfishing tackle while Volodya fetched his spinning rod from the shed. We walked down to the river bank to Volodya's boat, a battered aluminium craft with an outboard engine, similar to others along the shore and much the same as Ilya's boat that had brought me from Krasnoshchelye.

It was approaching midnight when we motored up the Ponoy away from the village under a dull cloudy sky. Buran, Volodya's Siberian laika dog, barked at the village as we left, and then placed himself strategically on the flat forepeak. I huddled low in the boat against the gusty south-west wind.

An hour later, as we turned a bend in the river, we spotted in the distance two men standing with their fishing rods on the low bank of a stretch of rapids, casting for salmon. On account of the downstream wind and the noise of the water they hadn't heard us. When they did see us they walked quickly back from the river and disappeared into the forest. Only when we drew close and they recognized Volodya at the rudder did they re-emerge and come over towards us.

Vladimir and Igor were from Lovozero. They were spending two months on the river fishing for salmon which they salted and planned to transport home for profit. Vladimir was most likely in his late sixties, with grey hair and a leathery face; Igor, who had kind, dark eyes and a soft, pale brown skin, was in his fifties, but both looked older, particularly with four weeks of growth on their faces. I wanted to know whether they were Saami or Russian but, as was usually the case during my early peregrinations, I felt unable to ask such a straightforward question. Of larger build overall than Volodya, they looked, I imagined, more Slavic. Perhaps they were of mixed race. Soiled and rough, their clothing patched and ragged, they would have frightened me had I encountered them on the river bank on my own. I was not yet accustomed to the transformation of the male of the Russian North once the smells of the forest and some campfire smoke have passed through his nostrils over the course of a few days.

As we drank tea the talk turned to fishing. I said I wanted to try my hand at the salmon but when the two men examined my tackle they pronounced all of it useless.

'This is what you need, my friend,' said Igor, holding up a metal spinner gadget, the main body of which was the size of a large kitchen spoon, apparently more suited to catching omnivorous sharks in rough muddy seas than the cautious-minded 'kings of the river'.

I walked the bank and studied the water. The others meanwhile were already at work, fishing close to each other as is the wont of spinning anglers everywhere, confidently throwing their large lumps of metal far across the river, laughing boisterously at their own jokes, and urging me to 'have a go' or 'get a move on and stop fiddling around with that fancy tackle'. Before I had even started, my neighbours, who had been casting for fifteen minutes without seeing a fish, had already lost patience and were now settled on the bank for a smoke, waiting to be entertained by the Englishman. This was the kind of situation where I invariably ended up with the line round my neck or a hook in the back of my jacket.

The gods, however, favoured me. My Spey casts cut the fierce wind and my presentation of the fly was evidently satisfactory for within the hour I had landed two fine salmon between six and seven kilograms. Igor and Vladimir's relentless bankside mockery, already somewhat subdued by my initial success, had stopped altogether by the time they watched me bring a third fish to the bank. As I was refining my tactics with a reluctant fourth fish and hardly felt like leaving the river, Volodya called us to eat.

On this occasion and on all our fishing outings in the years to come, Volodya's meals were copious and taken at frequent intervals. He was never short of provisions and he knew just how to serve them. His old canvas rucksack was invariably full of bread, reindeer meat, *salo* (pork fat), sugar and salt, salted fish, onions and various emergency tins with wholesome but often barely palatable contents such as cod livers. Tea was infused directly in an old blackened kettle. Sugar, like the salt, was kept in cloth pouches. If we had special company, there might also be some sweet biscuits, boiled candy or vodka. Volodya Zakharov always made me feel like one of the family, and for years thereafter, usually when eating on the river bank, it amused him greatly to recall how he had rescued me from the village hotel.

Vladimir and Igor, who had caught no fish since I had arrived, invited me to come into the forest to impress me with the week's catch, which Volodya was to take back to Kanevka. They had dug a shallow pit and lined it with polythene and wood. Here they stored the salmon after gutting and cleaning and rubbing salt into the two sides. More salt was then sprinkled liberally between the layers of fish in the pit, and the top was closed with sphagnum and branches.

From that time on Volodya regarded me as an expert angler, a reputation I had never previously enjoyed except with my godchildren before they grew older and wiser. He and the others could never understand how I was able to catch large fish on hooks which were rarely longer than fifteen millimetres and only sparsely dressed with fur or feather. I in turn was fascinated by their crude tackle: the short aluminium rods that telescoped to the length of a forearm, the large-diameter reels carrying coarse nylon, and the crude oversized lures. Volodya explained why the rods telescoped to such a small size: they could be stuffed down the trousers if river police should appear.

Volodya explained that we were fishing illegally. Theoretically it was possible to buy licences to fish a small part of the river near Kanevka with rod and line, but even for him as a villager it would be too expensive to pay for all the days when he went out for salmon.

'There are fishery inspectors on the river now. You never know when they're going to come, and these days they often arrive by boat. About sixty kilometres downstream from here there's a new fishing camp for foreigners which started up a short time ago. Inspectors fly regularly with the angling clients in the camp helicopter to and from

Murmansk airport, and then they borrow one of the camp's very fast jet boats. If you're lucky you hear them coming but they have ingenious ways of sneaking up into the wind or drifting back downstream with the motor turned off, usually during cloudy nights. They grab you on the bank or on the river. I've been caught many times with fish or nets in the boat and I've paid a lot in fines.

'The regulations forbid the river police or soldiers from searching your clothing so that's why we use these short rods. You can walk to rivers anywhere without causing suspicion, and – more important – it's easy to run away from the water's edge and into the woods with a rod like mine if you're taken by surprise.'

Though the waters still arguably belonged to the Saami, the Saami no longer had rights to fish and feed their families. The restrictions had begun in Soviet times, and then, following perestroika, a party of Americans explored the Ponoy for recreational fishing and set up a camp downriver at its confluence with the Ryabaga. When they first came they were all over the villagers with their money, promising good earnings for people like Volodya. He worked in the camp as a guide for the first year but they didn't ask him back. Nor did they employ local people. The camp was of no benefit to the locals.

The camp was going to buy out the traps and nets at the Ponoy's estuary, Volodya told me. That might have been good for the salmon because since the Stalin years too many fish had been taken every year, but if he wasn't allowed to fish his own river, what did that add up to? To buy licences he'd have to spend a fortune simply to feed his family and relatives, let alone make a little money selling fish. Now he was continually under threat from inspectors.

'They're sometimes accompanied by soldiers who act like paid bullies. They recently threatened to take away my engine. Take tonight for example. The wind is blowing downstream and if a jet boat were on its way upriver you wouldn't hear it until the last moment . . .'

'Get some sleep and we'll go out again soon,' shouted Volodya over the noise of the engine as we motored home. 'It looks like there's a good run on.'

But my first stay at Kanevka was cut short. When washing and shaving in the river the following afternoon I saw an old biplane, which had been circling in the vicinity, land at the sand airstrip a mile downriver. Volodya came running to find me; he knew I had been worried about getting back from the moment I arrived.

'That's the forestry plane. We had no idea it would call. You could go with them now if you really have to leave.'

I was sad to leave so early. Of Kanevka I had seen nothing and learned nothing. After I had been snatched from the hotel we had been too busy fishing to talk about much else. I had less than an hour to pack. Matryona Alekseyevna insisted on feeding me macaroni and reindeer.

'Eat up. In this part of the world,' she said melodramatically, 'you never know where you'll be tomorrow.' Then Volodya drove me through the forest on his ancient motor scooter – a miracle of home maintenance – with my rucksacks in a small cart behind.

I looked in rapt wonder at the aeroplane, a dark green Antonov-2 An-Dva biplane, which was sitting, like a suppliant spaniel, with its tail in the sand and its nose in the air, a design masterpiece of the 1940s. The overall effect was of ample and balanced curvaceousness: the deep-bellied, riveted aluminium fuselage, the round propeller housing, the four circular windows along each side, the twinned wing tips, the tail-fin and the tail-planes, all harmoniously rounded. The upper and lower wings, strengthened by diagonal rods, were covered with stretched and doped canvas that yielded to the touch; the mechanism exposed behind the smooth lips of the propeller housing was an aeronautical erogenous zone. To my mind there were to be few comparably attractive aircraft designs until the Concorde prototype of the sixties.

As hopeful travellers arrived hastily from the village, the departure time and passenger capacity became increasingly conjectural, but Volodya, who had meanwhile been talking in a confidential manner to the pilot on the other side of the fuselage, assured me that I would fly.

'He'll look after you,' he said as he thrust a metre-long brown paper package under my arm. It looked and smelled remarkably like a fish.

When the time came, there was an undignified scramble for the few places on the metal bench seats that ran along the walls of the plane interior. The pilot and his supernumerary struggled to impose their authority, turning away what they considered to be excess baggage and packages. How they decided whom or what was to be admitted was not clear, but the process certainly threw them into a temper, as it did the passengers and those wishing to send items of freight. Once we were seated, the pilot clambered over the bags and crates on his way to the cabin, introducing himself to me as he went. This seemed to be the cue to hand him my package.

The engine chugged and chortled as we taxied to the far end of the sand strip. The plane turned, let out a deep-throated roar, accelerated, and lifted above the trees. We banked over the village to head north-west towards Murmansk. Through the cabin door I watched the pilot at the controls. In their old leather flying-caps, he and his equally-seasoned co-pilot looked like veteran aviators of the Biggles era.

For the first half hour the plane tracked the river. From the porthole I followed the water's broad, shallow stretches and deep narrow runs through the trees and the hills, back to the open bog and wetlands where I had watched eagles and falcon with Sergey and met the Kapitan, seen the lake fishermen, travelled with a reticent boatman, and learned about old Saami places. The birch trees were in full leaf and there were no longer any pockets of snow. It was full summer.

The Skolt Saami

THREE MONTHS LATER, in late October, I made contact with the Saami from Finland who had driven me to Lovozero on the occasion of my initial search for Lapps and wilderness. This time I wanted him to take me in the other direction, on one of his return journeys, along the road that ran north-west out of Murmansk parallel to the coast and on to the border with Norway near Kirkenes. Having seen some of the Saami places in the east of the oblast, on the Kola Peninsula, I was eager to see the west. As a start I would visit at least one of the river estuaries on the north-west coast to which Saami had traditionally migrated each year for the summer months. My preferred destination was the estuary of the River Titovka, an old summer encampment of the Motovsky Saami.

My Finn reminded me that the coastal area was a closed zone and that we would be subject to military roadblocks and at least one internal border post but that if I was willing to take the risk and help him with the necessary finance we would make it. He agreed to put me down short of the international border and from there I could make my own way to the coast.

For his home runs the van was rarely empty and for the last year he had been regularly transporting people taking advantage of the newly relaxed border to visit Saami relations and contacts in Norway or Finland. On this occasion I shared the van with two girls who were crossing the border for the first time.

The history of Russia's north-west border with Norway and Finland as described by my driver was too complex for me to understand at the time above the noise of the engine, even though recounted in fluent English. It was only later when I read the English social anthropologist Tim Ingold's book on the Skolt Saami* that I grasped the full significance of the borderland's twentieth-century disruptions and diaspora resulting from three wars, one revolution and over four decades of forced collectivization.

The Skolt Lapps lived in the area that straddles the contiguous parts of modern Norway, Finland and Russia, approximately defined by the triangle between the Kola Gulf, Norway's Varanger Fjord, and the country south-east of Finland's Lake Inari. Conventionally included under the Skolt caption are seven territorially linked family groups of (from east to west) Kildin, Motov, Nota, Songel, Pechenga, Paz and Neiden.

When the first north-west border was drawn by the governments of Norway and Russia in 1826, the Skolt Saami were divided by nationality for the first time in their long history. After the October Revolution the Treaty of Dorpat, signed in 1920 between Finland and the new Bolshevik government, ceded to Finland broad strips of the border from the Gulf of Finland in the south to the Barents Sea in the north. Twenty years later, after the Soviet Union had invaded the Finns in the Winter War of 1939–40, these areas were taken back. The Finns lost their access to the sea and many Skolt Saami who had been Finnish for a time were subjected once again to Russian rule. When in June 1941 the Germans and Austrians unexpectedly invaded the Soviet Union in the north-west and crossed the borders with Finland and Norway, the Skolt Saami on both sides found themselves not only in the thick of the action again but this time with loyalties divided between Finland/Germany and the Soviet Union.

By 1944, when the Soviet Army had finally pushed the Germans and Austrians back into Norway – along the very road for which I was now aiming – Skolt Saami life on either side of the north-west border had been almost eradicated. Herds of reindeer had been slaughtered by the famished armies, and when the Germans retreated they maliciously destroyed what remained, from homes and barns to boats, nets and handcarts. German-occupied Kirkenes, a large port and an important naval base in north Norway which had been subjected to constant air raids by the Soviets for almost three years, was left with a depleted and exhausted population of Norwegians and less

* Tim Ingold, *The Skolt Lapps today*, Cambridge University Press, 1976.

than thirty houses from the original four or five hundred. In the border country further south the few Saami who returned to their lands after 1944, lived for a time in holes in the ground, scrabbling around in the ashes and ruins for nails to rebuild their homes and their barns.

For those who had managed to flee far from the war zone in a westerly direction during the invasion of 1941, the Finnish government designated areas around Lake Inari, near the border, where returning Skolts could regather, settle and build new homes at the end of the war. The Saami on the Soviet side of the border after the German retreat, however – some of whom had already suffered persecution and forced collectivization during the 1930s – were once again subjected to moves which dispersed traditional family groups and separated children from parents. To this day the Skolt Saami on the Russian side of the border have never been permitted to reclaim their territories. During the second half of the twentieth century the only people who were permitted to settle within their land were immigrants from Soviet bloc countries to the new mining towns, and men of the military and the Northern Fleet.

'The result of all that complicated history as it affects me ... as well as these girls,' said my driver, 'is that although some of the Saami in Lovozero are related to people in my region of Finland, it's only during the last few years that we've been able to meet up.'

The first police checkpoint on our route to the border was strategically placed on the far side of the bridge that crosses the Gulf at Kola. Here the road divided to run due west to Finland or northwest to Norway. Our large van was recognized and waved through. We drove out of the valley up on to the tundra, and for the next two hours we bumped along the open empty highway, weaving between potholes, only occasionally passing a car in either direction. The tundra of low rolling hills had recently received a thin layer of early snow. Under the weak October morning light, further subdued by low cloud, the landscape looked bleak and inhospitable.

Now that some of my Saami historical jigsaw pieces were falling into place, I was interested to learn more about the two girls in the van. Both had been ready to make small talk early in the journey as we left Lovozero, but as soon as I began to ask questions about their families and family life they looked uneasy. They introduced themselves unconvincingly after a pause as 'Natasha' and 'Olga' and muttered an incoherent family name, but I let it pass. My questions produced nothing and I found them increasingly withdrawn as if they trusted nobody, not even our Finn. They were not sisters but both were fairly small, and both had the same round head with childlike features, pronounced eyebrows and dark-brown eyes and hair. They wore no make-up and I judged them to be well short of twenty. They had heavy long woollen coats, both with old-fashioned fitted waists, but underneath they wore thin short dresses, hardly suitable for a stay in the country, and they appeared to have no hats or luggage. Again, it was only later that I learned more about the nature of the Finnish driver's 'special relationship' with 'cousins' at Lovozero. Although more and more Skolt families were indeed reuniting under official auspices for cultural exchange, these particular 'cousins' were going no further than the outskirts of Kirkenes, where they would be housed in a small room above a petrol station to engage in whatever social intercourse would turn a krone or two.

As the time approached for us to pass through the internal military border my two travel companions and even the rumbustious Finn had become subdued.

'Don't worry about the military,' he reassured us. 'I'll look after them. They all know me at the barrier. They won't bother us or search the van. They know better.' As the three of us climbed to the back of the vehicle, we saw the first of the guardhouses, and then the wire fencing running over the hills into the distance. At the barrier – the Russians use the evocative German word *shlagbaum* – our driver was greeted by name. The formalities were perfunctory and then the talk turned male and hearty before finishing with profuse thanks on both sides. We were on our way.

At this time I had little idea of the strategic importance of the north-west military bases, nor was I greatly interested. A few years later, when I did get to see the extensive military stockpiles and infrastructure, much of it obsolete or abandoned, that had accumulated around the battalions of infantry and armoured vehicle units stationed there and exercised across the tundra since before the Cold War, I was overwhelmed. The rows of guns, tanks and armoured personnel vehicles, the massive runway for bombers and carriers, the drab bases at Linakhamari, Sputnik, Luostari and Pechenga, the sheer volume of accumulated military matériel, all left me incredulous as I finally grasped its geographical proximity to NATO's European heartland.

On this first visit, however, my mind was full of Saami lore and life. I was heading towards Rybachy, the peninsula that protrudes eastwards into the Barents Sea 100 kilometres west of Murmansk and forms a large sheltered bay known as the Motovsky Gulf. In earlier times it demarcated the Arctic Ocean coast of the Russian Lapps to the east and the Scandinavian Norse to the west, separating the Murman from the Nurman (Norseman) coast.

Of the rivers that flow into the Gulf the Titovka was one of three – together with the West Litsa and the Ura – long favoured as a summer fishing place by the Motovsky Saami. The Saami used to arrive each May to trap and net in the estuary and to catch seal and fish in the open waters of the Gulf, returning inland to their winter homes in September. The Titovka estuary was additionally notable because by the early years of the twentieth century it had been transformed into a mixed community that included Finns, Norwegians and Russians, who had arrived as a result of Tsar Alexander III's incentives to settle and colonize the north-west. Unlike the migrating Saami these settlers stayed at Titovka the year round, saving hay, growing vegetables in the summer and tending cattle, sheep and deer. In time they developed the estuary settlement into a stable and materially wealthy community, and by the 1920s the settler population had grown to several hundred, with the Saami probably never numbering more than a few dozen. Settlers and Lapps lived in harmony and to mutual benefit. Some Saami families continued to live in their turf and birch *vezhi*, others copied the settlers' flat-roofed houses of wood, known as *koadty* or *tupy*. The anthropologist Charnolussky, who visited the Motovsky Saami in the late 1920s, remarked that their homes were bright, spacious and more organized than those on the Kola Peninsula to the east. There were iron stoves and chimneys rather than rough hearths; floors 'so clean that even babies could crawl around'; men were well dressed, clean, modest and 'sweet-natured'; and there was a noticeable mutual respect between the sexes.

In the days of Charnolussky the deep waters of the Gulf were visited by large numbers of whales. At the end of the twentieth century one was more likely to see a submarine – perhaps a nuclear-powered vessel of the Akula (Shark) Class – slipping from its base, making for the open sea and a far quarter of the globe. And where Saami and Finn had once moved over the tundra with the reindeer, one might nowadays encounter an infantry platoon advancing behind an armoured vehicle. The estuary of the River Titovka was cleared of its inhabitants ten years after Charnolussky saw it; at the end of the twentieth century it was still a military closed zone.

My plan was to leave the road after the barrier and then walk north to the estuary, returning to the road where I had fixed a rendez-vous with a friend of mine in Murmansk who had a car. From the moment I stepped out of the van I felt exposed and nervous. I knew I might have to avoid a further sentry post but I had no idea where it would turn up. Only the weather seemed in my favour; the clouds had disappeared and the sun gave the snow a sparkle, casting blue shadows on white. Minus two degrees Celsius was perfect weather for my twenty-kilometre walk. I moved off the tundra and bog and on to a rough track where I had seen heavy vehicles going towards the Titovka base and the military installations of Rybachy beyond. I wished I were alone in the landscape with the ptarmigan who were on the ground all around me, already in their mottled winter plumage and feeding on the last of the bilberries before the arrival of more snow.

I crossed the river by a derelict wooden bridge high above a set of rapids and proceeded along the river valley, but after a time I was compelled to walk up on to high ground and was once again worried about being exposed. This sensation was further aggravated by the appearance of a large truck which stopped at a brick hut on the opposite bank that I had just left. I could hear voices. I had no wish to be discovered. Never mind the inconvenience of the delays, the detention, and the inevitable, tedious interrogations – the fine for a foreigner found in a closed zone could amount to $5,000, and it would be hard to secure a Russian visa in the future.

In the early afternoon I caught sight of a large collection of multifarious barracks and sheds on the alluvial plain below me. The base seemed far enough away for me to choose the fast and easy option and continue along the footpath which I was on rather than move out of sight. This was a mistake: when the path took me past a junction I saw fresh prints of boots and vehicle tracks in the snow and, some minutes later, more fresh prints.

Then, unannounced and as if from nowhere, an all-terrain personnel carrier arrived on the tundra nearby. It was out of sight but it could not have been more than half a kilometre behind me, probably at the junction. I could hear the roar of its open exhaust engine as if I were sitting on top of it. Men's voices were shouting over the noise. There was a tone of excitement.

I would have to disappear into the surrounding hills for cover. I ran as fast as I could, stopping occasionally, hoping to locate the vehicle. I was expecting it to come into view below me but when I stopped and listened the loudest sound was my pounding heart. I had broken into a sweat and went aground for an hour. I could hear the vehicle and spasmodic voices but I never saw the soldiers. Such was my mental state that I imagined them holding the vantage of low ground below me, waiting for me to make a move.

After an hour I could no longer hear anything. I broke cover and, hoping for the best but still observing basic fieldcraft, headed for the coast.

Within a further hour I was rewarded. The expanse of the Motovsky Bay opened up before me and on the other side of the water I could see the snow-covered Rybachy Peninsula. Below me and to the left was the Titovka's estuary and, close to its left bank, the islands and inlets that were once so popular with the Saami. They looked picturesque: three small low-lying pieces of land offering protection from gales, good sites for houses, a perfect natural harbour with a narrow but easily navigable entrance, and enough water to sail at all tides. I had no difficulty imagining it as it was sixty years earlier, with smoke whisping from the colonists' cabins and the traditional branch-and-turf *vezhi* of the Saami families, and children running around in bare feet, playing games and shrieking with delight as they caught sight of boats coming home.

I took a last look along the coast and started to walk back. Having had the advantage of a reconnaissance on the outward car journey, I took a return route in a south-easterly direction, avoiding the military fence, and aiming for the road well inside the internal border post. As night drew in I felt less exposed and relied increasingly on my compass. My greatest apprehension, apart from the weather and the reliability of Slava's car, was the accuracy of my map regarding streams; I had a towel and a change of clothes but I had no wish to wade more than was absolutely necessary. I was fortunate: the autumn ground was well drained, the going good, and only two streams required wading. By 10 pm I had located Slava, fast asleep in the driver's seat. I tapped on the window. 'Home, James,' I said in my best English.

A few days after my return from the coast my own picture of the summer encampment at Titovka was brought to life and embellished for me by a small group of Saami now living in the modern village of Upper Tuloma not far from the original Motovsky inland winter *seit*. Felka Petrovna, a lively, smiling extrovert in her seventies, remembered Titovka in some detail even though she had not been there for sixty years, since she had been a child.

'Every summer all the families went off to the sea, some to Titovka, others to the bay at Litsa, all except the older grandmothers who stayed behind in the winter place. My parents had a small home on one of the estuary islands at Titovka. Everyone had boats. We were fishing all the time. To this day I remember the big fish catches of the summer of 1931. We caught a great number in the traps and also at sea in the seines. I even remember a whale getting washed up on the shore and decaying there. I don't know why we didn't render the oil as we used to years ago. Maybe there wasn't a market any more. All I remember was that some of the men built huts and benches out of the bones.

'There were deer up on the tundra all along the coast from Titovka to Litsa, which was where other Motovsky Saami families lived during the summer. We took skins to Kola town to sell or barter for flour and sugar.

'The little school at Titovka was Finnish and the teacher was Russian. We spoke Saami amongst ourselves but we also spoke Finnish and Russian.

'There were always foreign ships coming into the Gulf at that time, anchoring off Litsa or Titovka to buy fish or to trade. I remember being told of an Englishman who landed at Titovka one summer in the late 1800s and went off with two Saami girls. To everyone's surprise the "marriages" were a great success. The couple – or should I say the three of them – returned regularly from England with their children.

'It was a good life. We ate well and there was plenty of everything. We usually left Titovka in September just as the deer came off the tundra with their calves and made their way inland. We'd be back in the winter *seit* until the following spring.'

Felka's neighbour, Zoya, also in her seventies, gave me the grim details of what happened in the late 1930s and early '40s. Forced collectivization began, and many of those who resisted the NKVD reforms were arrested. Soldiers appeared out of the blue and marched away anybody under suspicion.

'In 1937, on the twenty-seventh of August, my father and grandfather were taken away to the south of Petrograd [St Petersburg] and shot. Three years later, in 1940 – February or March it was – all the families were given four hours to pack and leave. Just like that. Everything was taken away from us, including our cattle, sheep and deer. We had to go to Vosmos, the new collective nearby on the banks of the River Tuloma, and there we lived – Russian, Norwegian, Finnish and Saami families all together.

'Nobody went to the sea at Litsa or Titovka that spring, and I've not seen either place ever since. By the next year, 1941, we were at war and, as the front was only a few kilometres away, we were moved again, first to Shongui, near Murmansk, and then, when the Germans started to bomb Murmansk, a hundred kilometres further south to Olenegorsk. The German invasion – the Great Patriotic War as they like to call it – split up most of the Skolt families both sides of the border. You could say that what the NKVD had started, the war finished off.'

Aleksandr Gerasimov, a Notozersky Saami and the youngest of the group I was with, was born in 1951. He was a stocky, muscular man with smiling blue eyes and a generous red beard. That afternoon, walking behind Aleksandr, following in tracks made in the fresh snow by his deerskin boots, and keeping an eye on the red cone of his woollen hat moving ahead through the trees, I was led a few kilometres from the village to higher ground, to the site of a former summer *seit*, a place he called Rautseit – literally 'trout settlement'.

He showed me traces of houses visible beneath the snow. It looked an inconsequential place but, as he talked about it, describing how the thirty houses would have been sited on the side of the hill overlooking the small lake, sheltered by pines, with grass suitable for grazing domestic animals, I began to understand the place better.

'Before the Finnish War and the Second War the Notozersky went long distances to the west into Finland to trade skins, travelling by sledge in winter and using the waterways in summer. Today I can travel west again. The difference is that now I have to cross the border illegally and I don't trade skins; I only fish and hunt.'

Aleksandr then walked me back to the modern village and down to the River Tuloma, to the place where the Notozersky formerly owned a summer fishing place known as Padun (the Falls). There were still a few wooden houses there.

'Before we were forced to live in the collective, the Notozersky Saami had rights to the salmon that came up the Tuloma,' Aleksandr explained. 'The catch at this waterfall was always large, well over a hundred tonnes a year. My family took thousands of fish downriver to sell at Kola every year and made a good living that way, but by the 1940s most of the fish was going to the State. After the war the dam was built for a power station and the lake became a reservoir.'

Aleksandr took me a short way up the river to the enormous concrete wall of the reservoir dam and we looked west across the characteristically insipid water. 'Today a lot of fish go up the tributary Pecha, but it's nothing compared to what it was.'

Back at the modern village Felka Petrovna talked about life in a Saami *seit*. 'What I remember of the old days was the amount of work undertaken by women. Women seemed able to do almost anything that the men did, including hunting ptarmigan, capercaillie or hare, though perhaps not elk or bear. One moment we were doing dainty work like sewing beads on to our *shamshury* or our bags, then we'd be scraping skins for hours on end. One day it would be birch bark floats for the nets, then grass for shoes, then we'd be collecting lichen for winter feed or saving hay for days on end. I suppose that when we were marched off under guard to Vosmos to join the collective we were fit for anything. I remember living in a pit at first with my sister, sleeping on a bed of lichen. We worked in men's brigades, worked the same as men. I got blisters, which was unusual for me.

'During the war I worked in a military laundry on Rybachy Peninsula until 1945. Then I ended up in a bakery in Odessa before returning to Shongui near Murmansk. After that I worked for about fifteen years at sea as a cook. Then it was Shongui again in 1960. And here I am back near where I started. At least I've survived. Unlike a cousin of mine who escaped after the war from a strict regime labour camp not far from Leningrad and walked all the way home only to be killed by a bear a few weeks later.'

3

SETTLERS

Pomors

OCEANS OF VODKA. *Mountains of salmon. Come and get it!* The laconic note scrawled in capital letters on the back of a blank school report was all that Isaak and Feodosiya at Vologda had received in response to their long letter of detailed questions despatched weeks earlier to their friend Oleg, a supply teacher at Varzuga, a village on the large river of the same name that flows into the White Sea. As recent graduates they had been investigating teaching posts on offer away from home, preferably in the north. At Varzuga there were two open to them, both in mathematics. It was one of the few opportunities for married couples newly qualified in the same subject to work together.

Of the village itself there was little or nothing to discover. It was shown on most Russian maps, situated just below the Arctic Circle on the White Sea coast of the Kola Peninsula. A map belonging to Isaak's grandmother, printed before the Revolution, called the whole area 'Russian Lapland' and the southern coast the 'Ter' or 'Tersky' coast. A colour brochure sent by the Murmansk Regional Authority suggested that most of the roadless Peninsula was one large, unpopulated wilderness, but there was also a picture of Varzuga's church, a magnificent, tall wooden structure dating from the seventeenth century, with a steeple that dominated the panorama of the village and its river.

To an adventurous young couple like Isaak and Feodosiya taking their first step in a new career, Varzuga sounded irresistible. And then, when they remembered Oleg who had been sent there two years earlier, they had written to him immediately. The men and women conducting the interview for the Vologda Board of Education were 'not absolutely certain' that the school at Varzuga was a going concern but they knew that somebody was running at least the old-style classes. Just travel to Kandalaksha on the White Sea, they said. There should be a ferry along the coast. We think you'll do just fine.

Arriving at Kandalaksha, the first large town of Murmansk Oblast coming from the south, they found out that the ferry had ceased to run but, after some delays and a difficult overland journey, the couple finally reached the village and were shown to Oleg's house ready for their first term of teaching. What Oleg had not mentioned in his letter from Varzuga was his alcohol problem and that he was about to leave.

'The house had been abandoned,' Isaak told me ten years on. 'When we arrived there was nothing in it except an old bed, a few kitchen utensils, piles of bottles, and mountains of rubbish. It took us a week just to clear and clean the place.'

They spent their first weeks trying to get used to the lack of shops and the intermittent supply of electricity, but the young couple rapidly warmed to their new life. Their cheeks began to glow . . . for more reasons than one.

'One of the great advantages of having our own place at last, however derelict, was that for the first time we could enjoy our own company. We were so busy with you-know-what that we had difficulty getting on with the household jobs.'

Isaak's old 8-mm projector flickered hypnotically. I was sitting on the edge of a divan bed, three feet away from the small piece of white card that served as a screen, using my reading glasses to focus on the minute sepia moving images, the unfolding story of Isaak and Feodosiya's 1982 Varzuga adventure, their first summer at the village. The camera panned slowly across a settlement of wooden buildings standing on either side of a wide stretch of slow-moving water which emerged from the forest half a kilometre upstream and was some 400 metres wide when flowing past the houses. Small wooden rowing boats were taking villagers from one bank to the other, salmon making their way from the White Sea were leaping playfully, men and women were carrying pails of water up the steep river banks, and cattle were leaving their sheds for the day's grazing.

After the film show Feodosiya told me about Varzuga's history. 'The south coast of the Kola Peninsula has been home to pioneer settlers – real pioneers – for hundreds of years. The place is full of tradition, Varzuga in particular. It's all to do with the kind of people who started migrating here a thousand years ago.

'You've heard of the Pomors? The word means "coastal people". It's the name that was given to the people of the Novgorod Republic who came north to the White Sea originally in the quest for animal fur. They were joined by others from Karelia, south of Russian Lapland, and by the year 1200 traders and fishermen were beginning to see the advantages of living in the region all year round. Gradually they settled. And now we've come.

'Even today, after all the upsets of the twentieth century, the people of the Tersky coast think of themselves as an extended family. They're interested in their history and, luckily for us teachers, they're keen to get an education. Historically, the Tersky settlers were ardent Orthodox Christians with the mental resilience required for survival in the new lands. Today they still have a reputation for being well organized, competent and resourceful. Classic pioneers.'

Isaak and Feodosiya seemed to me like pioneers too. Perestroika Pomors.

*

At the beginning of my second summer visit to the region I had set out from Kandalaksha to go east along the Tersky coast, like Isaak and Feodosiya a decade earlier. I knew of Varzuga and its historic church but had little idea how I would get there. The good news was that there was a real road along the coast as far as Umba, and a bus was leaving that afternoon.

Umba is the administrative centre of the Tersky region which forms the south-east quarter of the Kola Peninsula, and is bordered by the River Ponoy to the north and the White Sea to the south. During the nineteenth century and Soviet times the small port had thrived on fish processing and timber but now its fish factory and sawmills were all but closed. As the bus came out of the trees I saw some of Umba's older wooden houses spread along the banks of a long narrow bay like a sea loch, but in the distance, through the trees, I glimpsed modern five-storey Soviet-style apartment houses.

The bus put me down alone in a small square. A young boy chattered at me, urging me to stay at his parents' home, but I opted for an old two-storey wooden house on the other side of the small square which improbably identified itself by a small hand-painted notice board: *Gostinitsa*. I was not expecting a repeat of my Kanevka adventure, but nothing could have looked less like a hotel from the outside. However, passing through the porch and finding myself in a hall which had a clean, painted wooden floor and looked into a family sitting room from which I was greeted by two women and a small child, I was immediately put at my ease. The hotel was warm and homely. I would be comfortable.

Returning from a short evening walk to the water I was summoned by the landlady. She informed me that tomorrow the *militsiya* – the police – would come for me. The very word filled me with apprehension; the only possible response was to thank her for her trouble and hope for the best.

When the police came for me the next morning I was up, washed and ready packed. My escort drove me in a blue jeep to a large two-storey wooden building, the regional administrative headquarters. I affected gratitude to the policeman but grew alarmed at the pragmatic urgency with which he performed his task, all but applying the handcuffs. And when he swept me up the stairs, along a spotless corridor that smelt institutionally of disinfectant and floor polish, and guided me swiftly through a spacious reception office with a secretary who seemed to be expecting us, I began to worry.

I was invited to continue straight ahead through double doors. As I entered the room, six men sitting at a long conference table turned to look at me. A boy of school age, evidently engaged as interpreter, came forward and greeted me politely in fluent formal English.

'Good day, sir. You are here at the order of the Regional Head of Administration, Viktor Sergeyevich Didenko. He wishes you to give an account of yourself and to explain the reason for your visit to Umba. Please sit down.'

The greeting was courteous but unsettling. The six men at the table might, before my arrival, have been discussing the regional budget or the Umba drains but to me the circumstances were ominous, and the men, probably on account of their black leather jackets, seemed sinister.

I explained that I had been on business in St Petersburg and, being an amateur ornithologist and naturalist, had decided to make a trip to

Murmansk Oblast and Varzuga. About this and my further intentions I was interrogated at length and, fortunately, the reason for my visit was found acceptable. However, not only was there no road to Varzuga but, for military reasons, the coast round Umba was a closed zone. My visa itinerary did not itemize the town. I would have to return to Kandalaksha. And there were minor formalities to observe beforehand, such as having my visa stamped. The relevant stamp-bearing officials were somewhere else, so I had to agree to come to the administration offices the following day on the chance that the officials had returned and could see to my paperwork.

I was awoken early the next day by yet another policeman. Did they not trust me to present my visa? Or did they simply wish to keep an eye on me?

'The Governor sends his regards. If you wish to proceed east to Varzuga we can organize this for you. Several large trucks are about to leave Umba for Varzuga. You can ride with them. We shall arrange everything. I just have to locate the Chairman of Varzuga village, Svyatoslav Mikhaylovich. He'll be travelling with the convoy. Wait here at the hotel until we collect you.'

Feast or famine, Russian-style. As I was increasingly to find on my travels, one is either completely lost for a next move, encountering every opposition, official and private, or one's Russian acquaintances of the moment, having decided to be helpful, provide every assistance: a waived regulation, three days' provisions, perhaps even a lift in a helicopter.

I waited. Outside it was snowing but without conviction. I thought, not for the first time, how pleasant it was this far north that travel plans from May to August were rarely affected by the time of day; the truck convoy could as well leave at midnight as at noon. Feeling that the tide had turned I asked no questions and kept my fingers crossed.

The six trucks travelling to Varzuga were enormous. Russian-built in the 1960s for the East German military, they had been brought back for reconditioning and sold on. Svyatoslav Mikhaylovich Kalyuzhen, the chairman of Varzuga's collective, of whom everyone had been speaking in respectful tones, had arrived and was organizing our departure as if we were setting off for the Front.

Each of the trucks was attached to long flatbed loaders carrying giant empty fuel-storage cylinders and, as we drew away from Umba and headed east through the forest, our convoy made an impressive sight. I had been directed to ride in the cabin of the leading truck. This was driven by a serious, taciturn young man who concentrated on the driving every minute of the way. Sitting rigidly upright, staring straight ahead, his strong broad hands on the ship-size wheel, he reassuringly exuded confidence, the very model of a Soviet hero.

The road to Varzuga, as far as it had been built at that time, was of beaten earth and easy going. Only at a few of the small rivers, where the bridges had been damaged by the spring spate and the trucks had to negotiate steep banks, did my nerve falter. On these occasions, in spite of my confidence in the hero at the wheel, I climbed down from the high cabin – a difficult physical undertaking in itself – and crossed the shallow rapids on foot. The road ran for a further 70 kilometres through pine and birch forest along the top of an escarpment parallel to the White Sea coast, and then petered out. At that point the convoy left the forest to make the steep, roadless descent towards the shore. The hair-raising task involved manoeuvring the trucks and cylinders down the hillside through the forest to the bog that lay between the escarpment and the seashore. At the foot of the escarpment most of us disembarked to make our own way to the shore on foot and watch the drivers handle the huge beasts which roared, rocked and bucked, churning the bog beneath them, sinking and rising, slowly edging ahead, all under the calm invigilation of Kalyuzhen. The sense of relief was sweet as the trucks emerged from the bog on to the hard shore and we climbed back up into the cabins.

Thereafter our easterly progress along the sea shore was swift. The drivers negotiated the deeper water slowly but took the dry sand flats at speed, putting up large flocks of waders and duck which peeled off the shore and away into the clear blue sky. The warming evening sun shone from behind, throwing everything into richly coloured relief. I thrilled to the vast flat and unpopulated seascape of the Tersky coast.

The convoy halted for tea near the village of Kashkarants. As I had already learned, the Russian invitation '*chay peet!*' promised more than just a cup of tea. A fire was lit among the dunes, several sacks and boxes of food were unpacked, and in the comparative warmth of the late spring evening we relaxed and talked. Kalyuzhen sat with a small group of men a short distance away, occasionally staring across at me without expression.

One of the vast cylinders was to be left at Kashkarants and this delay allowed me time to have my first look at a Tersky coast 'Pomor' settlement. Occupying a bleak exposed headland of the flat treeless shore, Kashkarants accommodated probably no more than twenty families and, as at Umba which I had just left, my first impression of the place was of dereliction and abandonment. From the outside the small wooden houses seemed uninhabitable and the areas between were strewn with used timber, scrap metal, old engines, rotten boats and the debris and detritus of everyday life. A noisy diesel generator was housed at the edge of the village in a shed from which a dozen bare cables emerged on to poles and roofs in a haphazard manner. Knowing that electricity involved keeping positive and negative apart, I was at a loss to understand how any current reached a homestead.

Some twenty kilometres short of the Varzuga's estuary the trucks turned north and inland for the final leg of our journey, driving once again through forest, now into the low night sun. I was beginning to feel impatient for a sight of the great river, whose presence to the east of us I could feel, but the going was heavy and slow. Finally, after hours of vehicular grunts and groans the convoy emerged on to open high ground with a breathtaking view of the valley below. Out of the distant forest came a broad smooth band of water, glistening under the night sun as it glided past Varzuga village and its church.

The descent to the village was problematic. Most of the track had been washed away by melting snow and the recent rains, and several wrecked vehicles from earlier years lay rotting at the bottom of the ravine. Passengers descended to the valley on foot. Nearly all the trucks made it except one that misjudged a turn. I watched in disbelief as the huge cylinder slowly overbalanced, detaching itself and its trailer from the cabin, to roll and crash into the ravine below, leaving the driver at the steering wheel, shaken but safe.

And then we arrived at the village. As trucks were abandoned in the rush for home, I was left holding my rucksack, wondering where to go.

Can a stranger in a Russian village ever feel welcome? I had already noticed in Umba that no passer-by offered or returned a greeting, and at first it was the same in Varzuga. Not a word or a nod as I walked and explored.

Varzuga lay on both sides of the river. The high right bank gave me a panoramic view: north into the forest, east across the water to the other half of the village, and south downstream as far as a bend in the river. The other side of the village was on lower ground and appeared prone to flooding. Small boats were occasionally rowed across the water, and this made me curious about the far bank but I felt too shy and unwelcome to ask how I could procure a lift, and decided that the crossing could await another day.

The majority of the houses on my side had been built back from the river where there was a busy path. On the river side of the path some of the householders had built small, toy-like bath sheds, each with a tin chimney. The wooden church, dedicated to the Assumption of the Virgin, with a magnificent octagonal steeple rising above a square base and four transepts to a height of 34 metres, held the strategic position on the highest part of the bank carved by the turning river. Commissioned by a Pomor merchant known to posterity simply as one 'Kliment', and finished in 1674, it was one of the best examples of pegged, 'tent-roofed' Karelian ecclesiastical architecture.

As if to make me feel really unwanted, Chairman Kalyuzhen had told me it was quite impossible for me to stay in the village, but by the end of the first day he had found me a home of sorts in a deserted two-roomed cabin with a stove, a table, a chair, and a bed with a mattress in each of the two rooms. The oven had collapsed but the roof was intact and the outside door closed. The indoor toilet was a boxed bench-seat above a pit. Less than a half-day's housework made the place habitable. I spread my sleeping bag on the bed and called the place home. I worked out a domestic routine and made the best of eating without an oven. I then washed some clothes and cleaned myself up, although once I had carried a few large containers of water up the steep sandy bank of the river and a hundred metres to the door, personal hygiene became less of a priority.

Several visitors had soon called at the cabin, looking uneasy about my presence, and to these I simply uttered the magic word Kalyuzhen. Drunkards who lurched through the door and straight into my room I was able to dispatch with my own brand of emphasis.

Late that first evening I called at the house of Chairman Kalyuzhen to thank him and let him know that I had settled in, but the door was opened instead by an assistant who told me the big man was not in. The cabin was modest, an undomesticated bachelor home in extremis. Kalyuzhen, who had achieved a reputation for efficient management of his community, had apparently neglected his own patch. Evidently no cleaning had been done for months and the oven looked sorely in need of repair. In an inner room I saw a large collapsed bed. Papers and personal items were scattered everywhere and the telephone rang incessantly (this was the first time I realized that Varzuga had telephones). Everyone, it seemed, wanted Kalyuzhen.

I returned to my home to find the door bolted from the inside. Nobody was visible through the windows and no amount of knocking produced a response. I was angry with myself for not using my own padlock but it occurred to me that perhaps it was I who was really the intruder. Hoping that none of the many vociferous village dogs would find me asleep during the night, I had no option but to settle down behind a woodpile at the back of the house.

In the morning, resuming my loud knocking, I managed to arouse the uninvited guests – a man and a woman – who after some time opened the door, stumbled out on to the porch muttering something under their alcoholic breath, and walked off in each other's arms. I rushed into the house fearing for my equipment but found nothing missing. I had been slow to grasp the role played in the community by the empty cabin in providing shelter and refuge for adulterous trysts.

The village shop, a large, heavily barred cabin at the end of the village, had a modest stock: clothes, stationery and household goods on one side, food on the other. Poor-quality Russian-made jackets, trousers and rubber boots were displayed haphazardly amidst underwear, socks and toothbrushes. I had no oven to cook on but I found plenty in the shop to keep me going: salt-fish, biscuits, jam from former Eastern Bloc countries of the kind I had not seen since my early schooldays, jars of plums, tea, crystallized fruit, fresh bread, local butter, honey, and irresistibly delicious wheaten biscuits that resembled flapjacks.

Everyone continued to ignore me apart from inquisitive house visitors and drunks. As I pondered my situation and my pathetic failure to link up with anybody, a small dog scampered through the open door of my house, wagging its tail urgently, followed by four children. They had brought me an urn of water, telling me that it was good for drinking, and explained where I could find the well. (I never did find it for myself; the children insisted on keeping me supplied daily throughout my stay.)

'This is Dolly,' said the eldest, pointing to their dog. Then, without being asked, they recited their names and ages like soldiers at roll-call, standing in line, decreasing proportionately in height and age from left to right: Darya ten, Yekaterina seven, Ilya six, and little Mikhail four. Dasha, Kasha, Isha, Misha.

'Our mother and father are both mathematics teachers at the school. They want you to come along with us to our home.'

After my relative isolation, I was delighted to accept the invitation. And that was how I came to be watching the film of Isaak and Feodosiya's Varzuga adventure.

*

After the film show Isaak drew back the curtains to let in the midnight sun, and Feodosiya went to the kitchen to prepare food. I sat back on the bed, smiling at the children, delighted that I had made some friends and was at last learning something about the place where I had arrived four days earlier.

I looked around the house. The entrance corridor was crammed to the ceiling with boxes, buckets, jars and tools. The sitting room, which doubled as a bedroom, was lined with thin wooden shelves bowing and groaning with academic journals and books. The children's bedroom was awash with their own paraphernalia. The kitchen was to my systematic mind idiosyncratic. A small room off the corridor housed the toilet, but it was in such demand as a storeroom that there was barely sufficient space between the shelves to manoeuvre oneself with any comfort on to the box-bench against the end wall.

The television news was running a long feature on the fiscal situation. The call was for taxes, taxes, taxes. But hyperinflation and the barter economy persisted, and businesses were obstinately continuing to settle bills in kind. Throughout Russia there was a great shortage of cash, but the Treasury spoke of raising rents and the price of utilities.

'At times like these,' observed Isaak and Feodosiya, 'we find our own village collective infinitely more encouraging than national economic indicators.'

A community had lived on and near the River Varzuga for at least six thousand years. The early, indigenous people of the Tersky, who may have been related to the Saami, lived isolated but self-sufficient lives, going to sea in boats for fish, seal and whale, and hunting the forests for game and fur-bearing animals. In medieval times, however, with the northward expansion of the Novgorod Republic and the burgeoning international trade in furs, these coastal people – by now clearly identifiable as Saami – became increasingly interwoven with the life of civilizations far removed to the south and west. Once the Saami's reputation as unfailing deliverers of high-quality pelts and skins had reached the merchants on the banks of Novgorod's River Volkhov and the chambers of the German Hanse, an increasing number of pioneer traders and seasonal fishermen annually travelled the long distance north by river and portage to the White Sea and the southern coast of the Kola Peninsula. The Karelians, who occupied lands between the Gulf of Finland and the White Sea, also settled for fishing and fur trading.

By the thirteenth century the Slavs from the south were so amply enriching themselves that they were incurring the envy of the Danes, Swedes and Norwegians who, having themselves exploited and terrorized the Lapps for centuries with impunity, felt threatened by the new settlers and the dash for fur. Under the leadership of Alexander Nevsky, Novgorod fought and famously defeated the Swedes on the Neva in 1240, but in eastern Lapland skirmishes continued for many years. In some cases these were substantial battles where indigenous Lapps fought alongside settler Slavs against the Scandinavian raiders. In 1416 a Norwegian seaborne raid almost annihilated the population of Varzuga.

In 1477 eastern Lapland came under the rule of Muscovy. Muscovite jurisdiction and influence, initially benign, had by 1575 acquired a signal brutality. When Ivan the Terrible sent a disciplinary force to sack Varzuga for failing to pay tribute, the village was once again nearly destroyed and the population halved to 45 households. Soon afterwards, however, the settlement was repopulated by families from the merchant classes on the run from the Tsar's infamous *oprichniki*, his vast army of shock-troops who were now on the rampage throughout the old Novgorod territories to the south.

It was from this time that the Tersky settlers, now predominantly involved in fishing and salt, acquired a reputation for high moral resilience and staunch Christian Orthodoxy, characteristics further complemented a hundred years later by the arrival from the south of the Old Believer families who had been anathematized for rejecting the 1653–56 reforms promulgated by Patriarch Nikon. The Old Believers – still to be found today around Kandalaksha – clung to their faith even throughout the Communist years, and have continued to observe a strict domestic practice similar to the *koshrut* of Orthodox Judaism.*

Varzuga was never out of the commercial mainstream for long. Even in spite of the increasingly prehensile behaviour of the Church, which had been granted extensive land rights by the Tsar throughout what was now known as *Russian* Lapland, Varzuga's resilient Pomors flourished. Their church of the Assumption bore witness to the village's talent for generating wealth.

The Saami, although meanwhile displaced from the coast, largely benefited from the Pomors' presence. Travelling long distances from the hinterland on reindeer-drawn sledges or downriver by boat to barter at Varzuga's famous markets, they found they could rely on the unfailing success of Varzugan self-promotion in the wider market-place. Throughout the eighteenth and nineteenth centuries in Moscow, St Petersburg and other large Russian towns, Varzuga's exports commanded premium prices, whether for salmon, pearls or pelts.

In the 1990s, after decades of Soviet mismanagement and four years of war with Germany that took almost all the young men of the village and dozens of women, post-perestroika Varzuga seemed set once again to position itself in the market-place, this time within the baffling economy of New Russia.

Whatever the material and financial prospects for the Varzuga collective, my new friends Isaak and Feodosiya were sceptical about the future of the community.

---

* In 1998 I was refused an interview by the Old Believer community in spite of a family introduction from a Pomor friend in Umba who vouched for me. 'We are wary of journalists,' said one of the elders. 'They only ever write frivolous anecdotes.'

'Kalyuzhen is our saviour, and with him we'll flourish financially. But he's Ukrainian. He'll probably eradicate the Pomor character of Varzuga because he's never understood it, and in the longer run that will harm us.'

Kalyuzhen was a bear of a man; not tall but with a vast girth and a rolling gait more like a ship riding a swell than a human being on feet. Unmistakable in his generously baggy camouflage fatigues and perennial baseball hat above a Zapata moustache, Mikhaylich, as he was affectionately known, commanded the respect of his people. Mostly as a result of his unflagging labours, they were among the few small rural communities throughout the Russian North that could justify a measure of optimism about the future.

Kalyuzhen had been raised in the Ukraine and gone to sea on a large ocean-going trawler. Quietly ambitious as a young man, he had achieved good qualifications and secured a place at one of the higher colleges much sought after by those with an eye to a career in the Party. In 1987 he was invited to run the collective at Varzuga, a post that many would have seen as a political cul-de-sac but which Kalyuzhen saw as an opportunity. At the age of thirty-two he took over a failing collective in a deteriorating village on a coast that was becoming increasingly isolated and irrelevant to the economy of the oblast, at a time when small and large collectives alike had become aware of the terminal condition of Russia's command economy. Chairmen appointed during the same period to other villages along the coast spent their time in offices in Murmansk, then gave up and moved on. Kalyuzhen stayed.

When he arrived at Varzuga there were just over a hundred inhabitants, and the young people were leaving. Now the population had tripled, was young and expanding, and there was a well-run school with nine teachers to about fifty pupils. The farm produced meat and milk, there was a good bakery – the best in the oblast, some said – and Varzuga was trading with Germany, using hard currency earned from the collective's sea-going trawlers. A generator was kept going by the skin of its teeth while Kalyuzhen was building a power line to bring mains electricity hundreds of kilometres through the forest. The farm sheds and most of the machinery dated from the old days but a freezer plant for salmon was planned for a business that would face fierce competition from the Norwegians.

'Kalyuzhen is everywhere,' one of his foremen said to me. 'The Chairman knows about everything and everyone. Even when he's not around you can sense he's looking over your shoulder checking your work. And when you see him climbing into a helicopter you can be sure that he'll be working like a dog on our behalf when he gets to wherever he's going. He really pushes them around in Murmansk, you know. Nobody messes with Kalyuzhen.'

In New Russia, where bosses at all levels were presumed to look first to their own pockets, the compliment came as a surprise. 'He's a real worker, that Mikhaylich. He kept his promise when he came here.'

And then that word again. 'He's a true Pomor.'

When I finally found him at home in his cramped, near-squalid wooden cabin, where I drank his tea and ate salmon from a can, he told me little. He was guarded, suspicious of my status and of my motives: I was neither a businessman nor a journalist. Kalyuzhen's head was anyway too full of other matters to focus on an uninvited foreign visitor asking tiresome questions, too full of plans for the refrigeration plant, the new power cable, the road, the six-vessel trawler fleet.

As to what motivated the mighty chairman, he didn't let on – not to me, anyway. If he lined his pockets he didn't do so at home. The man with a talent for solving post-Soviet problems, who controlled a small fleet of trawlers and bullied the oblast administration, hadn't had a cooked meal in weeks and sat on a collapsed bed wearing a T-shirt and long johns, constantly answering the telephone; he either trusted nobody or had never learned to deputize. He showed scant curiosity about the Western world and never asked me any questions about England. 'You Westerners have no idea,' he said. 'You're great at business and you build empires, but I had to rebuild Varzuga with absolutely no money.'

It was said he couldn't relax unless he was stretched out on his bed enjoying his library of pornographic videos and magazines, but this may have been just good-natured gossip generated by the women of the village who regularly strafed him about his bachelor status. On a helicopter stopover at the Upper Varzuga angling camp in 1995 I shared a *banya* with Kalyuzhen, two inspectors and two soldiers. In the cookhouse afterwards I observed him as he stood towelling his hair, remorselessly mocked by the Varzugan females of the kitchen.

'Look at you, Mikhaylich. Your body's a mess, you've so much weight on you you can hardly walk, your home is a slum, you never wash your clothes, you eat badly, you don't drink enough, and you dress like a backwoodsman. The village is full of pretty girls and you, our *predsedatel*, our great chairman, bring shame on us by being the unmarried oaf that you are.' The target of this virtuoso abuse was a man who had a sense of his own importance but also the self-confidence to take it on the chin.

The Varzuga collective's offices were housed in a large single-storey log building on the left bank of the village. I entered a spacious, uncluttered hallway with a stove that had heated the place to a comfortable temperature. From there I looked into three bright and orderly rooms of desks and office furniture. I had telephoned in advance. Yelena Leonidovna, the collective's secretary, rose from her desk and came to greet me.

'You probably think the Shoots of Communism collective is a primitive operation today, and wonder why we even keep the old name, but I can tell you, it's been transformed by Kalyuzhen,' she said with pride.

'In the old days it was easy to go anywhere by air. Then everything collapsed. No fuel, no flights, we could barely sell our fish, the shop was empty. Now we look forward to having a road all the way from Kandalaksha and Umba. The road was one of the first things that Mikaylich planned. To get the money to pay for this and all the things the village needed he bought a trawler that would work out of Murmansk. Now we have a fleet of six, and we're thinking of buying a cargo ship as well. We can earn hard currency from the trawlers, trade with Germany and Denmark, and also stock the shop.' I wondered, but didn't ask, how Kalyuzhen had managed to acquire the trawlers 'with no money'.

The collective embraced not only Varzuga but also smaller villages along the coast, ancient settlements of the Pomors. Without the wider collective effort, these diminished villages, some now with only a few families, would have disappeared completely.

The village on the left bank of the river contained most of the older and larger houses of Varzuga, many of them well over a hundred years old and painted in bright blues, yellows and reds. There was also the library and the meeting hall, the school, the bakery and two small churches – the first ruined, the second used for other purposes.

Walking along the path in the same direction as myself was a man shouldering an axe. He was wearing leather boots, a quilted cotton jacket, and a light fur hat with the ear-flaps hanging loose. Still desperately searching for my classic Pomor, I engaged him in conversation. In his late thirties with bold, broad features, deep blue eyes and a full red beard, he introduced himself as Yaroslav, and as we walked he told me a little of his Pomor ancestry. True to the old family name of Zaborshchikov, fish-trapper, he worked at the salmon fishery.

He pointed with his axe at the house where he had been born and where his mother now lived. The house had charm, its carved embellishments and old fittings contrasting with the unembellished Soviet-era houses on the other bank – 'my' bank. My new acquaintance called to his mother. She was tending six sheep which had a stall underneath the house and were now feeding in their wooden pen outside, stripping the bark off a recently felled sapling. She greeted us as we stood at the fence, introducing her sheep affectionately by name.

Round the kitchen table, over a bowl of *shchi* and fresh white bread from the bakery, Yaroslav's mother talked at length of how life was reputed to have been in the Tersky coast villages sixty years previously. Pomors were renowned for their adventurous sea journeys to unknown parts in small boats.

'*Neck-or-nothing* was a traditional saying in those days, before my time, before the Communists. Pomor fishermen loved to be out for days on end in their tiny *shnyaki*, bobbing around on big seas, flinging out several kilometres of hooked lines – *yarusy*, we call them – coming home loaded to the gunwales, usually having survived horrendous storms. Even when large foreign cargo ships foundered in gales on their way in and out of the White Sea, plying between Norway and Archangel, the crews in the *shnyaki* almost always came back alive.

'The men were expert at handling and navigating small boats. According to my father, one of our family once sailed with a few other Pomors and two Nenets men up to Vaigach Island to hunt walrus and seal. Vaigach Island! There aren't many people around here today who could even take a small boat up to the Barents and back. Think of it. Vaigach must be at least 1,000 kilometres away.'

I learned some years later about the detailed navigation logs kept by Pomor seamen and handed down over generations. It was an Archangel historian, Kseniya Gemp, married to an Englishman, who was largely responsible for researching and publishing these remarkable documents, some of them originating in the Middle Ages. Written in the Novgorod dialect, the manuscripts record tides, currents, depths of water, landmarks, fishing grounds, preferred routes from the White Sea to Norway, Novaya Zemlya or Spitzbergen, and the best trading places.

When Aleksandr Engelhart, Governor of Archangel – the region which included Russian Lapland until the creation of Murmansk Oblast in 1938 – visited Pomor homes in 1896, he found them invariably tidy, spacious, orderly and well equipped. If my new acquaintance Yaroslav Zaborshchikov and his wife Yevdokiya were of Pomor descent, his house reflected the fact, for it was one of the most ordered and tastefully disposed country homes that I have ever seen. In contrast to the average small Russian village household it gave the immediate impression of space, colour and light.

The entrance corridor, usually in Russia a dark and congested place crowded to the ceiling with clothes and containers of all kinds, was methodically arranged. Boots, coats, skins, hats and house slippers had been hung or placed in a way that was pleasing to the eye. Some of the walls were painted in fresh pale pink. The floorboards shone with varnish. There was no clutter. The wooden staircase to the small upper rooms was beautifully joined.

A door from the hall led down wide steps to the cellar and to what seemed like several lifetimes' worth of provisions: jars of jams and preserves, currants, berries and mushrooms at one end, and about 500 kilograms of potatoes, with sacks of essentials such as flour, salt and sugar, at the other. Salted meat swung from hooks in the ceiling, dried fish hung from strings and racks.

The front room of the house was a double-space sitting room with ample windows giving on to the river. There were some floral fabrics, the curtains were of thick full material, and the furniture was well made, rather modern in style, quite unlike the poorly assembled factory specimens that I had so far seen in both town and country.

Yaroslav and Yevdokiya Zaborshchikov offered the kind of hospitality that I cherished.

*

In August several years later, travelling the Ponoy by raft to the Peninsula's interior and on by river to the White Sea, I found myself on the Tersky coast for a second time. The old Pomor village of Strelna, which was once a thriving estuary village and an important member of the Varzuga collective, had been all but abandoned and was now visited in summer only by families who had moved out to Murmansk or St Petersburg. Making my way past the twelve or so remaining wooden houses, I approached three youths who were working outside a shed on a boat engine. They directed me towards the nearby house, a wooden building in good condition with a small garden and large piles of logs outside the entrance. Making my way through the *seni* with its full complement of seafarer's clothes and boots, I knocked on the inner door of the house of Aleksandr Petrovich Strelkov, whose settler ancestors had founded the village.

Inside I found a lively, cheerful group of people. Sitting at a table under the window, the old Pomor declared himself from across the room and then pointed out his wife as the small elderly woman who was taking dishes of food from the large oven. A man and woman in their thirties were introduced as Strelkov's daughter and son-in-law from Murmansk, and with them was their fourteen-year-old daughter and a young friend or relative who had travelled from Dagestan. A group of summer holiday neighbours, who filled the remaining space in the room, were waiting for the daily midday telephone connection to Umba.

Unkempt and bearded, I had hardly explained myself from the door when I was insistently seated at the table by the daughter. The 'superfluous' telephone visitors were sent packing, a bowl of water and a towel were set before me, and I was served fresh-baked bread with butter and jam.

After I had given an account of my river journey and what I had seen, Strelkov went to busy himself with the boat engine while his son-in-law walked me round the village. The Regional Authority at Murmansk had apparently ceased to concern itself with Strelna and the eastern end of the Tersky coast. Even more so than the village of Kashkarants, Strelna gave the appearance of having lost the battle with history and the elements. Now dominated by the tower of what was once a large nineteenth-century church, the Pomor village had been liquidated in the early 1980s. The salting and barrelling warehouses of the now-defunct fishing collective, of which Strelkov had been chairman for fifteen years, were in poor condition and used for little more than storing a few nets. The only positive news for the place's economic prospects had recently appeared in the form of prefabricated wooden huts, flown in by helicopter by the enterprising Mikhaylich and sited one kilometre upriver from the estuary ready to receive foreign salmon anglers paying for their sport in hard currency.

Seventy-five-year-old Aleksandr Petrovich, whose ancestors had arrived from Karelia and given their name to the place more centuries ago than he now knew, died one month after offering me the hospitality of his table. The sole and probably last Pomor resident of Strelna was buried in a grave behind the metal railings of the small village cemetery, sited on a sand dune close to the White Sea, well above the spring tides.

Strangers from the east

LONG AFTER the Pomors of Novgorod and Karelia had adopted the White Sea and much of Russian Lapland's coast, there were others – this time to the east, towards the Ural Mountains – who began to covet the rich wilderness of Russian Lapland's Kola Peninsula. The migration and settlement of the Pomors, a gradual process over hundreds of years, had been achieved more or less amicably, bringing trade, complementary skills and mutual wealth. Moreover, Pomor activity was largely confined to the sea and barely disrupted the traditional inland territories of the Saami or their seasonal migrations. The arrival of the Komi from the Pechora region of Western Siberia at the end of the nineteenth century, however, brought little or no benefit to the indigenous Saami, and had an immediate effect on the livelihood of the families living in the remote eastern territories.

The year before, on my way to the interior with the ornithologist Sergey Ganusevich, I had stopped briefly at the village of Krasnoshchelye in the centre of the Peninsula, which had been founded by Komi. On that occasion I had wanted to learn about the village and its founders but, with Sergey anxious to reach his survey areas, there had been no time to pursue my enquiries. Since that visit I had learned something of Krasnoshchelye and the Komi story; now I was eager to get a fuller picture.

During several days' wait in Lovozero for the helicopter to Krasnoshchelye, I succeeded in getting a telephone connection to Lyudmila Artiyeva, with whom Sergey and I had stayed on that first visit. She responded positively to the news of my imminent arrival and suggested that I stay as her guest once more, this time in her mother's old house.

The helicopter from Lovozero was overloaded. Provisions for the village shop and crates containing engine spares occupied most of the interior of the old Mi-8; the remaining space was filled by ten passengers, all of whom, including myself, had packed as if for life. We squeezed in along the side walls with our knees up to our chests, sitting among the baskets, sacks, cardboard boxes and brown paper parcels, all of which were carefully secured with rope and string. I read the family names on the handwritten labels, wondering which were Komi, which Saami and which Russian. As the engine roared into life and the rising fuselage shuddered, a laika puppy, which had been leaping excitedly over the cargo, sought refuge on my lap, where it responded to my soothing words by pushing its head under my shoulder for the next half-hour.

As we flew east the mid-summer evening sun threw the landscape into relief: the Lovozero hills behind us, the forest taiga ahead of us, and then the undulating Keyvy Ridge far to our left. The village of Krasnoshchelye on the Ponoy lay at the geographical centre of the Kola Peninsula, at the very heart of its roadless interior and, from an aerial vantage-point, appeared to justify its name, resonant in Russian but clumsily translated as Beautiful Opening. It consisted of less than a hundred wooden houses and barns extending in a T shape along the river bank and back into the forest. The airstrip was a swathe of sand cleared of trees. When we landed, the helicopter was surrounded: vintage motor bikes with sidecars, handcarts, bicycles, a grey horse and cart, children, wives and *babushki*, shouting and laughing, welcoming homecomers or anticipating long-awaited parcels.

I tumbled over the crates and bags and out through the freight door at the back, besieged already by ferocious mosquitoes. Amid the mêlée someone took me by the hand, assuring me that my rucksack would be looked after, and within moments I was riding pillion at speed through pine trees before emerging on to the wide sand street of the village. Houses flew past on either side; I was put down without ceremony outside a garden picket gate and then led by my unidentified driver through the outer hall and over the threshold where I was received immediately with welcoming handshakes.

Lyudmila's husband, Nikolay, who was Komi, had just arrived home from the sawmill and was in heavy-duty working clothes. A man of medium build in his late thirties, he had a striking, somewhat angular appearance, with thick black shoulder-length hair and piercing, slightly narrowed, dark brown eyes. Lyudmila, a Saami, was smaller, more roundly proportioned, and of fairer and gentler complexion. Their small younger son Sergey greeted me shyly from the corner.

I was introduced to Lyudmila's elderly mother, now no longer able to look after herself at home. In a small side bedroom she sat darning socks beneath a large framed sepia photograph of her late husband, the spit and image of Roy Orbison. She agreed that I should stay in her empty house and Lyudmila walked me the short distance through the pine trees.

The house was the preserve of an older generation and an earlier time. Everything was in place as if ready for the next day's work or the evening's cooking, with clean clothes and linen lying folded for a returning member of the household. It comprised a *seni* (unheated entrance room), a kitchen and a large living room. Parts were painted in blue or a warm, old-fashioned ochre. Built into a corner of the main room was a curtained bed; in another corner stood an old glass-fronted cupboard painted yellow, holding shelves of meticulously arranged linen and cloth. Printed fabrics framed the windows, draped the beds, covered small chests, or kept dust from bowls and jugs. The wide, painted floorboards were scattered with knotted rugs. Craft tools in metal and wood hung on the walls as if looking forward to a retirement on display after a long life of hard work. The kitchen had a wood-stove built into the wall, large enough to heat the two adjacent rooms as well as seeing off a family's cooking. Above it was a curtained sleeping space where one could be sure of a warm surface long after the main heat had left the body of the oven. On the opposite wall was a sink with an *umyvalnik* above and a drain bucket below, a carved wooden plate rack to the side, and bright blue and yellow painted cupboards for dishes. In the far corner of the kitchen, under the window near the padded inner entrance door, was a narrow couch which was to be my bed.

In the spacious *seni* I found boots, coats and hats of all shapes and materials – rubber, deerskin, leather, bear, seal, polar fox and muskrat – and numerous vessels for water, food, vegetables, flour, fish and fish-salting. Cupboards and shelves held glass jars and containers awaiting the autumn harvest of berries and mushrooms. From the *seni* a ladder took me up to an Aladdin's loft where heavy skins hung from the rafters and winter clothes were stored in trunks.

Outside, a few paces from the entrance, next to the *saray* (sheds), was the neatest of earth closets. Brooms and garden tools were propped in the near corner, and the seat was at the far end, with a small wooden box holding torn paper squares mounted on the wall beside it. This was a place to linger.

Later that night, standing in my pyjamas in the middle of the large room, contemplating the beauty of my unexpected new home, with the sun still streaming through its western windows, I caught the ghostlike strains of music: distant, faint and tinny but unmistakably a Bach cello suite. I traced the sound to a small bakelite speaker behind one of the curtains, connected to a thin, cloth–covered cable that disappeared mysteriously into the woodwork. I turned up the volume and lay on my kitchen couch hearing out the suite, drifting into sleep to Rossini's *Wilhelm Tell* overture.

I awoke half-way through the next morning to the sound of clanking pails and female laughter and looked out of my bedside window. Among the pine trees near the house, dressed in patterned summer frocks of the kind my sister had worn in her teens, were two young girls drawing water from a well, standing on the canopied wooden platform, working the handle of a large drum of rope and emptying each bucketful into an urn on a handcart. Was each morning's awakening at Krasnoshchelye to be like this?

Returning from her morning's administrative duties at the kindergarten, Lyudmila brought me some buckwheat *kasha* and then offered to show me to the shop and the bakery.

'The morning after a flight from Lovozero there's always a queue at the shop,' she said. 'People like to get there before it opens at two o'clock to take advantage of the new stock, particularly if there's some fruit.' After a long wait I purchased some traditional Russian sausages for boiling, some Chinese jam, a bag of sugar, and the last few oranges.

Lyudmila and I walked the length of the village, carrying our jugs to the dairy, passing cattle, sheep and a goat freely grazing among the houses and trees. The dairy buildings were at the edge of the forest. We stood patiently in line at one of the large barns, waiting to be served by the unseen, bad-tempered dairyman who was verbally abusing us from the hatch in the wall.

'One day you all want cream, then it's everyone wanting *smetana* [soured cream]. Thin cream this week, thick the next. Why are you all so difficult? Come on then. Give me your jugs ...' I handed my two through the hole, one for milk, one for *smetana*.

Following our shopping outing we returned to Lyudmila's kitchen where I sat and sipped tea as she prepared food. Bearing in mind that she herself was Saami, I took the opportunity to ask her about the immigrant Komi.

The families who migrated to Russian Lapland originated on the other side of the White Sea, to the west of the Urals, in the basin of the River Pechora between the tributary rivers Izhma and Usa. Known also as Izhemtsy or Zyryan Komi, they were largely a herding people but non-nomadic. During the eighteenth and nineteenth centuries, with the help of their Nenets reindeer-herding neighbours to the north, they evolved a method of reindeer husbandry on a large scale which became economically profitable. During the same period, however, the number of Izhemtsy Komi had grown rapidly, so that in time the combination of a swelled population and greatly enlarged herds created pressures on living space and land use. During the 1880s, following huge losses of animals to epidemics probably brought on by overgrazing, many of the Komi herding families were eager to emigrate.

Having heard from their own seamen about Russian Lapland and its large areas of undergrazed tundra and taiga, a few young Komi set out to forge themselves a new future. In the autumn of 1883 four families started the long trek west through Archangel Oblast and then round the White Sea, bringing with them about 9,000 reindeer and long trains of draught sledges. They arrived in Karelia, worked their way up the west coast of the White Sea, and by the spring of 1884 had crossed the ice of the Kandalaksha Bay, just before the melt. By any standard it was a physical and logistical achievement: there were difficult and risky summer passages across unknown bog and wet-lands, there was the Dvina to cross as well as many smaller rivers running into the White Sea, and there was also the problem of finding suitable forage.

'The Komi planned and thought about everything in detail,' remarked Lyudmila. 'That's how they are. That's why they've survived so well, even today.'

The Komi migrated with no official permission or government sanction and when they arrived in Russian Lapland they handed out money liberally, first to officials whom they encountered in Kandalaksha, and then to the Saami, most of whom resisted the proposed settlement. Gradually village councils relented, and in the winter of 1886–87, three and a half years after leaving home, four Komi families finally reached the inland, mixed Saami-Russian settlement of Lovozero, close to large expanses of grazing.

When the Komi arrived at Lovozero they found a small village of a few dozen modest wooden houses. It was a place that had been used by Saami as a winter home for at least the previous thousand years. A few Russians had moved into the region over the previous two hundred years, but their interests presented no conflict. Saami and Russian cohabited peacefully; Russians didn't require large tracts of land, and Saami were circumspect about miscegenation.

The arrival of the Komi was different. The Komi were enterprising and resourceful. They were competing for grazing and for land, and in reindeer husbandry they were commercially ambitious. They settled, they built grand houses – the first to have more than one floor – they spent money on a new church and communal buildings in Lovozero, and they set up suede tanneries. As word got home to other aspiring immigrants, the Komi population rapidly expanded. Within a few years they had bred and bought large herds of deer which soon almost equalled in size all the traditionally small Saami herds put together.

By the early twentieth century, within only twenty years of their first arrival, the Komi dominated life at Lovozero. They owned property, workshops and shops, they traded meat with St Petersburg and the West, and they sold animals to the Finns. They changed the traditional way of life in the Lovozero region, and they seduced many of the Saami with the new commerce. They had won the pockets if not the hearts of the majority around them.

'But it was with the reindeer that the trouble really started,' Lyudmila insisted. 'The reindeer mattered to the Saami more than anything else. Saami deer got lost among the large Komi herds and there was overgrazing. Problems with reindeer-herding caused a lot of friction.'

After leaving Lyudmila I walked towards the river. The village claimed about 800 inhabitants but there were few people in evidence that afternoon, just a few men pottering around small sheds at the water's edge. Men and sheds, I thought. The same everywhere. Sauntering along the yellow sand bank, I passed neat stacks of tree trunks that had been floated downriver on the higher spring flood, and gazed vacantly at the few boats which motored up and down, disappearing into the forest. I explored the sand paths and the grass areas between the wooden village houses, looking at gardens and barns where reindeer antlers, animal skins and strings of pike heads were drying in the sun. Motorbikes, mostly ancient Ural models, were the only form of motorized land transport, though on the sand streets I also came across large, well-worn *vezdekhody*, the ex-military personnel carriers which were indispensable across snow and bog. They looked as if they were waiting for spare parts which were unlikely to come.

East of the village, at the sawmill, I found Nikolay and his elder son Vladik working a large planking band-saw. Two other men were picking out spruce trunks from the stacks that had been floated down the river, ramping them up the bank and trimming them with their axes for the feed assembly. When the men stopped to talk they picked mosquitoes off each other's faces. Two dogs under the platform, also worried by mosquitoes, had dug themselves an escape hole in the pile of sawdust. Nikolay switched off the motor and jumped down from the sawmill platform, his stubbled face coated with grime and wood dust.

'I'm ready for some steam, Roger. How about you?'

He had already invited me to participate in the twice-weekly communal *banya* and we now returned towards the houses, joined by other villagers making their way to the large wooden building. Reminding myself of how few people I had seen that afternoon, I reckoned that everyone had either been hiding in their houses or had timed their return from the forest and the river for the pleasures of hot steam. I had long been anticipating the famed mysteries of the *banya* but had never before had the opportunity.

'*S lyogkim parom*,' ran the curious traditional greeting. 'With light steam.'

'*Spasibo*. Thank you,' I replied lamely, not certain of the appropriate response.

Inside the entrance to the bath-house we lined up at a booth as if purchasing tickets at a country cinema. Men filed off in one direction, women in the other. Lyudmila gave me a towel and I walked into the *predbanya* (changing rooms) where Nikolay took me in hand. Spirits were high and the banter ran round the large changing room as clothes were shed and pale skins were exposed below tanned and weathered stubbly necks and faces. Entering the steam room I waited for my eyes to adjust to the dark before edging past the large stove and climbing to a place among the flesh already racked on the terraces of slatted seats. Males of all shapes and sizes greeted me quietly as I clambered through the bodies.

'Don't overdo it,' advised Nikolay. 'Take an early break and a wash down with water before you start to bake.'

In the washing room everything was on an industrial scale. Water taps more appropriate to a ship's engine-room cascaded hot and cold water into large metal bowls and enamel jugs. Nikolay emptied bowls of warm water over me after I had soaped myself, and I reciprocated. Returning to the steam room he picked up some *veniki* – small branches of birch with the leaves intact – dipped them into a bowl of water and applied them to my back, then to my front, a few firm whacks followed by a short rubbing motion.

'Now me. Harder. Put some meat into it. *Muzhchina!* That's it.' We returned to our seats where others were also thrashing their neighbours with birch branches. I soaked up the enveloping heat and felt my pores opening. Back in the washing room, we doused with cold water, dried and dressed.

Returning along the river bank under the warm night sun we arrived at a half-finished, two-storey log house. It already had its roof, floors and stairs. Nikolay explained that, since I had last seen him, he and Lyudmila had decided to live apart.

'I'm living with my mother until I get the house ready,' he explained. I looked apologetic in the English manner.

'Don't be sorry. As the saying goes: *two bears are too many for one hole*.' Nikolay's carefree delivery of his marriage epitaph sounded less vulgar in Russian.

Later we were all seated at the table, Nikolay and Vladik included, in what I now thought of as 'Lyudmila's house', celebrating little Sergey's seventh birthday. The boy beamed with delight as mother, father, brother, grandmother and foreign guest toasted him with home-made cranberry wine. Lyudmila had made reindeer *kotlet* that looked like rissoles, a *kulibyaka* pie with fresh salmon, and a sweet, plaited bread called *plyushki*.

'Reindeer meat's full of goodness, Roger,' said Nikolay. 'Feel the fat on your lips. In the winter it gives you the protection you need from the wind and cold, you'll see.'

Nikolay, Vladik and I took smoking breaks in the *seni*, squatting among boots, fishing gear and food safes. Vladik was a reserved and quiet-spoken twenty-year-old. He had the distinctive narrow eyes of some Komi but the paler colouring and rounder face of his Saami mother and none of the extroversion of his Komi father.

Nikolay spoke of reindeer, asking Vladik about the herding brigade and prospects for the autumn corral and slaughter. Most of the herders were now at home in the village, fishing or gathering berries and mushrooms while the herd was far to the north for the summer. In late September, as the herd was returning from the coast to the winter pastures, the arduous work would begin. Vladik and his colleagues would leave on their sledges to locate the deer, trekking large distances, often through wetlands, chasing animals which had been running wild since the spring and had now grown strong from their summer forage of grasses, leaves, berries and mushrooms.

'Bringing the small groups together into one large herd is exciting but, after summer at home and working on the river or at the sawmill, I don't exactly look forward to it. It's hard going,' said Vladik, fiddling with a hide lasso that hung down from the coat-hooks. 'And I'll be mostly away for eight months.'

Vladik's work-cycle was indeed demanding. By late October his herd of about 8,000 had to be brought to the corral and checked. In November, after sufficient beasts had been slaughtered for local con-sumption, a large group would be herded 150 kilometres west to Lovozero, to the new Swedish-financed slaughterhouse, while the main herd back in the taiga needed to be watched by a small shift-team throughout the remaining winter. Then there was castration to be done through February and March, the calving during April and May, and after that the newborn – the *pyzhiki* – would have their ears cut with the owners' marks. Bulls for the draught sledges were also to be brought to the corral and selected.

'And before you know where you are, the deer are off north again. A few of us run with them as they move towards the coast but these days, by and large, the animals go free, and we get the summer to ourselves.'

Vladik made no comment about other, more personal, circumstances that were preying on his mind. He had his eye on a Krasnoshchelye girl and, because of her, was even thinking of giving up herding altogether. He was right to worry. His girlfriend, like most other young countrywomen since perestroika and the arrival of hard times, may not have been looking for the hand of a herder. In the old days a herder was a prestigious member of the community, better placed than most other villagers, and definitely a catch. But with the collapse of the state collective system and the evaporation of central subsidies, the herder was at the bottom of the pyramid and looked like being left behind in the rush for private business and hard cash. Until relatively recently whole families – or at least part families – lived with the herders for much of the year, particularly in the school holidays; now women seemed reluctant to learn the way of the tundra. Even the staple support of the *chumrabotnitsa*, the female tent-worker, was often lacking, and this all served to sap morale as standards slipped and alcohol took its hold.

Herders were uncertain how to play the future. Prospects for forming large-scale private herds seemed for the moment a step too far into the unknown and had not been seriously considered. There was plenty of meat to sell, and plenty of people in the larger region to eat it, but the Swedish slaughterhouse at Lovozero was the only major buyer, and prices were rarely more than $2–3 per kilogram of carcass meat. Lovozero was also a long way to herd deer to slaughter; the animals would not arrive in peak condition, and, if they then had to wait for a few days in a corral, with a shortage of lichen, they would deteriorate further, and much of the herders' profit would disappear. Also, the collective's administrative offices held the pursestrings, and by the time the money had worked its way through the Byzantine accounting systems, herders were not paid until around January, having usually been in debt to the collective since the previous April.

'Even when we take the initiative ourselves and get meat to the markets in Murmansk,' said Vladik, 'nobody buys it. The people there, who are mainly from the south, either don't like reindeer meat or they don't know how to cook it. And the few times I've seen it on the counters I didn't think it seemed very appetising either. It's usually been poorly butchered … It looks like it's time for me to learn to play the accordion.'

A week later – a Saturday again – the stove was lit in the small *banya* belonging to Nikolay's mother. The cabin was at the bottom of her garden, abutting wooden sheds which were home to a single ewe, a kid goat and a fine-looking red hen that was said to be a good layer. After Lyudmila and Nikolay's mother had finished steaming and washing clothes, Nikolay and I crossed the garden, skirting the large potato patch, and opened the small door to a scene reminiscent of a Chardin still life. The windows were hung with lace curtains through which the evening sun tinged the old copper vessels ranged along the shelves of the *predbanya,* the small outer chamber. Inside, I bumped my head on the ceiling beams several times and, forgetting that all water had to be drawn at the well, used more of it than I should have. I settled on the top plank. It was a good opportunity to ask Nikolay about his people, the Komi.

'After the Revolution the Komi at Lovozero sought out new places for villages and were granted permission to move east. In the early twenties they settled here at Krasnoshchelye and then further down the Ponoy at Chalmne Varre.'

The outside door of the little *banya* hut opened noisily. After much greeting and joking through the dividing wall, the unexpected visitor stepped naked into the inner room, a man in his forties with short brown hair and a beard.

'Chuprov, Stepan,' he introduced himself heartily, throwing almost enough water over the hot rocks on top of the stove to put the fire out completely. 'I'm a good friend of Nikolay,' he said, as if to apologize for interrupting our conversation. 'I heard Nikolay had the *banya* going.'

Chuprov, Stepan, his voice deep and gravelly, was deceptively rough-looking, for he soon gave the impression of having a lively, educated mind. Nikolay explained my interest in the village and in the Komi generally, and told Stepan of our various discussions, as if Stepan and he were accustomed to talking history. Stepan was, as I recognized from the family name, Komi. Nikolay continued the narrative.

'In about 1928 collectivization began. Some of the Saami were ordered to settle permanently in the villages and to work in larger groups. An unpleasant time for many of us, Komi and Saami alike, came with the process of *dekulakizatsiya*, the confiscation of "excess" property held by the kulaks. Sometimes confiscation was completely absurd: for example, a baby having two sets of clothing might have one taken from it, usually the warmer set.'

'My mother,' interjected Stepan, 'was a prominent person in the community, much respected and known for her clothes-making, particularly from reindeer skin, but our family, like most Komi, were immediately "listed" as well-off and privileged kulaks. We were turned out of our home and forced to live in other peoples' houses. We were not allowed to build our own house again until 1949. Our reindeer were all taken from us so we were left with almost nothing. The listing made everything difficult for us and we were demoralized.'

'The Saami were particularly badly affected. In the case of livestock and farm property many of the well-off Saami simply refused to comply, they preferred to destroy their cattle or their barns rather than hand them over. In some families there was suicide.'

I wondered whether this all caused resentment on the part of those who had more. The Komi, for example, owned more deer and larger houses, and were generally better off than the Saami.

'No it didn't. In many cases deer were taken from Komi and given to Saami, but relations between Saami and Komi were good.'

I wondered how correct Nikolay was in this respect. Although he was born in the 1950s, the traumatic events of the Stalin period must have left scars that reopened over the years. Even I, a newcomer, had formed in my mind a historical picture of almost continual friction between Saami and Komi since the 1880s. Lifestyles and farming practices were often incompatible. There were frequent disputes over ownership of animals. The Saami maintained that the Komi were not scrupulous about moving their herds and conserving the lichen, and that the new herder-bases built out on the tundra and taiga in turn caused more overgrazing as time went on. Moreover, the collectivization process and the larger herds did not make for the best results when it came to slaughtering; the Saami well knew that reindeer herding produced better results when on a small scale and privately managed.

I had heard from several sources, admittedly usually from those with a Saami bias, that collectivization came easily to the Komi. The Komi were said to be used to living in larger groups and sticking together as a family, whereas Saami had always tended to spread out – except perhaps in the winter months – with families and the newly married finding their own patch and keeping their distance. The Komi were also accustomed to adopting a formal and managed approach to agriculture. This was not a characteristic of the Saami who had always been small in number and lived off large areas, killing, hunting and breeding only for their immediate needs, and not seeking to expand commercially. They had never needed to address the practical problems that arose from large-scale, collective collaboration, especially not with outsiders.

During the 1930s the Sovietization of the eastern territories of Russian Lapland – that is, the Kola Peninsula itself – was relatively benign; the Saami were for a time allowed to live and work on their traditional lands and to fish their own waters. The harshest years were decidedly those after the Great Patriotic War when, in the 1960s, the government became obsessed with closing villages, condensing the population and developing enormous reindeer herds, managing everything at state-farm level and using machinery.

'Lyudmila's family lived further down the river at Chalmne Varre – Ivanovka, as the Komi used to call it – but the village was closed in the 1960s and they were moved here. The house you're sleeping in – her mother's house – was brought all the way by boat, log for log.'

The Saami removed from the eastern territories who ended up living in apartment blocks in Lovozero had the worst experience of all. The town was hardly prepared for the scale of such an influx, and competition over apartments was intense. What Nikolay had not mentioned was that the community leaders who administered the population movements were predominantly Komi; in the eyes of the Soviet authorities, the Komi were natural choices for brigade heads or community leaders. Disputes over housing were therefore often seen in tribal terms. The Saami sometimes found themselves living twelve or sixteen to a room and usually in the worst of the available apartments.

The consequences of the diaspora on the Peninsula are still evident today. The reindeer herders, who had previously enjoyed high status in the community, found themselves largely unable to cope with their new life at Lovozero. Their record has become one of severe alcoholism, petty crime, crimes of passion, and suicide. In 1990, for example, only twenty per cent of Saami deaths were from natural causes. In the case of male suicides, doctors often adopted a sympathetic approach and certified the deaths as natural, thereby protecting the widow's pension.

It is the women who have survived best. From the start they picked up the pieces and held families together, and in recent times Saami family heads have invariably been women. On the other hand, the new social status of Saami woman has also aggravated the situation as they have obtained a better education, moved away, married out, and sometimes even done their best *not* to be Saami.

When I had first asked Nikolay about the village's history he had suggested I visit a teacher at the Middle School, Dina Aleksandrovna. The school's premises was a large single-storey wooden building on the outskirts of the village. Dina Aleksandrovna came out to me at the door and introduced herself formally, ignoring my inappropriately offered handshake. I had come simply to arrange a future meeting, I explained, but she left instructions with her class and immediately walked me along the broad corridor. Most unusually there was barely a trace of the smell of children that habitually lingers in school corridors; more prominent were the flags and banners of a large display devoted to the Second World War – the Great Patriotic War – and a mural in the Soviet style across a large part of the end wall.

We settled at a table in an empty classroom. Dina Aleksandrovna, a correct woman in her thirties with pale brown hair and glasses, showed not the flicker of a smile – I was not yet familiar with the reserve and formality of professional women in Russia – as she pondered my initial enquiries.

'I am currently making a study of all the Komi on the Peninsula,' she said. 'In my opinion too much consideration has been shown to the Saami. This is a bias that needs to be adjusted.' And on the subject of the relationship between Saami and Komi she was emphatic.

'There was no social conflict. The Komi negotiated and paid for their right to settle along the Ponoy, and the two races have intermingled harmoniously. Even during the late twenties, when the famous "lists" of people's property and assets were compiled prior to collectivization, there was no revengeful behaviour, even though much was confiscated from the Komi and redistributed to the poorer Saami.'

I looked around the room. The rows of books looked as if they would fulfil needs well beyond the school curriculum, and instructive wall-charts ranged through natural and human history to geology and the jet engine. On the matter of the demographic history of Russian Lapland, however, I suspected that the historical syllabus for the foreseeable future would follow a safe, prescribed path with an emphasis on the Soviet heroes of the Great Patriotic War.

Village in winter

'YOU KNOW the village in summer, you know the river from Krasnoshchelye to Kanevka, and you know where the salmon lie,' Volodya Zakharov had said to me with exaggeration when I had hurried away from Kanevka village two years previously. 'You must visit us in winter and learn about logging, reindeer and hunting. Then you'll really know how to survive at Kanevka all year round, like a Saami or a Komi!'

This time I was to stay in Kanevka for several weeks. During the night before my arrival there had been a heavy fall of snow. Seen from the air the village was almost lost in the uniform whiteness of the forest. I had no salmon to barter for the flight this time; the co-pilot had simply bundled me on to the already overloaded plane – similar to the old green Antonov which had taken me prematurely away from Kanevka on my last visit – and made room for me among the boxes of provisions for the village shop, telling me to pay for my ticket at the other end.

On our arrival the plane was surrounded by excited villagers awaiting or proffering parcels to the co-pilot, the same women, men, and children, it seemed, with whom I had jostled when trying to secure a place on the outgoing aeroplane on my previous visit.

I made my way towards the edge of the forest where a two-storey log building doubled as control tower and hunters' doss-house. A hidden voice summoned me up the stepladder and through a trapdoor into an attic where I was welcomed by a man surrounded by banks of old military-green radio equipment. He knew my name and was already writing my ticket. The paperwork, which lasted some fifteen minutes, gave me the opportunity to absorb the ambience of his eyrie. The room held generations of communications paraphernalia. There were rows of softly glowing dials and quivering needles, the floor was a bed of tangled cables, and there was a lingering smell of solder. The place reminded me of those many-season sea-eagle nests, rich in prandial debris, built into the tops of pine trees, that I had been shown by Sergey Ganusevich in the Ponoy wilderness. The cloth-covered speakers crackled and hissed, eliciting occasional grunted responses into a microphone from the man himself. Glancing out of the window at the venerable biplane at rest on its skis, I felt I was playing the hero of a story in *Boys' Own Paper*, or travelling with Farley Mowat to the trappers of Hudson Bay.

On my last arrival at Kanevka I had been peremptorily deposited on the bank and from there had found my way to the village 'hotel'. Now Volodya was meeting me with his snowmobile. This was unexpected; when I had last seen the machine it had looked abandoned, and the dogs had scattered small engine parts around the garden.

'I was expecting to be met by reindeer,' I shouted over the racing engine which Volodya had to keep running.

'We're logging at the moment so you can travel with the deer tomorrow if you like. Sasha's waiting for you.' There was a hint of long-suffering in his voice; I was always asking about reindeer.

At the family house, Matryona Alekseyevna greeted me with a broad smile, her small frame wrapped in layers against the cold: two thick skirts over woollen leggings, her head as usual in a colourful scarf tied at the back. I embraced her, even though I knew she would be unaccustomed to the gesture. The small dog Lada yapped excitedly; even Zhuchka the tame reindeer joined in the welcome.

'Come and look at the new cabin,' said Volodya. 'There've been a few improvements. I've made it into a family home. You see, I'm married now.' This took me completely by surprise. Volodya had made no mention of this possibility on my previous visit. I had spent only a few days in Kanevka on that occasion but I never set eyes on a woman of marriageable age. In the post-perestroika 1990s what woman would wish to marry and settle in Kanevka? Without the support of the old collective system, survival in this small remote place was not proving easy.

The interior walls of the rough log cabin had been papered, and the ceiling boarded and painted. A TV dominated the corner together with a video recorder and piles of cassettes featuring some of

Hollywood's less notable productions. On the wall a large coloured calendar featured a topless blonde, kneeling on a Caribbean beach, smiling invitingly, her legs indelicately open. I contemplated the role of this imagery in the couple's new married life. On the table Volodya had considerately provided some light reading matter for his new wife, including issues of *SPEED* magazine (the title is coincidentally the Russian acronymous near-equivalent to AIDS), all racy showbiz gossip, agony columns, illustrated love stories, and pin-ups.

'You can sleep here on the couch; we'll sleep in there, in the little room.' On the other side of the curtained doorway there was a camp bed in the middle of the room and a double bunk for children.

'And a baby's on the way,' said Volodya, pre-empting my joke about being well prepared. 'Oh, and Inna has a little daughter, Lyuda. She's three years old.'

I immediately wanted to ask all the usual questions but I thought it best to wait for the right moment. When did they meet, and where? Was there a matchmaker somewhere in the picture? Did they have some sort of service or ceremony? Was she a local girl? Saami? Komi? Russian? Was she beautiful? Had she been married before? What about the child? How did Volodya's mother, Matryona Alekseyevna, take the news? She had always relied on Volodya for everything around the old house and home and she was a critical woman with high standards.

'If you want to do some work, come logging with us tomorrow,' Volodya said, just as I was on the point of asking questions. 'Try these on first so you don't freeze to death on the sledges.' He handed me *lipty* and *volpimy* – inner and outer boots made from reindeer skin – and a woollen *sovik* (smock). The *lipty* were made from fine calf's skin with the soft coat on the inside, the *volpimy* from the thick dark brown coat of a mature wild reindeer with the coat on the outside. I sank into them as if I were slipping in between the softest bed linen, and then I fixed both pairs to my belt with straps, rather like thigh waders.

The heavy and bulky deerskin *malitsa*, with the fur inside and the outside draped with a cotton shift, went over my head easily but I had a long struggle finding the opening of the hood. The garment came down well below my knees. The hood and the mittens were all part of the one garment. I stood there wondering how I would ever be

139

able to do anything in such all-enveloping clothes, when in walked a stoutly built woman in her thirties with a shy toddler hiding in her skirts, who introduced herself as Volodya's wife Inna. She had heavily bleached hair, prominent gold teeth and an engaging smile. I couldn't judge whether she was Russian, Saami, Komi, Nenets, or a mixture of any of these, but I realized immediately from her speech impediment and her difficulty in understanding me that she was deaf. My questions were likely to remain unanswered for a long time yet.

In the morning Volodya's brother Sasha arrived with a team of deer drawing two large sledges. Volodya and the other brother Aleksey loaded a third sledge behind the snowmobile with food, skis, axes and chain-saws, roping everything tightly. Volodya cranked the engine. It caught first time. Sasha was untangling the deer's harnesses while they fidgeted impatiently and pawed at the snow. He cursed them roundly. As so often, I looked on helplessly.

'Just sit down, *Rodzher!*' Volodya shouted as he moved ahead of us on the screaming snowmobile with Aleksey on the rear seat. 'Quick! Near the back. And hold tight!' I waddled hurriedly over to the reindeer, realizing my day rucksack was still in my hand when it should have been with our cargo, and hurried to do as I was told, sitting down on the sledge like a trussed turkey. Before I had taken breath I was thrown violently backwards with my feet in the air. I clutched unsuccessfully for a rope and fell off, but grabbed hold of the back of the sledge as it passed by my head. Finding that I was being dragged along the ground at speed, I struggled to regain my place and my dignity. Once I had worked my way back on to the sledge, sat upright and removed the snow from my face and hood, I saw that Sasha, oblivious of his passenger, had taken his place in front with the rein and the long *khorey* (driving pole), and that we were hurtling wildly down the long slope towards the river, enveloped in an explosion of snow, with all four reindeer throwing their heads in excitement. We continued for a further 200 metres before the deer, enjoying the easy compacted trail over the Ponoy ice, settled to a steady run. I had heard it said that reindeer are faster than horses and, although I doubted this could be true, I had just learned how fast deer could travel, especially when starting out fresh.

The two Siberian laikas were running behind us. The younger, light brown Norka, who disliked falling behind, kept her nose to within a few inches of the back of the sledge; the elder black-coated Vokan lagged behind because of a wounded leg. When we left the river and headed into the forest, the snow was deep and soft, even on the main route, and the dogs were constantly sinking. I marvelled at their stamina and began to understand why Amundsen took dogs to the South Pole.*

Volodya slowed the snowmobile engine and came alongside us.

'That's where we've already been felling this winter.' He pointed at the spruce and pine poles, trimmed and stacked at the side of the track. 'You can just make out our old tracks going up the slope through the trees. If other villagers see we've been working here they don't follow. They make their own way into the forest further on.'

We stopped at the felling site. Sasha unhitched the three deer and left them in harness to dig for lichen and nibble the black beard-moss on the tree trunks. I climbed off the sledge but immediately sank into the deep snow, filling the tops of my boots as the *malitsa* rode up to my waist.

'Try these skis, Roger,' said Aleksey. The skis were short and fairly broad, with two small metal clasps and strips of hide to hold the feet. Accustomed to large solid ski boots, I found it strange to be climbing into bindings with skin-thin boots that felt more like bedroom slippers. Bending with difficulty, and frequently standing upright to get my breath, I struggled for what seemed a very long time.

'You've got it now,' said Aleksey, who had been smoking a cigarette and giggling as he directed my flounderings and fiddlings. The three Zakharov brothers were also on skis and had stripped down to their pullovers. Aleksey took the chain-saw, moved through the trees, made his selection and started the felling; Volodya and Sasha worked after him with an axe, trimming and cutting. The three brothers moved well together, with flair and panache. They got pleasure from the work. Sasha, a different man now from the drunk of eighteen months earlier, threw me a broad gold-toothed smile whenever he

---

* In eastern Lapland dogs never became popular as draught animals. Around the villages and on the major routes Russians preferred horses, but for the Saami and Komi in the country reindeer were always the clear favourite. Deer can survive on lichen in winter but dogs require meat, which has to be caught or carried.

saw me watching. I attempted to do some trimming with my hatchet but my contribution was modest; I had difficulty staying in my bindings and nearly trimmed my own limbs instead.

At midday Volodya lit a fire in the snow. The temperature was about minus ten degrees Celsius, a good temperature for manual labour. The brothers put their overclothing back on and we were soon enjoying the warmth of the flames. While Volodya made the tea Aleksey produced a sack and picked out some untidy lumps of reindeer flesh which he cut into small pieces and placed on green sticks whittled by Sasha. These were stuck into the snow and leant towards the fire to cook. The next delicacy to emerge from the sack was the heart of an elk.

'Try it raw first,' said Aleksey, making a show of slicing the frozen heart into slithers with his sharp axe. 'It's a delicacy. We sometimes eat it raw when we're travelling through a storm and can't stop to cook.' As the fire burned, the surrounding snow melted. When we returned to the site in the afternoon the embers were sitting in a hole a metre down.

'After this week we won't take any more trees from here for a number of years,' Sasha said. 'We're selective with our logging. Over in the west, near the border with Finland, the Finns have been sold large tracts of forest, and the results are devastating. Corruption as usual.'

By the time we stopped for tea we had six trees on each reindeer sledge and twice that number behind the snowmobile, ready for pulling out of the forest and back on to the open track. The deer pulled together well and without much difficulty – Sasha knew the capacity of all his draught bulls – but the snowmobile made heavy weather of it and we had to lift and dig the machine from the deep snow every few metres. Volodya, who was a miracle worker when it came to engine repairs, had a wicked temper if his patient failed to recover. He cursed the engine, spat on the ground and berated it at length, treating it like a father confronting a spoilt and ungrateful child. It was hot work, particularly with a double layer of reindeer on my legs.

'We take most of the logs to the river and float them home when the ice has melted,' explained Volodya.

Before we started our homeward journey we secured as much

round wood on the sledges as we thought the machine and the animals could manage. Sasha had hitched two deer to his small driving sledge, and attached to that was a long draught sledge for the trees. Then came the other two deer drawing their own load. Behind the deer came Volodya's snowmobile with Aleksey riding pillion, and two sledges. I was told to perch on top of the load of the first snowmobile sledge. My place seemed precarious and untenable from the outset but there was little option and I did as I was bid.

We moved off. On a flat surface I had no difficulty in staying on board but it was a different matter as soon as we met bumpy surfaces or traversed a slope; within the first half hour I was thrown twice, once nearly catching myself under the oncoming second sledge. An additional hazard was that Volodya and Aleksey, who tended to forget about me, could not hear my shouts from the top of the pile over the din of the engine, and there was nothing behind us. Nobody noticed my first fall. I picked myself up and dusted myself down, watching the sledges disappearing through the trees. Later, as we were travelling at speed along a traverse and I was feeling pleased with myself for having mastered the balancing act, my sledge parted with its entire load. As the ropes snapped and the timber spilled wildly from under me I scrambled to throw myself clear, getting away with only a sharp blow to my back from the second sledge coming on.

Returning along the river, and now carrying the extra weight of the timber, I wondered about the strength of the ice; I knew that river ice was usually thinner than lake ice on account of the current. 'No problem,' Volodya told me later, pausing before adding: 'although towards the end of winter one or two snowmobiles do usually go through, and you have to wait until the river has melted before you can haul them out.' I wondered about their owners.

Matryona Alekseyevna fed us on arrival home, our fifth meal of the day. It included a few specialities that were new to me: salmon livers, cod tongues fried in batter (the cod came from one of Volodya's winter trips to the Barents coast), *frikadelki* – balls of elk meat with rice – and potatoes fried in elk marrow. Even after all that I could hardly resist the salted salmon and the salmon caviar. Matryona Alekseyevna was, as usual, pleased to see me overeating. 'Now you're beginning to eat like a forester.'

The logs from the forest had been stacked on the village path next to the woodshed. The following morning Aleksey sawed them into lengths, leaving me and Sasha to split them, and Volodya to stack them into golden piles up to the roof. I had some assistance from the tame young reindeer, a white calf adopted at five months when she had returned that September from her first summer on the tundra. Unlike the older Zhuchka, who always liked to be part of the family but would rarely allow herself to be approached, the 'baby' was demandingly affectionate. She had a small delicate velvet mouth with which she daintily picked the wisps of beard-lichen from the unsawn trunks before coming over to investigate me and my pockets. She offered help in return for backrubs.

During our absence in the forest the biplane had returned with more provisions for the village shop. Volodya had been hoping for a delivery of fuel but only a new fishing net arrived. Outside the shop I stood in line with ten women, keeping a place for Matryona Alekseyevna. I strained to catch news and local gossip but with my inadequate command of Russian and complete ignorance of Komi and Saami it was difficult.

At 11 am the shop opened. There was only one woman to serve the twelve people ahead of us in the queue, so it was a long wait. Biscuits had to be weighed, sugar was scooped from wooden boxes, buckwheat from sacks, and obscure cans and bottles of this and that, with labels in different languages, were brought from the back of the shop after several minutes' search. The woman at the counter conducted her duties without charm or humour. At intervals men could be heard stumbling up the outside steps before crashing through the door and lurching into the shop to engage us in the international language of drink. They were all politely and firmly ejected, only to take up ambush positions outside the porch, looking for handouts.

*

'The Kanev families came here in the winter of 1924–25,' said Matryona Alekseyevna. 'Pure Komi. Five brothers, three of them with families. The village was named after the family. My father was with them. My great uncle bought settling rights to this land from the Saami in the twenties. There was nothing here on the Ponoy before we arrived.'

We were sitting in the kitchen, Matryona Alekseyevna, Aleksey and myself. I had been asking Matryona for some time to tell me about the village and her life. That morning she was in the mood. She had emptied a large envelope of photographs on to the table. Volodya was coming and going, busy with snowmobile repairs as usual. Sasha appeared looking full of sleep, his narrow eyes squinting over a heavy stubble.

'I was born just after the Kanev families arrived,' she continued. 'I remember living in our *chum* at first, and then my father built a small log cabin just over there towards the river. It's still standing.' She pointed in the direction of a nearby house, smaller than Volodya's marital cabin. 'Later we built a larger home but that wasn't until there were eleven of us: my father and stepmother, five brothers and four sisters. I was my mother's only child – she died when I was four – and as I was the eldest I was kept busy from the moment I could pick up my baby stepbrother. By the age of seven I was salmon-fishing with my father, and at eleven I could help save hay. I remember as a girl travelling by boat with my father to the riverside meadows. We would all stay out there for two or three days at a time. We worked right through the sunny nights and I would just crawl into a stook and sleep there.

'We walked to our school at Ponoy village, at the estuary; the luggage went by boat. On foot the journey was about 90 kilometres. We all did it twice a year, in September at the start of school and back again at the end of May. Sometimes we came home by sledge for the holidays at New Year or in March. That was a treat.'

The *internat* boarding schools were a Soviet introduction and, for the Saami and Komi, a catastrophe. At these schools, in Ponoy, Lovozero, Murmansk, and across the whole of the Russian North, children were leached of their national identity and ethos. During Matryona's time the Saami and Komi languages, customs and dress were tolerated, and compulsory Russian was limited to the classroom and organized activities; in later years, notably after the Great Patriotic War, the regime became increasingly intolerant.

In 1941, after finishing school, Matryona Alekseyevna had married a Saami herdsman, who had almost immediately gone off to fight the Germans. He survived the war and lived until 1985. On cue Aleksey reverentially handed me two photographs of the burial service. Then

Matryona showed me a formal wedding photograph taken in Lovozero. Zakharov looked bewildered and out of sorts in his Russian suit and tie. Matryona was taller than him and self-confident. In the eyes of a herdsman of possibly modest circumstances a girl from the now-influential Kanev family would have been an attractive catch.

Matryona gave birth to nine children, of whom six survived. She now had nine grandchildren and four great-grandchildren. I asked whether she still felt she was 'one hundred per cent Komi'? And what about her boys and girls? For that matter, I thought to myself, what could anyone feel about their personal identity after the years of Soviet Communism.

'Well, we don't think about it much anymore. In Kanevka we're such a small crowd, and we've married into each other's families anyway.'

Sensing I couldn't question her any further about 'being Komi' or 'being Saami', I asked her to tell me more about Ponoy.

In the late sixties Ponoy village almost ceased to exist because it became a radar station and military base, so all the children in Kanevka had to go to the school in Lovozero. The closure of Ponoy village destroyed many families – Saami, Pomor and Russian. Most of the villagers there had been part of the fishing collective which was rich and successful, sending fish to Archangel or along the coast to Umba and Kandalaksha for canning. The salmon were the community's main livelihood. Today the Ponoy families have been prevented from resettling the village because of the small base that remains, but also because of the financial interests surrounding the salmon angling camp for foreigners, which was established some fifty kilometres upriver from the estuary in 1991.

A Saami neighbour of the Zakharov family had come into the kitchen and was also looking at Matryona's photographs. He was from a family of reindeer herders with territory on the River Lumbovka, north of Ponoy, who had been moved to Kanevka to add their herd to the village collective. He was of typically small, compact Saami stature, with keen dark eyes, apparently physically fit for his seventy years. Ivan Timofeyevich took over the narrative.

'In the late sixties the *internat* schools became even more intolerant of Saami and Komi children. We Saami especially – more so than the

Komi – were considered illiterate and stupid and were force-fed the state culture. All traces of the shamanistic tradition were outlawed. Like the kulaks, the shamans were declared 'enemies of the people'. I remember a mural in one of the schools depicting shamans being chased by children over a precipice. Our Saami children were even forced to eat Russian food, much of it strange and distasteful to us. Some were housed with juvenile delinquents or problem children from the towns, and were separated from their family background for such long periods that they would return home almost unable to speak their own language. In many cases they were sent to the far south and never saw their parents again. In time we Saami became fearful of admitting our origins. Can you believe it, some of us insisted we were Russian, particularly some of our girls!'

Few of these aspects had been touched on by Matryona who, I noticed, preferred to gloss over the unpleasant aspects of the past, or even by Aleksey, who with his brothers must have suffered from the post-war racist culture of the *internat* schools.

Matryona spoke about her sons, particularly the three still living in the village. Volodya, Matryona's cherished youngest child, was the family spokesman and more extrovert than the older brothers. Good-looking as they were, the two reticent bachelors would surely have difficulty finding marriage partners, a situation aggravated by their chronic weakness for the bottle.

'Aleksandr – my Sashka – is good with reindeer; Aleksey is the craftsman, particularly with the needle,' added Matryona, much to the embarrassment of the latter who tended to bouts of shyness, 'I have passed on all my sewing knowledge to him.' Telling Aleksey to make tea she went to the loft and came back with her arms full of some of her best work in deerskin.

There was a *malitsa*, a *parka*, some fine *lipty*, and a pair of knee-length boots, *toborki*, made from a patchwork of different-coloured reindeer skins. Her small *kangi* (summer boots) were sewn from calf's skin, decorated with coloured beads and a fur trim, and secured at the ankle with thin woollen straps. There were two beautiful hats, both for women: a *kokoshnik*, probably for summer, with geometrical bead decoration and coloured trim, and a 'best' winter hat made from thicker wool and fox fur.

'This is what I would take on a long journey.' Matryona produced a large strong deerskin patchwork bag. 'These smaller bags are for separate belongings.' They were superb examples of fine abstract beadwork and silk embroidery on closely woven wool. All of them were precious family heirlooms.

'My travel bag has been with me on the sledges many, many times, even as far as Murmansk. When I was young we made the journey to Murmansk probably every year. By the fifties it created a bit of a stir if a reindeer appeared there on the streets.

'When the children were small we also made the journey to the north coast, to Iokanga. Iokanga had always been a summer camp for the Saami so there were many wooden cabins there: large *tupy* belonging to the Pomors who lived there all the year round, and smaller huts for the people who came up from the south or Karelia for the fishing and sealing. Small trading ships visited the beautiful bay. It was very picturesque. Those were happy, special times ...' Matryona went quiet.

'But life changed. Iokanga and Lumbovka became a closed zone because of the submarine base and everybody was moved out at short notice. Most of the villagers were forced to live in Lovozero, in those horrible concrete apartment blocks. A few were moved here – like you, Ivan – and some to Krasnoshchelye.'

Ivan and his wife lost access to the salmon fishing in the River Lumbovka and to the flounder-fishing and seal-hunting in Lumbovka Bay. Large well-established herds of reindeer were confiscated. But when I questioned him about the move from the Lumbovka territories he was not bitter. Either time had healed the wounds or he would talk only about injustices in general.

'So Iokanga became a closed military zone,' repeated Matryona, 'and changed its name to Gremikha. Our family hasn't lost contact with it, though, because my daughter, who married a submariner, lives at the base. And Volodya makes the journey on the snowmobile twice every winter to barter salmon for fuel, food and anything else that's going.'

Then, beaming broadly, Matryona passed me what at first looked like fine chamois leather but which unfolded as a pair of underpants sewn from the thin soft skin of a hare.

'They're very rare these days.'

The kitchen door crashed open. I recognized the uninvited visitor as the blond young man of the previous year living among the drunks at the 'hotel'. He staggered straight for me muttering '... *dollari* ... *dengi* ... *vodka* ...', but Volodya had spotted him entering the house and had rushed from the garden to eject him, though not without a struggle.

'He has to go if he can't behave himself,' explained Sasha, whom ironically I had seen similarly ejected on my very first arrival at the Zakharov house.

'He's not an alcoholic anyway,' said Volodya later. 'People like him feign drunkenness because they're lazy and don't want to work. You should see them wake up when they're tied to a sledge by the neck!'

I asked Matryona Alekseyevna to tell me more about collectivization. She composed her thoughts.

'A mink farm started up. We also started making bricks for ovens but that closed down. Gradually collectivization became more serious. We worked larger herds, we spent much more time working for the collective, and more time together. Perhaps that drew Komi and Saami closer for the first time, because Saami and Komi were beginning to intermarry. Russian was the common language but many Komi started to speak Saami and some Saami even learned Komi. There were never many Russians in the village; only itinerant workers from time to time.

'We lived well and the village became wealthy. We lived comfortably right up to the eighties. We were probably the richest village on the Peninsula.'

I had heard this before, and the very next day I heard it again. On the recommendation of Nikolay Artiyev at Krasnoshchelye I called on a Komi acquaintance of his, Konstantin Chuprov, who had a small well-built log house near the 'hotel'. A knock on the door brought two small children to the door. They pointed up the hill to a man approaching us carrying farm tools over his shoulder. I introduced myself and offered him Artiyev's compliments.

'Very strange. Very strange indeed.' He looked puzzled and not so friendly.

'I'm interested in the history of the village. Perhaps you would like to talk.' A long silence.

'The village? History?' Another pause. I had turned up, as the Russians say, like snow falling from the sky. 'Well, you can see the history of the village here, there, all around you.' I worried lest I had found the village philosopher but, once Chuprov had gathered his thoughts, we enjoyed pleasant conversation. He was an open-faced, gentle-mannered man, broadly built, tall, no more than sixty, and he looked handsome in a bearskin hat and quilted jacket over a red shirt buttoned at the neck. His dark grey trousers were tucked into good-quality felt *valenki*. It was cold and I was not dressed well for outdoors. I looked hopefully towards the house but Chuprov apologized for not being able to invite me inside because his mother suffered from high blood pressure. We could talk outside, he suggested. He didn't want to miss the opportunity of talking to his 'first non-Scandinavian foreigner'. I kicked my boots to keep the circulation going.

Chuprov's great-aunt, his grandmother's sister, was one of the Kanev Komis who founded the village. He himself was a bachelor. His fiancée had left him when he was on military service, he said, looking at me earnestly with deep blue eyes. Since he obviously did not want to tell me about the village's past I asked him about its future. This had the desired effect.

'The future's not looking good at all. In the past we lived well here. There was a lot of coming and going, sometimes more than one plane a day, usually landing on the river right here in front of the houses. The hotel where you stayed used to be the airport office.' He smiled for the first time. 'Unfortunately there were few labourers and fewer artisans. Artisans had to be imported, usually Russians. Yes, we lived well.'

Some time later I asked Yevgeniya Yakovlevna Patsiya, the curator at the Apatity Museum and one of the region's more reliable, if less charitable, historians, about the so-called wealth of Kanevka village.

'Yes. The village was certainly comfortably off,' she said. 'It was closed to locals from the late 1960s because it was selected by the Party as a fishing and hunting place for *apparatchiki*. So the village was more than amply supplied. The shops contained a fabulous range of goods and food, and the villagers profited from their visitors. In time the Kanevtsy forgot how to work. So when the Party bosses and their hangers-on stopped coming after 1985, the village declined. A new bakery which was built with money donated by the American boss of the Ponoy angling camp burned down. I would say they actually burned it down themselves. As for the fishermen, they're not even prepared to go twenty kilometres to the good lakes like the Saami in the west. And they don't know things like how to store fish and meat under the snow …

'Morale is low. Alcoholism is also a great problem for Kanevka. You as a visitor wouldn't know the worst because people stay in their houses and don't tell you about these things. It's all hidden.'

Running to get warm after my meeting with Konstantin Chuprov, I hurried back to the comfort of Matryona's kitchen. Outside in the garden I found Aleksey sitting on a large log putting the finishing touches to a new axe handle. He handed it to me. The axe was perfectly balanced. Then he showed me a number of knives for which he had made new handles out of birch, the best wood for the job because it stays warm during cold weather.

Desperate for my long-awaited cup of hot sweet tea, I made for the kitchen. Aleksey called after me: 'I'm going hunting tomorrow. You're welcome to come with me. Get some warm clothes organized and try out Volodya's skis.'

As I sipped my tea I recalled my lame efforts on skis in the forest. I could hardly feel confident about the long-distance outing awaiting me in the morning.

According to archaeologists the Saami and their antecedents have been travelling on skis for thousands of years. Finds have been carbon-dated to 2,500 BC, and the rock-drawing of a skiing man found at the Vyg estuary, south-west of the White Sea, is well over 2,000 years old. Tacitus mentioned how Lapp men and women went hunting together on skis, and medieval historians remarked on the speed and skill with which Lapps travelled on their 'curious curved wooden footware'. When I watched the Zakharov brothers on skis I often thought of the woodcut in Olaus Magnus's sixteenth-century *Description of the Northern Peoples*, a rich source of pictorial information about Saami, which shows two men and a woman on skis, the woman with long flowing hair, travelling with their dogs into the hills after wild deer. All three are carrying a bow and a quiver of arrows. When Anthony Jenkinson, the explorer of Asia, anchored at the Holy Cape – now Gremikha – in 1557, he accompanied a group of Lapps as they hunted. They were 'very good at shooting,' he wrote.

'The women too.' During the Great Patriotic War the Saami on the northern front were so prized for their marksmanship and stalking on skis that they enjoyed special protection.

Aleksey proved as skilled and swift on his skis over a long distance as he was in the forest with an axe or chain-saw in his hands. On that day he was considerate towards me as I struggled and tumbled at the outset, noticing I had reached near-exhaustion after travelling eight kilometres into the forest.

'We'll move slowly now. This is a good place for ptarmigan. Keep your eyes open.' We had already put up a number of birds on the way but hunters traditionally refrained from taking wildlife close to their village.

Aleksey had an old gun. He called it a .545, although that meant little to me. It could kill a bear, an elk, a deer, or a bird, he said confidently. By early afternoon we had bagged a dozen white ptarmigan. Aleksey never missed and I think on one occasion he picked off two with one round.

'Have a shot, Roger. You can see it's easy,' he offered as I examined a still warm bird in my hands. I had seen these beautiful and delicate white creatures of the taiga and tundra in the summer months when both male and female were blackish brown, almost invisible against the forest floor and surprisingly tame. The hoarse croaking call of the male was instantly recognizable, and the female often stayed down until the last moment. During my late October walk to the Titovka estuary a year earlier I had seen the autumn plumage on hundreds of the birds – grey, finely mottled with black and buff – matching perfectly their partially snow-covered habitat. Now, in winter, I had watched them escaping the oncoming sledges, flying nervously away through the trees in full white winter plumage. I declined Aleksey's offer.

After a short absence Aleksey returned with a white mountain hare, a smaller species than the brown one I knew from home in Ireland, not much bigger than a rabbit, with shorter ears and large furry feet. 'The fur is very fine. I'm going to make a little hat for Volodya's new stepdaughter Lyuda. She'll like that. Let's start home now. I want to look at my traps on the way.'

I was not sure whether trapping was still legal but it didn't seem the right moment to ask. Aleksey had pointed out several spoors during our outing, most of which he could recognize immediately. He beckoned me towards a rocky outcrop where one of his traps had a victim: a small animal with a white coat and tail and touches of brown, a male, almost a metre long. It had frozen solid, and its pointed, sharp-toothed, whiskered muzzle was twisted hard round as if angry at having been bitten in the back. The eyes had been pecked, so that the creature's rigidified death-throes resembled a theatrical mask.

It was a long time since the wealth of this part of the world had been measured largely by its animal fur. Profiting greatly from the burgeoning trade in fine skins in the Middle Ages, Lapps had bartered with Russian and Novgorod merchants for centuries. The furs travelled throughout Russia. The finest skins might finish their journey in the coffers of a prestigious diplomatic delegation or as the Tsar's gift to an eastern potentate. Skins from the region were also eagerly sought by the West. Merchants sailed to Rybachy Peninsula – Kegor, as it was formerly known – or up the Gulf to the settlement of Kola, and then further east to Kildin Island, the small but cosmopolitan anchorage to the east of the Kola Gulf, or the bay at Holy Cape, where the Iokanga Lapps bartered ermine, marten, squirrel and polar fox for flax, hemp, buckwheat, sugar and eagerly awaited alcohol and tobacco.

The remnants of the trade had lingered on in recent times in the form of a fur-farm collective at Zverosovkhoz, near Murmansk, whose Bluesilver Fox furs had been awarded trophies at the international trade fairs of London and other major capitals, but even that was now almost defunct and I heard that workers were paid in kind. When I had last driven near the farm, I had passed individual sellers on the road, keeping warm in their parked old Lada cars, displaying single skins hanging from the end of a pole.

Aleksey and I returned to the village with our catch, to which we had added a red fox. Our bags were full and my green Russian rucksack well blooded. As we approached the houses Matryona Alekseyevna came out of the *banya* and made her way through the garden, glowing from the heat, her hair hanging damp and loose almost to her waist.

'*S lyogkim parom*,' I called. I looked forward to easing my own aches and pains of the day.

When we emerged from the *banya* we were called to the kitchen in the family house. Matryona Alekseyevna had lit the family's old samovar in honour of my last night at the village, and was placing more charcoal in the internal cylinder as we entered the kitchen. She had been making *pirozhki* while Aleksey and I had been steaming ourselves, and the last ones were sizzling in the fat. When served straight from the frying pan they are one of Russia's culinary delights – light and full of flavour.

Returning to the cabin that night, my fur slippers crunching dry snow, I could feel the cumulative effect of *banya, pirozhki, vodka*. Stretched on my bed, I listened to the wind blowing from the forest, the bark of a dog, and passing neighbours' conversations muffled by the snow. This was my last night at Kanevka village, the last for a long time, possibly the last ever. I switched on Volodya's TV. Tarantino's *Pulp Fiction* was a cruel intrusion and I gazed vacantly at the screen. At eleven o'clock the village generator, out of earshot in the forest, shut down. The room went dark, the TV crackled. My thoughts drifted from the visceral turmoil of Los Angeles to reindeer, their stubby white scuts up in the air as they dug through the snow for lichen, the sound of ptarmigan complaining loudly as they escaped our oncoming sledges to fly away through the trees, or the sight of the white hare that had run through the snow with such rhythmic fluency that I hadn't the heart to alert my companion who was standing nearby with his old .545 but looking the other way.

4

WARM FRONTS

The Fish Place

The *Pram* sounded her whistle, and we dropped anchor in the
stream of the Tuloma, abreast of the town. It was a rare circum-
stance, and we could see the inhabitants by the score crowding
to the point. The people of Kola had heard of disputes between
their Government and ours; and their fears suggested, we learned
afterwards, that the *Pram* was another British gunboat. If we had
chanced to fire a gun, they would have taken to the woods.

Edward Rae, *The White Sea Peninsula*,
London: John Murray, 1879

EDWARD RAE OF BIRKENHEAD, a Fellow of the Royal Geographical
Society with some experience of the Russian Arctic, sailed from
the River Tyne on the steamer *Aurora* for Norway and the North
Cape on the last day of May 1879. He and Henry Pilkington
Brandreth, a medical doctor, had planned an expedition to the
'White Sea Peninsula' for the summer months. Taking a small steam
yacht on from Vardø, they arrived a few days later in the Kola Gulf
with the intention of setting off for the interior.

Steaming up the Gulf flying British colours might have been
thought provocative. The *ostrog* – fortified settlement – of Kola had
been visited twice within living memory by British warships, once
in 1809 when Russia was conducting a blockade against Britain,
and again during the Crimean War. When the British frigate
Miranda shelled Kola in 1854, so many of its wooden buildings and
fortifications were destroyed by fire, including the fine sixteenth-
century church, that the trading settlement, which before the
Crimean confrontation was already losing out to competing
anchorages nearer the open sea and along the north coast, never

fully recovered. When Rae and Brandreth saw it in 1879 it was in a poor state.

Today's Kola, still situated at the confluence of the Kola and the Tuloma rivers, is almost contiguous with Murmansk and only a twenty-minute drive south. In Rae's day Murmansk did not exist. Travelling to Kola by taxi with my Murmansk friend Olga and her husband Yan, we took the high ridge road and enjoyed a panoramic view across the Gulf to the low hills of the open tundra in the west. As we returned towards sea level and clattered over the old steel bridge, crossing the rapids emptying into the Gulf and driving on towards the town's agglomeration of smokestacks, railway mar-shalling-yards and standard five- or nine-storey buildings, Kola appeared at first glance no more or less unattractive than Murmansk. Not yet accustomed to the look of dereliction that pervades most Russian towns today, I had actually been expecting to find the place in much the same condition as when visited by Rae and Brandreth over a hundred years earlier.

'Believe it or not,' said Yan, 'this dump-of-a-town used to be eastern Lapland's key commercial centre. In midwinter the Gulf Stream kept the Barents and these waters more or less free of ice. That made it possible to sail right up to this point all year round. The Kola and the Tuloma rivers provided an easy route for the Saami to come from the south and west to trade valuable pelts with seaborne merchants. And when you look back to that large hill – the Solovaraky – behind the town, with the River Kola rapids passing round it,' Yan turned me on the spot by the shoulders as if I were a compass, 'you're looking at the last few hundred metres of the great Kola Trakt, the historic waterway that connected this Gulf and the open sea with places over a thousand kilometres to the south.'

The Trakt route, which came to play an important role in the lives of many different people, was developed by the Pomors, the families that settled around the White Sea from the twelfth century. It evolved out of the old trade route that for centuries had linked the merchants of Novgorod and other southern trading centres with the Lapps. Once the Pomors had settled Karelia and the White Sea in numbers, they extended the old route to take them even further north, on through Lappish lands to the open sea where, throughout the warm months, they worked the fish-rich waters of eastern Lapland's Arctic coast. This northward extension crossed Lapland by a series of lakes and rivers between Kandalaksha on the White Sea and the Kola Gulf in the north. Winter travellers crossed the snow on sledges and skis, using the ice of the rivers and lakes, and in the summer and autumn they went by boat – an easy route requiring only one short portage at the half-way watershed.

In the middle of the sixteenth century, on the sands below Solovaraky Hill, Kola settlement – or *Guolle Dak*, Fish Place, as the Lapps called it – still consisted of only a few log cabins owned by Pomors and Russians. By the 1600s, however, when the Muscovy Trading Company, established in 1555, was generating a wealth of traffic between Archangel and Western Europe, seaborne trade around the North Cape was growing beyond recognition. And as European sea captains discovered the advantages of Lapland's ice-free coast, with its natural harbours and safe anchorages, the Kola Gulf became a much-favoured water for barter and ship repair. The Gulf was also a place where onbound goods could be offloaded from Western ships on to those sailing further east to the White Sea, and vice versa. Kola settlement flourished. By the 1600s it had trebled its population and could boast a fine large wooden church in the Karelian style. Both Ivan the Terrible and Peter the Great fortified Kola. In the eighteenth and early nineteenth centuries, when the fishing, whaling and sealing industries were reaching their peak, Pomor fishermen and boatmen in their thousands travelled the Trakt route to Kola on their way to the established fish stations along eastern Lapland's Arctic coast.

The British shelling of Kola heralded an ignominious coda to the Fish Place's prominent role in east-west trade. By 1854 ships were already becoming larger and deeper-keeled so that, on account of the lack of navigable water in the upper Gulf, seaborne trade was shifting to the natural deep-water harbour of Yekaterina near the mouth of the Gulf and the open sea.

In spite of the demise of Kola settlement itself, however, the increasing economic importance of the sea-based industries through-out this corner of the Empire began to require a more prominent government presence. By the late nineteenth century the Trakt, now also known as the Postal Trakt, was wired for telephone, controlled by a handful of Russian officials, and serviced by the Saami who were paid a small retainer by the government and remunerated by independent travellers for providing boats, guides and porters as well as food and shelter in waterside cabins. The more fortunate travellers, if spotted in advance, might even arrive at one of these huts to find tea and food ready waiting for them.

If the Trakt brought a good income for the Saami, it gave many foreigners and Russians their only contact with the indigenous people. Edward Rae, who sailed the entire coast of the Kola Peninsula but hardly ventured into the interior, travelled from Kandalaksha to Kola on his home leg. Journeying the Trakt for several days, he had his first opportunity to talk with Saami at length and visit families in their *vezhi*, turf houses.

'If you're entertaining any romantic notions of travelling the Trakt today,' Yan remarked, reading my mind with uncanny accuracy, 'I should forget it. You'll find no Lapps and not a few obstacles, like the nuclear power station at Polyarny Zory. And there are no reindeer sledges in winter around here now.'

(In spite of these discouraging remarks, I did fulfil a small ambition to travel at least the northern half of the Trakt. In February 1999 a Russian friend Ivan Vdovin and I had purchased a portable, two-metre rubber dinghy for expedition purposes, and in early June we decided to test the boat's behaviour on the nearby waters of the Kola Trakt. We had several days of wet pleasure but the dinghy, which was found to be too small for two men, rucksacks and food, was almost uncontrollable in fast water and we met near-disaster at the first rapids. In time we found the only reliable technique for running white water with this particular dinghy was for one person to perch up on the stern, read the water ahead, and communicate with the oarsman by pointing and by eye contact. Since this necessarily involved the rower travelling backwards, and because the Russian was disinclined to trust an English navigator, I ended up as oarsman not only on the Trakt route, but also for our next expedition on the River Iokanga, a 250-kilometre course from its tributary river Rova to the Barents estuary.)

'If we're going to call on Olga Vasilyevna we have to take her something,' Yan reminded me. Engrossed in our historical excursion, we had almost forgotten that we were paying a visit to the *provodnitsa* whose acquaintance I had made on my first train journey north from St Petersburg.

We traced the house address with difficulty and located her apartment after climbing three different sets of staircases. Her door was padded and studded with leather, the smartest of four on the shared top-floor landing of the 1950s block. 'She works on the railways,' said a half-dressed neighbour from within the safe distance of his own corridor, breathing alcohol fumes at us and scratching himself under his vest. 'You never know when she's going to be at home.' We left a note in the small metal post-box which had her hand-painted number and shared a wall on the second floor with nineteen identical boxes, some of them broken open with the doors swinging loose.

Our written greetings were answered as we walked back across the main square: Olga Vasilyevna had just arrived from Murmansk and had spotted me before I had even noticed her bus. She seemed pleased that she had recognized me instantly and we greeted each other as if we were old friends. She walked all three of us around the town, adroitly piloting us along the few tree-lined boulevards and encouraging us to concentrate on the vistas to the heights on the other side of the Gulf rather than on the less inspiring features of the town. She had been brought up in Kola and was proud of her historic town, now developed in the ponderous Soviet style.

We returned to Olga Vasilyevna's home. It was a typical, two-room apartment of one bedroom and one sitting room, with few items of any age or beauty but with a warm, welcoming atmosphere. After an improvised but ample meal, served on her best porcelain from the glass-fronted cabinet, our hostess produced her photograph albums. Yan and Olga were more interested in an authors' conference on the TV but to me the old albums were compelling.

Her grandfather, Vladimir Aleksandrovich Obnorsky, had been a priest. In 1934, when Stalin was closing churches and suppressing the priesthood, he was arrested in his parish in Vologda for 'anti-Soviet and counter-revolutionary agitation' and sent for five years to a labour camp in the Amur region of the far east. He returned in 1938, sick and feeble, and barely alive. Olga showed me a picture of a skeletal man with his head shaven, taken shortly after his return.

But he recovered his health. After the Great Patriotic War he moved to Murmansk, still in ruins, where he administered to

German prisoners-of-war while the family lived in a *zemlyanka*, a dug-out. In 1950 he was offered the parish at Kola, where the church still enjoyed an active congregation in spite of being continually harassed and periodically shut down from the early 1930s. Olga Vasilyevna showed me a photograph of a tiny log cabin in the grounds of the church, where the family lived and she was born. Vladimir Aleksandrovich had eleven children, of whom two survived. A large group picture of the priest's extended family taken in 1953 showed Olga as a pretty, self-assured, bonneted girl aged three, and the men's long beards blowing in the wind at an angle of 45 degrees.

This was a difficult time for priests and their families, and particularly for Olga's father who was a Party official. Vladimir Aleksandrovich nevertheless augmented his resilient congregation and never allowed the Party to subsume his role in the community. He died in 1958, much respected by many, even outside the church.

'The funeral was a major event. I remember it well,' Olga Vasilyevna remarked quietly. 'There were many more people than ever attended a Party rally.'

Olga described the relentless persecution by the KGB of active Christians in Kola – including her mother – after her grandfather's death. The church was finally closed in 1960 and converted into a school workshop, with the toilets intentionally sited where the altar had been. On our way to the bus station, Olga Vasilyevna pointed out fifteen tall poplars, planted by her grandfather in the grounds of the recently reconsecrated church almost forty years earlier.

Back in Murmansk I looked at my map of north-west Russia and found the series of waterways that formed the trade route from Novgorod to the White Sea, and the connecting Trakt route north from Kandalaksha. I now understood why eastern Lapland was sometimes known in the Middle Ages as 'Tersky Navolok' – translated broadly as 'the Ter land-astride-the-waters', *volok* meaning portage; it was probably the renowned Trakt waters that had generated this sobriquet.

The name 'Russian Lapland' was common currency internationally from the sixteenth century but, as a result of the Soviets' policy towards the indigenous people, it became embarrassingly oxymoronic and disappeared from general use. The name 'Kola Peninsula', which is widely but inaccurately used today to mean all of Murmansk Oblast, is relatively modern.

I was pleased to have learned something about the scruffy, second-division town of Kola. Its name had been adopted for some seventy years to describe a little-known colony closed to the outside world and even to the rest of the Soviet Union, but in the summer of the year 2000 its name sounded from millions of television sets around the globe and set hearts thumping as the Northern Fleet's nuclear-powered submarine *Kursk* with its entire crew lay crippled on the bed of the Barents Sea.

Merchants and adventurers

'A VETERAN OF Afghanistan,' shouted the co-pilot over the noise of the engine, noticing my expression as he ran me over to where the helicopter was standing with its rotor blades already spinning and the pilot looking impatiently from the cockpit. All the helicopters I had seen operating out of Murmansk were old; this Mi-8, its battered dark green fuselage painted in camouflage waves and blackened from fuel exhaust, must have seen active war service. Or perhaps the co-pilot was referring to his colleague.

The helicopter pulled away from Murmansk in a north-easterly direction towards the coast. The sparkling early autumn day gave me clear views all round. Within an hour we had left the last of the thin forest behind us and the bare tundra of the Murman coast came into view.

The Murman coast was so called after the Norsemen, or Nurmen, who regularly navigated it. Othere, a chieftain and merchant trader from Halgoland, spoke of it when relating his marine adventures in the Arctic Ocean and White Sea – the Ice Ocean and Bjarmeland, as he referred to them – to King Alfred of Wessex in AD 880. Some three thousand years before Othere, Stone Age settlers had learned how to work a living on the coast in a climate which could be as cruel in summer as in winter. For two thousand years thereafter, Lapp people had also lived there in summer on the estuaries and rivers.

During the fourth century AD the Ice Ocean began to attract the curiosity of adventurers from more remote shores. In 325 the navigator Pytheas of Marseilles, six days beyond England, reported rumours of vast northern seas yet to be charted. By the twelfth century a small number of the more adventurous Pomors from Karelia and the Novgorod regions had also sailed into the waters of the Ice Ocean, exploring possibilities for fishing, hunting or settling, and compiling detailed logs of how they sailed and what they encountered.

Of the first printed maps of Scandinavia and north-west Russia, that drawn by the Swedish Archbishop Olaus Magnus (Olaus Pedersson) and published in 1539 to accompany his widely distributed *Historia de gentibus septentrionalibus* brought this part of the northern world vividly to the attention of the West. The large and lavishly illustrated sheet shows the Oceanus Scithicus – later known as the Barents Sea – as a busy shipping lane, and the White Sea as a landlocked Lacus Albus. Bishop Olaus's Biarmia – Russian Lapland as it soon became known – is alive with animal and human activity: falcons are stooping at hares, reindeer are running the tundra, and archers are hunting stoats and foxes. We see Saami netting salmon in the estuaries and living in conical transportable *kuvaksy*, exactly as in modern times. The Pomors, distinguishable by their dress, travel *na volok* – by portage – dragging boats across the watershed from one river to another. Engravings of the time show fishing traffic at Rybachy (Fisherman) Peninsula near Norway, or trade between Saami and sea merchants at Kildin, the safe island anchorage to the east of the Kola Gulf. Cod are being dried or salted to be barrelled and shipped east or west. In the two hundred years leading up to the Russian Revolution the Murman coast was one of the world's most productive fishing grounds. With good reason the Pomors called it *nasha niva* – our furrow.

Bringing his head back in through the open window, pointing down at the rough sea and granite cliffs below us, Vasily the co-pilot shouted, 'Difficult waters. Storms go on for days. In summer too.' I reminded myself how lucky I was to be travelling in a helicopter. Having been repeatedly warned against trying to walk the north-east coast, I was fortunate to have been introduced to a Swede who was involved in purchasing fishing rights on the northern rivers. He had agreed to my travelling in his helicopter going north-east but had added: 'It's all right with me, but you'll have to check with Yury.'

I finally cornered Yury in Murmansk airport. Aged about thirty-five but trying to look older, he was dark-haired and sallow-skinned, of medium height but large and broad-shouldered. He was in conversation with three taller men, all wearing near-identical heavy black leather jackets and sunglasses. He heard out my reasons for wanting to walk the north-east coast but finally shook his head. 'I'm sorry. The regulations make it impossible for us to take you to the coast. It's a closed zone and you need special permission.' At this point a helpful friend on the airport staff argued a fluent case on my behalf.

'Very good,' said my patron gruffly with a magnanimous flourish, 'you may go. Have a good time. But don't go upsetting the military.'

I learned later that Yury had worked loyally for several years during the 1980s for a senior Party member who was now known to be involved in what was economically described as 'illegal trading'. The two men had formed a close working relationship and after the fall of Communism had continued as business colleagues. The older man was said to have been responsible for the disappearance of large sums of Party funds during the early days of perestroika. True or not, it sounded familiar.

'That's Rynda,' shouted Vasily. 'Only one family lives there now but a few more people are hoping to return and build homes at the estuary where the old fishing village used to be.'

Edward Rae sailed past Rynda in 1879 and saw its large church. There was no church now; just one or two log cabins.

'There are border guards at most of the places where the major settlements used to be, like the River Kharlovka estuary,' Vasily said, 'but you're unlikely to meet anybody if you keep inland. And you won't get lost unless there's a blizzard. Just follow the electric cable pylons. They go all the way to Gremikha.'

After another 30 kilometres the pilot took us down. Vasily threw my rucksack out of the door and I jumped the few feet after it, landing on soft ground. The helicopter lifted off noisily, banked to the west and receded to a faint clatter in the distance. In the ensuing silence I looked around me and filled my lungs with the bracing air coming from the Barents Sea. I was alone for the first time on the Arctic tundra Murman coast of the Kola Peninsula.

The pilot had put me down five kilometres west of the Kharlovka, one of the principal rivers that flow into the Barents from the Peninsula's interior. I had been told that there was an isolated radar station at the estuary so, because of the faint possibility of being sighted, I aimed to cross the river well upstream. The high ground was firm and the lichen and mosses covering the granite made the going easy but the route was mostly indirect and required me to skirt rocky outcrops or traverse steep slopes to avoid the small lakes and bogs on the lower ground. My rucksack seemed heavier than ever, and as usual I cursed myself for bringing too much. As I walked I encountered reindeer paths that were enticingly convenient but also misleading, for they often ended on the wrong side of a knoll. It was raining, my old oiljacket was no longer waterproof, and I tried not to worry about the steady drop in temperature as the wind increased to near gale force. September in the north can be notoriously uncomfortable.

At the brow of a hill I found myself looking down into the Kharlovka valley. A kilometre to the south a large waterfall emptied into a long deep pool with high rocky banks. Here the river was quite impassable but downstream it widened and looked sufficiently shallow to wade. Above the waterfall there was a lake with picturesque grass slopes and sheltered stands of birch, and there I chose my first campsite. By nine o'clock in the evening the gale had blown over and the sun was out, giving me the opportunity for a trout supper. I was not disappointed; after missing several lightning rises, I quickened my responses and returned to the tent with two small fish.

The next day I explored the river above the lake. There were birch trees and sheltered grassy dells similar to my campsite and, along the faster runs of the river, erosion had exposed the varied textures and colours of the granite, from pink through dark red to black. In the near distance a herd of reindeer was foraging on the move, following its slow seasonal route southward. I startled a small detached group in the undergrowth. As they scattered in all directions a small calf passed me almost within touching distance. The larger 'family' watched from the higher ground, the elders sporting large antlers, the few white deer conspicuous in the autumn landscape.

Climbing into the hills I could just make out the sea to the north. To the south of me the tundra ran on well out of sight – for some 70 kilometres according to my map – to Lake Lyavozero, the Kharlovka's source.

After the months of arduous and erratic excursions since my first arrival at Murmansk I was at last beginning to understand the apparently isolated and discrete wilderness of the Peninsula. I was learning how to read the landscape in terms of a time-honoured network of seasonally migrating animals and people. Somewhere near where I was standing was one of the former favoured summer camps of the Semiostrov (Seven Island) Saami. The herd near me now would shortly be travelling inland and south to spend the winter in the forests near the village of Krasnoshchelye where the Semiostrov Saami had their winter *seit*. Since the last phase of Cold War clearances in the 1960s and 1970s the Saami no longer enjoyed the privilege of migration; the reindeer, however, represented an enduring link to the past, to a lifestyle that had been ideologically condemned and eradicated but which in recent years had been showing signs of re-emergence.

The following afternoon the weather deteriorated dramatically into persistent rain squalls which regularly caught me away from shelter. Temperatures of four above felt like four below. For much of the next five days and nights, as the cold weather continued, it became impossible to catch fish and I was marooned by equinoctial gales, lying in my tent in wet socks, hungrily nibbling hard cheese and dried reindeer meat but disinclined to get up and cook. When the weather finally cleared I struck camp and headed north-east, reaching the coast opposite the easternmost of the Sem Ostrov, the string of Seven Islands that ran along the coast a short way offshore. Not a ship was in sight, nor a single log cabin, not a soul. It was all in stark contrast to the busy seaside community encountered at the coastal fishing stations by Edward Rae in the summer of 1879.

I wanted to continue along the coast to the estuary of the Eastern Litsa, the next large river to run into the Barents Sea, but the border post there was said to be efficiently manned by several guards and an officer, so I gave it a miss, fording the water well upstream. The terrain became progressively more arduous, requiring me to chart my way around the waterways and in and out of small valleys. After four days my first major goal came into sight: China Island, Nokuyev Bay.

In the early 1500s there was increasing speculation among sea traders of a navigable north-eastern sea route beyond the North Cape of Norway and on through the Arctic Oceanus Scithicus to Cathay (China). English merchant adventurers had long been interested in discovering a north-east route ever since the Southern Seas had become dominated by hostile Portuguese and Spanish shipping, but it was not until 1553 that the army commander Sir Hugh Willoughby and the navigator Richard Chancellor finally embarked from England to search for what became known as the North-East Passage. Three ships sailed from the Thames in May: the *Bona Confidentia*, the *Bona Esperanza*, and the *Edward Bonaventura*, all between 100 and 160 tons, carrying a total crew between them of 110 men, their keels reinforced against ice and their holds laden with cloth and other Western offerings.

The voyage that was to end in triumph for Chancellor, the pilot-general, was a disaster for Willoughby, its captain-general. After passing the North Cape his two ships were separated from Chancellor's *Edward Bonaventura* and swept north-east to Novaya Zemlya before working their way back south. Running along the Murman coast, they put into a sheltered deep-water bay near Nokuyev, a coastal island about 250 kilometres east of the Kola Gulf inlet, 250 kilometres west of the Gorlo channel to the White Sea, and anchored off a small island later commemoratively named China Island. Knowing the coast to be 'inhabited by Lappish people', Willoughby sent reconnaissance parties inland but found 'no people or similitude of inhabitants'. Had they landed one month earlier they would have found Lapps at the estuaries of most of the major rivers of the eastern Murman coast from Rynda to Iokanga. But by mid-September the migrant families, like the reindeer, had left the coast to make their way inland towards their winter homes in the taiga forest. Having lost the best of the weather, and probably apprehensive of returning to Vardø on the Norwegian North Cape where his tired crew might jump ship, Willoughby decided to lay up for the winter on the deserted Lapland coast and to recuperate before attempting to venture further east.

Richard Chancellor was also driven off course by relentless northerly gales, but by chance found himself swept into the White Sea well before the ice. Arriving at the small harbour of St Nicholas, west of the estuary of the River Dvina – near today's Archangel – he changed his plans and proceeded overland in winter to Moscow. There he secured an audience with Tsar Ivan and founded the famed trading alliance, the Muscovy Company, which brought more than ample compensation for the aborted north-eastern mission. For the Tsar, who had failed to build a Baltic alliance, the Muscovy Company established safe passage round the North Cape and stimulated Russia's first extensive contacts with Western Europe. Trade concessions granted to the English, including virtually exclusive rights at the Dvina Estuary, brought Queen Elizabeth enormous financial rewards and initiated an influential Russian partnership with the English, and later with the Scots, that flourished through generations of merchant families until the Bolshevik Army stormed into Archangel in 1920.

I arrived at Nokuyev Bay in September, at the same time of year as Willoughby, and, cold, wet and exhausted myself, looked down from the granite cliffs to the bay where the Englishman had anchored his two ships almost four and a half centuries earlier.

Sir Hugh Willoughby's last log entry in January 1554 had recorded that 'most of the companie' were alive, and news of Willoughby's survival had also reached the Dvina via Pomor fishermen, yet when English crews located the *Bona Esperanza* and the *Bona Confidentia* – even after two winters the ships were high at anchor and in good condition – they were taken aback by what they found. Boarding one of the vessels and going below, they found all the ships' officers in the mess, dead at table, with no trace of the 64 crew that had been recruited on the Thames in 1553.

Willoughby himself may have died well before his officers and men, but it remains a mystery why anybody should have perished at all, and why the officers were found in such unusual circumstances. Willoughby's log entries made no mention of illness or starvation; there would anyway have been fish and seal to eat and preserve, berries and mushrooms to conserve against scurvy, and seal oil to burn. The most compelling explanation is that of mutiny and desertion. After having nearly foundered in Arctic gales, and convinced that they were highly likely to perish when they continued on their way into the icy unknown, the crew of both ships may have been tempted to row for the port of Vardø and for freedom.

Reflecting on this enigmatic page in the history of England's marine exploration, I set about finding a spot for my tent where I would be suitably sheltered from the relentless north-east wind and the icy squalls that were drenching me. Conscious that I was ill prepared for this extreme of cold and wet, wondering how I was going to return home, and scolding myself for not having waited in the first place until I could persuade a more experienced traveller to come with me, I crawled into my sleeping bag, once again without trying to light a fire, drank some vodka, and scribbled a few lines in my own log. If men of the calibre of Willoughby's crews, who had survived three months of severe storms at sea, had abandoned the mission, I thought that I would be unlikely to last more than a month in this place.

A result of the new Muscovy Company trade was that the Kola Gulf steadily gained in significance. A large proportion of goods purchased by the English in Russia was brought from the Dvina to the Gulf – or to the anchorages at Kildin Island, Rybachy and Pechenga – to be sold on to other Western European seaborne merchants. Some of the more enterprising Russian traders even found it profitable to bring goods to the Gulf overland in winter or summer all the way from Karelia and other distant southern regions.

One of the natural harbours of the Murman coast entered by the ships searching for Willoughby was at the estuary of the River Iokanga, about 90 kilometres further east from China Island and Nokuyev Bay. Known to Russians as Svyatoy Nos (Holy Cape), this large deepwater bay became a favoured anchorage for ships sailing between the Kola Gulf and the White Sea. Holy Cape and the Iokanga's estuary were to be my own next destination.

Before leaving Murmansk, I had looked at my maps and thought that the coastal tundra walk would be easily managed; I would not have to navigate my way round large bogs, the tundra would be firm going throughout, and I could always just keep to the coast. All these things were indeed relevant but, as I now looked at the next leg of my walk that was to take me to the Iokanga estuary, I was amazed at my naïveté. This was not a place to travel alone, even if the terrain or route were familiar. The chief difference between the tundra here and the taiga that I had become accustomed to was the lack of shelter. Whereas in the south I might have taken cover from a rainstorm in the forest, where I could suspend a tarpaulin roof between trees and sit in front of a large fire, this was seldom possible in the open treeless littoral. Away from the valleys of larger rivers there was little fire-wood, and whatever was to be found was often wet; only the branches and roots of dead dwarf juniper would guarantee a fire . . . if I could find shelter to get it started.

Bilberries and crowberries gave me the vitamins I needed. I sometimes became so voracious for their sugar that I found myself abandoning the stoop-and-pick movement of humans in favour of the crawl-and-graze of herbivores, my eyes looking ahead to select a productive route, my fingers and mouth stained deep purple. There were prolific *boletus* mushrooms among the berries but in mid-September many were wet or past their time, and my capacity for them was anyway limited.

The going to Iokanga and Holy Cape was good but it took me five days walking against strong, wet easterlies to cover the distance. The day I finally reached my destination was calm and warm and, as I basked shirtless in the sunshine on sheltered high ground, I enjoyed a magnificent panoramic view of the sea and the bay. Granite cliffs and an archipelago of small islands contained a ten-kilometre stretch of blue water that formed a deep natural anchorage, and in the distance the long narrow promontory of the Cape stretched far out to sea, sheltering the nearby coast from north-easterly gales.

In 1557, when the English explorer Anthony Jenkinson dropped anchor in this bay, he immediately encountered native people. The ship was boarded excitedly by a group of Lapp men and women, some dressed in reindeer skin or sealskin boots, others in embroidered summer woollen smocks and caps. Going ashore, the Englishmen found a community of around one hundred, living in turf-covered huts and large reindeer-hide tents. The Lapps were working the inshore waters for cod, taking large salmon in the estuary of the Iokanga, watching their reindeer on the nearby tundra, and looking to barter fish and furs with passing ships.

Since the 1960s, however, as home to some of the Russian Northern Fleet's most advanced nuclear-powered submarines, the bay had enjoyed a different reputation. It had also had various names. Some people still knew it simply as Iokanga, but the military, who first named it Murmansk-140 and later designated it a 'closed territorial-administrative unit' – ZATO for short – now referred to it as Gremikha. My own map named it Ostrovnoy.

By the time I approached the bay I was sufficiently accustomed to the landscape to believe that I had a good chance of moving without being spotted by patrols or border guards, and that I would be able to look briefly at the base before walking further to make a reconnaissance of some of the former Saami summer places near the Iokanga's estuary.

Moving down the hill and closer to the naval base, I stopped to look through my binoculars. I was overwhelmed by what I saw. I had already studied coarse-grained black-and-white photographs of the bunkers, yards, docking bays, jetties and gantries, but on a fine summer day, seen through good lenses from the vantage-point of my high rock haven, and surrounded by wild tundra and circling sea birds, the true nature of the crude reinforced concrete architecture, the near-dereliction of many of the buildings, and the detritus of four decades of Soviet military occupation appeared even at a distance like a monstrous extrusion, a massive fault in an otherwise pristine corner of the earth's surface.

Offshore in the middle of the bay were tankers and tender vessels looking much like ships at anchor in any port of the world but, alongside the quays and repair yards, several nuclear-powered Victor-class submarines wallowed conspicuously like fat black seals. These were armed and in active service but there were also twenty others now laid up for decommissioning, rotting in special channels carved into the rock cliff, awaiting funds and technical resources unlikely to be available for decades. In the rock below me there were forty decaying nuclear reactors and about 900 uranium fuel assemblies in ageing canisters awaiting removal.

To the east, beyond the shipyards, on high sloping ground over-looking the bay, lay Ostrovnoy, with its apartment buildings for military and civilian personnel. In the 1980s its population had reached 35,000, but since 1991 it had fallen to 10,000, with service families taking every opportunity to leave.

I climbed back up the slope and on to the plateau. From here I intended to work my way a short distance inland in order to move on past the base to the banks of the Iokanga where the Saami at one time had lived in summer. This was not as easy as I had envisaged, and the paranoia which I had last experienced at the River Titovka's estuary two years earlier began to surface. Not only was it impossible to avoid high ground and exposing myself to view against the horizon from the town below, but another problem emerged in the shape of a large radar station sited on high ground to the south-east of me. Identifiable by its characteristically prominent, large white sphere, the station looked down on to part of the terrain that I wished to explore, and through my binoculars I could see people moving about. Although I was convinced that no guards, patrols or civilians would be in the least interested in my presence as long as I kept well away from the base, I failed to summon sufficient courage or nonchalance to stroll along in a straight line across open ground in the preferred direction. I also had to stop myself imagining that I would encounter a patrol of OMON personnel. These special-force soldiers, who had a reputation for brutality, were now sent throughout Russia to assist ordinary soldiers in border and sentry duties, and to accompany inspectors and rangers patrolling national parks or the major spawning grounds of sturgeon and salmon.

Once I had stealthily worked my way well inland and crossed three small valleys I relaxed a little, strolled the final kilometre in good cover, and arrived at the river where I pitched my tent in amongst trees near the left bank.

I rose early the next morning, filled the saucepan at the river for coffee and decided to treat myself to the last of my cherished smoked bacon. Russian *bekon* is no more than a distant relative of the cured English rasher, and even the best Colombian Medellin after a week or two in a rucksack can taste uncannily similar to Nescafé, but the tang of fried pork fat and the coffee aroma floating amongst the birch trees on that warm September morning were sufficient to make me feel irrationally optimistic about getting back safely. I had been so eager to get to the north-east coast that the return journey was a problem I had hitherto ignored.

My optimism that morning was further enhanced by the sight of the river itself. The Iokanga has a historic reputation for salmon and I decided to try my hand with rod and fly for an hour or two before proceeding downstream. Ideally I would catch a small fish, cook some of it for the first day and then salt it.

Two hours later I was still casting without success. I had just waded in deep towards the middle of a broad stretch of the river and was standing rolling a cigarette, contemplating the relationship between possible lies and the direction of the sun, when a helicopter suddenly swooped low overhead, followed the course of the river downstream, and disappeared. There was no question of my taking cover even if I had heard its approach above the roar of the water. And anyway, I was determined to enjoy the fishing.

Several hours later, as I sat brewing a cup of tea, I caught sight of two men in the distance, working their way up the river bank and traversing the steep rock overlooking the rapids. I could see through my binoculars that they were wearing camouflage fatigues. By the time they arrived I had identified them as border guards.

They introduced themselves formally and made some sort of preliminary charge using procedural vocabulary I barely understood. I had been spotted from the helicopter, they said, and they had been ordered by radio to find me. The more we spoke, the more my two visitors warmed to their task but, despite my apprehensions of the last two days, they seemed curiously unhostile, and even became embarrassed and worried once they realized I was a foreigner. Rather than seeing me as a security threat, they were concerned about my wellbeing. Was I lost, where was I staying, and – a hilarious question coming from two skin-and-bone lads – had I got enough food? Learning that I was from England, one of them ventured a few elementary sentences in English, and that broke the ice.

Then came the ubiquitous question 'How did you know about this place [Murmansk Region]?' I opted for a Russian-style response and shrugged my shoulders. The boys discussed me at length, examined my passport and visa, filled in a protocol sheet while I rolled them both a cigarette, handed me a copy of the charge, and made to leave.

'Walk to the base,' one of them said. 'If you leave within two hours you should easily arrive at the perimeter fence by 1500. A jeep and a small detail will be there to escort you. Just make sure you're there.' I said goodbye and watched them return down the river bank at a brisk pace and disappear around the rock face.

Determined to see more of the coast before handing myself over, I struck camp and climbed out of the valley on to the open tundra, moving north as quickly as I could go until I could see more of the inner bay near the estuary. This was the part of the bay where Anthony Jenkinson would have anchored, and where foreigners had long bartered metalware, tobacco and alcohol for furs, fish, oil and walrus tusks. Looking further west to where the base was today and seeing black smoke coming from the chimneys of Ostrovnoy's central-heating and hot-water plants, I was also reminded of the vast quantities of seal fat, whale blubber and cod liver that had been rendered and processed in this bay before the military had ousted the Iokanga people.

The Saami and Pomors had used and sold cod-liver oil for centuries. By the 1800s, the price that the refined oil was fetching from pharmacists in Russia and the West attracted outside capital, and the export of oil from the Murman coast became a substantial industry, enriching the major exporters and middlemen, and providing coastal people with a reliable cash income. Engravings and nineteenth-century photographs of the rendering houses on the Murman coast almost reek of putrescent flesh and boiling oil.

Seal oil, also known as trane or train oil, enjoyed an even wider sale. The fine liquid was used for oilcloth or for oiling wool; the bulk of the coarser residue was processed for soap and lamp oil. In Samuel Purchas's *Pilgrimes* (1625), Giles Fletcher describes 'wild Lapps' catching seals and making 'trane oyle, a very great and principal commoditie of Russia'. He recounts how the Lapps, at the onset of spring, drew their boats across the ice into the large bays and lived and hid in them. When a large haunt had gathered – ringed seals (*Phoca hispida*) were the preferred species – the Saami would club as many as 4,000–5,000 at a time. The seals were flensed and the flesh cut into lumps, most of which were then thrown into a pit and melted by hot rocks taken from a large fire. Trane oil continued to enjoy an international market until the wider switch to gas and mineral oil for lamps and the introduction of electric street lighting early in the twentieth century.

As well as killing seals, the Saami and their ancestors hunted beluga whales for at least 4,000 years. In modern times the waters around the Holy Cape, and the Motovsky Gulf to the west, were more likely to reveal a sleek, black-skinned, nuclear-powered submarine than a whale.

At two o'clock in the afternoon I left the estuary and hurried westwards. There was only one route towards Ostrovnoy and on my arrival I followed a footpath through the remnants of a wire perimeter fence and passed some large empty sheds. On the concrete road ahead of me was a parked military jeep facing in my direction. As I approached, an army officer stepped out, addressed me by name and ushered me through the passenger door and on to the back seat

1. Petroglyph at Lake Kanozero. One of many figurative and abstract images, some datable to 2,000 BC, discovered in 1997. The site adds significantly to the picture of migration and settlement in northern Europe, and relates iconographically to others in Karelia and at Alta, north Norway

2. A Lapp worshipping before a *seid*. Woodcut from Johann Scheffer's *Lapponia* (1673)

3. Medieval Slav Pomors travelling by portage from the Novgorod region to Lapland to barter for furs. Woodcut from Olaus Magnus's *Description of the Northern Peoples* (1555)

4. The anchorage of Kildin Island, east of the Kola Gulf. This engraving by Jan van Doetechum, included in Jan van Linschoten's *Voyagie ofte schip-vaert . . .* (1601), shows Saami bartering pelts. Also visible are Saami *vezhi* (turf houses), a reindeer-drawn boat-sledge and fish-drying racks

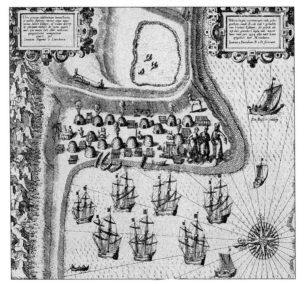

5. Saami at Rasnavolok, north-west Lake Imandra, 1903. As the word *volok* (portage) suggests, the place was a designated rest-station on the Kola Trakt route between Kandalaksha and Kola. Women and children, as well as the men, rowed travellers and provided food and shelter at waterside log-cabins the length of the 300-kilometre route

6. A highly productive fish-trap on the River Tuloma. The Notozersky Saami, who had rights to most of the river until collectivization in the 1930s, annually sold and bartered over 100 tonnes of salmon downstream at the port settlement of Kola

7. A *kuvaksa* or *chum*. A conical framework of birch poles may be encountered at convenient stopping places on lakes, rivers, tundra and taiga, over which the traveller can throw his own tarpaulins or skins. Departing campers traditionally leave logs and kindling for the next visitors

8. Aleksey Yakovlev, a Saami reindeer herder's son, watching the kettle boil. He is wearing a modern woollen cap and traditional deerskin thigh-boots

9. Two herders, Saami Yevdokin Kirillov and Nenets Nikolay Khatansey, with draught deer. Both men are wearing a traditional full-length deerskin *malitsa*

10. Vasily Nikolayevich Khatansey, Nenets herder, whose ancestors migrated with the Komi and their reindeer herds from Western Siberia to Russian Lapland in the 1890s; son of Nikolay Khatansey, shown above

11. Draught sledges in convoy

12. Corral

13. Teriberka, one of the busiest fishing villages of the Murman coast, around 1900

14. Pomor fishermen at Rynda on the Murman coast, around 1900

15. Murmansk, 1920: railway-wagon homes in the area of the port that came to be known as 'Shanghai'. By the time the line was nearing completion in 1916, the port had become a 'multicultural migration zone for the unruly and the discontented, the unemployed and the unemployable, a resting ground for the wounded, sick and dying'

16. Corpses of Bolsheviks on display towards the end of the Civil War in the north-west, January 1920. The photograph was subsequently widely circulated in Bolshevik propaganda

17. Murmansk during the winter of 1920–21

18. The cargo port at Murmansk, 1998

19. Khibinogorsk. Tents housing the first forced labourers in the Khibiny, about 1930

20. Aleksandr Yevgenevich Fersman (*centre*, *standing*), the talented and enterprising geochemist who pioneered the mineral exploitation of Russian Lapland, with colleagues in the field during the second petrological survey of the Khibiny, 1921. Women played a prominent role throughout the early years

21. Khibinogorsk. Strict regime labourers, many of them from the warm south, built the 20-kilometre branch railway to Fersman's mining town during the winter of 1931, working non-stop in shifts under intolerable conditions. A rare photograph (from Fersman's own albums) including two armed guards

22. Khibinogorsk. First apatite-ore chute, *c.* 1930. In time the vast deposits of the mineral apatite in the hills of Khibiny provided the Soviet Union with its entire requirement of phosphate fertilizer, even during Khrushchev's crazed agricultural policies of the 1950s and 1960s

23. Mortar crew, Litsa Front, winter 1942–43. Red Army soldiers showed remarkable adeptness in the use of mortars and small guns

24. The reindeer contribution to the war effort. Offloading bombs from a reindeer sledge on to a Russian Ilyushin

25. Murmansk after the bombing raid of June 1942. Murmanchaners claim that only Stalingrad endured more bombing; the town was almost completely destroyed, leaving most of the population living in dugouts and bomb shelters. Life of a kind endured, however, and fishing-fleet trawlers continued to put to sea, many of them crewed by women

26. Monument to the Great Patriotic War. The colossal concrete Red Army
infantryman, known affectionately to Murmanchaners as Alyosha, stands high above
Murmansk port, facing west across the Kola Gulf towards the River Litsa, where the
Soviets famously stopped the German invasion of June 1941. The Kandalaksha–Litsa
line held firm throughout the war, the only one to do so the entire length of the
Soviet front with Hitler from the Arctic Ocean to the Black Sea

27. The nickel smelter at Monchegorsk, Russian Lapland's first environmental black spot, built by and initially run on forced labour. Over a period of 60 years it has emitted into the atmosphere hundreds of thousands of tonnes of heavy metals and sulphur dioxide. Almost all plant life within a radius of some 20 kilometres has disappeared, and airborne particles have been carried on prevailing easterlies far into the neighbouring Scandinavian countries

28. Lovozero, 1999. Herders digging potatoes. Most Saami were forcibly relocated in substandard five- and nine-storey concrete apartment buildings in the 1960s–70s; a few still inhabit older wooden homes

29. Iokanga Bay, Holy Cape, Barents coast, summer 2000. Long occupied by Saami and Pomor fishermen during the summer months, and favoured as an anchorage by merchantmen plying between Western Europe and the Dvina Estuary, the bay was cleared by the military in the 1960s. Now known as Gremikha, Iokanga Bay houses some of the Northern Fleet's most advanced nuclear-powered strategic and attack submarines

30. The SSGN nuclear-powered attack submarine *Kursk* moored at its base shortly before meeting its tragic end in the Barents Sea during exercises in August 2000

31. River Ponoy, early morning. Petrol engines have shortened journey times, but animal skins still provide the best protection against the cold

where I squeezed myself between two young army conscripts. We drove in silence towards the centre of the town.

I tried not to show too keen an interest in my surroundings. Ostrovnoy was indeed in a state of serious neglect, its dreary aspect made more poignant by a statue of Lenin and two memorials to the naval dead of the Great Patriotic War. The cracked and pitted concrete road led us round and down the hill past civilian apartment buildings that had been abandoned, and the jeep pulled up in the enclosed yard of what appeared to be police headquarters.

The officer led me and my two escorts into the building, up a flight of stairs and along busy clean warm corridors to a small homely office containing a collection of pot plants, where I was left alone without explanation. After half an hour a woman of about thirty, wearing a neat grey suit, entered and addressed me in good English with a smile: 'I am English teacher. You will have difficulty understanding. I am your interpreter.'

I was then accompanied back to the jeep and driven through the town into open country and up the hill along a narrow road until we reached a plateau high above the bay where there was a large tarmac landing pad. At the far end of the tarmac sat the helicopter that had flown over me that same morning. Within a few minutes an open military truck holding a dozen armed soldiers also reached the top of the hill and parked nearby. This was followed by the arrival of a naval jeep, and I was invited to step out on to the tarmac. An officer in the smart dark blue uniform and white forage cap of Naval Intelligence, accompanied by a junior officer and a soldier, approached me briskly.

'I am Major Novikov. My identification.' He opened it close to my face. 'You have entered a restricted military zone. Please introduce yourself and explain the purpose of your arrival here.'

The other dramatis personae on the tarmac overlooking the wide sweep of the Barents Sea were briefly held in suspended animation: the armed soldiers who had jumped down from the truck were now loitering and smoking in the background; the helicopter pilot and his two crew stood near the cockpit, observing us blankly from below the drooping rotor blades; the two conscripts, hands in pockets, caps pushed to the back of their shaven heads, vacantly kicked the tyres of the jeep; only the clerical officer and the schoolteacher, standing upstage of Novikov and awaiting instructions, were directly engaged.

The warm air, carried across the tundra on a southerly breeze, smelt pure and sweet. As the cliffs and sea shimmered below me to my left, the late afternoon sun behind me was spasmodically reflected by the major's cap badge. A lark rose and fell high above us, addressing us with a ceaseless trill, as if to insist that nobody meant me harm or discourtesy.

Major Novikov was a spruce man in his thirties with jet-black hair and a thin-trimmed black moustache. He wore his pressed uniform with the flair and ease of a regular officer. His manner was calm, self-confident, impeccable, his speech fluent and elegant. He enjoyed a well-turned phrase, and the interrogation developed its own rhetoric. I explained that I was an Englishman on holiday. I was aware that I had entered a restricted zone but I had intended to walk back up the River Iokanga and move well away from the base. I wanted to walk and camp, live in the wild, and make notes on the flora and fauna. After a lengthy exchange, which was extended and elaborated by the interpretation and interjections of the schoolteacher, the questioning was concluded. The gist of Novikov's summary was that, while he understood my intentions and sympathized with my interests, he had no option other than to return me to Murmansk.

'Please step inside the jeep so that we can sit while our interview is written up and the protocols prepared for your signature.'

The clerical procedure occupied more than an hour. The junior officer recorded the discussion in detail, while the major was meticulous about nomenclature and phrasing, as if drafting a battlefield treaty for posterity and the scrutiny of historians.

As time went on our formal intercourse became interspersed with other topics. Novikov, who had opened my rod case while his clerk was scribbling, tenderly fingered the small trout rod.

'I have heard about flyfishing and I would like to learn. In Russia we have no imagination; all we know is how to throw crude metal lures at our beautiful fish, or catch them in nets. I would like to take you up the river to show you some ideal spots for salmon and some of the best places for campsites.' He talked at length about the tundra, the fish he had caught and the wildlife he had seen. He appeared to be familiar with a large part of the lower river. He would be my ideal companion.

The more Novikov talked about his days spent in the wild the more emotional he became. His eyes grew moist and he looked away. The teacher put her own case.

'I wish there were a way of allowing him to stay. Just think what pleasure it would give my children if he could attend some of our English classes. And he could talk to them about all the places around the world that he's seen. It would be a great inspiration to them. As for me,' she added softly, with gratitude bordering on affection, 'you're the first native English speaker I've met.'

Novikov turned back to us, sighed, and apologized at length about having to return me to Murmansk. He extended our conversation further but I was becoming irritated by the prevarication. I suggested that, unless I could be allowed to stay, we should complete the paperwork so that I could leave.

The transcript and protocol, written on coarse-grained, recycled paper, were read to me for approval and signature and I was handed a copy to retain.

The major saluted me smartly and we shook hands. The teacher was almost in tears. I looked into my own boots and turned away, overcome by the formal intimacy of our chance encounter. Seeing me pick up my rucksack and starting to walk towards the helicopter, the pilot climbed into the cockpit, fired the engine, and the rotor blades started to turn. As the helicopter lifted and took a westerly course into the setting sun, I said my goodbyes to the Murman coast and the Holy Cape – the historic haven of Norse traders, an anchorage for Western adventurers, the summer home of the Iokanga Saami, and now a rest-home for the beached whales of a naval fleet in decline.

Our bare furrow

AFTER MY EXPULSION from Gremikha I cursed the military for having closed the entire north coast to all indigenous and Russian people alike.

It was not always like this. There was a time when the Russian Government was anxious for people to settle there. When Russian cod was under threat in the 1860s, the Governor of Archangel Region wrote to Tsar Alexander II about the 'increasingly zealous incursions along our shores by Norwegian fishermen,' concluding: 'there is no order there ... one could maintain that the Murman coast belongs to no government.'

Realizing by the late 1860s that the threat was not only material – a cod war – but potentially also territorial, Alexander II initiated generous incentives to Russians and foreigners to settle this corner of the Empire. Settlers were offered a six-year exemption from taxes and other state obligations, and families received cash incentives. Pomor fishermen and seasonally hired workers, who normally returned south at the end of the fishing season in September to their family homes on the White Sea or in Karelia, were encouraged to build permanent homes and stay all year round. The Saami, present everywhere in small numbers, were urged to change their nomadic lifestyle and settle at the coast, living and working with Pomors and foreigners.

Within five years coastal settlements had sprung up to the west and east of the Kola Gulf. Law-abiding and industrious Norwegian and Finnish families adopted Russian nationality, Russian colonists brought skills and trading acumen, and Pomors began to stay put. Famine in the south and the 1861 emancipation of serfs also brought people north. There were disputes with the Saami over fishing and hunting rights, but by and large the new coastal communities and fish stations were deemed a success by most parties. Above all, the northern shores became demonstrably Russian.

Teriberka, the small settlement on the coast of the Barents Sea about 80 kilometres east of the Kola Gulf, epitomized the old pioneering spirit of the Murman coast. Thousands of Pomors from Karelia and the White Sea migrated there each spring to try their luck in the rich fishing grounds of the Arctic Ocean. The work was risky: many were drowned when fishing in big seas or were swept away on ice floes when hunting seal. It was also labour-intensive: many hands were needed to undertake the drying, salting and barrelling – mostly of cod and white halibut – and to load the trading ships going west to Europe or east into the White Sea to the insatiable Russian markets at the estuary of the Dvina. But there was ample opportunity for profit. When Edward Rae dropped anchor at the settlement in June 1879 there were already about 300 fishermen and 30 boats with a winter population of some 80 men and women.

*

'You can't just take a bus or car, Roger,' came the usual reply to my proposals to look at Teriberka for myself. 'The military stop vehicles and ask for documentation. Teriberka is in the closed coastal zone. Face up to it, you won't be going there.'

I made enquiries about checkpoints and found there were two likely places where a car would be stopped, and then left Murmansk with Slava, my car-owning friend, early one autumn morning. The road was initially tarmaced and fast but it soon turned rough. A few kilometres out of town we passed family groups walking to the woods to pick the last of the season's berries, and men with shotguns making their way to the lakes and ponds for duck and geese. Further on we came across the grimy barracks of the military airstrip Severomorsk III. Then, as we travelled further east, the tree-line fell away to the south to expose pristine open tundra, sprinkled here and there with early snow. I imagined the rolling carpet of rocks and lichen continuing uninterrupted for the next 500 kilometres all the way to the east coast where the Gorlo tides separated Russian Lapland from Cape Kanin, homeland of the Nenets.

The first barrier did not materialize but, as we passed through a series of narrow valleys running more or less north, with high granite cliffs on either side, and caught sight of the sea, we spotted the second. Slava pulled up and reversed the car into the undergrowth. The barrier was near the village and the bay; I could easily skirt the road by foot and make my own way to the coast. I set out, leaving Slava with instructions to make his own way home if I failed to return within the agreed period.

I was impatient to see the Barents again. I was going to have an easy climb out of the ravine, on to the high hills and across the tundra overlooking the sea, but I was anxious to avoid being spotted or giving cause for a search party; I knew that there would be border guards on patrol, equipped with radios. On the high ground, my first task was to skirt a tall radar tower, part of the security network that continued the length of the coast to the Norwegian border. There was a telephone cable running from it. Keeping to the dead ground, I stopped near the tower, crouching behind a rock, and then . . . stood up and burst into laughter. The glass had gone from the window and not all the cables were connected. I had been crawling past an abandoned building. With a sigh of relief I walked on. I could now make my way as I wished, remembering only to avoid throwing a profile on high ground.

My panoramic surroundings were beautiful. Variegated mosses and lichens covered every rock and boulder, the ground berries were prolific, and small pools in the bog gleamed darkly. The hill streams supported dwarf birch and small rowans, home to finch-like birds busy feeding before the onset of winter. I looked out to a single trawler moving across the calm sea, and then to the broad sweep of the Bay of Teriberka, a perfectly formed deep-water haven. As I walked across the high plateau above the river estuary, the village came into view below me, consisting of several dozen houses – some concrete, some old and wooden – and, beyond, a group of large military barracks that looked cold and neglected.

I descended into the village, uncertain as to whether or not the sight of someone approaching from the hills was commonplace. As I came into the outskirts I saw villagers, soldiers and one or two cars. I passed the central heating plant from where steam pipes, leaking copiously, snaked an apparently haphazard route towards the houses. Along the water's edge lay ramshackle sheds, workshops and garages where old cars were being maintained by their hopeful owners. Beyond these, among the dunes and the sedge grass, there were a few wooden boats and boathouses. The village seemed abandoned; during my travels on the Peninsula, I had never yet seen a place in such a state of decay. Before the Revolution Teriberka had been a substantial village with a church, a post office and a telegraph. It was particularly noted by the Russian hydrologist Knipovich, the leader of a long-term survey of the Barents at the turn of the century, as undergoing rapid development, even trading directly with companies in Hamburg, St Petersburg and Moscow. After the 1918–20 Civil War Teriberka was the first collective on the Murman, a model for the other fishing stations. Under the Soviets, it flourished and became a significant fishing base for Norwegian and Russian trawler fleets. The place I was now visiting had been abandoned by the regional authorities, deserted by the military, and left destitute, without even a fishing fleet.

Across the waste ground a man hurried towards me, stumbling through the dune grass, apparently the worse for drink. I sought refuge in the first of two shops housed inside large wooden buildings. There was a good stock of oranges, apples and bananas, frozen meat and the usual cans but, as is often the case in fishing villages, no fish.

'Where can I buy some fish?' I ventured. The shopkeeper shrugged her shoulders. The second shop, fifty yards further along the street, contained near-identical offerings and included fresh bread. 'If you want fish, just ask around,' a *babushka* suggested. I asked the next person I encountered on the street.

'Come with me. My neighbour may have some.' I followed my acquaintance, an elderly, kindly man with an open smiling face, towards one of the houses. Here we spoke with a burly man wearing *valenki* and a fur hat, working in his garden.

How many kilos? was the question I was expecting, this being a place where fish was probably bought in quantity. And I had wanted to ask: What kind of fish do you have? But there was no mention of species, weight or price. I was told to come back in an hour.

My acquaintance insisted on accompanying me across the concrete bridge over the river to the other half of the settlement. Seeing four soldiers in the distance I asked him about the military.

'Oh, the army mostly left. There are just a few soldiers now who are meant to guard the coastal border and check on movements in and out. The military kindly left us a big store of motor fuel. You know what we've done with it?' He beamed at me broadly. 'Some bright lads knew how to separate it chemically: one half for cars, the other half for drinking. Thousands of litres, can you imagine?

'This place used to be wealthy, we had an enormous traffic of people connected with fishing, and there was money around. Now we're completely isolated from the rest of the oblast, in fact we've become a laughing stock. Everything just evaporated or was creamed off by the criminals. The Administration can do nothing. In fact, they're more than likely the criminals themselves. Severomorsk is our administrative region but they don't want to pay us anything, don't want anything to do with us. Not even fish come through Teriberka now; well, none to speak of.'

Amidst the dereliction of present-day Teriberka there were still a few well-constructed two-storey wooden houses on high ground overlooking the bay. These must have been built before or soon after the Revolution, during Teriberka's heyday. Their size, their steep mansard roofs and their grand windows hinted at the wealthy merchant class who had made fortunes out of fish and seal, exploiting every opportunity for trade and barter with the coastal ships that called regularly en route between Archangel, Norway, England and Scotland.

Today's 'merchant adventurers' of Teriberka were, it seemed, still in existence, but well beyond the reach of the tax-gatherer and hardly benefiting the local population. 'A party of Norwegians was here the other day,' said my companion, 'and there's talk of a Norwegian fishing company setting up. We'd normally be delighted to hear this, of course, but we're too cynical to expect anything from such a venture. It'll be profitable for the major shareholders, whatever they have in mind.'

We returned to the man who was going to sell me fish and found him in his garden, ready with a large plastic bag. I caught some of the conversation. 'I can see he's a foreigner. Look at the hat. He's not Russian. He should be paying 14,000 roubles a kilo, not 11,000. If he's one of those Norwegian businessmen he should pay more.' My acquaintance agreed I was foreign but settled for 12,000 roubles and passed me the bag. I made a mental note about the hat for the future.

I took the short easy route back to the main road through the valley, passing the barrier within a few hundred yards. The single border guard on duty occupied a picturesque four-wheeled contraption like an old-fashioned tinker's caravan. It had wooden steps, two small high windows, and a tin chimney protruding at an angle from the roof.

Slava was waiting for me when I returned. He had been in the hills looking for berries. 'Then I was spotted by two soldiers travelling with a fish inspector. They must have been looking for people taking fish inland from the bay. They searched the car.' Perhaps Teriberka had become a smugglers' haven.

5

WATERSHED

WHEN ALEKSANDR ENGELHARDT, Governor of Archangel Province, returned home after his 1896 tour of Russian Lapland, he felt optimistic about the north-western corner of his domain. It lagged far behind in communications, transport and trade, but he believed he had seen its future. 'Yes, the Murman is now on the verge of a new era of prosperity and expansion,' he wrote, 'nor is the time far remote when even its political, as well as commercial, importance will receive the recognition which nature herself points out as its due.'

Engelhardt had both a visionary view and a practical understanding of the advantages that the ice-free Gulf Stream waters could bring to the Empire at large. 'Nor must we lose sight of the fact that in the port of Yekaterina harbour [at the mouth of the Kola Gulf], Russia is building for herself an open window with a broad and far-reaching view, looking out not only towards Europe, but on the whole world beyond.' He had already initiated telegraphic connection between Karelia and Kola. Only one ingredient now separated the Governor from his vision: a railway was needed, a link with the Empire's interior, a line running from St Petersburg to Karelia, and on to Kandalaksha, Kola and the Arctic coast.

The route for such a railway had in fact been discussed at the highest levels in Moscow since the 1860s, but Government had considered it a 'wild scheme'. The idea was reconsidered on a number of occasions but no decision was ever forthcoming. It was Engelhardt's enthusiasm, vision and understanding of his territory that finally swayed the opinion of his superiors, who at last began to project in their minds the substantial financial profit that could be generated by a railway line carrying Russian exports towards a Northern harbour that would be open and accessible to world shipping the whole year round.

If the export-minded politicians were slow to move, the outbreak of war in 1914 and the consequent urgent need for *imports* acted as the final catalyst. Russia and her Allies, under pressure on all sides, knew that the struggle against the overwhelming forces of the Central Powers would need a large and continual flow of imported supplies and ordnance. However, the Baltic ports were blockaded by the German navy and, on account of hostilities with Turkey, there was no egress through the Bosporus or the Dardanelles. Although the commercial port of Archangel could be depended upon for imports, it was frozen for six months of the year.

So it was that the significance of the Murman coast, a region still almost as strange to most Russians as to the rest of the world, was finally and indelibly impressed on the minds of the Russian and Allied leaders. As if a sign had appeared in the form of *aurora borealis* lights floating down the corridors of power, the Tsarist government of 1914 pursued the Murman railway project with all the haste and resources that could be mustered.

A widespread recruitment drive, notable for its ruthless agents, successfully attracted labourers to the railway from across the whole Empire, including Tatars, Khirgiz, and Finns. Many were from the less suitable and desirable pools of labour that remained after all able-bodied males had left for the war, last-chancers looking for fast easy money, or men with criminal records of no fixed address, but they came. On the promise of regular wages, thousands undertook long and arduous journeys to the railhead in cattle trucks: 15,000 navvies were transported from Harbin in China; the core hard-labour force was formed by 20,000 prisoners-of-war from the German and Austrian armies, including Czechs and Slovaks; timber and forestry labourers came from Karelia.

From the outset emphasis was given to speed. Few of the standard engineering norms were consistently observed. Much of the line was laid down without ballast and, since half the construction work was undertaken during the winter months when rods were rammed through the snow to test for rock, long stretches of rail were revealed in summer to have relied on little more than a bed of ice or bog. Bends in the route were frequently too sharp and gradients too steep.

The wooden bridges large and small that were required to cross the 1,100 rivers and streams were constructed mostly by ad hoc carpenters working by eye. There were the usual extremes in temperature, from 30 degrees Celsius in the summer – the mosquitoes providing an extra dimension to everybody's problems – to 40 degrees of cold in mid winter. These were conditions that southern recruits would have found barely tolerable under any circumstances but, since work had to be continued throughout the polar night under lamplight and with almost no thick winter clothing, casualties were enormous. Only the growing number of armed soldiers seemed suitably clothed.

Week by week, as wages failed to materialize, the civilian workforce began to realize that they were not wage slaves but labour slaves and, finding themselves in virtual captivity, many ran for the open spaces. Armed guards, who patrolled the line and guarded the work details in much the same way as their successors would watch over gulag workers twenty and more years later, fired on sight, not only at escaping prisoners-of-war but also at absconding civilians. Little food was available to any of the workers, whether civilians or prisoners. At times there was nothing beyond flour and dried peas. Death through starvation was commonplace and scurvy was rampant.*

On his reconnaissance in 1896 Governor Engelhardt had committed himself to the promotion of Yekaterina, the small natural harbour on the western side of the Kola Gulf very near the open sea. Once work on the railway line was under way, however, the focus of activity shifted fifteen kilometres upstream to the east bank of the Gulf, to a stretch of the shore relatively sheltered from the north-east gales, which enjoyed an ideal anchorage: safe, deep, no strong tides, and very large. There the first jetties were hastily pushed out from the shore in 1915 to offload ships bringing tools and timber for the railway, there the first shipments of ordnance and ammunition arrived for the Tsarist armies. There the present-day port of Murmansk sprang up.

* The casualties of the two-year railway project are difficult to quantify. The human suffering involved in the hurried construction of the 1,000 kilometres of narrow-gauge single track from Petrozavodsk in Karelia to the coast of the Barents Sea ranks in scale with that resulting from the building of the nearby Belomor Canal in the 1930s between the Baltic and the White Sea. The Murman railway's labour force over the two years totalled between 70,000 and 120,000. Some writers have estimated the lower figure without referring to fatalities; others have reckoned that prisoners of war alone numbered 70,000 and that casualties among them exceeded 25,000 dead.

Before the start of the Murmansk railway project this large, open-shore amphitheatre, then known as Semenov Bay, was inhabited all year round by one man in a log cabin and occasionally visited by Kildin Saami. As work on the line progressed, the small number of settled port workers was augmented by thousands of railway labourers advancing along the railway's route. By the time the line was nearing completion in 1916, the place had become a multicultural migration zone for the unruly and the discontented, the unemployed and the unemployable, a resting ground for the wounded, sick and dying, all of whom were now living in huts, converted railway wagons and dug-outs, sharing a common aimlessness but nevertheless hoping for some kind of future in the place where fate had landed them. Plans were hastily drawn up for the development of the shanty lands of Semenov Bay. The port was optimistically perceived as 'Western European', and on 29 June 1916 the shoreline shantylands were grandiosely named Romanov-na-Murmane. By November, the first trains had arrived from St Petersburg – or Petrograd as it was now known – and a year later, after the Revolution, the town was hurriedly renamed Murmansk. In further honour of events in Petrograd, the infamous railway line became known as the October Railway.

*

Walking through the main square of Murmansk, the Square of Five Corners, I caught sight of an inscribed stone plaque set into the wall above a shop window.

> *On 21 February 1920 in the town of Murmansk,*
> *revolutionaries led an uprising of seamen, port workers and*
> *railwaymen, and overcame the might of the Interventionists and*
> *the White Guard. Murmansk became for ever Soviet.*

I had only a vague idea about these events. The uprising to which the plaque referred was a battle which ended near where I was standing and brought to a close two years of civil war in the north-west of Russia. I was curious to learn more. I copied the text of the plaque on to the reverse of my afternoon shopping list and, pursued by the relentless techno-throb coming from the newly-arrived pirate music-cassette stalls beneath the Meridian Hotel, made my way to the other side of the square.

Between the square and the railway terminus was a small park dotted with a variety of mature trees. In its centre, where small groups of old and young and a few outcasts congregated to chat, smoke and drink, stood a white concrete construction about six metres high, a four-legged observation platform with two open staircases – a cold, unimaginative and enigmatic piece of architecture. It was a memorial 'to the dead of 1919–20', but reading these words on the plaque I was none the wiser. I decided to start my enquiries in the Regional Museum. Reminding myself that the museum's sense of twentieth-century history was more than usually selective, I walked through the rooms until I reached the exhibits devoted to the Revolution. There I found the display I wanted.

I learned how the so-called Interventionists, including detachments from Britain, France, America, Canada, Italy and Serbia, but principally Britain, had exploited the disarray caused by the Revolution and the collapse of the Russian armies. They had landed by sea in the north-west in 1918 – first at Murmansk, then at Archangel – with the intention of destroying the new Bolshevik government. The enormously superior invading Interventionists had advanced south, killing heroes of the Red Army and imprisoning Bolshevik partisans on the way, but finally Bolshevik troops had overcome the remnants of the Russian White Guard abandoned by the Allies at Murmansk and Archangel, and driven the foreigners into the sea.

Among the items in the display, under glass, there was a small, beautifully crafted cross-section model of a prison barrack. Inside the barrack human figures lay and crawled like maggots over three tiers of bunk beds. The original barrack had been constructed on the north-east coast near the Iokanga's estuary; it was a 'typical Interventionist prison' holding up to 500 prisoners. There were no stoves in these buildings; many prisoners occupying the lower bunks froze to death in winter, many on the upper bunks were asphyxiated from the stench and lack of oxygen. The text of the label accompanying the model was ambiguous but I understood that similar buildings in the region had admitted thousands of prisoners, and that of the 1,200 prisoners admitted at Iokanga only 500 had survived.

In the middle of the floor a large free-standing contoured model of Murmansk town and port showed the battle referred to on the plaque above the shop, the last moments of resistance in the face of the advancing Red Army. Superimposed on the model were large sweeping arrows of the kind usually employed to illustrate battle history, one set depicting the onslaught of the glorious Bolsheviks, another set for the defeated White Guard, the *Belogvardeytsy*.

I left the Museum better informed but far from satisfied with my findings. In the Lovozero Museum a short time later I learned much the same story. On this occasion I came across a map that marked villages along the White Sea coast of the Peninsula that had 'resisted call-up' (by whom?) and had been burned and looted in reprisal (again, by whom?). Pictograms of log cabins in flames and gallows with swinging bodies implied the extent of the suffering. Here again, mention was made of the prisons.

When I returned to England that winter I found that few people I asked knew about the Allied venture at Murmansk and Archangel during 1918 and 1919. Those who did spoke of it as an attempt to overthrow the Bolshevik regime, a campaign with confused motives and in some way unworthy of the participants. The events had received a bad press in Britain at the time and encountered strong opposition from the Labour Party. The British people had been, above all, impatient to have done with war and to see troops coming home rather than embarking on a new front with a nation to which they had until recently been allied.

*

After the October Revolution and the collapse of the Russian armies, the Treaty of Brest-Litovsk between the new revolutionary government and the Central Powers ended the war for Russia and freed large numbers of German and Austrian troops from the eastern front. While the treaty allowed the Germans to transfer the majority of these troops to the west, it also handed them a free rein in the east. Among their several treacherous – and illegal – post-Treaty moves was the despatch of several divisions to Finland with a view to occupying the ice-free ports of Pechenga and Murmansk. In the space of a single year following completion of the Murmansk railway, Germany had observed some 600,000 tons of military matériel and a similar tonnage of coal being landed by the Allies at the Kola Gulf for the Tsarist armies. Following Russia's withdrawal from the war, large quantities of munitions, rifles, armoured vehicles, wire and fuel were still stranded on the quays or en route south. In addition to benefiting from these large stockpiles, Germany intended to establish naval and submarine bases in the Barents Sea inlets, and to control the vital rail links from Murmansk to Petrograd, and from Archangel to Moscow.

In the face of the threat of 55,000 German and 50,000 anti-Bolshevik Finnish troops under the command of General van der Goltz a short distance away across the Finnish border, and with German U-boats entering the Barents, the Bolsheviks appealed to the Allies for assistance. Concerned by the October Revolution and the Treaty of Brest-Litovsk, the Allies were initially reluctant to commit troops to their former partners at a time when they were preparing for the critical conflict in France and Flanders. On 2 March 1918, however, an oral agreement, reached between the Allied military and the Murmansk Soviet, and sanctioned by War Commissar Leon Trotsky, determined that the Allies would assist in the protection of the northern ports and the White Sea. At the invitation of the new government in Moscow, a small initial British naval detachment was ordered to the Kola Gulf in April 1918, and a Russian commissar by the name of Natserenus was sent by Moscow to negotiate the common defence of the new town of Murmansk. He was also to co-ordinate the Allied troops and the newly-named Red Guards in the defence of the October Railway which ran vulnerably close to the Finnish border all the way from Russian Lapland to Petrograd. The Russian Northern Army at Archangel, expecting a German naval attack on their own port if Murmansk were to fall, also anxiously requested Allied assistance.

The Bolsheviks later changed their minds. The Moscow government, which was probably beginning to realize how few Russians or Karelians were likely to support the Bolshevik cause in the north-west, now cast the Allies as foreign invaders, and on 8 June 1918, without prior negotiation, Lenin instructed all Allied forces in the region to quit. The Murmansk Soviet, however, being more concerned with combating Germans than supporting Bolshevism, ignored Moscow's volte-face, and in June they welcomed the arrival at Murmansk of a further Allied expeditionary force, commanded by the English general Sir Charles Clarkson Maynard, comprising 2,000 English, French, Serb, Canadian and Italian soldiers. They not only formally rejected Moscow's order but, on 6 July 1918, signed an agreement with the Allies to form a joint Allied-Russian force to combat the threat from Germany and Finland.*

On his arrival by ship in the Kola Gulf with his expeditionary force, General Maynard was taken aback by what he saw. He was well aware of the hasty genesis of the port that had appeared on the shores of the ice-free Kola Gulf as if from nowhere, and of the important role the port had played since the autumn of 1916, receiving Allied and American-financed armaments and provisions for the stricken Russian armies. But he was hardly prepared for the vista of chaos before him. The railhead was a jumble of sheds, log warehouses, ramshackle work-cabins and tangled sidings interspersed with stacks of steel rails, sleepers and timber. The jetties and quayside were disordered and lacked rudimentary facilities such as cranes. Two Russian warships – there were 500 Russian sailors in town – which were apparently leaking had been beached nearby. Most of the small craft, apart from the few British vessels, appeared to have been abandoned and were in need of extensive repair.

Once ashore Maynard was directly confronted with the squalor of the infant port and the inhabitants themselves, many of whom were far from pleased to see the arrival of foreign troops known to be at odds with Moscow. 'Outside many of the huts was such a conglomeration of unsavory refuse,' he wrote, 'that one shrank from the very thought of ever being compelled to enter them ... Adding to the general look of squalidness was the appearance of the inhabitants themselves ... In addition to Russians, the population included Poles, Koreans, Letts, Chinese, and other foreigners – a motley and unprepossessing crowd.' When Maynard conferred with General Poole, the

---

* The displays at the Murmansk museum had at first led me to believe that Russian Lapland and Russian Karelia were hotbeds of revolutionary Bolshevik fervour. Certainly there was some anti-Tsarist enthusiasm in 1905 and some support for the Bolshevik cause in early 1917 in the form of small meetings and marches by sawmill workers at Kandalaksha and the White Sea village of Knyazhaya Guba, but Lenin was slow to understand the character of the region's peasants and entrepreneur Pomors. Most had become accustomed to a measure of self-determination and were hardly likely to greet any national policy that failed to recognize the peculiar needs of Northern society and its economy. Voters in the North had anyway recently turned out for the Socialist Party in overwhelming numbers. If in early 1918 the Bolshevik government assessed their support in the region as negligible they were in no doubt of it by June.

commander of the small naval detachment that had arrived before him in April 1918, on the available manpower, he calculated they had a total of 2,500. Of these nearly the entire Serb battalion was sick, the French artillery was ill-equipped and suffering from an influenza epidemic, and the 150 Russians and Poles had only just enlisted. It barely constituted a fighting force. At least their aim was unambiguous: to join with the Russian forces already in the region, to prepare defences against German and Finnish cross-border incursions, and to ready the port to defend against a German sea-borne invasion.

Once the Allies had signed the agreement with the Murmansk Soviet, General Maynard took an armed reconnaissance party by rail to the south. The line ran a short way up the Gulf as far as the old near-abandoned trading settlement of Kola, and there it turned inland and due south to follow the River Kola upstream. From his carriage window Maynard was overlooking the waters of the Trakt which for centuries had carried fishing gangs and travellers north. By the time the locomotive passed over the narrow strip of land 100 kilometres from the Gulf that formed the portage between the south- and north-flowing rivers of the Trakt, Maynard had begun to comprehend the nature of the terrain over which his battalions would be fighting. His army's routes would be determined not only by the major lakes and rivers but also by bogs. All of these could be traversed in winter, but from spring to autumn they would have to be avoided. It was hardly the kind of fighting country to which his troops could become accustomed within the course of a few weeks.

The train was agonizingly slow. Maynard discovered for himself the shortcomings of the engineering that had famously brought the rails from Petrozavodsk to the Arctic coast in such a hurry. Some of the bends were so tight as to be almost unnegotiable and, where there was a lack of ballast beneath the rails, the cars tilted dangerously. On some of the steeper hills the locomotive had to take a second run.*

* During the delays and in between assessing the problems of fighting among the forests and bogs, Maynard contemplated other strategies. In his own account of events he wrote: 'The only relief is when your train runs slowly alongside, or creeps yet more slowly across, some clear, swift-running river, haunted almost to a certainty by salmon, or at least by many a fine trout, which you picture as rising with a decisive swirl to your red palmer [fly]. Then for an instant you forget the monotony of your surroundings. Your thoughts fly back to the times when field-boots were replaced by waders and, armed with rod instead of revolver, you spent glorious hours luring hard-fighting trout from some Scottish stream.'

Maynard had encountered civilian disobedience among the motley crowd at Murmansk and was uncertain of what opposition to expect on his way south. He had his first taste of it after a further 50 kilometres. The train was running along the east bank of Lake Imandra beneath the still snow-capped heights of the Khibiny mountain range when it was shunted into the siding of a small station. A crowd of local people, who had gathered as if expecting the train's arrival, were noisily antagonistic towards the soldiers now putting their heads out of the carriages. Maynard went with an escort to find the station-master and learn the reason for the delay. When found, the man was abusive and refused to allow the train to travel further, saying he was acting under instructions, whereupon Maynard's English aide held a gun to the head of the recalcitrant railwayman and issued a new set of instructions. This had the desired effect. In the full light of the early July midnight sun the train pulled out of the siding and continued slowly southwards along the shore of the lake towards Kandalaksha and the White Sea.

As for the Red Guards somewhere on the line further south, who were now theoretically under Moscow's control and no longer allied to the British but who were perhaps not yet 'enemy', Maynard had no information. Nor had he any idea how they would react when encountered; he could only be prepared for all eventualities. Within several hours he was to find out. As the train came within sight of the White Sea and drew into the station at Kandalaksha, the Allied troops were surprised to see that they were drawing alongside a trainload of the opposition, several hundred of them, all likewise staring wide-eyed from the windows, their locomotive fully steamed, ready to make for Murmansk. Maynard summed up the situation and promptly commanded the British troops to parade directly in front of the Red Guards' locomotive, effectively preventing departure, while his aide was despatched to summon Spiridonov, the Russian commander, to parley.

Spiridonov was drunk, disinclined to move from his carriage, and had to be coaxed. Eventually ushered into Maynard's carriage, he sat with his escort party, all with pistols at the ready, and listened to the General's reasons, expressed in diplomatic and gentlemanly terms through the British interpreter, why the Red troops could not be permitted to proceed north to Murmansk. It was a delicate moment, made somewhat more difficult by the Russian's alcoholic impatience with a foreigner who had until a few days earlier been an ally and who was apparently conciliatory, but who was now being obstructive and making it unambiguously clear that force would be used against the Red troops if Spiridonov insisted on advancing. Fortunately for Maynard his bluff was not called. Although there were Allied forces already in Kandalaksha in the shape of Serb infantry and French artillery, these would have been no match at that moment for the very superior number of Red troops. Spiridornov could have chosen to steam northwards and on to Murmansk but, instead of sweeping the Englishman's threats aside, he stayed put and then retreated to Petrozavodsk.

Maynard later continued his reconnaissance, travelling south into Karelia and on to the White Sea port of Kem. There he learned that more Red Guards were shortly to be despatched from Petrograd in support of Spiridornov. Full engagement with the Bolsheviks from the front now seemed increasingly likely; and on Maynard's right flank 15,000 Finns and a greater number of Germans were poised to attack.

Maynard was acutely aware of the small size of his army. Russian recruits to the anti-Bolshevik cause were still minimal; of the thousands of potential candidates congregated around the port at Murmansk most had been too unhealthy, ill-fed or disenchanted to be of any use as a fighting force, and the rest he dismissed as 'useless riff-raff'. By good fortune, shortly after arriving in Kem, Maynard was able to recruit 1,200 Karelians, and when the skirmishes on the Finland border began in August, this paid dividends. Throughout the late summer and autumn of 1918 the Karelians under British and Canadian command inflicted a string of defeats and significant casualties on the invading Finns and their German commanders. They turned out to be stout-hearted allies, versatile in their use of the waterways and ingenious with their knowledge of the wetlands. Their womenfolk, who came up behind the men to keep the supply line going, proved no less resilient – they were, after all, defending their cherished homeland. On one occasion an isolated boatload of supplies being rowed upstream by two women was spotted by three Finnish soldiers who put out to intercept them. The Finns opened fire but the women turned their boat and rammed the enemy hard amidships, setting about the men with their oars, drowning two of them and seeing off the third. This incident, which was much celebrated locally, was recorded by Maynard who saw to it that both women were awarded the Military Medal.

The political situation at Archangel after the October Revolution was not dissimilar to that of the new small port of Murmansk. Archangel's large dockside population was politically volatile, but the established Pomor families and the influential and internationally-oriented merchant class of the old town were of a firmly independent caste. When in March 1918 a group of senior Bolshevik representatives, bearing the grandiose title of Extraordinary Committee for the Evacuation of the Port of Archangel, arrived from Moscow to expropriate the large stockpiles of armaments in and around the port, they were turned away by the town's leaders. They were reminded not only that their unofficial new government had not paid for the arms and ordnance, but also that the Bolsheviks had repudiated all loans secured during the Tsarist regime. The stockpiles therefore belonged to the Allies if not to the town of Archangel itself.

Efforts by the Bolsheviks to conscript men for the Red Army from among peasants throughout the Archangel region in June 1918 were also unsuccessful. Most of the locals considered themselves 'neutral', and probably in reaction to the recruiting drive there was an anti-Bolshevik uprising among peasants in Shenkursk, 300 kilometres to the south of Archangel. The influential sea-going Pomors tended likewise to be hostile towards the Bolshevik government, and this may have contributed a good deal to the success of the coup d'état of 1 August 1918 in Archangel, engineered by British agents and planned to coincide with the arrival of the first Allies by ship the following day.

All was not straightforward for the Allies at Archangel, however. The reception given to the British warships disembarking 1,500 Allied troops on to the Archangel quays on 2 August 1918 – four months after General Maynard's expeditionary force had arrived in Murmansk – epitomized the feelings of the wider population in the north-west: emphatically anti-German, predominantly anti-Bolshevik, but ambivalent towards a 'foreign incursion'.

If the British Cabinet and the British people were divided in their attitude towards reopening the eastern front and sending troops to Russia, President Woodrow Wilson proved to be the very embodiment of vacillation. But when Lenin's aggressive volte-face of June 1918 – ordering the Allies to quit – followed the Bolsheviks' breathtakingly treacherous betrayal and attempted massacre of a trainload of unarmed Czech troops at Irkutsk station in Siberia in May, Wilson began to reconsider. He became involved in Siberia by June, and by July he had committed American soldiers to assist the Russians on the White Sea. On 5 September 1918, 4,500 American infantrymen, along with engineers and support companies, disembarked at Archangel to join the smaller number of British and French already there. As on the Lapland/Karelia front, the operation was to be under the overall command of the British.

The US soldiers were mostly fresh young recruits from the Mid-West who had responded enthusiastically to their training in anticipation of chasing Germans across the fields of France and Flanders. When rumour reached them that they were destined for 'guard duty somewhere in Russia', they were understandably confused. Landing at Archangel with two-thirds of their number weak from influenza, they still had little conception of who these obscure 'Bolsheviks' were that their President now wished them to fight. All they knew was that the English and French, under pressure somewhere in the Russian forests and swamps far up the River Dvina, urgently needed their help. Germans were nowhere in the picture.

As the troops on both fronts, in Archangel and Lapland/Karelia, repeatedly dried their boots and socks and struggled with bogs, rain or blood-sucking insects, rumour had it that they were headed further south. The Archangel commander-in-chief, General Edmund Ironside, contrary to President Wilson's non-aggressive stance, was prepared to press ahead to the Trans-Siberian Railway to join with the White Russian commander-in-chief Admiral Kolchak, and also with the Czech troops who were now fully engaged in fighting the Red Guards. General Maynard on the Murmansk railway line was also considering an advance, all the way to Petrograd if necessary. The outlook on the Lapland/Karelia front during the autumn of 1918 was promising; the Russian recruits were showing some enthusiasm and coming forward in larger numbers.

In all of north-west Russia there was soon to be a total Allied and American force of 28,000 troops alongside some 20,000 Russian anti-Bolshevik 'Whites'.

By the time of the late October snows, however, it was clear that the Bolsheviks were set on taking Archangel. When, during the first days of November 1918, a four-day battle at Toulgas on the River Dvina nearly went in favour of the Bolsheviks who had brought forward a further 1,000 infantry, the immediate future seemed unlikely to promise any glorious southward marches on either front. Furthermore, continual unrest was regularly surfacing in the form of sabotage and mutiny.

When Germany and Austria-Hungary signed the Armistice on 11 November 1918, it was widely assumed throughout Russia that the British, the Americans and their Allies would withdraw from Murmansk and Archangel (as well as Siberia), and return home. Those who were most apprehensive about the Allies' response to the Armistice were, of course, the Murmansk Soviet and the Archangel leaders, together with the Russian soldiers and the 'White' Finns and Karelians who had worked and fought under British command for over six months. On the other hand there were civilians, peasants and soldiers who believed that perhaps the time had now come to resign themselves to Bolshevik rule in the North. Those who had consistently supported resistance to the Allied presence on Russian soil now vigorously manipulated wavering allegiances to increase agitation and the propaganda war.

Most British and American soldiers hoped and expected to hear of their imminent return home and were troubled when they learned that this was unlikely. When the Labour Party in England stepped up its campaign against what they called the Allies' 'meddling in Russian internal affairs', the soldiers' impatience occasionally surfaced as overt disobedience, presenting British officers with the task of quelling mutiny. On one occasion an entire battalion of the Yorkshire Regiment refused to go into battle.

Unrest among the Russian troops, caused by torn allegiances, news of Bolshevik advances, and leaflet propaganda threatening horrific recriminations, was even greater. Mutinies broke out with alarming frequency. Some of these were forestalled, others resulted in the imprisonment of ringleaders or executions by firing squad.

Whereas the Bolsheviks were able rapidly to strengthen their aims and offensives and to watch their propaganda working as well as, if not better than their bayonets, the Allied and White Russian cause was hindered by the vacillation of the Allied political leaders at home who seemed almost incapable of addressing the problems of the *de facto* war with Lenin. On the Archangel and Karelian fronts no clear instructions were received from London for many weeks. The frequent question 'Are we at war with the Bolsheviks?' was answered from home with a string of ambiguous official public statements.

Winston Churchill was among the few who thoroughly grasped the issues from a distance. He attempted an explanation to the House towards the end of the affair. 'Although to us who sit here at home in England it may seem very easy to say, "Clear out, evacuate, cut the loss, get the troops on board ship and come away" – and to arrive at that intellectual decision, yet on the spot, face to face with the people among whom you have been living, with the troops by the side of whom you have been fighting . . . when you get our officers and men involved like that on the spot, it is a matter of very great and painful difficulty to sever the ties and quit the scene.'

Whatever were the political or moral views expounded (not to mention the question of whether the Bolshevik Government was the legitimate and majority choice of the Russian people), there were three major considerations that prevented immediate withdrawal from the Russian north-west immediately following the Armistice of November 1918. First, it was impossible to sail from Archangel prior to the ice melt in June 1919, and this in turn determined the timing of any withdrawal from Murmansk. Secondly, it was necessary for the Allied and Russian forces to take certain aggressive actions against the Bolsheviks if a withdrawal by the Allies were to be conducted successfully and without excessive loss of life. Thirdly, under the terms of the campaign – one of the first international invasions of modern times – no withdrawal could take place without the approval of *all* the Allied governments.

The instructions that came from London were simply to stay on and hold the territory.

Regretting the indecision of their leaders at home, the Allied generals at Archangel and Murmansk prepared with some apprehension for the long winter of 1918–19. Having seen many of their men hospitalized with severe mosquito bites, they now had to try to guard against frostbite. Almost all the Allied troops were unfamiliar with extreme cold; only the few Canadians knew what it meant to live under the hazy Arctic sun for four months of the year in a seemingly endless wasteland of snow. The gloom of the northern days, with sometimes barely three hours of half light, did indeed take its toll on the morale of the British. As the snow started to settle and the going became more difficult they struggled to keep control of their minds, to maintain discipline and sustain a personal routine, to fight the lurking temptation to fall asleep in the open or remove gloves to repair a rifle or reorganize kit. There were long waits in subzero temperatures. Travel by sledge, far from being the easy option, produced numbing body temperatures within minutes, only partially alleviated by a tot of rum.

However, as winter advanced and thermometers at night regularly showed 30 degrees below zero, the Allied troops were surprised to find that in time they were adequately equipped and coping well after all. Many town lads, who had been thoroughly sceptical about even staying alive, found that they had forgotten the cold once they were busy learning about ponies from the Russians or how to keep the sled dogs from tangling their harnesses. And some would never forget their experience of living alongside the Saami, learning how to coax a team of reluctant and hungry reindeer in blizzard conditions, spending nights in smoke-filled 'wigwams', chewing raw reindeer meat, and listening to the strange little people chattering away in their own 'foreign'.

The engineers showed that they too had picked up a few extra skills from the locals when it came to constructing a log cabin. They morticed the logs with their axes, filled the chines with the right mosses and lichens, and insulated the base walls with sawdust and shavings, all in the ancient way of the northern settlers.

The not unexpected news of the Allies' decision to withdraw – the order itself did not reach Maynard and Ironside until July 1919 – was received by the Northern Russian Army commanders with acute disappointment but also, as Maynard pointed out, with pride and fortitude. 'There was no word of complaint,' he wrote, 'no hint of dissatisfaction; nothing but the expression of a fixed determination to continue the fight till victory should be assured. But beneath a brave exterior there lurked, I knew, the spectre of doubt – a spectre which I feared greatly that time's passage would fail to exorcize.'

General Maynard's own conduct of the campaign – in contrast to the disorder and confusion that prevailed under Generals Ironside and Miller in the Archangel theatre of operations – was from the start an example of talented administration, good soldiering and tactful diplomacy. His consideration for those under his command and his understanding of his Russian collaborators, together with his pragmatic but sensitive interpretation of every situation, produced successful skirmishes and advances, which in turn boosted morale and stimulated the recruiting process. By the summer of 1919 the number of Russian soldiers on the Lapland/Karelia front was to reach 7,000, not including the many Karelians loyal to the anti-Bolshevik cause.* When the order for withdrawal finally came, Maynard was leaving behind him an army under Russian command capable of holding its own and well positioned to advance.

The Americans who had disembarked at Archangel in September 1918 fought the Reds for nine long months and a particularly cold winter, and then departed on British ships in June 1919. Demoralized by propaganda and the prickly relationship with their British commanders, and pursued by a Red Army that had grown progressively larger, their survival and retreat was a close-run thing. They had won some pitched battles and proved inventive in close-quarter skirmishes but found that they were steadily losing ground to an enemy who was becoming increasingly skilled at hit-and-run tactics as well as firing howitzers. Even despite many technical advantages – such as the Royal Flying Corps' effective use of phosphorous bombs, a fact kept secret for many years – the Americans had failed to resist the Bolshevik advance. On the positive side, however, they had established good relationships with the predominantly anti-Bolshevik

---

* Karelia had been annexed to Russia since 1721. At the Armistice of 1918 the Karelians saw their chance for independence. This caused Maynard considerable trouble, not because the Karelians were unwilling to fight alongside the Allies, but because the Russian Governor Yermolov had publicly refused to support any Karelian move for independence. The Karelians thereafter refused to serve with Russians or under their command.

peasant villagers among whom they had spent long winter days and by whom help was freely given, and the American 'invasion' was in later years remembered with ironic affection by soldiers and peasants alike. But as they sailed out of the White Sea in June 1919, the Americans had to admit to themselves they were still unclear as to what it had all been about.

After the Americans departed from Archangel, matters there became increasingly unpleasant for the British. The troops who had been sent in May to hold the line and facilitate the American withdrawal encountered serious problems with mutinous Russians. One July morning in 1919 a hundred Russians deserted, murdered four of their own and three British officers in their billets and then turned to fight against their former comrades. General Yevgeny Miller, a seasoned Russian Tsarist campaigner, in spite of his English-sounding surname, who had joined the British command in January 1919, became excessively vindictive towards any local support for the advancing Bolsheviks, and this did little to win favour among Archangel's agitated and apprehensive population. As the British force made its final withdrawal by sea on 10 September, full-scale mutiny by Miller's Russian Northern Army was in the air.

Miller's army finally dispersed on 19 February 1920. Miller left by icebreaker, taking with him Russian officers, members of the Northern government, influential local merchants, and a number of foreigners whose families had traded at the Dvina Estuary since the establishment of the Muscovy Company in the sixteenth century. On the same day the 154th Red Army Infantry Regiment marched into Archangel.

Maynard contemplated his own exodus with reluctance, not only because it felt militarily inglorious but because, like Governor Engelhardt, he now understood the port's importance: 'This is the coming place as being an ice-free port, and we shall score a hundredfold if, at the end of all this pother, we are in a leading position to influence its future ... Needless to say, I have no personal desire to remain in this forsaken spot a moment longer than necessary. It has caused me to lose much of my hair and more of my temper.'

The last Allied ships left the Kola Gulf on 12 October 1919 with minimal loss of life. During the four winter months that followed, the unsupported Russians under Skobeltsin in Lapland/Karelia were no match for the Bolsheviks pressing steadily northwards and gaining in numbers as White troops deserted to avoid recriminations. Murmansk too surrendered on 21 February 1920 and 'became for ever Soviet.'

*

When I returned to the Square of Five Corners in the New Year I looked again at the plaque above the shop, and in the polar winter gloom walked over to the monument in the park. With snowflakes settling on my coat I stood in front of the strange staircase-and-platform construction and contemplated the hundreds of dead that had been buried in the soil beneath my feet in a mass grave dug by the Reds three weeks after the fall of Murmansk. I was no nearer understanding the story behind the concentration camp at Iokanga or the map at the Lovozero museum with its gallows and burning houses (it was said to relate to recruitment expeditions along the White Sea coast commanded by English officers). I also heard unsubstantiated stories of atrocities committed by the advancing Reds (villages were looted and burned, and opponents of Bolshevism put to forced labour, hanged or shot on the spot). But I was glad that I now knew at least something about the Civil War in the north-west of Russia. By 2001 the subject had become a hot topic of investigation among historians of both sides, but at the time of my initial enquiries some six years earlier, Russian historians and museum curators whom I approached for help were reluctant to do more than trot out their responses from the authorized Soviet publications.

The British have remained largely ignorant of these events but the Soviets wrote their own history, exploited it to the full, and regularly beat the Allies over the head with it in diplomatic situations, particularly the British and the Americans. When Nikita Khrushchev went to Los Angeles in 1959 he angrily alluded to 'the grim days when American and British soldiers went to our soil to combat the new revolution.'

After February 1920 the people of Archangel, Karelia and Russian Lapland, anxious to rebuild their lives – and impressed by the assurance that there would be no return to Tsarist rule – welcomed the advancing victors. The Saami, the Pomors and the new Komi immigrants were more sceptical than most about the future but, in a land where they would soon form an even smaller minority, their forebodings went largely unheeded.

The October Railway played a different role from any that Governor Engelhardt could have foreseen. Conceived initially in a spirit of commercial adventure similar to that of the old Muscovy Company – to enrich the Empire with exports and imports through a safe harbour – the railway started life by importing arms and allies at a critical time for the Russian Empire. Subsequently it brought from the south the soldiers, politicians, scientists and inquisitors who were to change the face of old Russian Lapland forever and subject it to a seventy-year regime which it barely survived and from which it now struggles to emerge.

6

ROCKS AND BLOOD

Slaves on the hill

This severe, barren, useless, northern wilderness has emerged in
reality as one of the richest.

Sergey Mironovich Kirov, First Secretary, Leningrad
Communist Party, 1930

IN MAY 1920, less than three months after the Bolsheviks had
swooped down from the heights overlooking Murmansk, a train
carrying a party of distinguished academics and economists left
Petrograd for Russian Lapland. The Northern Science Research
Expedition of the All-Russia Council for the National Economy
included a thirty-six-year-old geochemist, Aleksandr Yevgenevich
Fersman, a Russian of German extraction already well regarded in
geological circles. The Bolsheviks had consistently advocated the
more effective exploitation of the country's natural resources, especially in the northern regions, and when the Council of People's
Commissars, with Lenin's direct involvement, had been planning a
comprehensive programme of official research expeditions, Fersman
was considered an ideal participant.

The trip from Petrograd to Murmansk in May 1920 took longer
than expected. Long stretches of track were being relaid and shored
up with ballast. At frequent intervals the train slowed and crept past
labour-gangs working on the line day and night. As the train rolled
through the seamless forests of Karelia, past the White Sea and on to
Kandalaksha in Russian Lapland, the subsidence problems were com-
pounded by other damage caused a year or more earlier during the
'British invasion'. Bridges were in a bad state, and derailed locomo-
tives, wrecked coaches and lengths of twisted rail lay alongside the
repaired track.

On the east bank of Lake Imandra the Research Expedition's locomotive stopped for repair. This allowed passengers to leave the train for fresh air and a stroll. Seeing how close they were to the foothills of the Khibiny mountain range, Fersman walked up the nearest slopes and disappeared for several hours. When summoned by blasts on the whistle of the repaired locomotive, he returned in an excited condition, dirty, perspiring and breathless, apologizing for his long absence. Back on the train he animatedly justified his elation. On his walk, he said, he had encountered for the first time the fabulous mineral wealth of the Khibiny, all readily visible under his feet. As he wrote later: 'In the tedious grey landscape, amongst cliffs covered in lichens and mosses, I found a vast, variegated array of rare minerals: blood red or cherry eudialyte, flecks of astrophylite sparkling like gold, bright green aegirine, violet fluoric spars, golden sphene . . . It is impossible to convey the medley of colours that nature has granted this grey corner of the earth! I immediately realized that what I had discovered here was a vast, almost unlimited new source of wealth; a truly great opportunity for our nation.'*

In August of the same year Fersman gathered a small expedition of Petrograd students and postgraduates and returned north for three weeks. Initial indications were confirmed beyond his wildest expectations; the hand-picked group of colleagues and students from Petrograd, working long days and white nights, surprised Fersman on an almost daily basis with their mineralogical finds.

The summers of the 1920s on the Khibiny passed in a flurry of pioneer ferment. Most of the younger Petrograd-born men and women were experiencing wilderness for the first time in their lives. Tirelessly chipping rocks and taking sightings, they explored the network of valleys, walked the high tundra near grazing reindeer, and pitched their canvas tents by lakes and streams that yielded brown trout, whitefish, and even a rare species of charr. As summers moved into autumns, many in the fieldwork groups formed close and lasting bonds.†

---

* Fersman's excitement was to be immeasurably justified, but at the time he was somewhat disingenuous about his discoveries. The mineralogical importance of the Khibiny and Lovozero massifs had been established by the Swedish geologist Wilhelm Ramsay in the 1880s.

† For the first expedition in August and September 1920 – logistically one of the most difficult – Fersman's party of eleven consisted entirely of women. Professional women played a major role throughout the early petrological surveys of the Khibiny.

In 1923 they made a discovery that in Soviet agronomic terms was one of the most significant. In the hills that to this day are still referred to by their ancient Saami names of Kukisvumchorr, Yuksporr and Rasvumchorr, two of Fersman's colleagues discovered large deposits of apatite. This mineral, a principal source of phosphate for fertilizer, had hitherto been imported from Morocco, but now the urgent order was out for deposits to be discovered within Russia's own territories to enable low-cost agricultural development on a large scale. By 1926, following the early years of exploration and analysis, teams of reindeer were taking the first tonnes from Khibiny to the railway twenty kilometres away, and Fersman was directing large-scale removal of the ore by hand from the face of Mount Kukisvumchorr. Fersman's achievements, on top of his own professional reputation, brought him the high-level backing he needed. State input to the project began at a serious level. The Khibiny mine was to be one of the Party's first major development projects in the Russian North.

As time went on, the Khibiny project justified Fersman's vision. Not only did the hills prove to hold one of the world's most diverse ranges of rare alkaline minerals, but the apatite deposit appeared to be inexhaustible and probably the world's largest and most accessible. Over time, Fersman's mines were able to meet Russia's entire phosphate fertilizer requirement, even during Khrushchev's crazed agricultural expansion programme of the 1950s.

There was a less euphoric aspect to events. Fersman enjoyed the support of large numbers of happy and fulfilled academics, scientists, engineers, artisans and students, as well as political favour in Moscow. What he lacked was an infrastructure and a massive labour force to realize the dream. In 1929 the base camp of the operations was still no more than a chaotic assortment of large canvas tents and wooden cabins that had sprung up in the wild surroundings of Lake Vudyjavr near the foot of Mount Kukisvumchorr – not far, as it happened, from where Wilhelm Ramsay's expedition had pitched camp in 1891. First of all Fersman required a branch railway line. Then there were the mine shafts, the ore ducts, the workshops to process the ore, the offices, the living quarters, eventually a major settlement – the town of Khibinogorsk.

Following the victorious advance of the Bolsheviks through

Karelia and Russian Lapland in 1920, captured anti-Bolshevik soldiers were taken prisoner and put to work. When the Cheka arrived in the region, further hundreds of men and women suspected of being hostile to Bolshevism were rounded up. Some were put to work in the new port and town of Murmansk or on the October Railway, the remainder were transported or marched to the Khibiny to assist Fersman.

By the late 1920s political prisoners, criminals, exiles, kulaks, peasants and large groups of 'special settlers' were being moved in their thousands from one part of the Soviet Union to the other to feed the labour-hungry development projects of the Communist Party's New Economic Policy and Five-Year Plans. Many such people began to arrive at Khibiny. Fersman's project became the site of one of the largest forced labour camps in the Russian North.*

Such was the urgency for the twenty-kilometre connection to the main October Railway line running south that the shifts continued by kerosene lanterns under armed guard, non-stop day and night, throughout one whole winter. Most prisoners were dressed in the light clothing in which they had arrived. Provided with tools inadequate for working frozen soil, they resorted to pulling out roots and rocks by hand.

> Seven miles in a single winter month ... and why in one month? Couldn't it have been postponed till summer? ... And they called it earth? It was harder than any granite! ... Close your eyes and picture the scene: you are a helpless city dweller, a person who sighs and pines like a character out of Chekhov. And there you are in that icy hell! Or you are a Turkmenian in your embroidered skull-cap – your *tyubeteyka* – out there in that night blizzard! Digging out stumps.

> Aleksandr Solzhenitsyn, *The Gulag Archipelago, 1918–1956: an experiment in literary investigation*, translated by H.T. Willets, London, 1975

*

---

* Kulaks, who owned land or property and employed labour, were *ipso facto* opposed to Communism and collectivization and deemed 'enemies of the people'. All those not categorized as political offenders, exiles or common criminals were classed as *spetspereselentsy* or 'special settlers'.

Over sixty years later, also in winter but in the comfort of a heated modern railway carriage, I made my own way to the Khibiny mountains to see Fersman's mining town for myself. It was a slow service, stopping at every station the length of Lake Imandra, which was just what I wanted. On the east bank of the lake the train was boarded by a group of twenty rumbustious fishermen going home after a week on the lake and the river. From the window I could see many of their kind spread across the lake, peering into ice holes, sitting on stools in front of shelters of exotic and ingenious design clad in polythene sheeting. My high-spirited fellow-travellers were weighed down with operational equipment: boxes for tackle, boxes for food, rucksacks for clothes, and giant corkscrews for drilling the lake. From the pungent smell that had invaded the entire open compartment, it was clear they were carrying quantities of fish.

They settled into groups. Well-thumbed playing cards were produced and boxes cleaned up as playing surfaces. Soon the sound of slapped cards was amplified by inebriated but good-tempered shouting and cursing, raising the noise level by several decibels.

'Tickets!' A young woman of medium height with a head of fine auburn hair, no more than twenty-five years of age, slid open the compartment door. She had an unmistakably authoritative bearing, further complemented by a calf-length leather skirt, fur-lined leather boots and a shining brown leather money-satchel which, with an adroit single movement, she swung round to her front like a loaded pistol. If there wasn't one fishing licence between the whole lot in the carriage, there certainly wasn't a railway ticket. By an intuitive ability with which all ticket-collectors regardless of age seem to be endowed, the young woman silenced and subdued every one of her passengers, big, rough or rowdy. Whining their several excuses of hard times, sick wives, poorly-clothed children and unpaid wages, they meekly coughed up.

Looking at my fellow travellers as they quietly resumed their games, I wondered about their family backgrounds. Were some descended from the first workers at Khibiny, from the prisoners, convicts, exiles, or 'special settlers' brought here to fuel Fersman's great mining operation? Had their kin been sacrificed at the altar of the town called Khibinogorsk, in 1934 renamed Kirovsk in honour of Leningrad's First Secretary Kirov, shortly before he too was murdered by Stalin?

The weather on the way south had been cold, bright and blue-skied, making it a pleasant, brisk, early-winter day with good views of the lake and the snow-white mountains that overlooked the railway. Half an hour later, as the train turned away from the lake and climbed into the hills, we were moving into low cloud. What I could see of the mining town was enveloped in a thin pale yellow fog and looked forbidding. I had already heard it described as a 'godforsaken place, even in better times ... with the worst climate in the region'.

'It's a modern and progressive town, Kirovsk,' said one of the more sober fishermen, seeing me straining to look through the condensation trapped between the window panes. 'People come here for winter sports from all over Russia. We've had international championships. There are ski-lifts, plenty of snow, modern hotels.'

It was hard to believe from what I had seen that anyone would wish to go there to work, let alone play. I searched for redeeming features – there were a few stone or stuccoed municipal buildings here and there – but the familiar dead hand of Soviet architecture was everywhere in evidence.

I was on my way to meet the grandmother of a young acquaintance of mine, Sergey Osokin. She was among Khibinogorsk's first 'special settlers', arriving here with her mother as a four-year-old in 1930. Sergey was at the station to meet me. We telephoned his grandmother to say we were on our way and then walked to the far end of town, traversing the hill. Already feeling Kirovsk's extra cold I drew the flaps of my hat down over my ears and put up my collar.

The house was a five-storey *khrushchevka* concrete block of the 1960s, identical to many others, with the usual wrecked entrance to a dingy, dirty staircase. On the third floor a small woman opened the door to us. When we had crossed the threshold, removed our coats and put on the old slippers that she offered, Sergey introduced me.

The apartment consisted of a small kitchen, a bathroom and a sitting room with a bed. We settled in the sitting room without further conversation and my hostess brought from the kitchen two bowls of *shchi* – a wholesome vegetable soup with *smetana* and small pieces of meat – followed by *pelmeni*.

Maria Mikhaylovna was diminutive and elderly, compactly proportioned, upright and trim. Her head seemed tightly arranged, with a small sharp nose and thin lips, but she had a gentle, kindly face. Her close-cropped brown hair, only slightly touched with grey, was watered down and combed back straight with a parting. In a striped shirt buttoned at the collar, she appeared boyish. Throughout our whole conversation she sat upright, at first visibly nervous. I may have been the first Westerner she had met; I was almost certainly the first foreigner with whom she had had a conversation of a personal nature. Sergey, who enjoyed a close and affectionate relationship with his grandmother, comforted and soothed her throughout our interview, tenderly stroking her neck and shoulders as she spoke.

'My father was a farmer of pure Karelian stock,' Maria Mikhaylovna began. 'We were kulaks. We had a small estate in the Novgorod Oblast and we had workers. I would say we lived a healthy, happy country life. I have a clear memory of soldiers arriving out of the blue one winter and telling us we had to move. I was four years old at the time. My father had already escaped, running off before any of us realized what was happening. My mother was held by one soldier while the other two took our jewellery and swapped their worn-out *valenki* for my father's good new ones. My mother wasn't even allowed to keep her ring. In fact the soldiers were so horrible that people from the village were afraid to approach us and give us bread to take with us. We left by horse and cart, my mother in deep shock, and my brother and I wrapped up together in one big fur coat, my father's old hunting coat. We had no idea where they were taking us. I remember just travelling and travelling. Sometimes by train, sometimes in horse-drawn carts, always heavily guarded.

'And so we arrived at Khibinogorsk. Down where the hospital is now, near the river. There was a large flat area there with tents – *shalmany* they were called – each holding about thirty people. There was a low table and some straw, and that was our place. That's where we lived and slept. The winter was severe. At night we slept close for warmth and there was also a man my mother had befriended. I reckon we were saved by having my father's coat. In the mornings we usually had to dig ourselves out of the tent. There was almost no food apart from thin soup and bread but my mother had good breast milk and continued to keep me fed like that for a long time. So that helped, although I remember feeling shy about it even then.

'There was illness everywhere. Many died from typhoid and scarlet fever. The soldiers never allowed us to bury our own dead because of the risk of escape, so sometimes we buried people at night secretly. My báby brother died during the first winter.'

Within a year or so there were the first barracks, and mothers and children were moved into these. 'That was luxury,' said Maria Mikhaylovna, getting up to fetch tea from the kitchen. 'There were curtained partitions and we had more room; and of course it was much warmer.'

After three years, Maria Mikhaylovna's father appeared at the camp having traced his wife. He was actually a 'free man', a volunteer worker, going under an assumed name, while Maria Mikhaylovna's mother was an 'enemy of the people' – *vrag naroda*. The couple therefore met at night and for reasons of security were careful not to let their young daughter see her father. But in time they grew impatient with the surreptitiousness and told the authorities they had been courting. Their interrogator warned the suitor that he would jeopardize his status, but the officer-in-charge reacted sympathetically. They were allowed to marry, and Maria Mikhaylovna's mother took the bridegroom's name of Gromov.

Their lives took on a fresh outlook. The town was growing rapidly, there were many more barracks, a few brick houses, even a cinema.

'My mother gave birth to my two sisters during those pre-war years. The authorities seemed very pleased with her about that.

'One thing I remember quite clearly was being in the main square when Comrade Kirov made a visit. We had already learned at the frequent parades how much we owed this great man and how much he was going to enrich our lives as we built the town and worked the mine. But really he was only here once or twice and was assassinated shortly after the visit in 1934. The Big Man around here was really Fersman. It was Fersman who ruled and made all the decisions.'

When the War came the family was evacuated to the Tatar Autonomous Republic. It was a disappointment for Maria who was beginning to make friends at school, but the mines and the works were being bombed heavily by the Germans.

The train journey to Yutaza was some 3,000 kilometres. Maria's parents rented a stable for which the government paid, and then found work in the fields. Far from improved chances of food, there was widespread famine. Workers were forbidden to take anything from the fields for themselves, and given 100 grams of flour and 'a particular grass'. They all became sick, and Maria's father and one of her sisters died, probably from eating infected wheat.

After the War Maria's mother, very low, didn't want to return to Kirovsk, but when the time came Maria persuaded her that they should do so, and, to buy the tickets for the three of them, decided on her own to sell the sewing machine which her mother had used to make all their clothes and earn extra money.

'My mother cried a great deal at that time, but when we got back to Kirovsk I was happy. I must have been about nineteen, and I had managed to get my passport "cleaned", which was a great advantage. For the first time I considered myself an independent person even though I didn't find work for a long time. In the end I got a job in a school kitchen. As you can imagine, I gained a lot of weight in that job!'

Only the toughest survived in Kirovsk (Khibinogorsk) in the years after the Great Patriotic War. Maria's second sister never recovered from the deprivations of their time in Tatarstan and died in 1946.

'All the same we had fun, and we danced. I only had one dress but I still had a great time. I remember a friend turning up for a dance in military boots, and I had some really good lace-up boots that I got in Tatarstan. In 1946 I met my husband and we lived together for three years but when he wanted to go back to Tatarstan, to Kazan, I refused to leave. I had my first child by then and anyway the pay away from the north would have been almost nothing.

'After the war there were a lot of prisoners working in Kirovsk. Many of them were Russians, repatriated from German concentration camps but suspected of being antagonistic to the Communist Party because they had been out of the country. Prisoners worked under military supervision. There were dogs and machine-guns everywhere. Prisoners were killed trying to escape. That whole street over there, ulitsa Parkovaya, was built by prisoners.'

I asked Maria Mikhaylovna if Kirovsk had changed much in her lifetime.

'Yes, of course! I've spent nearly all my life in barracks. There are no barracks in Kirovsk now.'

At the Kirovsk Museum later that day, the curator was expecting me and greeted me formally at a distance, standing with a cue-stick in her hand. I politely declined the tour and set off around the exhibits on my own, trailed by one of the elderly women attendants.

I was pleased to see that the pioneer geologist Wilhelm Ramsay had been given the prominence he deserved, but it was Fersman and his colleagues who received pride of place. The rest of the displays were all statistics, tonnages, factory bosses and Party chiefs who turned up to bathe in reflected glory. Photos of Kirovsk in the early days made it look like a spa in the Austrian Alps, with healthy young people smiling at cameras and waving banners. I might almost have been convinced that the building of the town was a labour of love, carried along on a wave of Komsomol volunteer enthusiasm.

The creation of Kirovsk and its mining combine – 30,000 inhabitants by the beginning of the Second World War – in the mountains north of the Arctic Circle was indeed a 'bold experiment', a 'magnificent undertaking'. If only all had been achieved without slave labour, without loss of life, without the destruction of families. The heroes of the story were those of the first generation, now grandfathers and grandmothers, who had braved all weathers and all conditions to build the railway, work the mines, and create the town. And were the greater heroes those who had survived or those who had died?

In 1995 Kirovsk looked to me like an abandoned town. An acquaintance of mine, Yelena Kruglikova, who had a son working underground, told me the mine was barely operating productively. Moscow was in such disarray, and Yeltsin's men so incompetent at managing the new political and economic conditions, that it was impossible to get major decisions from anybody in power. Yelena's musician husband had been invited to Kirovsk twelve years earlier to lead the town's orchestra. It included some highly talented amateurs but, like so many other aspects of Kirovsk life, was unlikely to flourish for long.

'Everyone dreams of going back to their family in Middle Russia . . . if they've still got one,' said Yelena. The elderly without family would have to stay where they were; they had lost everything in the bank crashes at the beginning of the decade and were now living on pensions of steadily diminishing value as the rouble continued its inexorable slide.

I walked up to the highest point of the town where the road ended. A permit was needed to go through the security gate into the works and up to the mines. Men on the afternoon overnight shift were making their way up the hill past me. Urban disarray was all around: scrap metal, rubbish dumps, exhausted buildings, all avoiding my gaze and retreating under a further light dusting of white snow. The engines of the mine buses coming up the hill towards me sounded like the complaints of the elderly, worked too hard for too long.

Ski chair-lifts on the slopes were swinging in the breeze, waiting for the first customers of the season. Far below was the large Lake Vudyavr and the main body of Kirovsk spread along one shore. In the distance to my left one half of a large hill had disappeared, sliced in half for its ore. Although this was to me an extraordinary spectacle, it was almost negligible compared with the vast opencast mines at Mount Kuelpor higher up. A visiting English geologist, observing the scale at which rock had been removed, was said to have remarked: 'There's only one way that that amount of rock could have been moved, and that's by nuclear fission.' It later became known that nuclear tests did indeed take place underground at Kuelpor in 1974 and 1984.

Gemstones

> Our academic researches have awakened the Khibiny mountains
> and surrounding area from a deep age-old sleep, and attracted
> thousands of people full of vital energy to this wonderful place.
>
> A. Vinogradov and G. Ivanyuk, *The wonders of Khibiny*,
> Apatity: Kola Science Centre, 1998

AFTER THE GREAT PATRIOTIC WAR of 1941–45 the relentless pressure to raise mining production levels, as well as the need for new buildings and bomb-damage repair, brought more scientists and labourers to Fersman's busy Arctic pioneer town. By the 1950s, when Khrushchev's agricultural policy was placing millions of fresh acres under the plough from Kazakhstan to the Ukraine, phenomenal quantities of fertilizer were being shipped, almost all of it apatite phosphate from the mines at Kirovsk.

To attract the best scientists and engineers, Fersman built before the war a large lodge called 'Tietta', a kind of study centre with a library and a buffet, which sat among the trees and provided a congenial and picturesque setting for socializing as well as research. 'Tietta' was doubtless no 'I Tatti' but it played its role in attracting some of the best scientific and engineering minds of the time to the Khibiny. In the 1960s, rather than trying to expand Kirovsk within the constricted mountain valleys, Fersman's planners built a new town sited well away from the rough-and-tumble of the old place and with a milder climate. A suitable and picturesque area was found twenty kilometres to the south-west overlooking one of the large bays of Lake Imandra. It was eponymously named Apatity.

The first time I approached the town was by bus along the tree-lined banks of Lake Imandra in summer. On our left towards the east were the peaks of the Khibiny, on our right I could see what looked like holiday camps hidden amongst the birches and pine trees along the shore. The elderly woman seated beside me, seeing my interest, engaged me in conversation.

'Those are rest-camps belonging to the mining company. They're said to be very comfortable. It doesn't seem long ago that they weren't there at all. I spent my childhood on those banks.' The woman's father had moved there from the south in the 1950s to join a fishing collective at Zasheyek at the south of the lake, the rest of the family had followed, and they had built a log cabin on the shore that we were passing, part of a tiny community living off the land.

One day the bosses from the apatite works turned up and ordered the family to move. They were to live in the new town; the authorities had taken over the area for their rest-camps. Now my bus companion lived in a comfortable flat in Apatity but missed the country life of her childhood. As we passed a small peninsula on the lake she told me that the Yekostrov Lapps used to come there in the summer. Their camp had everything: fish, summer breezes, good reindeer forage, plenty of trees, and a cash income from the old Postal Trakt which passed by their door until after the Civil War when the railway became the main form of north-south transport.

'God knows where they are now,' she said.

Our bus made an unscheduled stop to take on board a group of forestry workers. The men and women filled the bus with ripe country smells and good humour.

When I first caught sight of Apatity it was as part of a generally pleasing panorama, dominated by the smooth-topped Khibiny mountains, with the tall and strikingly conical old timber-built mineral dressing works sitting at the foot of the slopes. The town itself was visible only as a few rooftops over the trees in the middle ground.

The bus slowed as it approached a police observation tower just short of the town. I had seen a number of these inauspicious buildings elsewhere, all built with the same dreary grey brick. We stopped for a moment at a barrier that reached half-way across the road. A few years earlier there would have been a passenger document check;

Apatity was, and still is, home to a northern branch of the Russian Academy and to a large number of Soviet scientists, many of whom were engaged in work of value to the Cold War effort.

One area of Fersman's academic town particularly appealed to me. The first buildings to appear in the new town of the 1960s were small, mostly single-storey wood and stucco cottages with steeply pitched roofs, grouped picturesquely in a birch wood which was now in the middle of town. Built by prisoners, these buildings provided the laboratory and research facilities which in time evolved into today's Kola Science Centre.

A woman typist in one of the offices, seeing my curiosity, leaned out of her window and invited me in.

'This area is sometimes called the Academic Quarter,' she explained. 'The buildings belong to the eleven different institutes that comprise the Science Centre.'

I asked her about the people who worked there.

'Well,' she paused. 'I don't want to sound disloyal, but they don't all relate to the ordinary people of the town. Some of them come from a different planet.'

The house in the woods, which consisted of four or five office rooms, had a homely ambience; Russians know how to humanize their interior work spaces and make them comfortable and warm. Before I took my leave, the secretary produced a glass of sweet tea decoratively served on a wooden tray together with buttery home-made biscuits and a cranberry compote the like of which I have not tasted since.

Leaving academe's sylvan grove and walking through a small park in the town centre, I spotted the aloof, self-important features of Aleksandr Yevgenevich himself. Sculpted in granite and ensconced on a tall column, Academician Fersman was looking down at the large rock specimens laid out formally across the park – like flowers, and all conveniently labelled: nephelines, apatites, granites, cyanites, pegmatites from the Khibiny, iron ore from Olenegorsk and copper nickel from infamous Monchegorsk and Zapolyarny which I was shortly to visit. Beyond Fersman stood a 1970s concrete building with wide porticoed steps leading up to two separate entrances. I made a note of the juxtaposed name-plates: 'Institute for Information and Mathematical Modelling of Technological Processes'; and, next door: 'Institute of Economic Problems'. It was just one of several such buildings in Fersmantown with very expansive titles, all of which left the visitor in no doubt of each organization's function.

In the main square I came across Vladimir Ilyich Ulyanov. He was staring across the traffic roundabout, grumbling about the cinema programme, undecided whether to reserve the last of his venom for Apatity's new discotheque next to the cinema or for the town administration on his left. I ignored him and hurried to the Science Centre's main building for my meeting with its Head Scientist, geophysicist Feliks Gorbatsevich.

Gorbatsevich greeted me at the foot of the main staircase, a tall well-built man in his late forties, dressed informally in a denim shirt and cotton twill trousers. He took me up the stairs, along corridors lined with old cabinets of geological specimens, and into a spacious, high-ceilinged office with a view.

I had met Gorbatsevich on an earlier occasion and in a different context. He was the chairman of the north-west branch of Memorial, the humanitarian organization that gathered information for the descendant families of gulag inmates. I had warmed to him from our first acquaintance when I was amused by his boyish excitement at being the proud new owner of a simple digital wristwatch that recorded barometric pressure. I could see even now as we talked that he would prefer to discuss fishing, his great pastime.

Shortly before my appointment with Feliks I had been asked by a senior town resident what I thought would attract foreign tourists to Apatity; the question addressed an issue of concern to many declining towns of the Russian North. Apatity seemed to me to have little to offer.

'You might have to be a geologist to understand how this place can excite you,' said Gorbatsevich. I risked asking him to give me a brief lesson, half-expecting him to roll his eyes in disappointment that I had not done my homework. He did and he didn't.

'The Khibiny mountains and the adjacent Lovozero range are large alkaline intrusions of nepheline syenite which crystallized nearly 400 million years ago out of molten magmatic rock. Not old in geological terms, of course. Nor are alkaline rock massifs rare – there are similar intrusions in Norway, Greenland, Canada and South Africa – but three features make these hills unique: first, they constitute the largest *accessible* alkaline massifs in the world; secondly, they contain a very large number of minerals – new ones are discovered and registered every year; thirdly, and most significantly, they have yielded a large quantity of industrially useful elements and mineral products. The Khibiny and Lovozero massifs form the rare combination of great geological range and great industrial potential.'

When I eventually read the Swedish geologist Wilhelm Ramsay's articles in the Finnish scientific journal *Fennia* I found that not even the man's dry German style could fail to evoke the excitement of discovery. When in 1887 Ramsay and his Finnish colleagues mounted the first comprehensive scientific expedition across the Peninsula, the botanist and expedition leader Dr A.O. Kihlman exaggerated when he said: 'We are the first here, this place has never before been visited by scientists, botanists or geologists', but to a degree he was correct. Hitherto, most travellers of a scientific mind had been limited to circumnavigating the north and south coasts and travelling the busy Trakt route from Kandalaksha to Kola.

Ramsay made a series of dramatic discoveries, establishing for the first time the geological importance – and differences – of the two massifs of Khibiny and adjacent Lovozero, recording them as the world's largest single nepheline syenite occurrence. His own first-time discovery in the Lovozero hills, now known as loparite, a natural source of niobium, tantalum and other rare earth elements, and of immense value to the Soviet Union's military-industrial complex in the next century, he labelled modestly as 'New mineral No.1'.

Gorbatsevich continued his short course. The 900 minerals that had been recorded throughout the oblast to date represented a *quarter of all the mineral species known to exist in the world today*, and of these 900 minerals a fifth were discovered in Murmansk Oblast *for the first time ever*. In the Khibiny massif 350 different minerals have been identified, and of the 340 minerals in the Lovozero massif, 73 were first-time discoveries – a world record for single geological occurrences. Apart from noting the range of mineral species and their elements, I recognized some of the names as being prominent in the defence and engineering industries, in particular niobium, zirconium (eudialyte), tantalum, uranium and thorium.

Yet another mineralogist's dream was to be found nearby. The

Bolshiye Keyvy, the ridge which runs through the central part of the Kola Peninsula from north-west to south-east, one billion years old, is an older magmatic intrusion. Many beautifully coloured and exotically named semi-precious rocks could be found in abundance throughout the ridge's rolling hills, mostly on or near the surface, there almost for the asking: blue and green amazonites, red and purple eudialytes, blue corundum and kyanite, red garnet-almandine, violet amethyst, golden brown astrophyllite, smoke and pink quartz, blood-red jasper, and countless coloured marbles.*

Crossing the room to an old wooden-frame, glass-fronted case, Feliks took out a fist-sized drill core and put it in my hand. It was light grey, finely grained, dense and heavy.

'That's from SG-3, our super-deep bore-hole in the north-west of the oblast. It stopped operating in 1993, but at 12 kilometres 261 metres it's the deepest hole in the world by a long way. The idea was originally to find out more about the earth's core. That piece in your hand came from 11.4 kilometres below the earth's surface.'

I handled it with awe, taking in its density, the fineness of the grain, the subtle tones of the grey veins, and wondering in my ignorance about radioactive levels in the earth's core.

'It's called gabbro. Nothing special,' said Feliks, taking it from me and lobbing it into the drawer of his desk. 'You can find rock like that lying around on the ground almost anywhere near here. They say it's good for grave headstones.'

---

* In the late 1990s the Keyvy Ridge was increasingly prone to plunder. I regularly encountered large tracked vehicles that had made the hazardous journey to the interior across deep bogs in summer to bring back literally tons of booty. Particularly popular were the small staurolite crystals which at that time could easily be sold in bulk at about US$10 each.

In the mid-1990s the gold deposits north of the Keyvy Ridge between Voronye and Lake Kolmozero were targeted for commercial exploitation and this constituted a serious threat to the Peninsula's wilderness areas and to the reindeer herds. The venture was, however, put on hold: the price of gold declined, the rouble collapsed (August 1998), and the international business community was at the end of its tether with Russian corporate governance.

Old Nick's Wasteland

As soon as the extent of the apatite deposits in the Khibiny mountains had been confirmed and First Secretary Kirov had authorized funds and labour for the great project, Soviet geologists were busy looking elsewhere in the region for exploitable mineral deposits. They had already found iron ore and magnetic rock in the tundra and taiga to the north-west of Lake Imandra where the Babinsky Saami fished in summer; and then, in June 1930, the geographer Gavril Rikhter showed Fersman specimens of sulphide ore with copper and nickel patches that he had found in a spot on the west bank of Lake Imandra, known to his Saami boatmen as *Monche guba*, Beautiful Bay. Copper-nickel ore, known since the eighteenth century as Old Nick's Copper, was still at the time notoriously difficult to prospect successfully, but Fersman, with characteristic professional flare and self-confidence, evaluated the deposit as potentially exploitable. Events moved ahead swiftly. Scientists, mining engineers and labourers came from Khibiny to Monche Bay, living in tents and huts just as they had done at Khibinogorsk, and survey work started on a big scale.

With the newly developed separation and refining processes entering the industrial picture, nickel was becoming increasingly valued not just for its corrosion resistance, its high ductility and many useful electronic properties but particularly as a constituent in the new high-strength steel alloys. These alloys, which later became known as super-alloys, were already fundamentally influencing the design and manufacture of tanks, guns, ammunition, naval vessels, submarines, spacecraft, missiles, and the entire aircraft industry. The rock lying underneath the bogs and forests of Monche was a vital new potential component in the Soviet Union's growing military capability.

By 1935 a few large wooden buildings with pitched roofs, quaintly known as *kotedzhy*, from the English, and sited near one of the smaller lakes, housed the offices of the new mining and smelting enterprise called Severonikel, Northern Nickel. The town of Monchegorsk was born.

My bus journey from Apatity to Monchegorsk lasted about two hours. As we drew away from the Khibiny range and crossed the bridge over the narrow Yekostrov strait to the west side of Lake Imandra to make our way north, the undulating mountains and forest gave way to open rolling taiga and bog. After one and a half hours, some 30 kilometres short of our destination, I began to notice how the spruces and pines seemed fewer and smaller – I would anyway have expected this as we moved north – but, as we travelled further and as if on cue, a mutation of sorts was happening. A few conifers here and there seemed to have atrophied, but soon I saw many more in the same condition. And then, after only a short distance, most were little more than dark skeletons, stripped bare of foliage, leaning ready to fall. After that, except for isolated standings on a few hill-sides, all the trees had been reduced to stumps, as if a fire had swept through the land two or three years earlier. Between the charred trees and stumps the soil surface was exposed, revealing grey moraine sand and rock, uncharacteristically bare of lichen. On lower ground the bog had lost colour and texture; there was no variety of mosses and berry foliage. In certain light the streams appeared tinged with an unnatural sheen, the tarns lacklustre. I was reminded immediately of photographs and paintings of the 1914–18 battlefields. And this was perhaps how a nuclear test would leave the landscape: not mortally wounded, not dead, just lifeless. And for some distance I had seen no birds, not even the ubiquitous hooded crow.

At first I didn't notice the slagheaps. They were far removed from my own experience of their diminutive English equivalents, nowadays often reclaimed, reshaped and replanted. The Monchegorsk slagheaps were so large and had blended and fused with the grey haze so imperceptibly that at first I assumed them to be hills, not the huge man-made extensions of the landscape that I now realized them to be. After the initial shock of scale I consoled myself with the thought that the nickel mines of Canada's INCO, the International Nickel Company of Sudbury, Ontario, were on a similar scale.

The bus turned off the main road towards the town. I had a good view of the nickel-smelting works to my right. Spread across a plain below the snow-covered hills of Monche Tundra was an assortment of large, low buildings and a prominent parade of twenty chimneys of varying size, half of them smoking. Even from a distance, the appearance of the ensemble was overwhelmingly one of disorder and desuetude. The small lakes in the foreground were grimy and polluted.

The town of Monchegorsk was as ruthlessly self-promotional as any town in the world that has either nothing to offer or everything to hide. 'Reputed to be the most beautiful town on the Kola Peninsula,' one brochure had promised, but this beauty had escaped me so far, and the wide boulevards lined with rowan and birch did little to alleviate the ambient sterility. I walked into the main square and towards the Cultural Centre, but had the sense of being nowhere in particular, as if the town's heart had been inappropriately and irrevocably sited too early in the planning process. The Cultural Centre was an optimistic Soviet building of the 1950s with large concourses and grand interior staircases; on the day of my visit it had transformed into a trading hall for bric-a-brac stallholders.

A taxi-driver, surprisingly unaccustomed to foreigners, responded enthusiastically to my request for a tour. In time it was his enthusiasm alone that cheered me. We looked at lakeside sculptures of miners gazing at mineral-rich hills, heroes of the Great Patriotic War, and finally at a large Orthodox church under construction. It was, of course, to have a copper dome.

I wanted to make a tour of the Severonikel works, so we drove to the main gates that I had seen from the bus and went into the guardhouse. We soon conceded defeat. Realizing I was a foreigner, the duty manager rolled his eyes and the security chief apologized profusely: 'Sorry, the answer is no. Each time we allow a foreigner or an environmentalist near us they give us trouble. Now we stop you at the gate. All you ever do is write bad things.'

We had indeed written 'bad things'. The environmental destruction caused by Monchegorsk's nickel-processing plants had long been of concern to the Norwegians and Finns, who had suffered airborne pollution since the 1940s. After glasnost, when the region was exposed internationally to physicians, biologists and metallurgists, the full horror of the biological and human damage was broadcast to the world. Sensational stories appeared in the press at the time, and authoritative scientific articles have appeared regularly ever since.

In the late 1930s Monchegorsk was joined by a new processing plant at Nikel and, in the 1950s, by a mine at Zapolyarny, both in the north-west of the oblast. All three, together with the major mines and plants at Norilsk (west Siberia), became part of the metals combine known as Norilsk Nikel with an output equivalent to twenty per cent of world demand for nickel. Given the combine's national importance during the Second World War, and then the Cold War and the years of the space race, as well as its ability to earn hard currency, the drive for increased production was relentless from the start. Production targets became the only priorities. In consequence the industry enjoyed fifty years of arm's-length state control and a completely free hand in the management of the smelting and refining works themselves. For fifty years bosses resorted routinely to technological short cuts, consistently ignoring normal industrial practice relating to environmental matters, regarding health and safety in the workplace more in terms of remedy than prophylaxis. The Norilsk Nikel Combine was responsible for emitting into the atmosphere such high levels of heavy metals and noxious gases, and over such a long term, that almost all plant life over very large tracts of land and water was destroyed. The Murmansk Oblast smelters alone contaminated thousands of square kilometres in Finland, Sweden and Norway, well beyond Russia's own border. In 1983, a year generally acknowledged to have seen peak production, the smelters at Monchegorsk and Nikel emitted into the atmosphere over 900,000 tonnes of polluting substances, including some 700,000 tonnes of sulphur dioxide and up to 50,000 tonnes of heavy metals including nickel, copper, cobalt and lead. With regard to terrestrial and water damages, the consensus was that regeneration would require many decades. Even if production were to have ceased immediately, lichens might recover within thirty years but full coniferous growth in the northern climate would require a century or more.

Leaving aside the methods that were employed in the first place to force labourers and prisoners to build and service Monchegorsk's industry and town during the 1930s and 1940s, the human cost over fifty years was considerable. Statistics and reports published during the 1990s by international environmental agencies are almost unbelievable indictments. The Monchegorsk community was exposed for so long to the plant's toxic emissions that the proportion calculated to have suffered directly associated diseases and chronic symptoms was thought to be unprecedented outside the Third World.

During the 1990s the effects of the drop in world demand for nickel, the fall-off in military orders, and the complete absence of capital, meant a dramatic reduction in output. This in turn caused hardship to the communities entirely dependent on the fortunes of the industry. Unable to find alternative employment in their own town, families had nowhere to go; second- and third-generation labour migrants or descendants of 'special settlers', many of whom had few or no relatives remaining in other parts of the former Soviet Union, were even less favourably placed. 'Who wants us now?' is a remark I often heard during the 1990s.

The nadir of Norilsk Nikel's fortunes came in 1993 when the combine's output fell by over 20 per cent. Whereas this news was at first greeted by environmentalists with jubilation because it would bring respite to the affected lands, surveys showed that the slowdown resulted in *no significant reduction in harmful emissions*. During the ten years from 1983 to 1993 the plant's machinery had simply become less efficient. The gas purifiers, most of which had not been renewed since the early 1970s, were ineffective and in many cases had been abandoned altogether. These factors, combined with laxity in technological procedures and incident reporting, meant that pollution had proceeded as usual.

I was disappointed to miss seeing the giant ore-crushers, the matte flotation chambers, the smelting and roasting shops, the electrolysis workshops and the giant baths of sulphuric acid at the Severonikel works. My driver tried to cheer me up: 'Our next stop is the Prophylactic Centre,' he announced. The health centre, which sat amongst trees on the outskirts of town, had been built by the combine in the 1960s. Once past the reception desk I was in a time warp: Soviet Russia of the post-war years. In the corridors I was greeted cheerfully by cleaning women and nurses in white tunics and tall white headgear, the likes of which I had previously seen only in old illustrated Soviet brochures. The 'prophylactic chambers' were a bewildering assortment of rooms for sauna, hot and cold pools, physiotherapy, massage and recuperation, all of them of the original design. The humidity, which I found almost overpowering, had at least stimulated the Centre's ubiquitous and well-tended plant collection into rampant growth.

'These days we're less busy,' I was told, 'That's because some payment is now usually required.' There were certainly few patients in evidence but, since I was so rarely given full answers to questions, I didn't pursue the topic.

Planners had sited the town according to the prevailing winds. During my time at Monchegorsk the brisk breeze blowing over the water fortunately came from the north-east, placing the town upwind of the smelters. If the wind came from the south-west, everyone did their best to stay at home with windows firmly closed against the noxious smog. Parents kept children indoors during the 'poison days' but, even so, the children's hospitals were always overcrowded in the weeks that followed the unfavourable winds and children's respiratory diseases here lasted twice the Russian average.

There were days in the year, for example, when it was almost impossible to stay out of doors for more than two or three hours; peoples' lungs were unable to cope with the smog and dust coming from the works, and once the coughing started it persisted. The adult mortality rate had increased since the 1980s, as had cardiac complaints, and, in addition to the high incidence of oncological and endocrine diseases, there was recent evidence that emissions caused response changes in the immune system.

I found some of Monchegorsk's older residents cavalier about their own or their family's health. They had worked hard for decades, they pointed out, with barely a visit to a hospital or a day off sick. Families were now exposed to Western standards and had grown soft. Others insisted that all the trouble had started when ore matte began to be transported from the mines at Norilsk in Siberia for processing at Monchegorsk.

'The pollution used not to be bad,' an older employee told me, 'until they started taking ore from Norilsk. The Norilsk ore has a sulphur content six times higher than our local ore. That's why the landscape got so destroyed.'

On the other hand, one reliable source told me of children living near the smelter works who suffered severe brain damage even during the very first years of smelting in the 1940s. 'Many were dysfunctional by the age of five,' she said.

*

One cold spring morning two years after my first visit to Monchegorsk I was able to take the bus – a four-hour journey – from Murmansk to Nikel and Zapolyarny, an area that had hitherto been closed to foreigners.* As we approached the frontier with Norway we entered the militarized zone. Barracks and armoured vehicle bases were visible from the road. Tanks, trucks and APCs sat in their hundreds near gimcrack sheds built from grey cement blocks. A young border guard who had stopped the bus was checking documentation. He looked pale and undernourished. At the next junction in the road a woman stepped off the bus. Dressed in a long pink woollen coat and a silver-fox-fur hat, she walked over the dirty, melting snow, treading carefully in white ankle boots, moving towards the distant barracks like a mannequin, a sartorially exquisite phantom floating through a brutish landscape.

For a further hour the road from Zapolyarny ran a gauntlet through despoliation and man-made hills before emerging above the valley of Nikel town. A thin, yellowish chemical smog that I knew to be a noxious cocktail of sulphide gases and heavy metal particles was drifting westwards towards the Norwegian tundra.

As the road curved down to the level of the lake and then up towards the town we passed several acres of allotments. People were making their way there in cheerful groups, carrying gardening tools over their shoulders, probably to work the soil for the first time since the spring thaw in anticipation of an early planting of vegetables. Even in Nikel's damaged countryside the people of the Motherland cherished their special relationship with Mother Nature.

'We have excellent berries here,' remarked a hearty Zapolyarny woman on the bus. I thought she was joking until she continued:

* Nikel (founded in 1940, population under 20,000 in 2001) and the neighbouring Zapolyarny (founded in 1955, population about 15,000 in 2001) are home to Pechenganikel, Murmansk Oblast's other division of the Norilsk Nikel combine. Zapolyarny still operates a mine, whereas the more accessible strata at Nikel have been exhausted.

'I've been picking and eating our cloudberries and bilberries for years. So have my children. We're fit.' To this day I can't believe she wasn't joking.

Nikel town was dominated by the smelter. The sulphurous gases caught my nose and throat when I stepped out of the bus. As I walked east up the hill, the chimney stacks seemed to get taller and taller. When I reached the brow and was confronted by the huge old works busily huffing and roaring, puffing and belching, I felt I was being drawn into the mouth of Beelzebub. I wandered around the town for some hours until the evening when, thoroughly distempered, I caught the return bus to Murmansk.

In the early 1990s, notwithstanding the scenario of reduced outputs, old technologies, decaying machinery, health problems, and unpaid workers looking to leave, the whole Norilsk Nikel Group continued to be viable and to earn much-needed foreign currency. But from all that I heard and read, it was suffering at the hands of its directors and senior managers; they were apparently more interested in building ancillary business empires and advancing their own financial or political careers than in planning a commercially viable and environmentally acceptable future for their industry and its communities.

In those post-privatization years, however, when it seemed to outsiders and employees as if managerial negligence and lack of funds would result in the closure of the plants at Nikel, Zapolyarny and Monchegorsk within ten years, the combine was imperceptibly falling into the capable hands of the oilman-banker oligarch Vladimir Potanin. Potanin and others of his breed like the media tycoon Boris Berezovsky, oil magnate Roman Abramovich of Sibneft, or Vladimir Guzinsky of Media Most, had begun to wield the real power in Russia during the mid-1990s, bringing influence to bear on government with their business acumen and access to international capital. Working through his own Uneximbank – and for a risible sum – Potanin secured a controlling interest in the entire Norilsk Group. When the world market for nickel unexpectedly sprang into life in 1999, the group reported doubled profits within a year and Potanin finessed. In 2000 he orchestrated a brilliant, prehensile restructuring of the group, marginalizing shareholders, securing more capital, increasing output, and securing greater control. Potanin's only obligation to government was to invest, and this he happily did. During 2000 the Group earmarked $350 million to reanimate the plants and to open a new mine at Zapolyarny. Employees rejoiced – full-capacity operation looked like being guaranteed for a further thirty years; environmentalists despaired. Little of any substance was said about emissions. In that respect it looked as if it would continue to be business as usual.

Return to barracks

'Up on top, Roger. That's where the men sit.'

I flinched. Valentin's remark sounded like an order. Sasha, our driver, had repaired the vehicle on to which I now had to climb, catching shins on sharp edges. The thought of spending each day 'up on top' alarmed me. I was prepared for machismo, but it was the middle of October and the average daily temperature was already three degrees Celsius. It could turn cold.

Our expedition transport had an aggressive look about it. I had never ridden a GTT. The Russians called them *vezdekhody* – 'go-everywheres'. What I was climbing was a large track-laying armoured personnel carrier, exactly like a tank but without the gun-turret. If one had no qualms about ploughing bog and virgin terrain, destroying every shrub, bush and tree in the way, and shattering the peace of the forest with the roar of large petrol engines, these all-terrain, ex-Army monsters were ideal for moving through the wilderness. Reindeer-herding collectives sometimes used a *vezdekhod* to monitor herds in summer. Thus do traditional lifestyles evolve.

The previous day I had no idea I would be on the outing. I was in the warm office of Apatity Museum historian Yevgeniya Yakovlevna Patsiya, learning about the Saami over a cup of tea – as museum curators are widely imagined to spend their working days – when Yevgeniya was called away from her desk. She stood in the corridor talking quietly for ten minutes with a woman wearing heavy-duty forestry clothing and a large fur hat. Returning to the office with her visitor, Yevgeniya introduced us.

'Roger, this is Galina Bodrova. Galina is about to leave on expedition and can take you with her. There'll be four others. You'll be gone for a week or more. In my opinion, this is an opportunity you shouldn't miss.'

Looking at her several layers of expedition clothing I could judge little about Galina except that she was of medium height, aged between twenty-five and fifty, and had hazel Slavic eyes. When she began to explain the aim of the expedition and tell me about Memorial, the sponsoring organization, I could judge that she was professionally disciplined and well-educated.

Memorial, she said, was a national network dedicated to gathering information about the regime that used to exist under the Chief Administration for Corrective Labour Camps – the Gulag – by recording sites, dates and personal details of individuals who were imprisoned or who perished under the system. Such a network had already existed informally, but glasnost had enabled the whole network to begin to function publicly and internationally; the north-west branch of Memorial, based in Apatity and Kirovsk, could now actively research the camps of Murmansk Oblast. Having learned from Yevgeniya Yakovlevna about my historical interests, Galina had agreed to take me along, presumably on the basis that the participation of a foreigner might lend extra relevance to the expedition.

At that time Memorial was particularly interested in the Soviet Interior Ministry's works project No. 509, started in the 1950s, to construct a railway line across the centre of the Kola Peninsula to the east and north-east coasts. Up to that time the lines that branched east from the main Leningrad-Murmansk October Railway ran only to Kirovsk (to Fersman's Khibiny mines, and to nearby Revda). The newly expanded Northern Fleet and the bases planned for construction at Holy Cape (Gremikha) and at the Ponoy estuary were to be connected by railway to the Murmansk line and thus to the whole of the Soviet south; the movement of ordnance, fuel and personnel would no longer be limited to seaborne transport.

The camps, or barracks, for the forced labourers were strung out at regular intervals along the projected route, which ran through bog and forest towards the Bolshiye Keyvy Ridge at the centre of the Peninsula, an area which used to be occupied by eastern Saami families in winter. Building progress was extraordinarily slow – the Soviet government never acknowledged the inefficiency of forced labour – and in the 1960s, when numbers in the gulag were greatly reduced, the project ground to a halt. Only half of the route's earthworks had been completed when everyone was said to have walked free. Memorial wanted the barracks to be recorded, photographed and filmed before they rotted and disappeared into the undergrowth.

Galina's timely arrival at the museum coincided with my curiosity about the contribution of forced labour to the development of the whole region in the Soviet years. Given the time available and my relatively limited command of Russian I had been finding it a diffi-cult task. A Lovozero woman in her fifties had denied several times that there had been prison camps in her district (there were several), archival material had been withheld from me, and the Murmansk Museum had only two small display items devoted to the subject. In time I learned that Murmansk Oblast owed at least its early industrial development entirely to forced labour, and today I know of thirty camps that used to be within its borders.

Our expedition comprised leader Galina, an Apatity-based jour-nalist, Vadim, an unfit, overweight retired builder, Mikhail the video cameraman and Sergey the photographer, both in their late twenties, Sasha, a thirty-five-year-old train-driver from Kirovsk, accompanied by his laika dog Lapka, and myself, with little to offer apart from broken Russian and a rucksack hurriedly packed with *kolbasa* and vodka. In addition we would pick up a forester to guide us.

Within three hours we had left the town, travelling the first leg of our journey in an all-terrain UAZ truck from the Science Centre. At dusk we were stuck fast. Crossing a large bog we had broken through the rotten logs of the old road and sunk into the black ooze below. No amount of levering or canterlevering of tree trunks would move our vehicle forward, and we were at least ten kilometres from where we had planned to collect the GTT and spend our first night before proceeding into the interior. It was not a promising start but we were in good spirits. Sasha, who was to drive the GTT, volunteered to walk ahead, return with the vehicle and tow us out. The rest of us stayed behind, sitting in the half-submerged truck, chatting and smoking, looking out across the wetlands illuminated far and wide by the full moon. One by one we fell asleep, with Vadim in the front snoring loudly.

At two o'clock in the morning the headlights of the *vezdekhod* emerged from the distant forest. Sasha made short work of hauling our truck across the bog, and within the hour we had arrived at the wooden house of the man who was to be our guide. Valentin came out to greet us. He was in his sixties, a large man-of-the-wild, quiet and gentle-mannered with deep-set eyes, generous eyebrows and an ample moustache. I liked him immediately, preferring his calmness to the boisterous behaviour of our team. He introduced his wife Zhanna, a handsome woman of around fifty, who seemed urbane and refined for one who spent most of her time in the forest alone with her husband and a pack of dogs. Valentin had formerly worked as a heavy machinery mechanic for the mining combine in Kirovsk; Zhanna had been a crane-driver but a bad injury had prompted her and Valentin to take the forestry job.

Our home for what remained of the night was the scrag-end of a hut. Built to house forestry gangs, it had an ill-used appearance and its barrel roof and tin chimney made it look appropriately like a converted railway carriage, but we were tired and the night was bitterly cold, and once the stove had taken and the candles were lit, it acquired a more congenial atmosphere.

In spite of the hour, a meal was soon in preparation. Galina had cooked a substantial urn of soup in advance and most of it disappeared quickly. Much of what I thought of as my large holding of sausage was also consumed, together with two large loaves of bread, some slabs of cheese and plenty of raw garlic and onions. Vodka flowed, and the empty bottles rolled from under the table. Even taking into account the ample amount of food we had loaded, I estimated we would be running short by day three.

I was somewhat apprehensive about the expedition. Spending days with strangers on top of a *vezdekhod* and nights in close proximity in small huts requires certain compatibilities. Galina, our leader, was understandably anxious that the expedition should be a disciplined affair; she therefore tended to be on edge or give orders at ill-chosen moments. At first I thought Vadim's role was senior historian or labour-camp eye-witness, but I came to the conclusion that he was just in it for the ride, the food and the drink. Our video cameraman Mikhail was polite, conscientious and good at his work; Sergey the photographer was unaccustomed to taking instructions from a woman. Sasha, our driver, was good-natured and boisterous but seemed likely to take control at some point.

I was as usual having difficulty understanding conversation around the table; I was also irritated with myself that I had never learned any jokes, *anekdoty*, in Russian. Fortunately my companions were quickly resigned to my shortcomings, and we reached an understanding: when I failed to follow a topic they left it to me to ask for explanations.

I climbed on to my bunk shelf, crawled into my bag, and fell asleep to the sounds of Sasha entertaining the others.

I was the first to wake in the morning. Overcome by the heat from the stove and the stifling odour of bodies and socks, I went outside. A walk through the woods took me to the bank of a short river which ran between two lakes. I chose the picturesque and inviting spot for my morning ablutions and, with autumn's first snow-flakes drifting out of a leaden sky, plunged into the refreshingly cold water, allowing the current to sweep me downstream into the lower lake.

When I returned I found only Galina up and about. She was fussing over the delay; we had far to go and it looked like being a long wait for the others. After the late breakfast Valentin came over from his house and we loaded the vehicle.

The engine of the *vezdekhod* roared into life, coughing clouds of dense black smoke. Valentin shouted to me over the noise: 'Up on top, Roger . . .'

We moved off down the forest track, 'men on top'. Near me were Mikhail and Sergey with the cameras. Valentin sat over the cockpit, a gun on his lap, wrapped in several pullovers underneath a woollen *sovik* topped by a sleeveless leather jerkin and a long waterproof over-jacket. When he turned around periodically to check on me, his bonnet, pulled down to the eyes, showed only his prominent nose and his moustache above a broad grin. What was the gun for? Were we expecting bears?

Everybody seemed settled but I had no idea how I was going to prevent myself from freezing to death or being thrown from my seat. There was nothing to hold on to. The fumes from the ventilator were flying into my face, but our 'tank' was remarkable. Within a few kilo-metres it had already proved itself across a variety of terrains. Each of the two vehicle track belts was controlled by levers held by the driver in either hand and pulled or pushed for the desired direction. Sasha looked competent. He certainly had the muscles for the job.

In the late afternoon we were following a broad sand track through forest with a richly varicoloured ground cover when Valentin yelled an order to Sasha in the cockpit. We abruptly turned right on to a narrow path cut straight through the trees. Ahead of us I could see the remains of tall wooden gate-posts leaning at an angle; nearby were the fallen doors, rotting in grass amidst rolls of rusted barbed wire. We rolled on slowly through the camp entrance. Stretching into the forest to our right and left were the perimeter fences, mostly now collapsed. They ran in two stages: an inner fence to head height and an outer fence four metres high with about twenty strands of wire, closer together towards ground level. The vehicle stopped in a clearing and we jumped down on to the soft forest floor. The respite from the engine noise was welcome, the quiet almost tangible.

In all directions, camouflaged by lichens, mosses and shrubs, were the remains of the barracks. The walls had collapsed so that each building was no more that a pile of its parts, lying as they had fallen. It was difficult to determine the function of each building but there were still gable ends, foundations, drains, latrine ditches, and the rock and rubble bases of stoves. I made a guess at one pile of timber as against another: here could have been kitchens, there a workshop of sorts, there a dormitory. The roof coverings were made from small, finely sliced shingles of pine, held in position by tingles. The delicacy of the shingles and the skill with which the roofs had been laid were in striking contrast to the crude concrete architecture that we had left behind.

There seemed to be little method or programme to our visit. I wandered alone. Galina talked into a dictaphone as she walked, Mikhail took stills, Sergey explored with his camera in and around every building and ditch. Sasha and Valentin seemed to be doing what I was doing: gazing, contemplating the significance of the place.

I lifted beams and roof fragments, kicking debris aside. My foot made a dull clanking sound as it hit metal. From under the leaf mould I lifted a shallow dish – aluminium, about twenty centimetres in diameter, standard issue for every *zek*, or prisoner. It was oxidized. I cleaned it with grass and took it with me, feeling a little uneasy about my acquisition.

Galina came towards me, talking into her machine. 'How many

prisoners were there here, do you think?' I asked. She reckoned about one and a half thousand.

'Quite a few will have got away,' she added. 'It's only eighty kilometres to the main railway, the escape route to the south. That's why the camp was heavily guarded and fenced. The camps further east into the Bolshiye Keyvy have no wire; it was unlikely anybody could have found their way or been fit enough to survive the distance.'

Just outside the camp entrance were the remains of a guardhouse and several guards' buildings, more commodious than the other buildings and less like sheds. Just inside the perimeter fence Galina and I found the remains of a small hut that on closer scrutiny seemed to have been a solitary confinement cell, large enough for one person to stand but not to lie down. On the ground nearby was a steel door with an observation hole and a narrow food hatch. Not far from the camp perimeter there were signs of a common grave. I could imagine the long pit, the bodies covered by a thin layer of soil and lime, lost to families without trace or record. We bent down to pick the last of the season's bilberries which were everywhere, full of juice and sugar. Our fingers and mouths were stained black. The delicate birches and autumnal colours of the forest floor presented an idyllic backdrop to our grim historical scavenge.

The next leg of the journey took us through forest and out into the open undulating hills of the Bolshiye Keyvy Ridge. Everywhere there were huge rocks of snow-white quartz and green amazonite, a reminder of the mineral wealth of the area.

Then came our first major breakdown. The engine had been overheating and Sasha and Valentin had been regularly filling the water tank from streams, but eventually the engine flooded and the exhaust started to belch water and black fumes. The leak would have to be located. We made a fire by the side of the track for warmth and to boil a kettle. Sasha and Valentin raised the engine hatches and dismantled much of the upper engine. Piping had to be rebuilt and the main gasket repaired. It needed a few hours. Galina was upset; it was already late afternoon and darkness was due shortly.

We had plenty of food and plenty of vodka. Vadim spotted the opportunity and was soon tucking in; our mechanics stopped only for tea. Conversation eventually gravitated towards me. Vadim, reinforced by alcohol, wanted to know more about the Englishman. What kind of education did I have, how did I find employment after university, how much did I earn, had I inherited wealth, was I from a privileged family? Above all, what was I really doing in Russia, and why should I be allowed to roam and run with the reindeer? I assured him I was not allowed to go wherever I wanted, but the questioning continued. The more he probed, the more vociferous and pugnacious he became, screwing his piggy eyes at me, stabbing his finger, and plying me with more vodka to make me lose my patience. The others, seeing my discomfort, came to my help diplomatically, not by telling Vadim to leave me alone but by ostensibly accepting my answers.

The repair was completed after dark. Sasha had been intrigued by the headtorch which I lent him, and this gave him additional enthusiasm. By nine o'clock we were travelling on under bright moonlight, our stomachs warmed by vodka, with Vadim in his cups spreadeagled on top of our food and gear in the main cabin below.

Emerging from the pine forest, we looked south towards the crisp profile of the three-peak Pana Mountains against the night sky. We located a log cabin for the night. Standing in open tundra near a few scattered pines and low scrub, the cabin was a typical one-room *izba* with a small porch for shelter and storage. The north and east sides had been insulated with sheets of polythene.

'This hut was built last year by a young geologist,' said Valentin. 'For several seasons he pitched a tent but when he got married he built this for his bride.'

Inside the hut, smaller but more salubrious than the previous night's rendezvous, there was the same arrangement of wooden bunks, with a table under the window and a stove near the door. There was not room for all of us to sleep on the bunks; Valentin volunteered for the floor.

We were all awake and up by eight in the morning, and away within the hour. The barrack that we reached in mid-morning was in the depth of a spruce forest. We found a series of collapsed wooden buildings, standing on either side of the old track, with the same shingled roofs, the same foundations, ditches and mounds as at the previous site. Valentin said the camp would have held about 500 *zeki*. He claimed it was closed by the late 1950s 'after Stalin', but nobody ever wanted to admit to forced labour continuing after Stalin's death in 1953; the place had almost certainly been in use until the 1970s. The camp structures looked relatively fresh, the spruce saplings that now dominated the barrack area itself were no older than twenty years, and I found a green enamel mug which could be dated to the 1970s. Nearby I found a soup ladle, rubber clogs and two wheels from a small horse-cart.

Valentin showed me a contraption for making the roof shingles, a wooden workbench arrangement four or more metres square on stout legs. A large steel blade, hinged at one end, was drawn from side to side, guillotining the timber into fine slices as it was fed across the bench surface. The technique of making shingles must have been imported by prisoners from the south; it had never been employed elsewhere in the region. Planks, birch bark and turf had sufficed in the past for the roofs of log cabins in Russian Lapland.

A long track, overgrown with tall sedge grasses, stretched straight ahead through the undulating forest and into the far distance. It was a well preserved example of railway earthwork. The ghosts of many workgroups were still marching the track in convoy, escorted by armed guards and dog handlers.

We came into open country. The low snow-covered hills of the Keyvy Ridge were to our left, a large bog ahead. Our ship plunged and ploughed through the shivering floor which was not soft enough to sink us but required frequent reversing. The engine roared and screamed, black sods were flying, and parallel scars stretched into the distance behind us as we struggled to make headway. The two dogs, Sasha's Lapka and Valentin's older Vega, had followed us tirelessly all the way every day and were now enjoying the challenge of the bog. I looked back to see them sinking up to their necks, then swimming the streams to emerge slightly less black than when they had gone in. Lapka waited with unstinting loyalty for her slower older companion, even on the faster stretches when this often meant losing sight of us for an hour or two.

Much of our route had taken us parallel to the poles of the old trans-peninsular telephone cable. In the early evening of the next day we stopped at a substantial wooden cabin, built for telephone engineers but clearly also once a private home. There were small sheds near the cabin, and two fenced vegetable plots, now overgrown. The idyllic spot had been the most eastern point of the main railway work before the project petered out.

The cabin itself, which was slightly raised off the ground, had a full-length open porch, two bedrooms, and a central room dominated by a large, antiquated piece of telephone equipment looking like an electrical substation. Vadim was stringing dried fish on to a line across the room while Galina attended to the hot food. We settled in with glee. One of the bedrooms was for Galina, the remainder of us settled for the other, which had its own stove and a platform at knee height that ran the width of the room under the window and where we five men could sleep, side by side like sardines.

I awoke before dawn with a splitting headache from the heat of the stove, the lack of oxygen and the usual personal odours. I eased myself from the sardine pile and took myself outside, admiring once again the lichen shimmering almost white under the last of the night's moonlight before putting my sleeping bag down outside on the floor of the porch.

At dawn Valentin's dog Vega was standing over me, squeaking impatiently. I dressed and walked with her towards the river. The cabin stood on raised ground above a sharp bend in the Kulyok, a small tributary of the Ponoy, bordered by pines and birches. Wooden steps, now decayed, led down to the river bank and on to a small platform for filling water buckets.

I came across earthwork remains of the original gulag barrack foundations, as well as some beams and other building materials half buried by lichen and moss. Little remained of the series of prison huts that had once lined the river bank. I was beginning to sense the scale of suffering and death, and the hugely disproportionate effort, that had gone into this relatively small railway engineering task as it had for over half a century into the hundreds of forced labour projects across the width of the Soviet empire. In the early sun and the freshness of our surroundings, however, watching snow-bunting and waxwing moving busily in the trees, and mergansers, scaups and dippers on the river, I found it hard to imagine the misery of barrack life.

We turned for home, travelling longer distances, visiting a few more camps, photographing and filming. To Galina's irritation Sergey considered his work finished and had borrowed Sasha's shotgun. When we sighted ptarmigan or capercaillie Sergey yelled to Sasha to stop the *vezdekhod*, jumped down and made for the forest at speed before slowing to tip-toe stalking pace, gun at the ready, a most unconvincing huntsman. There was always a ten-minute silence before we heard two shots, followed by a pause and another empty-ing of barrels, after which Sergey reappeared. I would not have wanted to entrust the killing or catching of my supper to him. Valentin was noticeably silent.

'They flew off, did they?' we asked routinely.

7

COLD FRONTS

Ignoble and heroic wars

W E WERE TRAVELLING so fast that for the first time ever I was truly afraid for my life. I wondered breathlessly for whom the accident was going to be fatal. We had just glanced someone or something at speed, but Sasha was determined to make a seamless journey from the centre of Murmansk to his home in the northern suburbs. Traffic lights were ignored.

I had placed myself blindly in the hands of a chance acquaintance and his companion – also called Sasha – who had invited me to join them on a fishing expedition along two of the rivers that flowed to the north-west coast. I had immediately been interested to go, not only because that particular area of the closed coastal zone required an all-terrain vehicle, but because the rivers – the West Litsa in particular – had at one time played an important role in the region's history.

For three years of the Second World War, from 1941 to 1944, the West Litsa River of north-west Russian Lapland marked the right flank of the Soviets' northern front with Germany. During three years of almost unimaginable suffering and loss of life the 500-kilometre stretch from the Barents Sea through Kandalaksha to Northern Karelia was the only line along Russia's entire Second World War front with Germany – from the Arctic to the Black Sea – that held firm for the whole three years between Hitler's invasion of the Soviet Union in June 1941 and his retreat in 1944. I wanted to pay tribute to this outstandingly heroic yet little-known battle-ground.

There was another twentieth-century point of interest: these rivers, with their fjord-like estuaries, were home to some of the Northern Fleet's newest nuclear-powered submarines. I had already seen a little of the north-west military seaboard when I explored the former summer territory of the Skolt Saami at the Titovka estuary. Here was an opportunity for me to complete the picture.

Sasha's apartment block, for which we were heading at such suicidal speed before setting off on our expedition, was amongst a group of nine-storey concrete buildings of more than usual ugliness in the heart of Rosta, the naval neighbourhood that stood on high ground overlooking the shipyards of Murmansk. The approach was across ground that looked as if it were pitted with mortar-shell craters. We slowed down, and advanced through waves of gleeful children and dogs, football matches and mock gun battles.

The staircase and lift in Sasha's building were just as wrecked as the external approaches. His wife greeted us with the long-suffering expression of married partners world-wide. Over a generous meal of beef, chicken, salmon and vodka I learned a little about the family. Sasha, of Armenian extraction, was *na pensiye*, a pensioner at the age of forty, although I failed to ascertain from what work he had been pensioned. As he glibly expressed it, he had now gone 'into commerce'. His four other brothers and two sisters lived in the States and the UK, one of the sisters having recently married 'a banker'. Sasha and his wider family apparently enjoyed a certain wealth although, as we conversed, I recognized the responses of someone experienced in glossing over details.

Our departure for the hunting grounds was convoluted, requiring further stops at eight houses after leaving Rosta. We had transferred into a red truck with large tyres – Sasha had hurled in his fishing tackle as if it were so much scrap metal – and men came out of the houses where we stopped, as if they had been waiting for us. Other men got in and out of the truck, packets were exchanged for money but the talk and the banter was of salmon.

The Kola Gulf's only bridge is twelve kilometres upstream of Murmansk, at Kola town, at the confluence of the Kola and Tuloma rivers. As Sasha's truck rattled noisily over the old bridge and we headed west into the night sun I was hoping that the two-hour expedition preamble was at an end. In the back of the truck now was the other Sasha – blond Sasha – and a man called Valery who said he was 'not interested in fishing'.

After the bridge we motored uphill and on to high ground overlooking the Gulf. Seen from the warm sitting room of a tall apartment on the other side of the water, the west bank tundra land-scape always looked dramatic, but at close quarters it became progressively more bleak as we travelled west, no less awesome now in June than when I had last seen it in late autumn under a dusting of snow. On one or two of the distant hills I could see masts and radar surveillance installations.

'We're on our way now. You'll soon be at the salmon, Roger. The spring run is on,' roared Sasha over the noise of the engine. We were stopped at two military checkpoints on the way but the soldiers, guessing we were locals on our way to the rivers, seemed interested more in driving licences than in passports. After two hours we turned off the road and headed north.

We stopped among trees a short walk from the Litsa. Within a few moments Sasha had changed clothing and assembled his tackle from the tangle on the floor of the truck; judging by the size of his gaff he was expecting large fish. As I busied myself with the necessarily lengthy procedure of assembling my three-piece rod – purchased at some expense from Messrs Farlow of Pall Mall – mounting one of two reels, preparing the line, sorting out my box of flies, and then struggling into a pair of green rubber chest-waders and putting on my English cap, the others looked on, exchanging a flow of remarks and jokes at my expense. I couldn't follow, but I caught the mockery of the words *angliysky dzhentelman*.

It was a clear evening with a bitter north wind blowing up the river. Not a single salmon rose to my fly. After three hours I gave up and sat down on the bank shivering, my knees drawn up into the cape I had borrowed from Sasha, consoling myself with the fattest cigarette I could roll. Sasha was relentlessly targeting the top of a long steep rapid, hoping to catch the eye of a salmon as it arrived and rested in quieter water. When I saw that he had hooked a fish, I ran downstream, happy to abandon my own efforts and bathe in his reflected glory. The fight lasted a full twenty minutes. The fish ran for sea, back into the fast water. Prevented from returning down the rapid, it used the shelter of large rocks. Sasha had confidence in his thick nylon line and large hook to use plenty of strength but the beast proved difficult to move into the open. Sasha waded into the water, filling his thigh boots as he slipped and stumbled. When it began to tire, the salmon showed itself and came upstream leaping and thrashing, a mighty cock fish. When it finally succumbed to the pressure of Sasha's line and came in short, I watched the gaff smash into the silver body. Blood poured from the gills as it lay gasping on the bank well back from the water. Valery and blond Sasha, who had disappeared shortly after we reached the water, arrived for the kill as if from nowhere, threw the fish into a sack and vanished again.

'It's a magnificent fish you've caught,' I said, having stroked all one and a half metres of its heaving side. Sasha's only response was that my salmon flies were 'a complete waste of time'.

'The trouble with you, Roger, is that you're all detail. And being British, you have a different sense of scale from us Russians.' At nine o'clock the following morning Sasha and I were stretched out in front of a warm birchwood fire finishing our breakfast. We had spent the last hour discussing not the shortcomings of my fishing methods but the Second World War. Sasha was finding my interpretation of certain causes and events less than satisfactory.

'You had it easy in the War – I mean the British and the Americans. You didn't lose the millions that we did, and you weren't invaded. Russians will never forget how the Germans swarmed over our borders in June 1941. Right here, along the banks of the West Litsa alone, between 1941 and 1944, hundreds of thousands of our men were killed in action or froze to death.'

Walking along the banks of the Litsa with our fishing rods, Sasha had already shown me evidence of the three years of armed struggle: barbed wire, cable, metal fragments, gun parts, spent shells, shattered pieces of vehicles and tanks, and the overgrown remains of trenches. The very road that we had taken from Murmansk was built to bring men and arms here to the battlegrounds of the Red Army's far northern flank.

When Operation Barbarossa swept the Axis divisions into Russia on the morning of 22 June 1941, the tundra near Pechenga/Petsamo in the north-west corner of Murmansk Oblast, and the forests and lakes west of Kandalaksha to the south, were bristling with German, Austrian and Finnish troops and armour.

What Sasha had objected to was my insistence on discussing the sequence of events that had led up to this treacherous volte-face on the part of Hitler. As I tried to explain to Sasha, the world had been equally astonished by the Soviet Union's own treachery during the two years prior to the German invasion. The shock of Operation Barbarossa was particularly ironic in the context of far north-west Russia.

During the two years before the German invasion, the Soviets had themselves been engaged in violating the lands and lives of other nations. They had occupied eastern Poland in September 1939, concluded a secret protocol with the Germans to secure Lithuania within the Soviet sphere of influence, and then moved to constrain all three Baltic States to admit Soviet garrisons. Finland had refused to comply with similar demands and new territorial claims by the Soviets, and mobilized along the length of the border with Russia. On 28 November 1939 Stalin invaded Finland.

The Winter War – sometimes also known by Russians as the Border Campaign – is a bleak chapter in the history of the Soviet Union and its Red Army which most informed Russians prefer to forget. Among my own Russian acquaintances I never found anyone over the age of fifty willing to discuss the events with me, and almost nobody under the age of fifty who knew much about them. At any rate the war ended in a costly victory for the Soviets: half a million men spent four months fighting; of the 3,200 Russian tanks dispatched, the Finns captured or destroyed 1,600; of the thousands of Russian planes that flew, over 900 were shot down. At least 200,000 Soviet troops lost their lives, an astonishing total when compared with Finland's 25,000 killed or missing.

After the fall of Smolensk in July 1941 the Germans were predicting a sweep through Murmansk, Leningrad, Moscow and Stalingrad within a matter of weeks. Hitler already held the Baltic. He knew that if Murmansk were to fall, Archangel would follow, and the Barents and White Seas would come within Germany's control. If Kandalaksha, 100 kilometres to the south of Murmansk, could also be taken, a German advance to Moscow and Leningrad would be assured.

But that was not to be. On the far northern front – or Karelian Front, as it was widely known – Pechenga/Petsamo, with its valuable new nickel mine and smelter, was overrun just as easily as it had been by the Soviets in the winter of 1939 going in the other direction but, much to everyone's surprise, the German advance of 1941 was stopped 100 kilometres west of Kandalaksha and also at the banks of the West Litsa – where I now found myself – 80 kilometres short of the cherished goals of Murmansk port and the October Railway line to Leningrad. Hitler's Norway Army, under the overall command of General Falkenhorst, initially outnumbered the Soviet 14th Army by two to one, with massive superiority in the air, but, in spite of three early concerted assaults in 1941, the line between Kandalaksha and Litsa miraculously held firm.

The absence of tanks may have been a greater disadvantage to the Germans than to the Soviets. The Germans had been relying on tanks to push them through to Murmansk and Kandalaksha, but they were soon found to be next to useless in the steep, rocky landscape of the tundra or over the wetlands and bogs of the taiga further south. For similar reasons, and particularly on account of the lack of roads, the Russian Katyusha rocket-launchers, which inflicted damage everywhere else throughout the Second World War, were only used in the far north towards the end of hostilities. It was the old-fashioned, toy-like Maksim machine-gun, with its little barrel on wheels, easily carried in parts or dragged across any terrain winter and summer, which came to the rescue. In addition, the factories at Kandalaksha manufactured at short notice a similar gun of their own design for local use.

At the outset of hostilities the Russians had few operative aeroplanes in the north – their Ilyushin-15s were too old, and the MiG-3s, which had no radios, were probably more dangerous to Russians than to the enemy – but in August 1941 the British dispatched a shipload of Hurricanes, accompanied by an RAF wing assembled specially to train Russian pilots, and these switched the balance. Based at Vaenga – today's Severomorsk, north of Murmansk – the British put Russian pilots and ground crews through their paces: 'They learn fast as hell, and they're flat out to do anything for us,' wrote H. Griffith, one of the senior British instructors. By the end of October the Russians could be left on their own. Many more British and American planes arrived on the convoy ships shortly after, and in time there were Hurricanes and American Tomahawks active the length of the northern front.

'It's difficult to imagine how we would have managed without the

Hurricanes,' said one Red Army infantry officer in Murmansk, home from the trenches in 1944, 'particularly in the early part of the war.'

The situation for the Soviets in September 1941, however, was desperate. Many Red Army soldiers who had been taken prisoner by the Finns in 1939 and 1940 and therefore convicted as 'spies' on their return home and put to work on major engineering projects, were rushed from forced-labour camps as far away as Siberia. Arriving at the West Litsa, the healthy men were poured into the breaches; the sick and weak were marshalled into the tattered ranks of the 'penal battalions', advancing in front of the NKVD infantry and gun crews, reducing casualties among the fit combatants and saving valuable armour by triggering land mines.

Another response to the crisis was the formation of a special unit called the Polar Division. This was hurriedly made up of men from the region, one-third ordinary Murmanchaners and two-thirds prisoners or forced-labourers from local mining towns such as Kirovsk and Revda.* When the Polar Division arrived at the front it faced almost impossible circumstances. The overall casualty rate was increasing and the whole Litsa struggle was hanging in the balance after German units had crossed the river and advanced the line a short distance eastwards, forming an ominous bulge. The Polar Division recruits were short of rifles – there was one for every three men – and even their ammunition was deficient, but when these few thousand men moved into the battle zone and confronted the enemy at close range, they fought so fiercely that the Germans and Austrians called them the Wild Division. Having been instructed during their brief training period by talented and ruthless officers to 'rush the foe and go for the throat', the Polar Division is said to have done just that, solving their weapons shortage by wresting rifles and ammunition from the hands of bewildered and sometimes panic-stricken enemy infantrymen, eventually pushing the bulge back across the river once and for all.

The Polar Division's success at that critical time may have been as much luck as the result of suicide tactics. The demise of a brigade of fresh young recruits that advanced along the road from Murmansk a

* Among the forced-labourers were men who, having been captured by the Finns in the Winter War, had been sent as 'convicts' or 'spies' to work the mines of Revda, a new town south of Murmansk, where many were unknowingly irradiated in the mines for a whole year.

few months later, in April 1942, showed how quickly things could go wrong on the open tundra in severe weather with logistics in disarray. When the brigade marched from Murmansk it was sunny, dry, and well above freezing, but half-way to the Litsa there was a heavy downpour of rain followed by a drop in temperature to minus two Celsius. This was hardly cold but it was enough to freeze an infantryman's sodden clothing. When a long storm followed, bringing one and a half metres of fresh snow, this took its toll: five hundred men froze to death and a thousand were transported back to hospital with frostbite or hypothermia, rendering the brigade inoperative.

'In the long dark winters,' said Sasha, 'thousands of Soviet soldiers continued to freeze to death here, even towards the end of the campaign when they were much better clothed and better equipped than at the start. The Germans froze to death too.'

The miraculous survival of the Soviet forces during the first year of the war will be understandable to anyone who has worked under stress or in arduous physical circumstances alongside Russians. As one English friend put it to me irreverently: 'They couldn't plan a vodka party in advance, but when the situation is really desperate they're good at being heroes.'

Although by this time officially considered 'nationals' rather than 'natives', the indigenous peoples of the Russian North were not obliged to join up. Yet in the far north-west they did so readily. Responding to the call to 'defend the great achievements of October to their last drop of blood', the Saami, Komi and Nenets distinguished themselves throughout the war, building an unrivalled reputation as guides and marksmen. The Saami's reconnaissance and patrol skills in particular were soon considered so vital that everything was to be done to save their lives: in the event of enemy shelling or heavy gunfire, Russian soldiers were ordered to throw themselves on top of their indispensable colleagues.

Herders from the east – from Lovozero, Voronye, Kanevka, Krasnoshchelye, Varzino and Iokanga – brought their reindeer to assist the war effort. In November 1941 Vladimir Kanev, the son of Kanevka's founder, travelled west with herding dogs, driving several hundred head to the railway and thence to Murmansk.

'We crossed the shallow Gulf waters at Kola and rushed to the front, transporting as many shells and mines as we could load on the sledges. After that we spent all the winter running between Murmansk and Litsa. Often working under fire, we wrapped the wounded in deerskins, tied them down on the sledges and ran them to the hospitals. Then we came back almost straight away, bringing men, ammunition, medical supplies and food, pushing the animals as hard as we dared. That winter the road was impassable. We provided the only transport there was.'

Looking through newspaper articles and archives about the war I frequently came across the names of Saami and Komi reindeer-herding families that I had met or heard about: Galkin, Sorvanov, Yulin, the Zakharovs, the Matryokhin brothers, Chuprov, Terentev, and the Nenets family Khatanzey who had trekked to Lapland with the first Komi herders. They supplied over 5,000 reindeer for work or meat, and during the winter of 1941 alone ran 6,000 soldiers of the 14th Army back to Murmansk suffering from severe wounds or frost-bite – a not inconsiderable total for animals the size of a donkey. Eight hundred *kayuri* (herders) went to the northern front. Six hundred returned.

'And when our own planes and pilots came down on our side of the line,' said herder Mayzerov, 'we were usually the people who found them. Sometimes we even towed the planes themselves home so that they could be put back into service.'

In early 1942 more reindeer herders arrived, from the Pechora region, 900 kilometres east of Archangel, having travelled 2,600 kilo-metres across the snow to Murmansk with 4,500 head of deer. When they arrived in the north-west in March, the men and the 3,600 animals that had survived were hardly able to stand, but they under-went two weeks of hard training in March near Murmansk, and joined the 14th Army on the southern flank of the Litsa line in mid-April.

Russian soldiers who were drafted into the reindeer transport pla-toons, the *olenetransportnyye otryady*, found the workload heavy. Not only did they have to provide covering fire while loading and driving, but they had the ongoing task of providing fodder for the deer. Tons of seaweed were brought from the shore, and in winter, if there was no lichen under the snow, the deer were fed hay, leaves and branches, all of which had been saved in the summer.

Tales from the ski brigades, the *lizhniye brigady*, sounded no less heroic. Throughout the war many raiding parties moved behind enemy lines, sniping and laying ambushes, carrying mines, destroying buildings and detonating arms dumps. Anatoly Bredov, a Murmansk boy, also earned his place in war history when he repelled repeated attacks of the crack Austrian Alpine Jäger, killing the last of the enemy with hand grenades and sacrificing his own life in the process. It was such small-scale but relentless contributions that helped finally tip the balance in favour of the Soviets.

Despite the participation of Hurricanes and Tomahawks, the port of Murmansk was constantly bombed and strafed by Heinkels, Junkers and Stukas, and in June 1942 the town itself was almost completely destroyed. Murmanchaners claim that only Stalingrad endured more bombing.

'What about the Arctic convoys?' I asked Sasha, stoking the fire and preparing my fishing tackle for our next onslaught on the salmon. I wanted to test his selective memory. He caught the tone of my voice and took time to reply.

'I know you sent millions of tonnes of planes and ordnance and that many Allied sailors and merchant seamen died, but Britain and America exaggerated their help to the Soviet Union. At the time Stalin complained bitterly that your tanks, planes and vehicles were next to useless. Some people now say that the Arctic convoy cargoes only amounted to a very small percentage of Soviet military-industrial production.'*

Over the three years 1941–44, in fact, some four million tonnes of arms, ordnance, fuel and food reached Russian soil, an indisputably important ingredient in the Red Army's performance. But a heavy price was paid. German U-boats and destroyers sailed from bases in Norway to dispatch shells and torpedoes. Junkers and Stukas – the same planes that were strafing the Litsa trenches and the port of Murmansk – flew out to sea from Kirkenes in a 500-kilometre radius to deliver bombs and machine-gun fire at the slow-moving convoys and their naval escorts. In spite of the celebrated achievements of individual fighter pilots like Boris Safonov, who was decorated by

* The Soviet figure is 4 per cent; Western experts place the figure about four times higher.

both the Soviets and the British before being shot down over the Barents Sea, support from Russians flying from the Murmansk airfields was limited. Many of the early convoys barely survived the passage, and in the course of the four years hundreds of men and women went to their deaths in Arctic waters.

Winston Churchill had evidently been exposed to the Soviet readiness to expend lives. 'The operation is justified,' he once said of the convoys, 'if even *half* get through.' The fate of the convoy PQ17 during June and July 1942 – 35 merchantmen carrying 290 aircraft, 590 tanks, over 4,000 lorries and gun-carriers, and 150,000 tonnes of military cargo – marked the nadir of the convoy record and was one of Britain's greatest disasters at sea.

The heavy bombing of Murmansk in June 1942 had made it impossible for the PQ17 convoy to proceed to the Kola Gulf; the Admiralty therefore ordered all vessels except eight American ships to proceed instead to Archangel. This not only meant longer exposure of the ships as they made their way towards the Gorlo, the narrow channel into the White Sea, but it was also during the season of white nights when German shipping and U-boats enjoyed 24-hour visibility. Having slipped out of the Icelandic port of Hvalfjord for the last leg of their voyage, the PQ17 ships were spotted almost immediately by the Luftwaffe. Admiral Dönitz's U-boats from Pechenga/Petsamo were already at sea; Heinkel torpedo-armed seaplanes, Junkers bombers and Stuka dive-bombers at the Pechenga and Kirkenes airbases were placed on standby to fly out to the convoy as soon as it was within range. A series of inaccurate reports then received in London by the First Sea Lord, Admiral Sir Dudley Pound, about German battleships and destroyers reputedly at sea, induced Admiralty fears of severe losses of naval vessels urgently required elsewhere. The escort fleet was ordered to return home and to leave the merchantmen to make their own way after passing Bear Island.

'Owing to threat from surface ships, convoy is to disperse', was the signal received on board the destroyer HMS *Keppel* by Commander Jack Broome. 'Convoy is to scatter', came a second, unambiguous order. Of the 35 merchant ships that left Iceland, only ten reached Archangel; 210 bombers, 430 tanks, 3,350 vehicles and almost 100,000 tonnes of ammunition sank to the bed of the Barents Sea; 153 men lost their lives.

When Churchill proposed the postponement of PQ18 and even suggested the cancellation of all further convoys on account of the risks posed by the now very considerable German naval presence off Norway, Stalin ranted at Churchill and belittled the British navy. On this occasion Stalin's behaviour, which sorely tried Churchill at every turn during 1942, paid dividends. Convoy PQ18 sailed in September 1942 and when it did, it enjoyed such unusually heavy protection from Allied naval vessels and from the bombers and Spitfires flying out of the Russian bases that it was a success with consequences. The damage inflicted on German planes was such that the Luftwaffe never again launched such mass attacks on a convoy.

Looking down on to the town and port of Murmansk in August 2001 with a group of white-bereted British and US veterans who had arrived to commemorate the sixtieth anniversary of the first Arctic convoy, I listened to men in their late seventies recalling their experiences.

Morris Mitchell from St Helen's near Liverpool, a gunner on the light cruiser HMS *Scylla*, sailed to Murmansk with PQ18. On the way home his ship carried 200 of the PQ17 survivors. 'There was a lot of bitterness over PQ17,' he said. 'The name of Admiral Pound was on every sailor's lips. If one or two of them could have got their hands on him he would have been a dead man.'

To all the veterans, whatever the season of their arrival, the Murman coast was 'a cold, bleak, Godforsaken place'. The town of Murmansk itself – 'a few wooden houses surrounded by scrubland' was how one veteran described it – came to most sailors as a shock. 'Is this what we've been killing ourselves for?' some had muttered, thinking more in terms of their stomachs and loins than the war effort. 'It didn't look like a place where you could get a drink and meet a few girls.' For the early convoys, at least, this proved to be the case. The Soviet servicemen and civilians at Murmansk, Vaenga (Severomorsk) and Polyarny, who were regularly warned not to speak to the foreigners, were suspicious, withdrawn and frequently antagonistic.

The veterans spoke about the overstretched hospitals where they visited their shipmates lying among the Russian soldiers from the Litsa front. Most hospitals were in schools and ramshackle places, primitively equipped like field units. The Allied wounded – if they were conscious at all – complained bitterly, begging to be operated on by their own professionals on board one of the ships in the port. Moreover, Murmansk hospital conditions were often exacerbated by the attitude of the Russian doctors, many of whom were unable to cope and unwilling to admit shortcomings or discuss problems – a notable trait of Russians – and relationships tended to deteriorate. Against this, however, are to be set such experiences as that of Engineer Officer William Short whose ship SS *Induna* was torpedoed and who was miraculously kept alive by a Russian surgeon following the amputation of both legs.

In time the human need for communication and companionship overcame mutual suspicion. In the submarine port of Polyarny at the mouth of the Kola Gulf, the British were permitted to mark out a soccer pitch. On the ice-hard or stony ground – according to the season – fierce east-west rivalries flourished and stimulated real friendship. Men from both sides were the better for letting off steam. In Murmansk in 1943 the InterClub, which had shown Russian films five nights a week, started to screen American and English films on Thursdays and Sundays. After the show foreign visitors were allowed to dance with officially approved local partners.

'It wasn't great but there was nowhere else to go in the evenings,' said Terence Gillingham, who spent much of 1944 in the port operating a heavy crane on board one of the Empire ships. 'When you arrived at the door you were greeted by an older woman – we nick-named her Tatty Anna – and you met Russian girls, but the language was pidgin and it was all very chaste; the women knew they could be jailed for the smallest misdemeanours. What drove us mad, though, was that they only had two records for the gramophone: *Harvest Moon* and *Victory Polka*. They got played over and over.'

Terence Gillingham was either unlucky or else he was being discreet about what had been available during shore leave. In 1943 a hall was opened in Murmansk where Allied seamen were welcome and to which Murmansk's most attractive and respectable young women were invited. Whether this was the result of official policy or private profit-making initiative, local folklore does not relate, but the enterprise encouraged relationships to thaw. To attract the foreigners, the hall managers went so far as to call the place *Dom Druzhby, imeni*

Uinstona Churchkhilya – The Winston Churchill House of Friendship. There was the usual food, music and dancing, but the house's special offering was to be found in well-appointed premises at the rear of the building where the women provided a high-class personal service. This was a well-kept open secret until Murmansk husbands and boy-friends began to find out, after which time there were some changes in the workforce.

The Churchill House fulfilled another, more valuable role. Before the House opened it was often remarked that the young people of Murmansk, who held a larger stock of chocolate, cigarettes and money than anybody else, played an abnormally prominent role in the ever-active marketplace for barter. With very few mature women available for intimate companionship, many of the foreigners had inevitably, and in the time-honoured manner of sailors, turned to these importunate and ubiquitous boys and girls for sexual gratifica-tion. The children and their extended families found the exchanges highly profitable, but with the opening of the Churchill House the activity was said to have diminished.

Not until almost sixty years later did the full extent of the NKVD's response to circumstances such as Churchill House become fully known. In the 1990s a journalist from Archangel, Olga Golubtsova, gathered the stories of fourteen women who had been sentenced to prison and hard labour for up to ten years for associating with British troops. One of the more heart-rending aspects of these stories was that, after they left Murmansk and Archangel, almost every soldier or sailor had remained in ignorance of the suffering of the women who had been their close friends or lovers and, in some cases, the mother of their child.*

Perhaps the easing of relationships in Murmansk from 1943 onwards reflected the Soviet Union's own overall position in the war, for at that time the tide seemed to be turning. At the end of January General Paulus had surrendered at Stalingrad and, during each of the months that followed, towns and cities were retaken from the retreat-ing Germans. By 1944 the Russian production of armaments had multiplied fourfold since the Winter War, reinforcements were

---

* Olga Golubtsova, *Voyennaya lyubov po-angliyski*, Severodvinsk: N.N. Kuchurov, 2001.

reaching all fronts in a steady stream, and Red Army soldiers were now better equipped and better clothed.

In June 1944 the southern flank of the Karelian Front pressed through to Vyborg in Finland, producing a ceasefire by September and moving much of the border back to where it had been before the 1920 Treaty of Dorpat, causing Finland to lose its access to the Arctic and large areas of timber forest.

On the far northern flank, along the banks of the West Litsa and in the forest to the west of Kandalaksha, casualties continued to be large but, on the Litsa, 53,000 Germans now found themselves facing 97,000 Red Army soldiers who had three times as many guns and were supported in the air by four times as many planes. In October 1944 Marshal Shcherbakov's 14th Army finally pushed the Germans out of Soviet territory, past Pechenga/Petsamo, beyond Kirkenes, and into the sea.

'When the advance into Norway started,' said Saami reindeer-herder Galkin, 'we harnessed all the deer we could and ran with the rest of the Army, swimming the deer across countless rivers and streams, floating ourselves across on cape-tents stuffed with moss. It was a great to be chasing the enemy. Sometimes we even caught isolated German soldiers by lasso!' The border changes secured by the Soviets, however, also resulted in the migration of thousands of Finns and many Skolt Saami families, all anxious to avoid living under Communist rule.

As we drove away from the Litsa, with salmon in the truck, Sasha pointed out a number of small war monuments set back at intervals from the road. One of them was an anti-aircraft gun set on a small hill, pointing west; another had been constructed from the tail of a crashed Hurricane and positioned prominently on a birch-covered bluff.

'On each and every day of the campaign up here, from the seizure of Pechenga by the Germans in June 1941 till their retreat to Neiden in October 1944, there were deaths,' Sasha told me. 'Thousands of our troops were buried in mass graves during the three years of action along the Litsa. In the 1980s we exhumed many of the bodies and took them to graveyards near Murmansk. It was a macabre business but a very moving occasion.'

Many bodies had indeed been buried in mass graves but that was mostly after the war, and Sasha might more accurately have pointed out one of the differences between the opposing armies on the Litsa: the Germans had a policy of removing their dead, whereas the Soviets left their men where they fell and dug shallow graves, usually consisting of a few shovels of hard-gained soil and some stones on top. This made war records particularly difficult, and the overworked authorities often resorted, perhaps understandably, to issuing fictitious death certificates for individual soldiers. Sergeant Pyotr Nikolayevich Koryakovsky was listed as killed in action in Karelia, but in 1998 his remains were identified in a shallow grave exposed by natural erosion, found on the outskirts of Zapolyarny, the mining town north-west of Murmansk, some 600 kilometres from the Karelian battleground listed on the certificate.

On the way home from the coast two days later Sasha took me to the main war memorial out on the tundra, not far from the front, set back from the side of the road to Norway. I walked up and down the hundred-metre wall, reading engraved plaques commemorating the many *ryadovye* (private soldiers) who had perished along the Litsa. And then I looked for the names of the Russian, Saami and Komi families that I would recognize.

'BOW YOUR HEADS TO THE IMMORTAL HEROES,' ran the inscription in giant letters. 'BE WORTHY OF THE MEMORY OF THE PERISHED,' exhorted another.

The memorial wall holding the plaques was constructed from galvanized steel that looked as if it might originally have come off the roof of a factory, and the wall's base had been clumsily put together with steel rods and cement. Where the paint was peeling, fresh had recently been applied with almost indecent haste.

Spyfishing

THROUGHOUT THE NEXT DAY Sasha and I fished the river at a leisurely pace, intermittently sleeping on the bank after the exertions and excitements of our encounters with large fish. When it came to evening and time for the expedition to the submarine base that I had been planning, I had had more than enough sport. At about ten o'clock Sasha walked me further down the river and into the open landscape. From there he pointed out the best route to the estuary and then turned to me, taking me aback by extending his hand, as if to say goodbye.

'But Sasha, I'll be back in a few hours. I'm only going to look at a few boats.'

'*Uvidem, tovarishch!* We shall see, Comrade.' Sasha smiled briefly, performing a mock naval salute. As a loyal Russian, he didn't approve of my illegal peregrinations. He interpreted them as a lack of respect for the military and hence for the entire Russian people. Only after some persuasion had he agreed to wait for me to return from the base.

I had reached my own conclusions about closed zones. During the Cold War years the Russian Navy, obsessed with security, established exclusion zones over unnecessarily vast swathes of land surrounding their bases and coastal surveillance installations. Following glasnost the Navy no longer had many valuable strategic or technical secrets but were worried instead lest the outside world should learn about the now seriously decayed condition of their bases and fleets; considerations of prestige were just as significant to Russian sensibilities as concerns over spent nuclear fuel and radioactive waste.

I explained to Sasha that I certainly intended to have a look at the submarines at the Zapadnaya (Western) Litsa base because I had

267

heard so much about them, but I was genuinely more interested in the coastal terrain and in the bay itself. I wanted to imagine how it had been when Saami and Nordic colonists lived there sixty years earlier, and to see how it looked today under the present incumbents. I wanted to walk the coastal territories where the Saami ran with reindeer for the summer months and camped near the estuary for the salmon. To me the Northern Fleet and its submarines were parvenus.

'Well, we'll see what the Navy has to say to that,' Sasha had responded finally to my case with a shrug of the shoulders, like an examining officer closing my file and pushing it to the side of his desk for the consideration of his superior.

I turned from Sasha and started walking north at a good pace. The wind subsided and the sky cleared, and then the June night sun, still high above the horizon, warmed me up. The route along the western side of the Litsa Bay was at times arduous. I had the benefit of a track for some of the way but then, as I moved towards the bay and the coast, trying to stay hidden, the hills and contours pinched me into a sequence of steep scrambles which resulted in some tumbles and not a few curses. The tundra itself, with its floor of lichen and berries and its fissured granite bluffs, presented a romantic, wild spectacle. The low ground was dotted with small tarns. There were occasional pockets of snow. Then, as I moved ahead, much of the Litsa Bay – what Norwegians would call a fjord – opened up in front of me, giving glimpses of the open sea beyond.

I realized I was still carrying my fishing rod but as I was about to stow it into my rucksack, I changed my mind and decided to hold on to it, following a half-serious theory that in the eyes of a patrolling guard who had to detain me this attribute would brand me as a sportsman angler and not a spy. Perhaps he would even treat me as an *angliyskiy dzhentelman*.

Like the Titovka estuary that I had seen in early winter, the large Litsa Bay had been an ideal summer camp for the Saami. The conformation of the estuary with its sandbank giving on to deep water was ideal for incoming salmon and practicable for setting fish traps. The open sea was within easy access, there was a tide to help take boats out to sea or back when winds were contrary, the bay was sheltered from all directions, and there was nutritious ground cover for the wild or domestic reindeer grazing the mosquito-free high ground where I was standing.

I recalled my conversations with the elderly Skolt Saami women who had spent happy childhood summers here at Litsa and elsewhere along the Motovsky Gulf. Nobody among the Saami could possibly have foreseen – even in the 1920s, following the first phase of collectivization – what was to become of them at the hands of the NKVD that fateful August in 1937, the year in which the coastal families were given a few hours to pack and leave.

During our conversations one of them had questioned a companion as to why the NKVD was so adamant about never allowing any of the Gulf inhabitants near the coast again. Another had replied that it was 'something to do with the Germans. Some agreement or other.' At the time I had no idea what the woman was saying – I thought I had misheard her – and I didn't write it in my notebook. In the years following that discussion I occasionally wondered whether there was in fact any such 'agreement' in the air between Hitler and the Soviets in the years leading up to 1941.*

Whether this was the case or not, what was in no doubt was the enthusiasm shown for the Motovsky Gulf by the Soviet Government themselves at the start of the Cold War a decade or so later. Not for the first time Moscow politicians fingered their office globes and reminded themselves of the location's valuable assets: sheltered bays, deep inshore waters, and easy, ice-free access to the North Atlantic.

And then K-3 arrived. On a July day in 1958 the first nuclear-powered vessel of the November-class, built at Severodvinsk, the shipyard in the White Sea west of Archangel, moved cautiously into the mouth of the fjord, advancing safely in 80 metres of water, exploring the bays that by the 1970s were to house part of the world's largest submarine fleet.

My own first reaction when I saw the whole stretch of the bay was that of a small boy. I recalled long childhood days spent with my sister 'playing ships' in the garden pond or among the rocks of our local bay. Being the younger sibling I never got the best harbours but now, with the bay and waters below under my sole control (and the base

---

* Given that at this time the Soviets were bartering with the Germans for Baltic influence while also having an eye on future Atlantic conflicts, it now appears feasible that German naval access to north-west Russian waters and the Motovsky Gulf was under consideration.

not yet in view), I set about disposing my fleet and planning my docks and quays, and sat down to eat some of the food Sasha had thoughtfully piled into my rucksack. Thanking the heavens it was a warm and windless night I chased my thermos of tea with a shot of vodka and fell asleep.

A loud metallic clang, which woke me with a start and echoed around the bay, brought me back to the present, reminding me that I was in a closed zone. I walked on for another fifteen minutes and the base came into sight. Not for the first time in the oblast I experienced shock when I caught sight of the abused and damaged landscape – the litter of the docks, yards and sheds, the gantries, the ship debris, the shabby buildings, the grey administration blocks. The least offensive sight was the submarines themselves which lay alongside their quays like seals at rest, or with their heads on the shore and lower bodies wallowing in the water.

The Second World War proved beyond doubt the strategic and tactical advantage of a large submarine capability in broad-theatre conflict. The decision by the Supreme Soviet in 1952 to build nuclear-powered submarines, with an ability to run great distances without refuelling and even to remain permanently submerged, was one of the most significant moves of the Cold War.

The emphasis of the Soviet Navy's nuclear-power development was in the north. In the relatively short period from 1950 to 1970, the Northern Fleet grew from being the smallest of the Soviet fleets to being larger and more important than those of the Black Sea, the Pacific and the Baltic. Six new naval bases, some with nuclear submarine facilities, were rapidly established along the Murman coast from Zapadnaya Litsa in the west to Gremikha in the east, and five large naval yards were built in Murmansk Oblast and at Severodvinsk, near Archangel. It was not long before the power of the Soviet submarine fleet surpassed that of the American. By the late 1980s, 245 nuclear submarines and four nuclear-powered battle cruisers had been delivered to the Navy, 82 of the submarines to the Northern Fleet. In the year 1989 the Soviet Navy had its largest-ever number of nuclear submarines in active operation – 120 in total – and the vessels and territories of the Northern Fleet alone housed over one-fifth of the world's entire nuclear reactor capability.

By the end of the millennium, however, after more than a decade of perestroika and a series of economic crises, the Russian Navy was barely recognizable. Having established itself as an ocean-going force with a world-wide influence, it was rapidly reduced to patrolling home waters. While American submarines continued to move globally and lurk offshore in the Barents Sea, the Northern Fleet's presence in the Atlantic was negligible. By 1995, the year when I made my way to the Litsa base, only some 70 submarines remained in active service with the Northern Fleet; by 2001 less than 40 were taking part in exercises.

For decades the Northern Fleet managed to sit on the lid of its Pandora's box, withholding the truth about the condition of its bases and infrastructure, its management of nuclear fuel, and the catalogue of fleet accidents. By the mid-1990s a small Oslo-based environmental campaign group, which had embarked on a series of investigations into the Russian Navy, began to expose the Northern Fleet. Following the pioneer work of the Norwegian Bellona Foundation and the dramatic publication of a well-researched report in 1994, the world had its first comprehensive picture of the Russian Navy's parlous condition, and in time Bellona was directly instrumental even in turning Soviet martial law with regard to military secrets on its head.

From the early 1960s, it was now learned, there had been a large number of Northern Fleet accidents at sea and on land. Even the very first of the nuclear-powered submarines, the 100-metre November-class K-3, the first to sail into the Litsa Bay in 1958, was dogged by misfortune. In 1962 it suffered a fire, after which its two reactors were cut out, towed to the Kara Sea and dumped, one with all its fuel remaining inside. In 1967 another similar fire put it out of service permanently. Its first cousin, the K-8, had an accident off the British coast, leaking radioactivity into the sea before sinking in the Bay of Biscay. The K-8's successor, the K-11, experienced an uncontrolled chain reaction following a fire, and dumped its two live nuclear reactors in the sea off Novaya Zemlya. In the 1970s one of the Hotel-class torpedo submarines was so accident-prone that it acquired the nickname *Hiroshima*.

Before the tragic demise of the *Kursk*, the Oscar II-class submarine, in August 2000, the only Northern Fleet incident that had aroused world-wide concern was the sinking of the submarine *Komsomolets* in the Norwegian Sea, 180 kilometres south of Bear Island, in 1989. A fire broke out at sea, causing a complete failure of the electrical systems, and this in turn triggered further fires. After struggling for a day to save the situation, survivors watched as the submarine sank and exploded with 42 of their fellow crew trapped inside.

Among the alarming aspects of the *Komsomolets* accident was that a few months earlier the submarine had shown several deficiencies when undergoing a security test. In spite of regulations that categorically prescribed a return to the shipyard there and then, the *Komsomolets* continued its patrol. In 2002, after ongoing plans for a raising operation and one unsuccessful attempt, the *Komsomolets* still lay in the clay of the sea bed at a depth of 1,700 metres, carrying two nuclear reactors and two nuclear warheads. Uranium leaks were predicted.

From the start of the Soviet Union's naval expansion programme before the Second World War, Moscow placed relentless pressure on those in local command to meet unreasonable deadlines. As a result of this pressure, the aspirations, research skills and mechanical genius that built what became the world's technologically most advanced fleet were accompanied by a lamentable labour record and enormous cost in human lives. At the large naval shipyard of Severodvinsk on the White Sea – to offer an early example – which was founded in 1936 and built by gulag prisoners, conditions were particularly hard. During the years 1936 to 1953 at the labour camp there, which on average had a population of 60,000 inmates, approximately 25,000 prisoners were recorded as having died, an average over the seventeen years of almost 1,500 deaths annually. The undernourished prisoner-labourers were augmented by conscripts unfit for active service, with the end result that the labour force was unmotivated, poorly disciplined, and inclined to take short cuts.* As a result of this kind of

* It was also characteristic of bases, shipyards and closed towns that they had a succession of different names. Severodvinsk was founded by Stalin as Sudostroy and renamed Molotovsk after his foreign minister before being finally known as Severodvinsk from 1958. Zapadnaya Litsa was known first as Murmansk-150, then Zaozerny, then Severomorsk-7. Gremikha has been known as Iokanga, Murmansk-140, and Ostrovnoy.

pressure, most naval bases proved to be impractical and, ultimately, dangerous. Also in spite of the relentless development of ship technology and nuclear power, training and infrastructure almost never kept pace. In the north-west, for example, many of the buildings, naval and civilian, were designed by military personnel who lacked sufficient experience of harsh-climate construction and, typically at the Northern Fleet bases, several years might elapse before the onshore infrastructure matched newly commissioned vessels.

By the 1970s the Zapadnaya (Western) Litsa base, also known as Andreyeva Bay after one of its four docking areas, was home to some of the technologically most advanced nuclear-powered submarines of the world, and the housing quarters, consisting of grim concrete buildings standing back from the water, could accommodate a naval and civilian population of up to 20,000. Andreyeva, on the west side of the bay, held the storage facilities for radioactive waste and spent nuclear fuel. From where I was walking I could see most of the buildings and bunkers that housed the storage pools, the purification plants and the decontamination units, all of which were known to fall well short of internationally acknowledged safety levels.

Of the risks involved in the operation of nuclear-powered vessels the refuelling process demands the most stringent procedures. Fuel-assemblies – the part of a reactor which includes the fissionable, enriched uranium rods – have a tendency to crack when a reactor is in operation, making handling and storage of spent fuel a hazardous and protracted business. At worst, the smallest human error raises the possibility of chain reaction between fuel rods and the release of hazardous amounts of radioactivity over a large area. From the Fleet's earliest days of nuclear power the storage of spent fuel and radioactive waste was deficient. Suitably graded facilities for the secure handling and storage of spent fuel and radioactive waste always existed on drawing boards, but priority was rarely given to actual construction. Nor was much consideration given to the safety of naval personnel or the base's civilian population, and for many years there were no radiation limits at all set for shipyard workers. By the end of the century the legacy of these shortcomings – many of them aggravated by incompetence, lack of regulation and underskilled handling – was concentrating the minds of nuclear specialists and relevant environmental organizations around the world.

A series of incidents with spent-fuel storage at Zapadnaya Litsa in the 1980s, which became an international issue, was a classic though not isolated example of the Fleet's infrastructure shortcomings, combined with obsessive secrecy. In 1982 a leak of radioactive waste water was discovered. The concrete and steel lining of one of the large storage pools for spent fuel-assemblies, standing 350 metres from the sea, had become cracked because of substandard building methods and the effects of frost, and was spilling its cooling-water on to the surrounding land. The leakage started at 30 litres, increased to 100 litres a day, and briefly reached an alarming ten tonnes an hour. The water in the pool, which could not be replenished quickly enough, was sinking to such a low level that there was a possibility that the fuel-assembly containers would no longer be covered, resulting in heavy radioactive outfall. Atomic Energy Ministry technicians called in by the Navy failed to stop the leak, whereupon the naval commanders resorted to drastic short-term measures, constructed a lead and iron cover to the pool and poured large quantities of concrete over it. In 1989, when the level of radioactivity had decreased, it was decided to empty this pool, as well as an adjacent storage pool that had also been leaking, and transfer the solid fuel to a new storage building at the same base. During this stage of the operation an additional difficulty emerged. As a result of lax handling procedures in the past, half of the fuel-assemblies had been damaged; some had even fallen out of their containers and were lying loose.

As at Chernobyl, volunteers came forward. A dozen specialists transferred the intact fuel-assembly containers and then undertook the delicate and hazardous operation of lifting the hundreds of loose, damaged fuel rods piece by piece from the floor of the pools. The most dangerous part of the work lay in placing the damaged assemblies into newly built containers. The radiation at close proximity to the fuel rods was so high that one minute of exposure at close quarters would have been the equivalent to a lethal dose for a human being. Not surprisingly, in view of the long-term environmental threat posed by the incident, all the circumstances had remained secret until the Bellona Foundation exposures.

From my own early-morning vantage point above Andreyeva I

could see the building containing the old storage pools. I could also see an open-air pad where about thirty cylindrical containers stood exposed to the elements. Seen from a distance through binoculars their necks and domed caps made them look like rusting versions of the TV Dalek robots. Some of these cylinders, which between them contained hundreds of spent fuel-assemblies, had been there for up to 35 years and, because of corrosion and cracking and other related technical problems, could not now be moved for reprocessing. But the reason for the excessive accumulation of spent fuel and radioactive waste matter was overwhelmingly the result of misguided priorities: the refuelling of new submarines or of submarines in operation had always taken pride of place.

The Northern Fleet's record relating to dumping at sea was scarcely better. Its programme not only exceeded that of all other nuclear nations put together, but it had taken place in unapproved waters and in contravention even of the Soviet Government's own directives. In July 1988 at the London Convention – the forum for the International Atomic Energy Agency – the Soviet delegates declared that the dumping of radioactive waste at sea was 'prohibited by Soviet law; the Soviet Union has never dumped radioactive waste in the sea, nor does it intend to do so in the future.' In fact the Northern Fleet had dumped radioactive liquid waste annually since the 1960s in the Barents Sea and off the west coast of Novaya Zemlya. Solid waste had also been dropped, mostly in the waters to the east of Novaya Zemlya and in the Kara Sea. The dumped material included ships and lighters containing radioactive waste, nuclear reactors from submarines each with Uranium^{235} remaining in the reactors, and at least one submarine, K-27, scuttled in its entirety with two damaged reactors in a small shallow bay near the southern tip of Novaya Zemlya.

The Soviet Union constructed a plant for reprocessing nuclear fuel at Mayak in western Siberia in the 1960s, and in 1973 the first special wagons travelled from Murmansk. But this was a lengthy and difficult process, and by the 1980s, with Russia's new internal pricing policy in force, and with priority given to refuelling new or active submarines, there was a tendency to duck the expense of transportation, leave the fuel on land or afloat in service lighters, or simply to leave it in the reactors of laid-up submarines. In the sunny early hours of the

June morning when I stood on the slopes downwind of Andreyeva there were still over 20,000 spent assemblies awaiting transportation and reprocessing. These corresponded to fuel from about 80 nuclear reactors.

In spite of the relentless production of nuclear-powered submarines that continued unabated until the 1980s, there was no cradle-to-grave policy, no formal programme for the decommissioning – that is, the dismantling and scrapping – of submarines retired from active service. The issue was never fully addressed, and there were never sufficient funds or trained personnel; priorities lay elsewhere. Dozens of old submarines simply sat rotting alongside jetties at Severodvinsk or in the bases of the Murman coast, many of them with their reactors still containing uranium fuel-rods.

In 1991, following a Supreme Soviet resolution, the Russian Navy did finally establish guidelines and targets for the dismantling of their laid-up submarines but this had little effect; in 1996 the Bellona Foundation reckoned that not one single nuclear-powered submarine had been decommissioned to acceptable international standards. If as a result of the exposures by the Bellona Foundation the Navy became schizophrenic in its approach to the problem, it became even more so after the global publicity of the *Kursk* disaster in the year 2000. The Russian Government had invited the assistance of interested parties, not least the governments of Norway and the United Kingdom together with their naval and environmental advisors, yet the many visits by foreign delegations initially produced limited results. While the Russian Government showed almost indecent haste to get its hands on the millions of dollars required for the clean-up even at a primary level, naval bosses regularly refused full access to specialist foreign teams. They were reluctant to allow base visits even by prime ministers or senior ministers from the very countries who were offering technical and financial help. By 1998 dollars were starting to flow from the US Defense Department to break up submarines, but these monies related to the Start-II Treaty and were designed to decommission only SSBN submarines carrying intercontinental ballistic missiles. A wider appeal for funds to dismantle retired cruise-missile or general-purpose attack-submarines fell on stonier ground.

While governments talked and envoys failed to reach agreements, others forged ahead as best they could. Nerpa shipyard boss Pavel Steblin – as much for the yard's future financial security as for meeting the urgency of the situation – canvassed US senators and potential collaborators for finance, and despatched representatives to major international conferences. Given the funds, his yard alone could decommission up to six submarines a year. The West, however, having already suffered throughout the 1990s at the hands of Russian business governance and lack of transparency, and having repeatedly observed international funds go astray, was reluctant to help.

There were further factors in the Northern Fleet's demise. Most naval and shipyard pay was months in arrears, and pay-related strikes and demonstrations had become almost a common feature. In 1998, with wages unpaid for six months, 9,000 employees of Murmansk's Sevmorput naval yard held a one-day strike. 'You will have a second Chernobyl here in the north, more frightening than the first,' shipyard workers are reported to have said. 'Remember, we have nuclear-powered subs in our hands.'

There was also a desperate shortage of food; sailors and soldiers were often to be seen in Murmansk earning a pittance sweeping the streets or working on civil engineering sites. Naval commanders began to cast around for patronage among the communities in Central and Southern Russia from which their crews had been recruited, but even this measure proved largely unfruitful.

In 1999 the Defence Ministry's debt to just one of the major ship-yards at Severomorsk, near Murmansk, stood at $600,000.* With the December cold exacerbating the anguish of food and wage short-ages, workers from the yard attempted a blockade of the road con-necting Murmank and Severomorsk with the aim of severing vital communications and military supplies and withholding one of the newly repaired large Typhoon-class nuclear submarines shortly to leave dry dock. A similar action had been successful on two previous occasions, resulting in wage arrears being sent by the Ministry to the Northern Fleet at the last moment; it was hoped this would work again. It did.

* At the end of 1996 the Russian Government's total debt to shipyards involved in the decommissioning of nuclear-powered submarines was said to have reached US$26 million (source: the Bellona Foundation).

There was tension among naval crews. One incident in particular was indicative of the desperation of young conscripts in a demoralized navy. In September 1998 the alarm was sounded from one of the large Akula attack-submarines moored at the Skalisty base. An eighteen-year-old military-service sailor had started a quarrel and resolved the dispute by shooting his colleague with a Kalashnikov and going through the submarine killing seven other conscripts in their beds before barricading himself into a torpedo compartment. An armed siege ensued. Negotiators tried to persuade the mutinous sailor to give himself up but the affair ended in suicide.

But that was all in the future. When I was at Zapadnaya Litsa I felt like a spy and the Cold War seemed to be lingering on. Seeing signs of early morning activity around the base I packed my binoculars, picked up my fishing rod, and circled back towards the road, avoiding the guardhouse and road barrier, to begin the return walk to Sasha, thankful that I had had the sense to change my cumbersome chest waders for walking boots. Uppermost in my mind were thoughts of the vodka that Sasha had promised to keep for me, '. . . if I can keep it hidden from the others . . . and if you return, that is,' he had said.

'Ah, there you are! The spy will need some refreshment,' he said as I arrived at the rendez-vous, not altogether in jest, producing a full half-bottle of vodka to go with the last of the sausage and bread.

As we drove towards home I told him what I had observed. He was happy to see me safely back, but that didn't mean he had changed his attitude.

'I'm pleased that we still have a large navy, and the sooner our boys are paid up to date and fed properly the better. We have to be on our guard, you know. Don't forget that, as far as most Russians are concerned, you're a nuclear threat, and we have a vast border to protect, not a small coast from Dover to Hull like you English. And if you'd been brought up in Murmansk like me, and seen the rubble of Murmansk before it was rebuilt after the war, you wouldn't be so worried about a bit of radioactive spill.'

Eco wars

IN JUNE 1995 workers at the Bellona Foundation's Murmansk office suspected that their telephones were being tapped by the FSB, the Federal Security Service. Far from being alarmed, they could hardly believe that it hadn't happened earlier. For four years the Oslo-based environmental campaigners had been taking a close interest in Russia's Northern Fleet; already by 1992 they were circulating security-sensitive information, and by March 1994 they had published the first of their major reports.

The 1994 report, entitled *Sources of radioactive contamination in Murmansk and Archangel counties*, an illustrated and fully annotated 150-page booklet, itemized all the known potential sources of contamination resulting from the use of nuclear fuel in north-west Russia. It included: an overview of the Northern Fleet and the region's nuclear-powered icebreakers; a review of the region's only nuclear-power plant (reckoned to be the world's most dangerous); an almost complete record of nuclear test explosions and radioactive dumping since the 1960s; and, most significantly, details about spent nuclear fuel and nuclear waste. It was a devastating exposure of irresponsible management.

This report, the result of a two-year survey within the Russian border, was the first internationally important achievement of the small environmental group founded in 1986 by the Norwegian Frederic Hauge, and named Bellona after the Roman goddess of war. When Hauge, still in his twenties in 1990, had turned his interest to neighbouring Russia, he already had some successful campaigns under his belt relating to pollution and industrial dumping. His credibility was further enhanced by his positive views: 'Industry is not society's enemy,' he would say, 'Only the mess it makes. We want to fight bad technologies with better technologies. If car engines pollute the air we need better engines. It makes no sense to turn back the clock ...'

At the top of Hauge's list for attention were the nickel smelters at Monchegorsk and Nikel that for many years had concerned the Norwegians as well as the Finns and Swedes. But he also began to learn about the Northern Fleet and its record of nuclear-fuel management. Alarmed by his initial discoveries, he changed tack. His first colleagues were an environmental journalist, Thomas Nilsen, already working in the Russian North, and Nils Bohmer, a young nuclear physicist experienced in the field from his work for the Norwegian Radiation Protection Authority.

The arbitrary dumping of nuclear waste and the scuttling of decommissioned vessels in the region of Novaya Zemlya since the 1960s had been in the news for some years. That the Soviet Union had been detonating nuclear devices on and near Novaya Zemlya from the 1960s to the 1990s was also widely known. What was not known was the insecure and volatile condition of large quantities of the Northern Fleet's spent nuclear fuel and nuclear waste – at Zapadnaya Litsa, for example – and the number of fuelled submarines deteriorating at quaysides awaiting decommissioning. Prior to Hauge's work with Nilsen and Bohmer, most Scandinavians had perceived the principal threat from the Soviet Union to be the Northern Fleet's arsenal of nuclear weapons, a short distance the other side of the border.

The boldness, scope and sheer professionalism of Bellona's first report shocked the Russian Navy and the security service. The FSB, which had been observing Bellona's interest in the Northern Fleet since at least 1992, might have been expected to have taken earlier action, but Bellona's work had coincided with a period of post-perestroika paralysis afflicting certain government departments. Official reactions eventually surfaced when, on the evening of 5 October 1995, the FSB ransacked Bellona's office in Murmansk, confiscated files and computer hardware and, during the same night, raided the apartments and offices of Bellona contacts elsewhere. The FSB justified these actions by claiming that Bellona's next report, which was in preparation at the time and was devoted entirely to the Russian Northern Fleet, contained state secrets.

When I went to find Bellona's Murmansk office in 1996 it had moved, perhaps as a result of the raid. I was eventually directed to a small room next to the offices of the fish industry newspaper, *Rybnyy Zhurnal*, where I introduced myself to two young Bellona workers, Sergey Fillipov and Lyuba Kovalyova, both Murmanchaners with a relaxed and courteous manner. While Sergey prepared me a coffee Lyuba was at her computer, surrounded by press cuttings, updating the organization's extensive data bank.

'I don't know where we would be if we were an entirely Russian outfit,' Sergey said in fluent English. 'Without the hardware that we get from Norway we just wouldn't be effective. We use reliable Norwegian telephone lines with Norwegian numbers for international communication and electronic data, and that enables us to be in daily contact with our Oslo office. Otherwise we couldn't dial beyond this area of the town. Even the FSB are jealous of our communications.

'Igor Kudrik is really responsible for this section, but he was working at the Oslo office when the raid happened, and since he's Russian he can't risk coming home. The FSB are making everything difficult. It's almost impossible for foreign Bellona workers to obtain visas now.'

When Frederic Hauge sailed his boat *Genius* for Murmansk and arrived in the Kola Gulf in 1993 amidst much publicity, hundreds of Murmanchaners, many of whom were employed in the shipyards or on the nuclear-powered icebreakers, came on board to offer encouragement and shake his hand. However, I knew Russians who had mixed feelings about Bellona. Of the older generation I always expected a negative attitude but even some of my younger acquaintances were not happy with the way Bellona operated. There was no doubting the accuracy of Bellona's reports, they agreed, and it was right to expose Government and Navy negligence, not least in the matter of nuclear hazards. It was difficult, however, to face the truth about the scale of the incompetence and irresponsibility at every level.

'I'm embarrassed and depressed,' is how a student friend put it to me. 'I'm a law-abiding Russian about to embark on a teaching career, trying to feel optimistic about my country's place in the world order, and we're told by foreigners that we're not capable of running a nuclear power plant competently.'

'The hysteria stirred up by Bellona won't help,' said another. 'Their reports might be accurate but they'll turn out to be counter-productive, you wait and see. That's why that office of theirs finally got sacked. It was public opinion that pressured the FSB finally *to do something*. Bellona were publishing information that compromised our Navy. It was as simple as that. Their confrontational tactics won't work in Russia. They've no understanding of the way the Russian mind works. We're too proud and sensitive, and foreigners don't see that, including you sometimes, Roger. You're all criticism.'

Russians have particular difficulty in coming to terms with their past. In conversations on this subject even the accident at Chernobyl was often overlooked or dismissed as 'an exaggeration', or 'something our enemies enjoyed getting their teeth into at the time when Ukraine was part of the Soviet Union'. With my limited command of Russian I usually avoided confrontations about national shortcomings, but with the Bellona opponents I felt a duty to try my best, emphasizing that, if there were an accident involving radioactive material at one of the bases or in the port at Murmansk, it was going to be an international issue.

'When it comes to nuclear mismanagement we Russians aren't the only offenders,' was one immediate counter. 'The shipyard workers in Britain in the 1950s and 1960s were never told they had been seriously irradiated. And you're still ignoring international protests and pouring radioactive waste into the Irish Sea. Why don't you close Winscale down? Or is it Sellafield you call it now?'

After the mid-1990s I rarely heard such virulent anti-Bellona views. It may have been that younger Russians had started to come to terms with their past as well as their present. Nationwide demonstrations at the time, however, evinced a last yearning gasp for the old regime of order and national pride. Not long after my visit to the Bellona office in Murmansk I encountered a column of marchers coming away from the central square, and took up position under the war memorial for Anatoly Bredov, the grenade-throwing hero of the Litsa Front, as they passed. Unpaid public service workers and pensioners across the nation had announced a national day of marches and, not for the first time since Gorbachev's days, millions came on to the streets of Russia's larger towns. The elderly were out in force. State pensioners and bemedalled war veterans, alternating between marching and shuffling, produced a colourful mix, like a tailor's bag of ends, but held their heads high. The younger demonstrators mostly called for Yelstin's resignation or a government shake-up. A short distance from me an overwrought woman in tears was quietly and sustainedly wailing and holding up a board with a photograph of V.I. Ulyanov. The caption read: 'Dear Lenin. Look what's happened.'

Throughout much of Russia at this time the consensus was that foreigners should be 'sent packing', and the West's consumerist culture – at the least everything American – firmly abjured. One of the difficulties faced by the FSB, however, was that, although they claimed Bellona's work constituted espionage and involved state secrets, and was generally contrary to the interests of national security, they had difficulty in filing charges; the principal individuals involved in the compilation of the 1994 report and Bellona's other working papers were not Russian.

When Bellona took on a new recruit, a former naval captain by the name of Aleksandr Nikitin, the picture changed. Nikitin had served with the Northern Fleet until 1985 and had then transferred to the Ministry of Defence's Department for Nuclear Safety, where he was privy to Northern Fleet secrets involving nuclear fuel. When he left the Navy he was taken on by Bellona under contract specifically to work on the Foundation's next report which was scheduled for publication in 1996 and devoted entirely to the Northern Fleet.

During the months following the office raid, the FSB reviewed the status of the information already held by Bellona and the material being assembled by Nikitin. On 6 February 1996, at his home in St Petersburg, Nikitin was arrested, taken into custody and charged with high treason on grounds of espionage and divulging state secrets. The maximum sentence contained the death penalty but Nikitin, remanded in custody in St Petersburg for ten months after his arrest, was not allowed access to advisers of his choosing; much of the indictment against him was based on Ministry of Defence and Presidential decrees which were secret, and the state required that all participant lawyers in security trials had official clearance.*

* Coverage of the events and legal issues surrounding Aleksandr Nikitin's trial can be found at the Bellona website (http://www.bellona.no). I am grateful to the Foundation for their permission to quote from their web pages.

While Nikitin remained in custody through the summer of 1996 the new report was published and circulated world-wide. The recently restructured FSB, whose confidence and political standing meanwhile had grown, and who were determined to show a strong hand at every turn, responded by intimidating distributors and book-shops, and confiscating hundreds of copies of the report as they arrived at customs entry points – an absurd action since the whole illustrated report was also broadcast on Bellona's website.

Nikitin's arrest triggered enormous response. Alarmist articles about the Northern Fleet started to appear around the world, all of them benefiting from Nilsen and Bohmer's succinct, authoritative research, and the trial of Aleksandr Nikitin became an international issue. Questions were asked in the United States Senate as well as at the Council of Europe and the European Parliament. The matter was raised at meetings of the G7+1 powers and at other gatherings which included President Boris Yeltsin, such as the Helsinki summit of 1997. When ten US members of the House of Representatives met with Russian Ambassador Vorontsov on Capitol Hill, it was pointed out to Vorontsov that some of the secret decrees invoked for Nikitin's indictment were retroactive and did not even exist at the time of the act with which Nikitin was charged. Alcee Hastings from Florida, who sat on the International Relations Committee that approved aid to Russia, used blunter arguments. 'It is difficult to explain to the many poor voters in my district,' he said, 'that US money is well spent in Russia, especially with stories such as Nikitin's in the news.' These conversations were conducted at a time when the international banking community was being approached by the Russian Government for substantial loans and when many investors had already come to grief at the hands of Russian business partners.

As the time of the trial approached there was a broad understand-ing throughout the developed world that the Russian legal system was at a crossroads. The issue was whether the court could bring itself to act independently of the Federal Security Service and the St Petersburg Prosecutor. In cases brought by the security services in the past the courts were routinely expected to accept and pursue the line of argument established by the prosecution. There was almost no prospect of acquittal in such instances. As the then chairman of the

Soviet Supreme Court, A.F. Gorkhin, said in the 1960s, 'the Soviet Courts and the State security agencies were brought together by the identity of their tasks.'

The Russian Criminal Procedural Code of 1960 still actually prevented a court from making an acquittal based on grounds of lack of evidence. Moreover, in order to acquit, the court would have to submit in writing an itemized rebuttal of the indictment. This would be almost impossible in Nikitin's case: the indictment was simply too vague. As the *Moscow Times*, in its editorial of 31 October 1998, put it: 'If the prosecution can't bring a proper case against Nikitin, then Nikitin should be acquitted – but Nikitin can't be acquitted if the prosecution can't bring a proper case against him.'

The court was in effect torn between the limitations of the old 1960 Code and the norms now enshrined in Russia's new Constitution and post-Soviet international treaties. The FSB was ordered on several occasions by the Prosecutor General *not* to base the charges against Nikitin on secret and retroactive legislation, but these orders were repeatedly ignored in successive revised versions of the indictment. During the two years and eight months between Nikitin's arrest and the opening trial the FSB did little more than play for time, exerting pressure on the court as to how the case might be conducted.

When the trial finally opened in St Petersburg City Court in October 1998 and the indictment's 'secret military decrees' were read out in court, Nikitin's lawyers realized that there was little to fear from this direction. As defence counsel Reznyk said after the first day in the courtroom, '[The decrees] are not legal documents. They would fit better on the comic pages of a popular magazine ... I believe that the prosecution must have been embarrassed by the decrees ...'

Military experts called by the prosecution performed even less impressively. Confirming that the charges were based on secret and retroactive Ministry of Defence decrees, one such 'expert', a military officer named Oleg Romanov, said in court that he was confused as to why he had been asked to evaluate the secrecy status of the material under consideration. 'Our system for classifying secret information has worked well for decades,' he said. 'Now the law has messed everything up.'

The presiding judge's verdict, after only a few days in court, was strongly critical of the FSB: he found the indictment legally vague and, as it stood, it prevented Nikitin's lawyers from assembling a fair defence. The case was returned to the St Petersburg Prosecutor with instructions for FSB investigations to be renewed, with particular attention to the defence's claim that Nikitin and Bellona had only ever used information that was publicly accessible. This was a sensational start for Nikitin's lawyers, even if the judge did order the city arrest to be prolonged.

At the second City Court hearing in December 1999, St Petersburg Procurator Aleksandr Gutsan pulled out all the stops, using desperately specious arguments and new Defence Ministry documents to support the validity of the secret decrees used in the indictment, but on 29 December, as if in time for the new millennium, Judge Golets announced that the Court had acquitted Aleksandr Nikitin of all charges.

At appeal the verdict was upheld. In the autumn of year 2000, the Supreme Court disallowed all attempts to reverse the acquittal; the decision was final and could not be appealed. As the defence happily remarked, this was 'the first time in the history of the Russian Security Police – the successor of the KGB – that a person charged with high treason has been fully acquitted.'

Jon Gauslaa, Nikitin's legal advisor, said after the Supreme Court ruling: 'The principles established in the acquittal will in future force those whose case relies on secret information to respect the Constitution and Federal law. Categories of information relating to state secrets will from now on be determined by the law and not by secret decrees. It will no longer be the ministry "experts" who will determine whether an item of information is secret or not; it will be the Courts. This is a huge step forward.'

For many Russians Nikitin's acquittal was hard to swallow. Nikitin was still widely seen as a traitor and a spy. Speaking after the trial, one of my younger acquaintances sounded like a naval spokesperson: 'Nikitin was an officer in our Navy. We gave him top-class security clearance and access to state secrets. How do you think we felt when we learned that he had abused his privilege and helped a *foreign* organization to humiliate the Navy and the FSB ... and for money? Why didn't he work with one of *our* environmental organizations, who manage to campaign without upsetting everybody? Whatever the court ruled, Nikitin's a spy. It's as simple as that.'

Some time after my Bellona visit my wife Pat arrived in Murmansk by bus from Kirkenes. Among the first items out of her suitcase was a pocket-sized gamma-ray meter purchased in Canada, and two irradiation discs that she wanted us to wear under our jackets.

'But darling, the irradiation problem is not so much here and now as in the future,' I said. 'The major disaster is *in the making*. One large fire or major handling error and we shall certainly have something to record.'

'You seem to have forgotten the story about the Japanese that you told me yourself,' Pat replied. She was referring to a party of Japanese on a world tour who were said to have stopped at Murmansk. They had asked to be shown the port, particularly the icebreakers, and they happened to be carrying a geiger-counter. On finding that they had a positive reading, the Japanese panicked, vacated the port immediately and flew out of Murmansk the same day.

'You're going to wear this from now on,' Pat insisted, pinning the disc under my jacket and briefing me about bequerel and alpha, beta, gamma particles. 'I want to see the port and I'm not going near it without a meter.'

Standing on high ground near the giant soldier memorial to the Great Patriotic War overlooking the Kola Gulf, bracing ourselves against a fierce southerly wind, we took in the view of Murmansk's civilian port complex with its array of shipping, forest of cranes and gantries, jungle of sheds and railyards, and then the apartment blocks striding across the higher ground. I considered the port through the eyes of the Soviet leaders of the 1950s: if the Barents was strategically so critical during both World Wars, then the Soviet Navy could surely continue to benefit in the decades that followed. But by the same token, the region was vulnerable. Warsaw Pact countries provided a buffer zone in the event of NATO attack from the West, but no such protection existed in the north. In time, as the Soviets' nuclear submarine fleet expanded and then patrolled for months undetected under the ice north and east of the Kola Peninsula, it seemed that planet Earth had shifted its axis. The Arctic Circle had moved from the 'lost' area at the top of our terrestrial globes and repositioned itself somewhere around the 'centre', where the equator used to be. At the same time, Soviet neuroses about the vulnerability of the country's entire northern boundary were intensified; it was as if the Russian Empire had exchanged its troublesome southern borders of the old era with those of the north. By the 1960s the historical threat of invasion from Central Asia or the Caucasus had been largely replaced by the threat from the Americans, now recognized as polar neighbours who since 1958 could send their own submarines under the North Pole and into the waters of the Northern Sea Route, about which the Soviets were fiercely possessive.

We travelled in a friend's car north towards Severomorsk, the closed-town headquarters of the Northern Fleet, 25 kilometres down the Gulf from Murmansk in the direction of the open sea. Entry to Severomorsk normally required a pass – for a foreigner this was a difficult and lengthy application – but my friend had planned the trip for me and I said nothing, on the understanding that he had experience of the circumstances and was proceeding accordingly. On the way we passed the four-kilometre airstrip that serviced the Northern Fleet HQ. Further on we looked from a distance at heavily guarded buildings which were the Fleet's major storage facilities for nuclear missiles and conventional arms. In 1984 there had been a large explosion and fire at the store, when much of the conventional ordnance was destroyed. It was an inauspicious occurrence for the half-million residents within a 25-five kilometre radius.

The town of Severomorsk, whose population had reached 70,000 in the 1980s, was larger than I had expected. Approaching from the hills we looked over a mélée of naval administration buildings, the usual concrete parade of high-rise living quarters, and, at the water's edge, the shipyards themselves. There were no submarines within sight but surface vessels of all sizes were everywhere: in the docks, at the quays, and sitting at moorings.

Our driver pointed across the water to a large grey ship at anchor, probably over 250 metres in length with the large numbers '080' on its hull. It had an elegant elongated prow and bristled with warlike superstructures. I confessed to finding it beautiful, and once again recalled my days as a small boy when I gazed in wonderment at the battleships and destroyers which regularly passed through the Straits of Dover.

'That's the nuclear-powered battle cruiser *Peter the Great*. It has a crew of 800, two pressurized water-cooled reactors and plenty of missiles; even the helicopters on board carry nuclear weapons. Unfortunately it was fated from the start. On the way here there was an accident which left six crew dead and, because it took over ten years to construct, the design of the ship is now seriously out-of-date, making it almost impossible to upgrade. There are two other cruisers of the same class, built in the 1980s, but they're out of operation at the moment because the Navy can't afford to maintain them or refuel the reactors.'

Our companion saw the look on my face.

'We're truly fucked. The truth is, though, try as we may to swear at the US for all our ills, we fucked ourselves. Fucked ourselves for years and, what is more, just watched everything go wrong.'

I was cold and so was Pat. Fascinated as we were by our view of Severomorsk and what we could see of the fleet, I was also nervous about being discovered. Taking a last look at the Fleet headquarters and the hills above, busy with masts and paraphernalia for radar and communications, we drove away. Taking the coast road, we passed through the shipyards at Safonovo and Roslyakovo where we saw floating dry docks, including one of the Navy's largest, used for repairing the Typhoon-class ballistic missile-carrying submarines. Even though I had glimpsed only a small part of the Northern Fleet on my travels and had never set eyes on the other bases and yards nearer the open sea at Polyarny, Skalisty and Snezhnogorsk, I was overwhelmed by the magnitude of the military-industrial complex. I wished I had Governor Engelhardt with me to witness the outcome of his 'open-window' vision. His small port at Yekaterina, now known as Polyarny, had spawned a monster that extended throughout the Murman, not attracting the world and its wealth *into* Russia, as he had hoped, but holding it at arm's length and bringing increasing financial hardship until October 1987, when Mikhail Gorbachev arrived at the Gulf, stood beneath the giant war memorial, and proposed alternative strategies.

We drove on through the naval quarter of Rosta, a northern extension of Murmansk, and descended to sea level where we got out of the car. We walked from the road over rough land towards the water.

'Welcome to Murmansk's naval graveyard,' my friend announced. We had arrived near the shipyard of Sevmorput – a truncation of the words 'northern sea voyage' – also a dumping ground for hulks and unserviceable ships. It was difficult to make out what was what. Some ships looked as if they had sunk where they had been moored, others had been drawn up on dry land to rust and wait for decommissioning. There was little sign of ongoing activity. Clearly none of these ships would make another 'northern sea voyage'. I photographed the mess before me and we walked on.

'If you need to get your hands on some uranium just follow me,' our companion joked, indicating from the collapsed security fences how easy it would be to penetrate Sevmorput's inner premises. There was a history of uranium disappearing from these yards. Only recently police in the Caucasus had seized some enriched uranium suitable for making bombs from a man offering it for sale in a metal cylinder inside a lead container.

Soon after the collapse of the Soviet Union a market, often coordinated by naval officers, had been established not only for uranium and caesium but also for other precious metals. On several occasions nuclear submarines were disabled following thefts of filtration powder, a popular target; the powder, which cleaned the air when a submarine was submerged, contained valuable palladium. In 1999, a Northern Fleet conscript put an attack-submarine out of operation after he stole some lengths of cabling. The coiled palladium-vanadium wire was used in the communications systems of certain control devices and its removal incapacitated the entire reactor circuit.

One of the more frightening aspects of these incidents was the ignorance of some of the thieves. In 2000 two sailors sneaked into the nuclear reactor compartment of a submarine at a naval base and stole catalysts used for activating the reactor because they contained palladium, but they also stole some calibrating plates without knowing that the material was highly radioactive. Earlier in the same year five sailors were locked in a compartment of their submarine when going after saleable metal parts, and were asphyxiated to death.

The North-East Passage – or the Northern Sea Route, as it became known – which runs north of Siberia from the Barents Sea to the

Bering Straits and was eventually travelled for the first time in a single season in 1932, was extensively explored and studied by the Soviet scientific genius of the Russian North, Otto Yulyevich Shmidt, during the 1930s. When his and other expeditions contributed to Soviet advances in nuclear-power technology and hull design in the 1950s, the geopolitical map of the Arctic was transformed. A fleet of nuclear-powered icebreakers was planned – the first, the *Lenin,* was laid-down in the 1950s – which could not only cut through permanent ice of two metres but could also run without refuelling for up to four years. The fleet would enable freight to be moved in and out of the estuaries of Siberia's great northern rivers all year round, and to cut a route for naval surface attack-vessels and support-ships, enabling them to move across icebound waters at will throughout the year. The Soviet Union formed Arctic strategies, civil and naval, on a new scale.*

We drove to Atomflot, the shipyard where the Murmansk Shipping Company serviced and repaired its fleet of seven nuclear- and three diesel-powered icebreakers and one nuclear-powered container ship. Icebreakers are impressive to look at, distinguishable from other vessels by their superstructure and the shape of their bows and their hull. The hulls are strong enough to withstand continual impact with ice and are designed with a cutaway under the prow to enable the ship to rise over the ice and break it. The engines, driven by two reactors, are formidable: modern icebreakers like the Murmansk Shipping Company's *Yamal* has a propulsion power of over 50 MW, or 75,000 horsepower.

The yard seemed busy and, in contrast to the naval yards I had seen, gave the impression of being a going concern. The Murmansk Shipping Company, a joint stock company since 1993 and 35 per cent owned by the state, was a major business, involved in world cargo as well as icebreaking. Its five million tonnes of cargo a year, most of it foreign, was profitable business but, in spite of its currency earnings, the company was making a loss and the icebreakers had to be subsidized; when it came to Russian customers the company had difficulty getting paid. At the time of my visit in 1996 the Norilsk Nickel

---

* The world's first vessel constructed solely for icebreaking worked out of Murmansk. The *Yermak*, designed by the polymath Admiral Makarov and laid-down in England in 1897 at Armstrong's yard in Newcastle-upon-Tyne, was a beautiful vessel in the best traditions of quality shipbuilding. Its last voyage was in 1963, although by that time it had long ceased to be used for icebreaking.

Combine had owed millions of roubles for cargo and icebreaking work for several years.

With the collapse of the old economy and the restraints of the new, the Murmansk Shipping Company was in effect in similar straits to the Northern Fleet, and with both fleets actively looking for alternative methods of generating income, they were becoming commercial competitors. Since 1989 the icebreakers had been taking foreign tourists on summer trips to the Siberian coast and up to the North Pole, and because the icebreakers were well-appointed and rather lavishly furnished, the Company was able to demand handsome prices. The submarines also were interested in getting a slice of the tourist cake and taking passengers to the North Pole, two hundred at a time. They were reckoning that they too could ask prices similar to the $25,000 a passenger charged by the icebreakers.

In addition to looking at opportunities for earning foreign currency, the Navy had already used one or two of their submarines for freight and were said to be considering transport of nickel matte from the River Yenisey in Western Siberia to the civil port at Murmansk. Two of the technologically sophisticated Akula-class submarines, which were theoretically destined for decommissioning under the Start-II Treaty, were to be stripped of their missile- and torpedo-launchers and provided with large loading hatches at a cost of well over $50 million each. With cargo space for about 10,000 tonnes of nickel matte and the ability to make the 1,500-kilometre journey under ice where necessary and without icebreaker support, this enterprise promised substantial savings for the mining company and a long-term income for the Navy.

The environmentalists, however, were up in arms. Nils Bohmer at Bellona thought it was crazy to have a nuclear submarine commuting through the shallow waters of the Yenisey estuary and the Kara Sea. 'It's yet another recipe for a major disaster,' he said. Familiar as I now was with the Northern Fleet's proneness to accidents and its seemingly limitless incompetence, I was inclined to agree.

'I'm going to show you a ship of your worst nightmares,' I said to Pat, taking her along one of the quays and past a yellow nuclear hazard notice and towards a small coastal vessel. 'It's called the *Lepse*.'

The *Lepse* used to be a nuclear fuel supply ship, also used for dumping radioactive liquid waste off Novaya Zemlya. In 1981 it was taken out of service and moored in Murmansk as a long-term storage ship for spent fuel-assemblies and high-level radioactive waste. Many of the fuel-assemblies were damaged when transferred to the *Lepse* and therefore refused by the reprocessing centre at Mayak. We were looking at a bomb which could go off at any time, with the added danger of collision with other ships in the dock – indeed any accident, and so close to the town. There were 600 spent fuel-assemblies sitting in the *Lepse* with some 20,000 fuel-rods encased in concrete. Some of the rods were 40 years old and came from the *Lenin*. After a serious reactor accident on the *Lenin* in 1967, 300 fuel-rods were transferred but, because the rods had been deprived of coolant for a time, they had expanded and many would not fit into the *Lepse* storage containers. Workers took to using sledgehammers with the result that rods had shattered and were lying loose at the bottom of the ship's compartments. Some of these were encased in concrete but there was still a radiation problem. There was hardly a relevant environmental organization in the world that was not aware of the *Lepse*, particularly since Bellona had broadcast the information on the Internet.

The case of the *Lepse* later provided a good illustration of the problems that constantly beset clean-up projects involving international collaboration. In 1995 the International Atomic Energy Agency set up a committee to coordinate the offloading and processing of spent fuel from the *Lepse*. French and English engineers came up with a robotic, remote-controlled solution to the fuel-handling problem which would dramatically reduce irradiation doses received by workers. Adequate funds were promised, but in 1997 the project collapsed. Agreement could not be reached on issues of liability and Russian tax-exemption. Since the crew of the *Lepse* were therefore continuing to receive excessive radiation, the Bellona Foundation, searching for early practical solutions to larger problems, provided temporary dockside premises including laboratories, radiation control zones with showers, and living quarters with kitchens. It was some consolation that international debate about the *Lepse* had at last begun; the Russian Government's solution hitherto had been to 'scuttle the whole ship off Novaya Zemlya'.

I went in search of Pat whom I found in another part of the yard operating her gamma-ray meter. It stubbornly read negative.

8

NEW NORTHERNERS

Raid on the Varzina

ON A JUNE DAY in 1995 an Englishman of mature years from the Home Counties was spending a week on the northern coast of Russian Lapland as a client of the American-owned sportangling company Kola Salmon. It was a week that he would include among highlights in a life dedicated to fishing some of the world's finest streams and rivers. In the tradition of country-loving Englishmen since Isaac Walton, he had honed and nurtured his flyfishing knowledge and skill to the point of an art form. Wading stealthily downstream through the water, his line periodically sweeping and curling through the air, the hunter-angler was at one with his natural surroundings. Granite cliffs rose on either side of the fast-flowing water. Across the open tundra above him, either side of the river gorge, reindeer were moving towards the coast with new-born calves, grazing the grasses and shrubs emerging from under seven months of snow.

As the birch trees lining the river were coming into leaf, the salmon of the Kola Peninsula's northern rivers were migrating from the Atlantic, rounding the North Cape, running the coast as their species had done since before the arrival of Mesolithic man on those shores, and swimming into the estuaries of the Murman rivers. Salmon gathering near the offshore Nokuyev Island scented the water before making the final leg of their genetically preordained route. Once in the estuary of the Varzina they would recognize the water where they had been spawned.

The American operator had claimed to offer some of the world's most challenging salmon angling, with clients almost guaranteed to catch fish during their week's stay. A year earlier, in 1994, a salmon had been caught weighing over 30 kilograms and measuring 145 centimetres in length and 40 centimetres deep. Released to pass on its genes to subsequent generations, it may have been the largest Atlantic salmon ever caught on the fly. Only a few clients, however, were likely to land the largest and liveliest specimens; in wild north-west Russia the wiser British angler soon learned to adjust his theories about salmon behaviour gleaned from fathers and elders on the banks of Scottish and Irish rivers.

Isolated by the sound of the water and his own absorption, the Englishman barely noticed the helicopter as it passed overhead. It was an Mi-8, used by the camp to bring clients and provisions from Murmansk airport. He gave it little thought but guessed that the camp staff were bringing in provisions. 'Perhaps some fine Georgian wines and Russian caviar,' he mused. After all, this was a costly outing for which he and his companions had paid thousands of dollars. What he could not have guessed was that the helicopter was carrying representatives of the Lovozero District Administration, accompanied by OMON special forces personnel.

'I was eating my picnic lunch by the falls when the helicopter returned and landed nearby,' the angler told me later. 'I wasn't surprised when it arrived but I didn't expect to see inspectors. As the uniformed men approached I noticed there was something untoward about the way they walked, and I couldn't help noticing that written across their hats was the name of the company set up by the American operator's Finnish rival Eero Pettersson: Nature Unlimited. The same name was painted on the side of the helicopter.

'They produced identification and then formally advised us that our licences were not in order and we were fishing illegally. We were told to return with them to the camp. There I saw hooded and armed soldiers standing guard. Bill Davies, the boss of Kola Salmon, was there, surrounded by the Head of the Lovozero District, Petr Prins, and several of his departmental heads. They were handing him paper after paper, writing protocols and serving formal notice to close the operation. The camp was said to contravene a number of safety regulations – perhaps the most serious of these was that there were no evacuation instructions posted in the separate cabins – and it was quite clear that they had come to kick him out. Our rods and reels were confiscated. Bill advised us to pack. We would be leaving in the morning.'

*

The Saami's own salmon-fishing activity on the River Varzina had been abruptly brought to an end 30 years earlier, in the 1960s, as a result of the build-up of the Northern Fleet along the Murman coast and the construction of the base at Gremikha. Most of the families now lived in Lovozero.

Following the break-up of the Soviet Union, those Saami who still retained family rights on the north coast rivers entertained the hope that these rights might now be restored. Their hopes were in vain, and their continued absence from the whole north coast during the critical years following perestroika presented a commercial opportunity to fast-dealing Russian and foreign business adventurers that would pose an even greater long-term threat to their rights.

Although sportfishing during the Soviet era was illegal, certain salmon rivers on the Kola Peninsula had been reserved exclusively for the *nomenklatura*, who were flown from Moscow to picturesque spots and guided to the best salmon lies. When in 1987 a group of foreign businessmen working in Murmansk had asked the local Intourist if they too could put in a few days fishing before returning home, the regional KGB obliged, and the visitors were so pleased with the fishing that they pressed dollars into the palms of those at Intourist who had with some difficulty secured the relevant permissions. Legend has it that someone in authority in the Murmansk Region Administration at the time spotted the potential of selling salmon angling to rich visitors – Russian or foreign – and for dollars. By the time the new 'open market' mentality had taken root in Murmansk in the early 1990s, certain Russian businessmen, already involved unofficially in local and regional government, got wind of the opportunity and stepped in. Within a few years many of the salmon-rich rivers of Murmansk Oblast had become the domain of wealthy foreigners and a few 'New Russians', lured to the area in search of some of the world's best salmon angling. As regards the question of Saami fishing rights, entrepreneurs targeting the northern and eastern rivers claimed conveniently that 'this has been answered by the course of the region's history'.

The development of angling camps for foreigners on the Kola Peninsula is a murky story. Few operators emerged with their hands clean and reputations intact; there was even a convenient foreigner scapegoat in a North American, Bill Davies, from Tempe, Arizona, whose experiences give an idea of the kind of challenges encountered in business ventures in early post-Soviet Russia.

Davies arrived on the scene in 1985. He had wanted to start a new career and had decided on Russia. He mastered the basics of the language and struck on the idea of sportfishing for profit. His original official contact was through a *fatshchik*, a convicted homosexual released from jail in return for reporting to the KGB on foreigners. Through him Davies made contact with a recognized organization of indeterminate competence and bearing the unpronounceable title of Russokhotrybolovsoyuz – the Russian Association for Hunting and Angling. The initial pretext for all the meetings was 'the exchange of information on the management of endangered species' and subsequently Davies hit on the idea of proposing a sportfishing programme that would generate income to fund an environmental study programme.

The Soviets were understandably nervous of this liaison (Mikhail Gorbachev had only just been elected General Secretary of the Communist Party), so Davies lent the exercise a formal note by arranging that the proposed cultural exchange be mentioned in a 'speech on the floor of the US Senate', a procedure that students of US protocol will know to be next to meaningless.

This did the trick. A group of Soviet bureaucrats travelled to the United States where they learned the principles of catch-and-release angling. A contract was signed in 1989, and from 1990 onwards all agreements for angling camps in Russia contained the catch-and-release clause. Under Soviet rule the catching of anadromous fish (fish that return to their native rivers to spawn) was reserved for the collectives and forbidden to individuals. Although now, some years later, it would seem that most creatures in Russia with a sale value are nearing extinction as a result of unbridled poaching, it is worth recording that it was Bill Davies who was instrumental in placing angling in Russia on a legally and environmentally sound new footing. Where foreign fishermen would go – so ran the argument – the catch-and-release method would allow more fish to spawn, the camps would provide environmentally friendly tourism with local employment, and contracts could be structured to accommodate local interests. The overriding principle behind the new contracts and regulations was the survival of the species *Salmo salar*; all else was of secondary importance. Indeed, without the new foreign presence it was likely that the status of Atlantic salmon on the Kola Peninsula rivers would soon have reached the distressed levels recorded in most other countries within the species' migration range.

From then on, after a promising test-fishing session in 1989, events turned against Bill Davies and by 1990 competitors were at his heels. Organizational problems and rivalry on the part of those who had gained access – largely through Davies's efforts – to the Russian officials controlling leases and licences resulted in a succession of disagreements between Davies and his collaborators, foreign and local. The outcome was that the Swedish company Flyfish on Kola went to the Umba where Bill Davies had started out, the English company Roxton Bailey Robinson swiftly established itself on the Varzuga system in the south, and a consortium including the renowned American angler Gary Loomis and Eero Pettersson secured a lease on the Ponoy in the east, obtaining some of the world's highest fees for sportangling. Davies himself was now obliged to head off to the remote north-east to explore the rivers that flowed into the Barents Sea.*

These were pioneer times. Christopher Robinson, head of Roxton's international angling programme, spoke in nostalgic tones of his first expedition to the Kola Peninsula.

'There were countless delays getting there, not least those caused by the Intourist people in London and Moscow who insisted we would do better to fish for carp in the Caspian. When we arrived at the River Umba Bill Davies was already there. On our first day we worked the Krivets rapids. We were into fish within minutes ...

'I caught and released more fish in three hours than I had ever caught in a week anywhere else. We had struck gold ...

'We tested other rivers along the Tersky coast, fishing our hearts out and sleeping on the banks under the midnight sun. They were the happiest moments ... it was an angler's paradise.'

Later, the hard work started. 'We clinched the Varzuga contract for ourselves, Bill Davies having fallen foul of the local head man Kalyuzhen, and by May 1992 we had three camps with paying

* Gary Loomis sold his controlling interest in the River Ponoy Company almost immediately in 1995. In 1996 Pettersson also withdrew.

clients. It was all highly unpredictable. The river had to be sold to clients on the basis of an adventure . . .'

After years of exhaustive negotiations it seemed by 1995 as if a measure of equilibrium had been achieved in the matter of sportangling camps. Bill Davies, delighted by the scenic and challenging northern rivers, signed a contract with the Lovozero District in 1994 to fish the East Litsa, Kharlovka and Rynda, and added the Varzina to his portfolio for the 1995 season. His contract also took into consideration the needs of the few Saami who had regained access to the nearby River Drozdovka whom he aimed to employ and train and to whom he also flew timber for cabins. The future was at last looking promising. After ten years of talking and cajoling through the changing political and financial landscape of post-perestroika Russia, he had secured contracts for three camps and seven rivers. The Varzina, he assured his clients, was 'the most desirable salmon river in the world'.

*

Hardened as he was to ten years of disappointments and setbacks, Bill Davies was deeply shocked and emotionally overwhelmed by the outrageous helicopter raid of June 1995. Moreover, the event had directly involved his clients with whom it was critically important to retain credibility. When his Varzina clients had departed the morning following the confiscation of their rods, Davies flew west to his other camp on the River Rynda, preparing himself for the task of breaking the news to clients there, but quite unprepared for what confronted him on landing. A raid of a different sort had taken place.

'I found an even bigger circus, and a different crowd,' is how Davies described it to me three years later. 'In total contravention of our contract, my partner – the Russian leaseholder of the river – had invited the Mayor of Murmansk, the Head of Severomorsk Region and ten fee-paying Russian businessmen to fly out to Rynda, and I had walked in on a noisy birthday party.

'My own people there told me that the Russians had arrived out of the blue. When asked who they were, the businessmen had roared with laughter and replied: "Who are we? We're *biznesmeny*! We're here for a birthday party!"

'My clients were having a good time too. As one of them

remarked: "You promised me an adventure, Bill, and I'm sure as hell having one here." At that point I hadn't yet told my clients that their dream holiday was at an end and that they were going to have to leave for home the next day. Faced with the sheer lawlessness of the situation I had no option but to close the camp. I simply had to shut the shop and disappoint my precious clients.'

Davies may have been half expecting the worst. In January 1995, five months before the raid and one year after he had secured rights to the northern rivers (he had also contributed a substantial sum towards the Murmanrybvod Rivers Authority 'to conduct environmental surveys') he had received a letter from the Head of Lovozero District peremptorily informing him that the contract signed for the Varzina had been cancelled and that the lease was to be offered for tender in February. The tender was awarded to Pettersson's company, Nature Unlimited. Davies commented later that it was just like the old days of the Soviet Union when 'the law is what I say it is'.

With the angling season of 1995 fast approaching, Davies sued for breach of contract, and Lovozero countersued. Believing his own legal position to be sound, and with paid-up clients on the way from North America and England, Davies proceeded with the 1995 season.

The June 1995 'armed invasion' became a *cause célèbre,* with ramifications beyond the Kola Peninsula. There were representations at consular and ambassadorial level, and for a time the Americans imposed some small-scale trade sanctions. The Governor of Murmansk Oblast was heavily implicated, and several individuals holding senior political and administrative posts in the region were also cast in an unfavourable light. Petr Prins, the Head of Lovozero District, had simply disappeared, said many Lovozero locals. The Lovozero District Court upheld all aspects of Davies's case but dragged out the process by referring to the Stockholm Arbitration Institute. In 1998 Stockholm found in Davies's favour, establishing that the Varzina contract was valid, that Lovozero's revised tender was illegal, and that the inspectors' confiscations and subsequent fines were also illegal. Davies was awarded damages and costs amounting to almost US$1 million, not including interest, and the Stockholm ruling was finally upheld by the Russian Supreme Court in Moscow. Davies was fully vindicated.

The Stockholm and Moscow rulings may have concerned only one man's rights to salmon fishing but there were many observers, Russians among them, who were relieved that justice had been done. At a time in Russia when many in authority had scant regard for the legal process or for equitable and honourable procedure in matters of business, a small but important precedent had been established.*

---

* The year of the Varzina raid, 1995, was also an *annus horrendus* for local interests. On the River Ponoy, under the terms of the original Loomis/Pettersson contract, the collective at the estuary was to benefit in kind to a value of $50,000 annually. After Loomis sold out in 1995 a new contract was proposed, extending the rental period, reducing the rent by 75 per cent, and annulling the in-kind benefit. The collective's leader 'retired to an apartment in Murmansk', the collective acquiesced, and a fish-research programme was used to justify the closure of the netting station. The collective lost this source of food and income without compensation, leaving them only their reindeer. Subsequently their territory was hunted in winter by clients of Pettersson for a modest fee.

The Saami regained access to the rivers Drozdovka and Lumbovka but lost their riverside cabins to fire. The circumstances and cause of the fires were unclear but it was generally suspected that the camps were burned by the military acting on behalf of outsider interests. In 1995 the Drozdovka was fished by foreigners, clients of Nature Unlimited.

Pettersson became a large presence on the Kola Peninsula, a political and economic point of focus for the Murmansk administration, a thorn in the side of many Saami and Komi, and the object of heated debate among those with an interest in the future of salmon angling in north-west Russia. He died of a heart attack while hunting in Lithuania in 1999.

Catch-or-release

River Varzuga, May–June 1995
Arriving at Varzuga village for a second visit, more in search of salmon than of history, I was introduced to a silent, fair-haired youth called Sasha who picked up my rucksack, walked towards the river and beckoned me down the steep sandy bank towards a small wooden boat. The river at that point was some 300 metres wide, slow-moving and flat. As we moved off downstream and away from the village, the banks closed in on us, the water narrowed and quickened, and we were swept out of sight into the roar and rush of a long bend of rapids. With our small boat tossing to and fro, and the high melt-waters running us at full speed towards a steep cliff on the outside bend, Sasha calmly worked the boat back across the white water towards the slack, and within moments we were at the low inside bank. Still carrying my rucksack, Sasha jumped out ahead of me, painter in hand, drew the boat a short way up the sand and returned to help, treating me like precious cargo.

When we reached the top of the grass bank I was unprepared for the sight ahead. Towering above me, squatting like giant cormorants airing their wings, were two silver-grey helicopters, parked on a grass clearing among birch trees. I was hardly expecting to see Saami *kuvaksi* or tethered teams of summer reindeer, but it came as a surprise to hear a Home Counties accent.

'We know all about you. You're very welcome. I'm Rory Pilkington, the camp manager, and this is Alex.' A young man, wearing angling clothing of the best manufacture, shook my hand warmly and then introduced a smiling woman in her twenties. As we chatted and swapped information I looked around me. The camp comprised four large prefabricated wooden lodges and four traditional log cabins that all sat on flat ground beneath a steep wooded slope, overlooking the tail of the rapids which I had just passed through. Beyond the helicopters were two very large cylinders like the ones I had seen transported to Varzuga by truck, which I correctly assumed provided accommodation for pilots and fishing guides. We walked across the open grass and I was ushered into one of the larger wooden cabins where I was sat down immediately, Russian style, to a generous meal from the adjoining kitchen.

I had arrived at the salmon angling camp run by the English company Roxton Bailey Robinson, at the beginning of their fifth season on the Varzuga. The Varzuga was the most prolific Atlantic salmon river in Russian Lapland. There seemed to be no shortage of clients, particularly from the UK, happy to pay up to $7,000 a week for the fishing alone. When I arrived it was a Saturday and the helicopters had just brought the first week's clients from Murmansk, an hour's flight away. Veteran and first-time visitors were already down at the river, making an early start to their seven-day-seven-night indulgence. The skilled anglers would catch well over a hundred salmon that week.

There are said to be particular characteristics about the salmon run on the Varzuga that guarantee to make the first weeks on the river in spring especially productive for the angler. Thousands of large mature fish arrive at the estuary in late autumn and run a short way upstream. Finding they are entering an already freezing and falling river, they tend to retreat. The White Sea is not only rich in food but unusually deep not far from the estuary, and can therefore provide warmer water for the fish to winter.* In spring these wintering fish leave the deep and return under the sea ice to the estuary where they wait beneath the floes. Once the river starts to clear, the salmon – which are usually in fine condition – all move upstream in a glorious, instinct-driven rush, making the Varzuga one of the great, if not the world's greatest river for the Atlantic salmon, *Salmo salar*. In some spring seasons, when the river rises well above the low scrub on the banks, hundreds of fish can be seen together swimming through the

---

* The White Sea water in Kandalaksha Bay between the estuaries of the Varzuga and Umba rivers reaches depths of 300 metres. Being relatively near to the shipyards of Severodvinsk, Archangel, it is also used for submarine testing.

bushes and trees, avoiding the strong flood, making their way in just a few inches of water.

Roxton's were lucky to have landed in harness with the chairman of Varzuga's collective. In the 'fat controller' Svyatoslav Mikhaylovich Kalyuzhen, whom the English affectionately called Svet, who had total control over the river and leased the camps and fishing to Roxton's, they had a tough and tireless collaborator, who seemed as determined to meet English requirements as he was to make the enterprise a commercial success for his collective and to bring employment to the Varzuga villagers.

At first I felt uneasy about my arrival; I was not in a position to purchase even a day's fishing. But I was curious about life in the angling camps; like the Bellona Foundation – albeit for very different reasons – the camps had brought the far north-west region of Russia into the international news. However, I need not have worried; I was made to feel entirely at home by Rory and Alex and also by Christopher Robinson, a partner of Roxton's, who was currently paying his annual visit to the camp. I walked around and explored. The communal cabin, which was next to the small and chaotic kitchen where I had breakfasted, was divided into two with a large dining area at one end and a sitting room with a bar, easy chairs and an open fire at the other. The individual cabins were not lavish, but they had showers, comfortable beds and all the necessary bits and pieces. Each had a small porch for waders and wet-weather gear, and outside there were rod racks where expensive tackle sat waiting in justifiable anticipation.

I strolled down to the river, studied the water, listened to the cuckoo on the opposite bank, audible even above the roar of the rapids, and watched the Arctic terns as they flew up and down and swooped on the shoals of smolts making their first downstream journey. I then watched both the expert and the inexpert enjoying the first thrills of their holiday. Christopher Robinson, an insatiably experimental angler of many years' experience, was working the fast bigger water, catching strong sea-run salmon of up to four kilograms using a six-foot trout-stream rod. He had already snapped and patched two. It was an unforgettable exhibition of 'fishing light'.

Later in the evening I met some of the clients. They were a varied assortment of cheerful characters from different parts of Britain, all immediately identifiable as anglers. The older ones were exhausted from their first session of wading, casting and playing fish in big water, and all of them were overflowing with excitement. The renowned Michael Evans, whom I knew to be high in the angling hierarchy, was at large in the sitting room cabin before dinner, standing near the fire with a drink in his hand, waxing lyrical about the river and its fish, sharing the benefits of his long experience. I listened rapt as this rosy-cheeked man of indeterminate years and schoolboy appearance, wearing plus-fours, thick woollen socks and brown brogues, lectured on his gentle art.

The camp staff also liked to fish and they tended to indulge themselves at night when guests were asleep. Although two of the more motivated guides had learned how to cast a fly, most of the Russians used more modest tackle, to wit: one medium-size can with wooden handle fixed across diameter of open end; one hundred metres of monofilament wound around body of can; one heavy-duty spoon-shaped metal spinner; one large treble-hook with barbs. The favoured technique, which failed to match the charm of the tackle itself, was to hold the can by the handle, hurl the spinner *upstream* allowing the monofilament to shoot off the can, and then wind the monofilament back on to the can as fast as possible in the hope that it might surprise a salmon moving upstream through the fast water and snag it on the nose or body. Aware of the kind of sums that most camp clients spent on their tackle and angling wardrobe, one camp worker, a kitchen lad called Vitaly, pronounced his set-up as 'good value for money'.

That night, anxious not to overstay my welcome, I started to take my leave with a view to sleeping out in the woods or returning to the village, but Christopher Robinson insisted on my staying the night. The camp was full but I was offered one of the two comfortable settees in the communal lodge, and Christopher slept on the other.

In the morning I flew by helicopter with Rory and other camp staff in a north-westerly direction following the river up to its confluence with the Pana, and here we landed at one of the company's smaller camps, a picturesque riverside setting of commodious blue canvas tents and a log cabin dining lodge. The place was awash with the braying tones of aristocratic English, for the camp had been rented in its entirety by an English peer and his guests, lending it the ambience and bonhomie of a fishing lodge in Scotland.

A century before, other well-born Englishmen were already making their way to Russian Lapland to enjoy the fishing. The Russian traveller-diarist Nemirovich-Danchenko described two Englishmen who arrived at Kola town in the 1870s and created a stir. They also were peers – or members of parliament, it is difficult to tell from the text. They stayed a number of days in the village, spoke almost no Russian and, according to the diarist, 'mixed up *vodka* with *lodka* [boat], but went often to church and prayed in their own way.' Initially they confused and worried the *ispravnik*, the local police chief, as to what they were really up to. Relationships improved when the Englishmen, who were generous with their cash, bought large quantities of the best food and drink that could be found and persuaded the townsfolk to organize a party and to round up any available musicians for some dancing. An accordion-player was found and the Englishmen's enthusiasm proved infectious for, by the time the evening had been arranged, people came 'from beyond the immediate region' (probably from the Saami *seit* at Lake Kildin, a short distance away) to join in the fun. In honour of the occasion the visitors, in the manner of English gentlemen, appeared in white tie and tails. This proved a major attraction.

'The town had been bored to death,' wrote Nemirovich-Danchenko. 'The Englishmen were a breath of fresh air. They were extremely civilized and the population loved them, especially since they gave their calling cards to everyone – as if they were handing out tickets.' One local crone was not at all convinced of their bona fides and pronounced them *yurodivyye* – holy men living wild, soothsayers untrammelled by daily life.

The naturalist G.F. Gebel, who heard about the 'English milords' but never met them, wrote that they asked the Notozersky Saami to allow them to fish for salmon above the great falls on the Tuloma (the same falls which I myself had visited, following in the steps of Edward Rae). The Englishmen had remarkable sport, catching 250 *pud* of fish – over 200 large fish each – and handing to the Saami everything beyond their own needs. Everyone was so pleased that the Saami agreed to build two lodges on the river to which the Englishmen could return in following years for a rent of 250 roubles.

Next day I found Rory and his colleague Alex coping with the morning's quota of dramas: the Russian staff were querulous; a water pump had broken; local visitors had been helping themselves to food in the kitchen; the gas bottles were finished; one of the boat engines was giving trouble; and two clients who had barely known how to hold a rod when they arrived were complaining that they had caught only three salmon between them by the end of day two. Rory was coping admirably, unruffled and unsurprised by Russian behaviour or by the failure of Russian machinery. He was a quintessentially sanguine Englishman in the face of insurmountable problems, a gentleman of officer calibre, the sort you could follow into battle. To set up and run the camp clearly required tenacity and stamina; perhaps one of his solutions was not to learn how to speak the language.

Alex, a seasoned traveller from Australia of similar equanimity whose sparkling personality was rarely diminished by her demanding work, was new to Russia and was faring with some difficulty. Alex's domain was the kitchen, an almost unworkable space, and that morning, when she brought me a plate of fried eggs with a (rare and highly valued) English sausage, she confessed that she had been 'near to losing her cool' for the first time. Marina, her colleague from the village, catered for the Russian guides and Russian visitors, and an important part of her task was to keep these wolves away from the kitchen, but on that morning the Russian visitors had run amok and, in addition to the exhausting lupine harassment, Alex had to fend off one of the more excitable fish inspectors.

Among the visitors to the camp were two soldiers patrolling for poachers, who were becoming increasingly organized and commercial as harder times arrived. Neither of the men, one of whom was a pale, rat-faced teenager, had a smile or a friendly word for anyone; they were armed with light machine-guns and took their business seriously. A few days earlier they had shot at a man running away from them into the woods, and they also liked to fire at the poachers they couldn't reach on the other bank. Hearing that they and a group of fish inspectors were about to mount a raid on one of the nearby lakes, I invited myself for the ride.

All the passenger seats in the helicopter had been removed to make room for two inflatable rubber boats and three outboard engines, as well as boxes, sacks and large fuel drums. We lifted off from the camp.

The soldiers and inspectors were in camouflage fatigues, the rat-faced youth sitting with his sub-machine-gun in the lap of his spread legs, and Rafael, one of the fishery inspectors, looked grim – or perhaps just hung over – like a trooper on his last mission. Kalyuzhen, who was also with us, was serious and ruminative as usual and gave me an unfriendly glare as if to ask what I was doing on such an outing.

The whole repertoire of the terrain was spread before us as we travelled north-west. The river curled through pine and birch forest, its flat glides interspersed with rapids of white water. I saw myriad small lakes and streams below us, drumlins with small pockets of snow remaining in the shaded hollows, and more snow on the low, mineral-rich mountains of the Bolshiye Keyvy Ridge far to the north. The bog varied in texture from mire to berry-rich ground cover, from black to viridian. The lichen formed silver-grey-green carpets between the spruce, pine and silver birch. Traces of sledge and snowcart routes were visible from the air – winter trails that went in straight lines across bog and lake.

We crossed a watershed. The lake below us now fed a river that flowed west, emptying into the Umba system. Since the whole area was accessible from Umba village by track, there was a heavy poaching problem. Ever since Umba had lost its logging industry and the port had gone quiet, Umba men had been looking for ways to turn a few roubles. Over the years I saw many of them at work with their nets.

The helicopter banked, descended quickly, hovered a few feet above the ground and the doors flew open. Boats, engines, sacks, boxes and fuel drums flew out of the back doors with the 'storm troops' close behind. It all took less than thirty seconds before we lifted away up into the air, curling back towards Varzuga. I could already imagine Umba poachers, surprised by inspectors, dropping their nets and running breathlessly from the water into the forest, chased by the rat-faced boy firing his sub-machine gun into the trees above their heads.

As poaching activity on the Kola Peninsula increasingly threatened to become more than just subsistence fishing for the locals, these melodramatic activities by fish inspectors and their armed supporters may have been justifiable, especially in view of the demise of salmon world-wide. However, when they directly concerned friends of mine

– families that had been fishing the rivers for hundreds of years as part of their livelihood and who could historically justify their presence on the water – I was in two minds. While the advantage to the salmon population of the camps' catch-and release principle was evident, it was unfortunate that, where the river authorities were in the pockets of the entrepreneurs, the protection policies tended to be indiscriminate and excessive. The tactics of the inspectors, who now had access to large areas of their territory by helicopter or speed-boats supplied by the camp companies, were harassing single fisher-men working for their families – like my friend Volodya of Kanevka on the Ponoy – but failing to catch the major operators.

*

River Ponoy, September–October
Volodya stopped the boat at the nets which he had set at a small tribu-tary a short distance downstream of Kanevka, and collected the modest catch of six fish. All were tinged red, signifying that they had been in the river for some weeks. We then motored further to the confluence of one of the larger tributaries, over a hundred kilometres from the estuary and well away from the favoured lies of the American camp. I had promised to teach Volodya's Russian friend Valery how to cast a fly line. Valery was an enthusiastic cameraman; the previous year he had filmed me at the same stretch of the river and then spent long winter hours studying spey-casting and other skills, from tackling up to landing fish. He was a model pupil and took to the task with remarkable aptitude, hooking a grayling within the first hour. By the time Volodya's familiar mealtime call reached us from the bank – '*Rodzher, chay peet!*' – my friend had permanently discarded his spinning inclination in favour of the superior attractions of the fly.

The habitual picnic spot was at the top of a high bank with an upstream panorama of the low forested hills on either side of the Ponoy and a tantalizing view of the salmon lies at the confluence. Volodya's wife Inna tipped tea-leaves into the boiling kettle and checked the sticks of elk meat, while Volodya produced vodka to wash down the large slabs of bread, cheese and onion and an unla-belled can of meat which Valery opened in the Russian manner – one stab of the knife followed by a firm circular sweep as if paring a soft fruit.

Volodya had brought along a friend called Katya, a woman in her forties who worked part-time at the Lovozero airstrip as a meteorologist and made regular visits to the Ponoy villages earning extra money as a hairdresser. She liked to join fishing outings but she was never one to compromise her wardrobe with the kind of heavy-duty clothing that most people found necessary, summer or winter. She always looked elegant, and held my fascination by her extensive wardrobe and extravagant hairstyle. (I was never sure she actually liked me – she had the usual Russian suspicion of a foreigner – for in spite of spoiling me with some of the best *bliny* and jam puffs that I had ever eaten and which she brought to the airstrip when she knew I was waiting, she had a tiresome habit of confusing me with scraps of information about weather and flights and then watching as my mood swung between boyish delight, tearful frustration and sheer bad temper.) Earlier that summer day on the Ponoy, when I helped her step from the village bank into Volodya's boat, she was wearing elegant tasselled leather boots and a fine fox-fur hat. Now propped up in front of the fire in the lee of a large rock, cocooned by three white reindeer skins, she held her enamel mug of tea as if she were in an English drawing room. She was in good spirits. Inviting me closer and drawing me on to the reindeer skins, she put her arm around me.

'Roger, you must learn about Russian women.' Fair enough.

'And I shall teach you,' she added. I blessed Volodya and the usually reticent Valery who, seeing my blushes and habitual sheepish grin, leapt into the breach and sprung the decoy by vociferously extolling the virtues of Russian women.

'We shall be lovers tonight,' said Katya in a stage whisper.

I never did see Katya that evening, but the night was not without entertainment and not untypical of nights spent in remote communities. I was seldom well informed about what was going on in Kanevka village and sometimes I was kept in the dark on purpose. When I occasionally asked bold questions about what such-and-such a person was doing, the response was often a shrug of the shoulders. Whereas the villages during the day might seem abnormally quiet, with few people walking the paths and little sign of work, the nights were characteristically active: people were at large, there were noisy disputes, a struggle or two, and callers at all hours. From staying with

Volodya and Inna, I learned something about the protocol of these calls: disputes were conducted outside the porch door whatever the weather; ordinary callers were received in the *seni*, friends were admitted through the inner door; and a serious discussion with a member of the family or a close friend might be conducted *za stolom*, with feet under the kitchen table. When the nights were dark, some of the visits could be unnerving to an outsider. Volodya was continually beset by callers anxious for something or other. He always seemed to be 'in the money': sometimes the need was petrol, more often than not it was vodka or high-grade *spirt*, neither of which was to be had from the village shop.

Valery, Katya and about three other people had arrived at the village with me a few days earlier and there were business negotiations under way. I seemed to be witnessing – though not understanding – more than the usual number of earnest exchanges or plots as they were hatched around the houses or on our fishing outings. A further member of the cast, a pilot who had just made a delivery in a small twin-rotor helicopter, had appeared that evening. After a late dinner, which Volodya's mother had prepared for us on our return from fishing, Valery and I retired to the small guest cabin to sleep. Valery turned out his light uncharacteristically earlier than the 11 pm shutdown of the village generator, and I dozed, musing over the next day's fishing, but after an hour Valery got up and left me alone in the cabin. A further hour or two had passed when I was awoken by a knock at the outer door. I made my way to the *seni* and opened up without thinking, expecting Valery. I was confronted instead by a rough-looking drunk asking for Katya and also muttering something about *kamera* (room or closed space), which confused me. Behind him stood a woman. I assured them Katya was not with me, nor did I know anything about a *kamera*. When the man started to fight me for the door I gave him a shove which sent him reeling back and gave me time to lock the doors. There followed fifteen minutes of abuse from outside before they finally went away. At 3 am there was yet another call at the door. A middle-aged woman clearly needed help but I had no idea why and I closed the door in her face.

Drink was a constant problem at Kanevka village and I witnessed at close quarters how it affected Volodya's brothers, Aleksey and Sasha. I had seen both of them working assiduously in winter but during the summer months they were hardly recognizable: unsociable, querulous, unwashed and incoherent day after day. One night when I was on my own in the cabin and Aleksey had failed to secure adequate supplies of vodka – he was never helped out by Volodya who was a confirmed teetotal – he circled the cabin about six times between one o'clock and four o'clock in the morning, knocking on the window pleading for money.

Next morning, which had a touch of autumn, I lit the stove and sat at the table, writing and gazing vacantly out of the window. The tame reindeer Zhuchka lay asleep on the grass nearby. The dogs ran up and down the paths, scrapping and barking. The place was always full of dogs: tough Siberian laikas and other husky-like creatures that stayed outside through the winter. Valery returned in the late morning but disappeared again without a word, and there was no sign of Katya. I was curious to know what they were up to but I couldn't imagine how I would phrase the question. Perhaps nothing at all.

I went outside and ambled over to the family home where I found Volodya busy in his *pogreb*, the small cellar where he stored his salted salmon. It was his very personal place – not public like the garden sheds – and I was never sure he welcomed my gaze as he cleaned, filleted and salted innumerable lengths of pink flesh, packing them carefully into wooden boxes and barrels, sprinkling salt between the layers. As long as Volodya was able to catch hundreds of fish every year and barter or sell at between five and six dollars a kilo his family and his extended family in Murmansk and Gremikha would flourish.

'From today we'll have to keep our eyes and ears open when we're on the river,' Volodya remarked. Yesterday a helicopter had passed overhead on its way to the American camp and Volodya learned that there were inspectors and soldiers on board.

'They usually arrive about now because the large autumn run is about to begin and there'll be village people out with nets or spinning rods. Go up to that house there and see if you can purchase a villager's permit.' Villagers were at that time allowed a few day-licences with a catch limit of one salmon.

Katya turned up with a suitcase which Volodya filled with about fifteen kilograms of salted fish. She was to sell some of the fish when she returned to Lovozero. Volodya reminded me to take one of my fish with me when the time came to leave; a salmon would guarantee a seat on the plane or helicopter if demand outstripped supply, as it usually did.

The day's fishing party was the same as before with the addition of Anatoly, the helicopter pilot and the source of our information about fish inspectors. Valery and I were fishing side by side, Volodya was at the water's edge working on the boat. On the opposite bank there were two villagers with spinning rods. The first hour produced four fish all round.

There was a strong downstream wind. None of us heard the jet boat until it had rounded the bend of the river at speed. It was one of the boats from the American camp, carrying two uniformed inspectors and one soldier. The two villagers on the opposite bank, taken completely by surprise, were straight in line for the knock. One was rooted to the spot, the other threw down his rod and scrambled up the steep bank towards the forest. The boat was so swift and was run up on to the bank so adroitly that the soldier was soon in pursuit, his pistol drawn, shouting at the fugitive to stop. The angler kept scrambling and made the top of the bank, but when a shot rang out he froze. The soldier ran further into the forest to check for others, and then returned to the bank where the two fishermen were being questioned. Identification was requested, protocols were written, documents exchanged, and tackle confiscated.

The boat turned away from the bank and came over to our side of the river. I was relieved that both Valery and I had purchased permits. The senior inspector was confused to find me, a foreigner, fishing there but was satisfied with our permits. Valery and I were anxious about the two salmon we had recently caught and placed behind one of the boulders on the shore; our permits allowed only one fish a day. To our joy the inspectors left and motored on upstream.

Valery and Katya were to leave for Lovozero; I was going to stay on. As we all arrived at the airstrip, Anatoly, the pilot, who had been standing below the cockpit, strolled off across the sand in the other direction. Volodya, who had rolled a large drum across the strip, now moved it alongside and, using a hosepipe, drew petrol from the helicopter's tank for a full fifteen minutes. I wondered what complicated set of negotiations I might have missed when we were talking around the fire on the river bank. On that occasion the pilot Anatoly, a coarse, hard-drinking Russian, had turned to me saying 'Barter is the way things are done here' and that he was 'well connected'. If there was anything I needed, or if I wished to fly anywhere, he could arrange it. When the helicopter had left I helped Volodya to roll the 100-litre drum to the boat and then from the boat up to the village and into the sheds behind the house. If my barter information was correct, the drum of petrol might have cost no more than three litres of Volodya's best salmon eggs.

In the evening Volodya, Inna and I headed out on to the river for more fishing. The season had now closed, which meant none of the villagers could purchase a day permit, but we were expecting the large autumn salmon run to reach our part of the river at any moment and Volodya had set a few nets. He put me ashore to fish alone and motored further downstream. An hour had passed when I heard a boat engine approaching. Fearing inspectors, I retreated towards the bushes gathering my line as best as I could. Having reached the trees, I saw that it was Volodya's boat returning and I broke cover to show myself but, as I did so, I could see Inna frantically beckoning me to retreat again. Then I heard the now-familiar sound of the jet boat. Inspectors had spotted Volodya and were in pursuit.

Volodya was signalled to beach his boat and from the trees I watched them question my friend's movements and the reason for his being on the river at all. Volodya and Inna had already picked several baskets of berries, and that was to be their alibi, but I doubted this would receive the scantiest acknowledgement from sceptical inspectors. During the interview, as if they had seen Volodya setting his nets, the younger inspector drifted the boat a short way and pulled a net on board. Volodya was questioned but played dumb; he knew they would have had to catch him in possession for a prosecution to stick. I fled into the trees, hid my rod, and made some distance.

An hour later Volodya came walking through the forest calling for me. The inspectors had left. They had asked whether I had been fishing that day. Volodya had escaped with a warning.

It had turned into a mild sunny evening. We were standing on the shingle of the confluence near the lies and I wanted to continue casting but Volodya thought this would be foolhardy. I dismantled my rod ready for the journey home.

'Better lie in the bottom of the boat,' Volodya suggested, 'just in case we pass the inspectors on the way home.'

The inspectors were nearer than we thought. Camouflaged among the bushes of the far bank less than half a kilometre away, they were watching our movements in the dying evening light through infrared binoculars. When we left the shore their boat appeared ahead of us at speed and came alongside. From my position on the floor of the boat I found myself staring up into the faces of the two inspectors looking down at me from the height of their own boat, the senior man wearing a wry smile.

'*Dobry den*! Good day!' they both intoned sarcastically. 'Please beach the boat and climb out. We're going to search.' Fortunately Volodya had no fish in the boat and had washed off any fresh scales. He also gave an explanation for my presence – which I didn't understand – but when my rod was discovered I instinctively felt that the time of reckoning was upon us. When my rod was removed from its case the senior inspector observed that it was wet. He also found my wet waders. 'The rod has been in the boat since yesterday,' I replied lamely. And where was my reel? (In my jacket pocket.) 'The reel is at home in the village.'

The situation was not looking good. The grim-faced younger inspector was baying for blood. A long conversation ensued between Volodya and the senior inspector. My rod was confiscated and placed in the inspector's boat. We looked set for some protocol-writing, followed by a formal questioning at the Fishery headquarters in Murmansk at some point in the future. I had already been threatened by the Fisheries that if I was found with *brakoneri* (poachers) my future visa applications would be blocked. But a disagreement arose between the inspectors: the senior man was clearly uncertain about the consequences of apprehending a foreigner and, to the irritation of the younger official, my rod was returned, the matter was dropped, and the inspectors departed downstream.

We headed for the village. Volodya, who had been in constant collision with inspectors ever since the arrival of the American camp on the Ponoy and usually liked to be brazen about these encounters, was visibly apprehensive. What I longed to know was whether his trading influence and family connections within the closed circles of Lovozero ever eased his predicament. Did the inspectors see Volodya as a Saami plying his traditional trade or as just another *brakoner*, a common poacher with a nose for profit?

'Give the fishing a break for a few days,' urged Volodya's mother who was weary from the stress and anxiety that was generated in the household whenever the inspectors were at large. But the salmon were running, superb deep-bellied fish from the feeding grounds of the North Atlantic that would spend a year in the river before spawning and then a further six months after that before returning to sea. The following morning Volodya was caught on the way home from his nets with several prize fish in the boat. This would mean a fine of $200, and if he were apprehended again on the river his boat engine would be confiscated.

The local helicopter had still not come to the village after a delay of over a week, so when the forestry biplane appeared unannounced over the tree tops there was the usual rush for the airstrip. The competition for seats was going to be intense and there seemed to be an abnormal amount of parcels, small barrels and food containers. Volodya was anxious to get a large consignment away and I helped him load a dozen stout brown cardboard boxes from the cellar onto his cart. I estimated that the total weight was 50 kilograms, over 100 pounds of salted salmon. I was fearful that Volodya was risking so much of his stock on one flight.

He had not forgotten to wrap up two of my own fish.

'You may need to give one to the pilot, but take one with you to England when you go next week. You bought a licence, remember, so you're entitled to be carrying one salmon.'

Unknown to Volodya, the forestry plane had also brought a fishery inspector accompanied by a soldier, and when we had wheeled the boxes to join the other villagers' luggage heaped near the biplane, these two emerged from the log cabin control tower at the edge of the trees. I recognized neither of them. The inspector was young, aristocratic and self-confident, the soldier was his complement – young, well turned out, and certainly not a conscript; each was as fine a specimen of his own species as the best of those they were protecting. Both men nonchalantly circled the plane and the piles of freight before coming to a standstill next to the handcart containing Volodya's boxes. I could see no escape; some of the boxes were even stained with fish oil. I went to Volodya and thrust the last of my currency into his hand, a $100 bill.

'You're in real trouble. If it needs money, for heaven's sake use this.'

'It won't need that much,' replied Volodya, a little too haughtily, I thought, for his own good.

'Well, take it anyway.'

The inspector asked the owner of the handcart to identity himself and then asked Volodya to open one or two boxes.

'They're not mine. And it's too much trouble to open them up now. Look at all the string.' To my mind the boxes were inadequately tied and hardly looked as if they would tolerate one more handling; nor was the inspector impressed with this slip of an excuse. In this he was supported by the soldier who reminded Volodya that the inspector had every right to examine the contents. Volodya stood his ground.

'Well, I can't open them. That's all there is too it. As I said, they're not mine.'

An acrimonious exchange followed, including the suggestion that Volodya take the inspector to the owner. At this point I confidently predicted the outcome.

There then followed a pause, during which we all looked over towards the approaching figure of the pilot. It was Viktor, an elderly bonhomous character who had flown me on several occasions. When he reached us the pilot grasped the situation immediately and, with astonishing aplomb, appointed himself arbiter in the matter. Both parties put their case – although why the inspector felt obliged to do so was beyond me – and the pilot swiftly summed up. The speed of the discussion was beyond me but I understood that the pilot deemed it 'unreasonable' of the inspector to demand an examination of the boxes. Whether there was some trading in the deal, whether the inspectors relied excessively on the forestry plane – as they relied on the fishing camp helicopters – I could only guess. There was no time to get an explanation from Volodya either, for the pilot ordered everyone to start loading and we were swept up in the usual pandemonium.

'What's in here?' the co-pilot asked a woman who was offering up a white plastic drum.

'Mushrooms. They're for someone in hospital on a special diet.'

'I'm not taking them. We're not a charity,' he replied abruptly.

'And this?' he asked a *babushka* who was holding up two buckets of berries, closed at the top with a checked cloth tied with string. I preferred to think that the vitamin C was on its way to one of those pale undernourished youths on military service at a border post; the co-pilot, however, saw them as currency.

'They're not starving in Murmansk, you know. And you'll only get forty roubles a bucket for them anyway.'

Year one, year zero

RETURNING TO MURMANSK in February 1998 after an extended absence in England I found the town under a thick mantle of fresh snow. It was altogether more becoming, more welcoming than when I had last seen it on a cold, bleak, blustery day in autumn. The white undulating tundra hills on the far side of the Kola Gulf and the heights behind the town were gleaming under the blue sky. Older buildings stood out colourfully against the snow. Even the nine-storey apartment blocks – the brutalist concrete *devyatietazhki* – assumed a more benign aspect: less aggressive, less jerry-built than when in their summer undress. The place now seemed more at ease with its identity; even the classical stuccoed administration buildings on Lenin Prospekt had gained in authority and self-confidence.

From my first day's perambulations in Murmansk, the impression was that I had arrived amidst a comfortable bourgeois community such as one might find in provincial Austria. Were these Murmanchan Pomors the same townsfolk that I remembered? Could this really be the same drab Soviet port where I had once encountered overbearing hotel floor managers, ill-tempered shop-workers, suspicious museum janitors and pale young Anya, wearing her mother's hand-me-downs and slaving behind a food counter? Where had the modish couples that I now glimpsed in stores and passing cars come from? Who were the soigné men in well-cut suits? Murmansk women, young and mature, were wearing ankle-length coats of fox or mink complemented with stylishly cut fur hats and elegant, laced leather ankle-boots. Stern-faced matrons with more than their fair share of middle-age corpulence were moving with new-found style beneath the long swaying skins.

In the centre of town I chanced upon a money-changing friend. 'Nice jacket,' I remarked casually, noticing the Gore Tex label.

'Business has been good, Roger. I was expecting to give up this work but it's been worth carrying on. Foreigner business, yes; but Russians have money these days. It's boom town. You'll find it's not the place you remember.'

To outward appearances it certainly wasn't. The food shops held a larger range of foreign and quality goods, and their charmless cashiers, who used to be housed in raised glass booths, had disappeared. A few cafés had opened where you could sit and be served without feeling you were at a works canteen. There were fewer old cars, and many four-track vehicles of the kind that could now be seen in the fashionable quarters of any Western city. Off Lenin Prospekt new small shops were offering fine perfumes, designer fashions, and premium international brands in healthcare and household goods. Some of them had even erected signs advertising their wares. Inside I was asked by smiling sales assistants whether they could help me. The former *Beryozka* hard-currency shops for jewellery, watches, pens and fur coats, where the staff had looked askance at my expedition clothing on my first visit to Murmansk, were now open to all and any Russian and foreigner with money. The cold draught of competition was blowing under their door; the market economy boom that had started gradually in Moscow and St Petersburg even before the days of market liberalization had finally reached some of the 400,000 inhabitants of Murmansk.

Looking through the window of a newly opened clothes shop, I felt a tap on my shoulder and turned around to a young woman whom I didn't recognize. She could have been any one of the fur-coated beauties around Murmansk that seemed to have sprung from nowhere. Her skin was fine and pale in contrast to the rich fur of her hat, and her deep brown eyes were fixed on me securely from her slightly bowed head. Her lips, boldly painted in the Russian manner, were held in a smile, and she said nothing, challenging me to recognition. Not wanting to make the wrong guess, I played her at her own game. She removed her hat. The cascade of glistening auburn hair that fell to her shoulders and which she then loosened with a flick of her raised head immediately identified her as Anya – Anya Viktorevna. How could I have failed to recognize this girl with the

323

magnificent hair who had left school at sixteen to earn a small part-time wage at her local food store?

'Shame on you. You didn't recognize me. You're in Murmansk and you haven't even called my parents. You promised us.'

I protested that I had only just returned to the city.

'Well, I'm not going to let you escape now. You'll come with me for a coffee and a dessert – that sounds very American, don't you think? – and after that you can talk about fish with my father as long as you like.'

Anya's natural beauty was such that even when dressed in her mother's hand-me-downs or in a shop assistant's tall starched cap and long white coat – which is how I had first met her when with her father – she was instantly remarkable. I had come to admire her modesty and good nature, born in her case, I decided, of kind and intelligent parents.

'Well, I hardly know where to start.' She leant forward over her Murmansk-style cappuccino, eager to tell me of her recent experiences but blushing strongly.

Anya had been introduced by one of her older girlfriends to a businessman called Oleg, a forty-five-year-old Russian from the Caucasus. Oleg worked, I was told, in the import-export business and had joined up with a group of Murmanchaners to do business with the States and Western Europe – mostly Germany. Anya did not elaborate and I sensed she would not do so, even if asked. Judging from her boss's contacts with Monchegorsk, Nikel and Zapolyarny I guessed the business was to do with metals.

'I have to be on call all the time and available at short notice to go anywhere with my boss and his colleagues. That's all. I haven't learned anything. I mean I'm not really a secretary. I'm what you'd call a personal assistant, I suppose. It's easy. And we travel everywhere, all the time. Düsseldorf, Hamburg, Paris, sometimes New York. The most interesting people I meet are the young assistants – mostly men – who look after the financial and computerized side of things: the accounts, the cashflow, the international transactions. They're mostly university graduates with lots of qualifications. Just boys, but such responsibility.'

I refrained from asking Anya where she thought all this was taking her. She was on a roll, happy and relaxed; a life of well-remunerated prostitution was certainly good enough for the time being. She found herself accommodated in the world's finest hotels and, now and again, a luxurious private house or villa. Since starting work she had recruited a few of her own friends who, like her, had left school early. Substantial sums of money were flowing into the girls' pockets, and much of it on to their families and relations in Murmansk and elsewhere.

Why Anya felt she could confide in me – and sometimes in such detail – I was not sure. At her parents' home, she showed me her wardrobe. The extravagance and quality of her clothes, seen in the mean and colourless ambience of a standard one-bedroom Russian apartment, saddened me. Moreover, her parents had not arrived home from work and I felt unrelaxed in the situation. I took my leave but before doing so asked her for a small token, a keepsake: a lock of her unique auburn hair that I would make into a salmon fly. She responded to my request without hesitation but looked at me in complete puzzlement.

'Ask your father to explain, Anya. He'll understand.'

'The Russians are cherished clients all over the world,' said Larry, warming to a business analysis for me. 'There are hundreds of wealthy people in this town wanting to spend large sums of money overseas, and the people to whom we send our clients are delighted to welcome them through the door. Our experience is that if Russians spend, they spend lavishly. And if you can put up with their outrageous demands, you're in clover.'

I had been walking through the Volna shopping centre, an ugly late Sixties building on three floors which together with the Arktika and Meridian Hotel dominated Murmansk's central Five Corners Square. A tall, smartly dressed young woman carrying a clipboard had approached me, inviting me to answer a few simple questions and take part in a holiday competition. Realizing I was a foreigner she apologized and backed away, but I was interested in her work, and I asked her what her company was selling. That is how I came to be talking to Larry Temple in a small suite of offices on the sixth floor of the Meridian. (The loss-making Meridian, formerly the Northern Fleet's favoured hotel, had converted two floors to offices. They had also saved money by dismissing most of the women floor-managers who had intimidated me when I was first in Murmansk).

Larry Temple, a short, well-built man in his forties with close-cropped hair, came from Gravesend. He had a forthright, no-nonsense manner, with all the gifts of a South London barrow boy, and was frank about his business.

'Timeshare has a bad name, and it always will, however good the firm. The problem is often the clients: they get carried away, they don't read the small print, they decide too late they don't have the money after all, and when the competition gets to them, they're easily convinced that the company they've just dealt with is a con outfit. We do read the small print to them, but people here in Murmansk get excited about their freedom and newly acquired cash, and they don't even consult a lawyer ... You'll have to excuse me now. We have a client presentation.'

When Larry left the room I had the opportunity to talk with some of the sales staff. Lana, Boris, Yevgeniya and their colleagues were all graduates in their early twenties. They spoke fluent English, were charming, sophisticated, well-dressed, and motivated by the new profit-oriented work ethic flowing through Murmansk.

'Some Murmansk employees still get the Arctic premium on top of their pay,' said Boris, 'usually around 80 per cent – but salaries in the standard jobs are low, particularly when you consider that consumer prices might be 70 per cent higher here in the north and that to have a holiday we have to travel twice as far. Private enterprise is the thing. We can see it working, and we're going to be part of it. It's great. You set the business up right, you work hard, nobody gets in your way, and the money comes in. For some of us this is our first job, and to judge from the kind of life our parents have had, there's no chance of our going back to the old ways.'

'As a state-employed junior manager,' said Yevgeniya, ' I might get US$200 a month. Even as a fully-qualified business translator I'd never get $400 a month. That's a modest wage, particularly if you want to have your own place, raise children and live anywhere near the standards of people in the West. If I work for a private business and I'm good, I might get $1,000 a month within two years. The timeshare business is doing well, really well.'*

* These pre-August 1998 salaries were high. A shop assistant's pay would have been around $50 per month, the old-age pension rarely more than $30 per month; a well-qualified State teacher, working long hours in a higher institution, might expect (when paid) $300 per month.

I asked them about the 'unorthodox' jobs that seemed to be on offer everywhere. Would they work for an organization they knew to be outside the law? The peals of laughter died down and we talked salaries again. I could imagine the temptations. *Biznesmeny* were recruiting young men and women not only to the strongarm end of their operations; they were actively seeking through orthodox channels the brightest and sharpest graduates from the universities. There were high salaries on offer for those with good qualifications. Many young people had parents who had lost all their savings during the market liberalization of 1992 and the hyperinflation and banking shenanigans of the Gaidar era. There was therefore every incentive to bypass the State, which had betrayed the small depositor, and to find an organization which needed your skills, where you would be mentally stretched and where brains and initiative were handsomely rewarded.

Larry returned and offered me a cup of English-style tea-with-milk in his office. 'Unfortunately we also suffer from the attentions of the business world's lower orders.'

Larry explained to me how his firm had been targeted by the mafia. 'As soon as we started to generate a profit I had a visit. He was a big strong boy, a representative from what I would call the Physical Department. Later the same day somebody went through the books. We agreed on the sum payable to the "roofers" – as they're called here – and that was that. We just pay up every week. Fortunately we can afford it. God help us when we can't.'

Two weeks before I arrived in Murmansk there had been a spate of assassinations, one or two of them particularly brazen. A businessman had been shot on Lenin Prospekt in the middle of the day. By 1997 in Moscow or St Petersburg this kind of killing had become less frequent – or less prominent – but in Murmansk the territories were still being carved. Turf warfare was a messy business. Murmansk was in Year One.

Where was the blood money ending up? The microeconomy of Murmansk appeared to be flourishing: there was a substantial new turnover of foreign goods, there was more cash in circulation, and it was clear that much of this cash was benefiting employees' extended families. But what effect was illegal capital outflow from

Russia having on the macroeconomy? A year or so later I raised the matter of capital flight with Mark Galeotti, an English academic at Hull University in England and an adviser to the UK Government. He believed that by 1996 a substantial proportion of criminal and illegally exported capital was flowing back into the Russian economy. Professor Philip Hanson of Birmingham University, an economist and former diplomat with wide experience of pre- and post-perestroika Russia, was able in 1998 to confirm that for one quarter of 1997 there was an official net capital inflow to Russia.

Mark Galeotti also observed that historical factors had contributed to the phenomenal rise of organized crime. From the time of the ethnic purges and diasporae under Stalin, when national and international boundaries ceased to be sacrosanct, the Soviet peoples could be said to have developed a natural cross-border vision. They then grew so accustomed to the lack of support and succour from the State, and were reliant for so long on crime to conduct business or to secure a service, that allegiances and channels of communication were in place from one end of the former Soviet Union to the other. According to Galeotti, the lax eighteen-year Brezhnev era that came later particularly stimulated Russia's modern criminal alliances.

Thus when Russian, Ukrainian, Chechen, Georgian, Uzbek and other ethnic post-Soviet groupings sent their representatives to the conference tables of the world's criminal organizations, they came with immaculate credentials, tried and tested and well suited to global market operations. In the early years links were formed with Italian, Colombian and North American partners, and agreements were reached in relation to all the principal activities: narcotics, vice, protection, illegal arms, contract killing, importing stolen Western goods, exporting minerals and metals, conducting illegal financial transfers, fraud, counterfeiting, and money-laundering. According to Galeotti, the turnover of the organized black economy soon reached 15–18 per cent of the entire Russian defence budget, and by 1993 four per cent of *all* crime in Germany was under Russian control. By the millennium it had become possible to observe the extraordinary tide of Russian or Russian-owned talent in unorthodox business world-wide.

What was disheartening for the majority of Russians was to see not only how impotent the G7 countries were in the face of the tidal wave but also how the world's leading economies adopted a cynically practical approach to the problem of New Russian capital and money-laundering. In the United Kingdom, for example, the regulatory bodies, overwhelmed by the task of tracing the source and title of the many opaque transactions and registrations in the City of London, felt obliged to turn a blind eye. It was decided that from an agreed date the status of all depositors was to be acknowledged and Russians thereafter welcomed to the mainstream banking system on condition that – or in the hope that – new business would henceforth behave ethically. To most ordinary people this all sounded like 'acceptable levels of corruption' and normal City practice. The UK Treasury dubbed the policy Year Zero.

In spite of the customer-friendly transformation of the Meridian Hotel, I had decided in advance of this winter visit that I would rent an apartment as my expedition base. The two-bedroom home that had been found for me by my Murmansk friends Yan and Olga was located in an old quarter north of the centre, overlooking the shipyards, a part of town completely destroyed by the German blanket bombing of June 1942. Karl Liebknecht Street had been rebuilt immediately after the war with small houses rendered in sienna and yellow stucco over wooden frames, which glowed warmly next to the clean white snow. My own block, a blue-painted, five-floor building of the Khrushchev era, had by the 1990s acquired a certain antiquarian appeal. It had the further practical advantage of being close to the main open-air market. The staircase smelt of sewage, the apartment itself was grimy and, since it had been recently let to two seamen, it felt and smelt like a doss-house. But it was my new headquarters. Notwithstanding the company of myriad cockroaches – even in my bed – I expected to be more happy there than at the Meridian. The furniture was old-Soviet at its worst and the sitting room was dominated by an enormous deficient television, but after a day's bargain-hunting with a copy of a daily newspaper to hand, followed by a few hours of housework and a chemical-warfare strategy as to cockroaches, the household was up and running.

Yan had asked me to hold an English language class, so I broke off from the second day of household chores to make my way up the hill to the institute where he and his wife Olga had recently joined the teaching staff. The establishment was one of a small number of new fee-paying schools in Murmansk, with a large English language department for children from the age of ten and business management courses for those in their late teens. Yan told me the fees were substantial. These pupils were from financially privileged homes, the offspring of those who had benefited from the economic and political upheavals of the early 1990s.

I was formally introduced to the dozen eleven-year-old pupils by their teacher Tatyana Aleksandrovna. I was impressed by the class. Most were near-fluent in English, having started from scratch only eighteen months earlier. Even given that they had rehearsed many of their questions and recitations, the children were skilled at answering the follow-up questions that I fired at them – hardly the products of old Soviet parrot-fashion learning.

Most of the personal questions addressed to me were predictably materialist. How many cars did I have and what makes? How large was my home (presumed to be a substantial detached house in London's Hampstead or Highgate, now sought after by wealthy Russians)? How much was my salary, and did I eat in expensive restaurants? The narrow range of interrogation topics was broken by a boy who asked me what my hobby was. This made me laugh because it was also a favourite question of my late father who found that, as the twentieth century proceeded, fewer and fewer people were able to answer satisfactorily.

As I questioned them about their lives and interests, it became apparent that not one of the children had ventured locally out of Murmansk. They had almost no concept of the land in which they were living, either geographically or historically. They were also completely unaware of environmental matters. In other topics these children showed awareness and knowledge, and enjoyed a sophisticated lifestyle. They had travelled internationally, had an outline awareness of other European countries, and probably knew Sheremetevo international departure lounge as well as I did the equivalent at Heathrow or Stansted.

I spoke to them about Russian Lapland, its tundra and forests, its wildlife, its rivers and lakes, the indigenous Saami, the medieval

Pomor settler families, and the remote villages. But this was all foreign to them, and not part of their life and education. There were, I mused on the way home, reindeer galore in the forest not many kilometres away, ready for eating. There were dozens of people who would be happy to sell the meat. But not one of my class that day had ever eaten reindeer meat.

I returned to the class a few days later, but it was my last. Tatyana was pleased to have a native English speaker, but she appeared uneasy with my questions and the way in which I expanded the topics of discussion. I thought my value lay not in rehearsing grammar and syntax but in discussing challenging topics in a foreign language; she on the other hand had envisaged my task as simply to stand and correct the children's English. Tatyana observed me patiently throughout one half of a lesson as I drew the kids away from their materialist preoccupation towards global or environmental issues – even to talk about people less financially fortunate than themselves. She did not invite me to return.

Walking towards my apartment that evening I was spotted by some of the local children. They had had their eye on me since I was first sighted at the local market where they had insisted on making my acquaintance, calculating my value as a potential source of sweets or pocket money. I had realized that by taking an apartment in this district I was probably exposing myself to petty theft; even local adults observing my comings and goings might have thought me good for a $100 bill when weighed down with shopping. Also, the unlit staircase of number 40 Karl Liebknecht was dark from about 3 pm and there was an area just inside the street door which would be ideal for an ambush. As I approached the street door I always prepared myself for an encounter and ensured that my money was put away and that my apartment key was ready but not in my hand.

I proposed a tactical alliance with the children on a quid-pro-quo basis. I would control the arsenal of multinational confectionery and soft drinks; they guaranteed permanent patrol personnel, all with campaign experience of the local terrain. They provided a useful service; friends would call unannounced when I was out or away on expedition, and my team usually had names and messages for me when I returned.

After a period of familiarization I allowed the less hyperactive of the girls and boys to visit me. Cameras, radios and other enticing items were locked away, and the children were instructed to wash their hands and faces and not run around. They sat quietly, read magazines, played cards, chess or draughts, used my computer, or just talked, and if they behaved themselves they earned Coca Cola, chocolate and anything they wanted from the kitchen. None of them ever asked for alcohol and whenever they tasted my beer or Russian champagne they declared it undrinkable.

My best behaved visitors – though not my best security – were a young boy and his two sisters. I knew their parents by sight and occasionally greeted them. Oksana, at thirteen, was not the oldest but was the leader. The three of them were always unkempt, as if they had spent much of the day scrapping, and this gave them the appearance of fallen angels.

Katya, at fourteen, was undergoing a seasonal moult. She tired quickly of cards and even chocolate, and spent long periods looking at herself in the bathroom mirror, becoming increasingly dissatisfied with her dishevelled tomboy image. One week her pocket-money – or was it rich pickings? – secured her her first cosmetics. These were squirrelled into the bathroom on arrival, and later she emerged with lipstick, lip gloss, eye shadow and glitter liberally applied. She steadily lost interest in chess and our other activities and thereafter visited me less. When I did see her she was never without make-up.

There was a six-month interval before I saw the three children again. They were loitering late one warm evening to the side of the Arktika Hotel in an area which at the time had its own particular microclimate and 'wildlife'. Oksana, the leader, had not changed. She was now fourteen but still undersize, rough, tough and authoritative; I had learned early in our acquaintance not to cross her. Little Volodya stood quiet and contemplative by her side.

Katya, still thin and undernourished, still a child, had metamorphosed. She hardly looked me in the eye and persistently gazed at the toes of her shuffling feet. The blonde Russian gamine was disturbingly similar to the fashion images seen in upmarket Western magazines, their bruised *pauvre* faces and baleful expressions suggestive of manipulated, premature sexuality.

Katya's fashionable long cashmere coat had certainly not been purchased by her parents. As she fidgeted under my gaze, the front of the coat parted. The simple black cotton tank-top, which fitted tightly over her flat chest and exposed her tiny midriff, could have been worn by any of the older girls dancing in the discotheque above us. Her lower garments told a different story. Trimmed with lace at the hem, Katya's tiny skirt was high on her fleshless thighs, revealing the tops of black stay-up stockings. Her fine leather ankle-boots were chic but the tall heels brought her knees forward, giving her a slight stoop. She seemed off-balance, as if the metamorphosis was too much for her to comprehend or physically contain.

I became uneasy in the company of the children, these three good young friends whose hilarious sense of fun and humour I had greatly enjoyed, and whose cruel mockery of my spoken Russian I had happily endured. There was a pause in our perfunctory conversation. Katya raised her eyes. I did not recognize the smile. Sister Oksana fixed me with a cold hard stare. She moved closer to take my arm but I had started to leave. As I turned away I wished that the solid thud of the music from the club above were louder, loud enough to have drowned Oksana's words. For a long time I denied to myself that I had heard the lascivious ingratiations, the lewd propositions that had poured so fluently from her child's mouth.

'That would have been impossible a few years ago,' Edik, a longtime Murmansk friend, said over the disco music. 'Children never had the freedom to loiter; parents simply didn't allow it, and neighbours cut up a big fuss if children got seriously out of line.'

Edik had offered to give me a round trip of the nightspots in Murmansk, and we had ended up at a new discotheque which had been installed at one end of the Meridian Hotel. (Was this, I wondered, another part of the same business plan that had laid off the hotel *dezhurnyye*? Was I imagining it, or was the middle-aged woman working at the coat counter and under pressure from teenage customers really one of the officious, outrageously nosy women who had bossed me and reported my movements when I first stayed at the Meridian?)

333

'The new generation who grew up with perestroika,' Edik said unnecessarily, 'have no idea of their history. They're just mad for rock-'n-roll and trendy clothes. The girls of rich parents go out probably twice a week. The poorer girls you can see on Saturday afternoons on Lenina literally begging the club entrance fee; once inside they claw money from someone somehow.'

Edik, who didn't like dancing and was more at ease in male drinking company, said after a while. 'I'll leave you here to get on with it. But watch the *dinamo* girls – the freeloaders, Roger, they'll fleece you rotten. There are quite a few here.'

Soon after his departure I did receive the attentions of a young woman. She was less than half my age and could hardly have found me as attractive as she insisted, but I was interested to let the procedure run its course and joined her group of friends at a table. The gathering was under the auspices of a boy still in his teens but clearly aspiring to the new business classes. He soon invited me to treat him and three of the girls to dinner at the club restaurant; I suggested a round of drinks. Having offered to collect the drinks from the bar and now standing next to me ready to take a sum of money equivalent to his high estimate of the cost, he grabbed the roubles I was holding and in the same movement thrust his other hand into my other pocket which contained my dollars. Alone and deep inside enemy lines, I was tempted to count my losses and retreat. Nobody was more surprised than I when my challenge secured the return of the loot.

Walking through town one afternoon I came across a shop selling video films and computer game CDs that had opened since I was last in Murmansk. I was curious about the clientele and went inside. The shoppers were mostly boys and girls in their early teens. One of the boys was keeping two of the assistants particularly busy, asking for one CD after another to be handed to him from the shelves behind the counter.

'I've got that one, and that one. I bought this one last week. Yes, I know that one. Have you got anything new?' The assistants showed immense patience. From the back of the shop they produced a box of the most recent games from Moscow.

The boy stood on tiptoe and reached up over the counter with his roubles. 'I'm in a hurry. I'll take any three.' Following the boy from the shop, I noticed him climbing into a new Mitsubishi four-track. The two adults in the front seats, presumably his parents, were typical of a type that I had begun to notice regularly around Murmansk. The New Northerners were out in force.

9

RUNNING WITH HISTORY

THROUGHOUT MY EXPLORATIONS of the remote tundra and the empty coastal stretches of Russian Lapland, either alone or in company, I not unnaturally encountered few people. When Russians did appear in the middle of nowhere they were often engaged in illegal activities or driving the ominous, tank-like *vezdekhody*, loaded with anything from salmon and elk to rare minerals. On these occasions I found myself irrationally behaving in an almost proprietorial manner, rather like the Federal Security Service itself, whose regional officers were still uneasy about anybody's motives for moving anywhere beyond the urban tarmac.*

Early one summer night I was sitting on the bank of the River Umba with a friend, museum curator Ivan Vdovin, enjoying a quiet campsite supper on the second day of our expedition, when a shape appeared on the water at the turn of the river, drifting down towards us on the steady current. As it approached us in the half-light, the shape transformed into a log raft on rubber flotation tubes, with four men paddling at the corners. Believing them to be poachers – the Umba, which was not remote, was popular with locals – and expecting them to move on without so much as a nod of the head in our direction, I was taken aback when they steered directly for us and then greeted us good-naturedly as soon as they came within earshot. Instead of being suspicious of their motives I now became indignant about our provisions; prior to my departure from Murmansk – and greatly looking forward to the company of my favourite travel companion – I had stocked up with the best that

* The FSB, who were probably short of work by 2001, still pursued my elderly landlady – an old-style 'staircase informer' if ever I knew one – for snippets of information about me.

new-era Murmansk shopping could offer, including fine salami, smoked meat, coffee, cognac and good vodka. Ashamed of my English meanness, I drank up my coffee, hurried to hide the bottles – we would have to sacrifice our large pot of reindeer stew, of that I was certain – and sat awaiting the men's arrival and the usual persistent interrogations.

Accustomed to the rough-hewn and sometimes aggressive appearance of those poachers I had met, I was surprised by our visitors on this occasion who, although dishevelled from their travels, seemed remarkably genteel. They climbed the bank deferentially, as if entering our home, settled calmly round our fire and, contrary to my expectations, were more interested in our company than our larder. They declined every sustenance we offered except conversation and sweet tea.

The four *dzhentelmen* turned out to be former Moscow school friends, now living apart and in their late sixties – though looking to me more like octogenarians – who in their youth had cherished an ambition to travel two of the larger rivers of Murmansk Oblast by canoe, but with the arrival of the Cold War and the build-up of the military presence in the area, had been refused permission by the KGB. The men had therefore recently decided on a 'last adventure' and had left home a week earlier for the north-west. Like boys on their first-ever independent outing in the school holidays, they savoured the encounter of kindred spirits and looked wide-eyed at us, our campsite, our tent and our belongings. Their own raft and equipment, all of which was mature and of sound but heavy, old-fashioned materials, looked as if for decades it had been patiently awaiting a last glorious call to service.

Our visitors seemed to know little about Russian Lapland but, like myself years earlier, had been romantically curious about the wild, empty Kola Peninsula. When I told them that I was interested in the area's history, this caused hilarity.

'History?' one of them muttered, repeating the word rather like the man at Kanevka whom I had asked about his village out of the blue. 'Well, that won't keep you very busy here. There's not much history in these parts.' When the men later climbed on to their raft to move on, they wished me 'good luck with the history' and laughed loudly as they turned away and took up their paddles.

That May I had been waiting impatiently for the rivers to melt. The previous summer I had received news from Ivan of an astonishing archaeological discovery. The events were pure happenstance. Yury Ivanov, Ivan's young assistant at Revda Museum, had been rafting the length of the Umba with friends. When they reached Lake Kanozero, about half-way to the White Sea, they had stopped at a wooded island of about three hectares near the lake's east bank and pitched camp under trees near a large stretch of smooth rock that sloped down directly into the water. At one o'clock in the morning, as Yury was about to crawl into his tent, his eye was caught by the raking light of the sun, now low on the horizon. When he looked at the nearby shimmering rock, he noticed small markings on its surface that immediately struck him as unnatural. As he approached the rock, the markings, which were like shallow engravings and seemed man-made, revealed distinct shapes. On closer examination, one of them transformed into the profile of a boat rowed by eight men, its long prow resembling the head of a reindeer. After more searches across the same stretch of rock, Yury found other incisions – 'petroglyphs', Ivan had called them over the telephone – of men in frontal outline.

After a few hours' sleep, and believing that he must have been dreaming, Yury hurried back to the rock to find that the shapes had indeed disappeared. After a few minutes of half-hearted and sceptical searching, however, they began to re-emerge, but only indistinctly, as if the higher, eastern light of morning were reluctant to perform the night-time trick in the same way. As Yury's eye became accustomed to the differences between nature's striations and man's incisions, and as he followed the images across the smooth rock and lifted the lichen at its edges, he found other images.

When Yury returned to the island later that summer with Ivan Vdovin and Vladimir Shumkin of the St Petersburg Institute of Archaeology, a further two hundred or more man-made images were discovered within a few days, and a wider pictorial repertoire began to appear. Looked at collectively, the figurative drawings seemed almost to be telling the story of Russian Lapland. First came reindeer, then fish and whales (beluga in the White Sea), followed by men, women, couples holding hands, couples holding offspring, and a drawing of a male with curious attributes – not least that of outsize genitals – that might have represented a shaman. Thereafter the team uncovered representations of men with reindeer, men harpooning whales, and a man fishing with a rod and line – one of the earliest known representations of angling. All these incisions were confidently dated by Shumkin variously between 3,000 BC and the Bronze Age, some 2,000 years ago.

Eager to experience this archaeological windfall for myself, I had set off for Lake Kanozero with Ivan the summer following the discovery. As we entered the lake in the evening, rowing into a strong cold breeze, the island came into view in the distance, a mere lump of rock topped by pine trees. As we drew up to the sloping rock-face Ivan told me that the surface was slippery where wet but, in my haste, I forgot to heed the warning. My enduring memory of our arrival at the historic site was stepping from the boat on to the smooth rock and finishing the movement fully submerged in the cold waters of Kanozero. When I had dried my clothes in front of a fire I joined Ivan. He was crouched over a large sheet of paper laid across the rock a metre or two above water-level, making a rubbing. When he removed the paper I saw an array of figurative and abstract pictures. Then, walking me up the slope, he showed me more engraved images which until the previous summer had probably remained hidden by lichen since the era in which they were made.

It was not until around midnight, however, that I grasped the full beauty of the extraordinary Kanozero scratchings. When the sun moved into the northern quarters of its arc and cast its magic I was overcome by the animation and vitality of the shapes. They were not unlike the reindeer and human images on the smooth rock below Kapitan Nikolay's Ponoy cabin at Chalmne Varre, and they reminded me also of photographs I had seen of petroglyphs on Lake Onega and the River Vyg on the White Sea coast, as well as the world-famous rocks at Alta in northern Norway. In iconographical and anthropological terms their importance in building a picture of early man's migration and settlement in Northern Europe could not be overestimated.

The following morning, encouraged by Ivan to do some searching of my own, I was rewarded within the hour. When I lifted some mosses not a hundred metres from our tent I found a shape that at first I thought was a large reindeer but which Ivan identified as an elk, distinguishable by the shape of its head and its beard. On removing moss from the adjacent rock which had become separated from the first by a split, I saw that the elk was swimming, chased by a boat with eleven oarsmen and a man standing at the bow brandishing a spear. Later the same day I sat musing over the simple but telling image of a small man running with his reindeer, the two species moving together in harmony, and now exposed after some two millennia for my private contemplation.

Full of my Kanozero experience I returned to Murmansk on my way home to England feeling uplifted about the land that I had come to know so well. The region, still home to almost one million people, many of whom had been born of parents sent north to serve the Soviet Union's over-ambitious economic industrial plans, seemed now to be walking a tightrope with its various identities. The Kanozero panoply reminded me, amongst these thoughts, that eastern Lapland still offered its settlers traditional terms of mutually beneficial cohabitation and a future irrevocably associated with reindeer and the other creatures of its land and its waters.

Walking through town, I was greeted by Olga Konyukhova, my very first Murmansk acquaintance. 'Yan and I have got some news for you. We'll soon be going south. We're moving to Novgorod. I can't wait to get there. I just can't wait to leave this place.'

History's bells rang in my head.

'Novgorod. Novgorod,' I repeated to myself in the very same way as the Russian gentlemen-rafters and the man at Kanevka. For hundreds of years – before the Russians, before the October Revolution, before the Soviet Union – the spring and early summer traffic had gone in the opposite direction to that now being taken by young Olga and Yan with their small daughter Yelisaveta. Since the Middle Ages men and their families from the south had rushed optimistically northwards, travelling up and down rivers and across watershed portages to seek bounty in the fish-rich seas of the Arctic or to barter fur with Lapps, and return home with their pockets full.

Olga and Yan were typical of thousands of young Murmanchaners whose parents, like latter-day Pomors, had come north. In the wealthy 1970s, Yan and Olga's parents earned good salaries, lived comfortably, and raised a family under circumstances more favourable than those they had left behind in the south. Until the late 1980s

Murmansk had enjoyed positive immigration, but with the changed post-perestroika economy, the privileges of working in the north had steadily eroded and families were now returning south to their roots.

When I returned to my own home, I felt, like Richard Chancellor, that I had chanced upon a remarkable land 'where natural treasure falls from the sky'. I turned again to Tacitus, whose description of the Lapps in his *Germania* – also scratched two millennia earlier – concludes with the tantalizing sentences:

> They esteem their life a happier one than if it were spent in groaning over the clods and labouring to build houses, dreading ever to lose what has already been gained. Careless of what man may do or God decree, they have achieved the most difficult of all conditions to attain, in that they have nothing more to pray for.
>
> Farther than this everything dissolves into myths ... Of these I know nothing, and choose therefore to leave well alone.*

---

* *Germania*, translated by J.B. Rives, Oxford: Clarendon Press, 1999.

Glossary

Note: Stressed syllables are indicated where necessary

apparatchik	lit. operator. Slang term for high-level Soviet bureaucrat or Communist Party Member
bàbushka	lit. grandmother. A respectful word for any elderly woman
banya	steam-bath, or building where steam-bathing takes place
blin/bliny	pancake / pancakes, traditionally made with buckwheat flour and yeast
brakonèr	poacher
CHEKA/GPU/ NKVD/KGB/ FSB	abbreviations of Soviet government departments administering the secret police or state security service, from the Civil War to the 1990s
chum (Komi)	large tent formed with conical framework of poles covered by canvas or skins
dacha	any second family home in the country, from a log-cabin to a palace
devyatietàzhka	standard modular, nine-storey apartment building in the Soviet Union, 1970–90s
dezhùrnaya	lit. duty-person. Hotel floor-manager
glasnost	lit. openness. Socio-political climate resulting from Communist Party Secretary Gorbachev's policies of the late 1980s
gostìnitsa	hotel
GTT	see *vezdekhòd*
gulag	Russian acronym of Chief Administration for Corrective Labour Camps. The term can denote either one of these camps or the whole system
internàt	Soviet-era boarding-school
izbà/ìzby	small, one-room, short-stay log cabin/cabins for workers or travellers
khrushchèvka (pronounced khrushchòvka)	standard five-storey apartment building of the Khrushchev era
kolbasà	sausage, often salami

kulak	farmer of any scale owning land and employing workers
kuvàksa (Saami)	small, easily transportable tent formed with conical framework of poles covered by canvas or skins
Lop/Lopań	Lapp/Lapps. Russian words (now regarded as derogatory) for Saami
màlitsa	full-length, one-piece garment of reindeer skin including hood and mittens, with the fur inside
milìtsiya	civil police
muzhchìna	man
noàid	shaman of eastern Lapland
nomenklatura	members of the higher political echelons under the Soviet system
Oblast	County or Province, usually loosely translated as 'Region'
OMON	Special Purpose Militia, established in 1987
oprìchnina/ oprìchniki	special territorial and administrative domain established by Ivan the Terrible. The *oprìchniki* elite eventually abused their status and acquired a reputation for brutality
ostròg	fortified town, settlement or trading post
payk (Saami)	territory of a group of families, comprising several seasonal encampments, known as *seity*
pelmèni	a kind of ravioli
perestroika	lit. restructuring. The process of social and economic change that resulted from Communist Party Secretary Gorbachev's policies of the 1980s
pirozhòk/piròzhki	pie or pasty (which seldom lives up to its reputation as a national delicacy)
pogòst	archaic Novgorod word erroneously used by Russians to mean Saami winter home/settlement, or *seit*
polyarky	lit. polars. The premium earned in the Soviet Union by those working north of the Arctic Circle
Pomor	lit. by the sea (*po more*). The name given to those who came from medieval Novgorod and Karelia to settle the White Sea and Lapland coasts. Now also used in a self-promotional context, implying motivation and a high work-ethic
provòdnik/ provòdnitsa	guard on a train or superintendent of a sleeping car
ryumka	small drinking glass, usually shot-glass for spirit
sàlo	fat, usually cured pork fat
sarafàn	Russian woman's traditional dress, without sleeves, buttoning in front
sarày	shed/sheds
seid (Saami)	holy stone or rock venerated by Saami, often large and prominent, sometimes anthropomorphic
seit (Saami)	(in Russian Lapland perhaps more 'correctly' transliterated as *syyyt*; also known as *siit, siid, sijd*). One of several seasonal settlements within a territory or *payk*. Hence *tallv seit*, winter settlement; *letniy seit*, summer encampment; *chekhg seit*, autumn encampment

Glossary

seni	unheated multi-purpose entrance room between outer and inner entrance doors, used particularly for boots and outdoor clothing, and for the storage of food, skins and equipment
shamshùr (Saami)	low cylindrical hat, usually embroidered and beaded
shashlỳk	small pieces of meat grilled on a skewer
shchi	cabbage or vegetable soup, often embellished with a meat-bone and *smetana*
shnyak	single-masted smack of up to 15 metres in length, favoured by the Pomors both for coastal fishing and the open sea
smetàna	soured cream
sovìk	thick woollen smock, sometimes with a hood, popular in summer and winter
spetspereselèntsy	lit. special settlers. Those forcibly resettled during the Soviet era, usually to new industrial or mining towns
spirt	spirit or high-grade alcohol, often diluted with water as a vodka substitute
SSBN	strategic ballistic missile submarine, nuclear-powered
SSGN	cruise missile-firing submarine, nuclear-powered
SSN	fleet (attack) submarine, nuclear-powered
stalìnka	standard concrete, five-storey apartment building of the Stalin era
UAZ	Ulyanov Automobile Factory
vàlenki	felt boots
vezdekhòd	lit. go-everywhere-vehicle. A tracked tank-like vehicle but without a gun turret
vezhà	Saami home constructed from a framework of timber covered with birch-bark, turf and branches
yuròdivy	'God's Fool' or idiot, believed to possess a divine gift of prophecy
ZATO	Closed Administrative-Territorial Formation or closed military town
zavàrnik	small 'brewing' teapot
zek	slang, derived from *zaklyuchennyy* or prisoner

Further Reading

Murmansk Oblast played an important economic and strategic role in European Russia throughout the twentieth century; its scientific bibliography is therefore extensive. There are, however, no English language publications that offer an overview of its natural and human history. Nor, inconveniently, are there any English language journals that have consistently treated particular issues concerning the region. An extended version of the present bibliography, including Russian language titles, is available at the library of the Scott Polar Research Institute, Cambridge University.

The region at a glance
Utrolige Kola [Incredible Kola] (Kirkenes, Norway: Kappelens, 1994), edited by Kare Tannvik with a parallel English text, is an amply illustrated general survey with six authoritative essays on the region today.

Geology and mineralogy
The scientific bibliographies, particularly on mineralogy, are huge, but no non-specialist publication in English or Russian captures the whole region's geology and mineralogy between two covers. Igor Pekov, *Lovozero massif: history, pegmatites, minerals* (Moscow: Ocean Pictures, 2000) offers a lavishly illustrated and relatively comprehensible insight into the wonderful world of geology, if only for one particular geological occurrence.

Lapps/Saami
The best known of the early sources for the Lapps (Saami) are Tacitus' *Germania* of AD 98 (see J.B. Rives, *Tacitus Germania*, Oxford: Clarendon Press, 1999) and Saxo Grammaticus' *Gesta Danorum*, c. 1208 (tr. Oliver Elton, London: David Nutt, 1894).

Perhaps the most enjoyable reading of all is the still-unrivalled *Historia de gentibus septentrionalibus* by Olaus Magnus (Venice, 1539), which is copiously illustrated with woodcuts and a large separate pictorial map, and marvellously animates the entire life-cycle of the Lapps (available in translation in the *Journal of the Hakluyt Society*, 2nd series, vols 182, 187, 188). Johann Scheffer's famous *Lapponia* of 1673 (published in translation in Oxford in 1674) is a valuable contemporaneous summary of Lapland studies.

An early specific mention of eastern (later Russian) Lapland is made by the Viking chieftain Othere, who regularly circumnavigated the Peninsula to enter the White Sea in the ninth century. His journeys, recounted to King Alfred of Wessex and included in Alfred's Anglo-Saxon version of Orosius' *World history*, c. 880 (London: Joseph Bosworth, 1855) provide some of the first descriptions of coastal Lapps as they trapped, fished, hunted sea mammals and traded.

Saami studies were pursued internationally from the 1930s as academic interest in indigenous peoples gathered pace (by the 1960s they had generated a minor industry) and the bibliographies are extensive and accessible. General surveys, none of which makes more than a mention of the Russian Lapps, include: Roberto Bosi, *The Lapps*, London: Thames and Hudson, 1960; Ernst Manker, *People of eight seasons*, English edition, London: C.A. Watts, 1965; Walter Marsden, *Lapland*, Amsterdam: Time Life, 1976; and Arthur Spencer, *The Lapps*, New York: Crane, Russack, 1978.

On the Russian Saami, see: Tim Ingold, *The Skolt Lapps today*, Cambridge University Press, 1976; Tatyana Lukyanchenko, 'Lapps in the Soviet Union' in N. Broadbent (ed.), *Readings in Saami history, culture and language*, Umea: Centre for Arctic Cultural Research, 1989; and Leif Rantala, 'The Russian Saami of today' in Bjorklund, Moller and Reymert (eds), *The Barents Region*, University of Tromso, 1995. For a brief introduction to issues of Saami land rights, see: John Henriksen, 'The legal status of Saamiland rights in Finland, Russia, Norway and Sweden', *Indigenous Affairs*, 2, 1996.

The early settlement of eastern Lapland

Lars Ivar Hansen's *Interaction between Northern European sub-arctic societies during the Middle Ages* (Oslo: Research Council of Norway. Research Programme for Culture and Tradition, paper no. 66, 1996) is a detailed and riveting account of the movements of early medieval peoples near and into southern and eastern Lapland. Terence Armstrong's classic *Russian settlement of the North* (Cambridge University Press, 1965), pp. 9–14, describes Novgorod's colonization of the White Sea.

On the early fur trade between the Hanse, Novgorod and the Lapps, see: Robert Kerner, *The urge to the sea*, New York: Russell and Russell, 1971; and Janet Martin, *Treasure of the land of darkness*, Cambridge University Press, 1986.

Adventurers and explorers

Willoughby and Chancellor's famous and fated 1553 attempt at the northern sea route to Cathay (China), which resulted in the establishment of the Muscovy Company and regular marine traffic between Western Europe and Russia, is recounted by Samuel Purchas (*Hakluytus Posthumus, or Purchas his Pilgrimes*, London, 1625) and Richard Hakluyt (*Principal navigations, voyages and discoveries of the English nation*, London, 1589–1600).

Further Reading

Russian Lapland in the late nineteenth century

For an overview of the region's burgeoning society and economy prior to Bolshevism, see: Alexander Engelhardt, *A Russian province of the North*, London: Constable, 1899; Theodor Homen et al., *East Karelia and Kola Lappmark*, Helsingfors and London, 1921.

Edward Rae of Birkenhead, who circumnavigated the Kola Peninsula and met Lapps, Pomors and Russians during the summer of 1879, gives a vivid account of the region during this period (*The White Sea Peninsula*, London: John Murray, 1881). See also: Henry Pearson, *Three summers among the birds of Russian Lapland*, London: Porter, 1904.

The Komi-Izhemets migration

For the immigration of the Komi-Izhemets from the late 1880s, and for questions of the legitimacy of their settlement among the Saami, see: Z.I. Bryleva, 'The history of the Kola Peninsular Komi-Izhemets' in I. Seurujarvi-Kari and U.-M. Kulonen (eds), *Essays on indigenous identity and rights*, Helsinki University Press, 1996.

Civil War and the Allied Intervention

The events of 1918–20, when the Allies fought alongside the 'White' Russians south of Murmansk and Archangel, bred contention among Russians and Allies alike for more than 70 years. They are now (2002) a hot topic of investigation among historians of both sides. For a British military view of the confrontations in Russian Lapland and Karelia, see Major-General Sir Charles Maynard, *The Murmansk venture*, London: Hodder & Stoughton, 1928. Edward Halliday's account of the Archangel front (*The ignorant armies*, London: Weidenfeld & Nicolson, 1961) is thoroughly researched from the American point of view, and is a good read.

All Soviet writing was of limited value until the recent work of Vladislav Goldin, who publishes almost entirely in Russian. See, inter alia: V. Goldin, 'The Russian Revolution and the North', *International politics*, 33, 1998.

Communism, collectivization, slave labour and the Saami clearances

Terence Armstrong's *Russian settlement in the North* (Cambridge, 1965) gives the wider political and socio-economic scene in which Russian Lapland was developed and forcibly settled by the Communists from the 1920s. A classic study of the GULag prison camp system is David Dalin and Boris Nikolayevsky's *Forced labour in Soviet Russia* (New Haven: Yale University Press, 1947). On the Soviet 'reforms' of Northern peoples, see: Yuri Slezkine, *Arctic mirrors: Russia and the small peoples of the North*, Ithaca: Cornell University Press, 1994.

The Russian Saami experience in the face of the northern reforms and clearances is exampled briefly by Marju Sarv, 'Changes in the social life of the Kola Saami' in I. Seurujarvi-Kari and U.-M. Kulonen (eds), *Essays on indigenous identity and rights*, Helsinki University Press, 1996.

Further Reading

The 'Winter War' or 'Border War' with Finland, and the Great Patriotic War

For the Soviet Union's 1939–40 invasion of Finland see, inter alia: Richard Condon, *The Winter War: Russia against Finland*, New York: Ballantine, 1972.

Richard Woodman's well-researched *Arctic convoys* (London: John Murray, 1994) contains perhaps the best account of the Murmansk convoys and of Russian and Allied wartime life in the town and port of Murmansk itself. It can profitably be read alongside Hubert Griffith's *RAF in Russia* (London: Hammond, 1942), which recounts the experiences of the RAF Wing dispatched to train Russian pilots to fly Spitfires and Hurricanes in 1941.

Circumpolar geopolitics, the military and the Northern Fleet

Denis Snowman, *Pole positions: the polar regions and the future of the planet* (London: Hodder and Stoughton, 1993) places north-west Russia in the context of twentieth-century Arctic politics.

On the region's military presence, see: T. Ries and J. Skorve, *Investigating Kola: a study of military bases using satellite photography*, London: Brassey's Defence Publishers, 1982; and Geir Honneland and Anne-Kristin Jorgensen, *Integration vs. autonomy: civil-military relations on the Kola Peninsula*, Aldershot: Ashgate, 1999, which focuses on the military's social and structural challenges.

Thomas Nilsen, Igor Kudrik, and Aleksandr Nikitin, *The Russian Northern Fleet* (Oslo: Bellona Foundation, 1996) is the report which reached the world and helped change the course of jurisprudence in Russia. The Bellona website is at http://www.bellona.no

Environmental contamination and health

G.E. Vilchek et al., 'The environment in the Russian Arctic' (*Polar Geography*, 20, 1996) gives the all-North Russia viewpoint. AMAP Norway's *Arctic pollution issues: a state of the Arctic environment report* (Oslo: Arctic Monitoring and Assessment Programme, 1997) can also be downloaded from their website: http://www.amap.no

Airborne pollution from the oblast's nickel smelters was extensively monitored in the 1990s and documented in specialist articles. A good layperson's guide to the terrestrial damages is Eero Tikkanen and Irja Niemeia, *Kola Peninsula pollutants and forest ecosystems in Lapland* (Helsinki: Ministry of Agriculture and Forestry, 1995).

The Bellona Foundation's reports that address the threat of nuclear contamination from the Northern Fleet are essential and compelling reading: Thomas Nilsen and Nils Bøhmer, *Sources of radioactive pollution in Murmansk and Archangel Counties*, 1994; and Bøhmer, Nikitin, Kudrik, Nilsen, McGovern and Zolotkov, *The Arctic nuclear challenge*, 2001. Those who are forever confused between ballistic missiles and cruise missiles, Start Treaties and North Atlantic Treaties should read Steven Sawhill and Ann-Kristin Jorgensen, *Military nuclear waste and international cooperation in north-west Russia* (Lysaker, Oslo: Fridtjof Hansen Institute, 2001).

The journal *Barentswatch* (published by Svanhovd Environmental Centre, Svanvik, Norway) contains colour-illustrated articles on environmental matters written by professionals in lay language.

351

Further Reading

Reindeer herding

Reindeer are at the cultural and emotional heart of the tundra-related communities, and reindeer herding today, more than ever, has strong potential for improving living conditions for northern peoples. Reindeer herding on the Kola Peninsula, however, is in a critical state. See: Hugh Beach, 'Reindeer herding on the Kola Peninsula: report of a visit with Saami herders of Sovkhov Tundra' in Minority Rights Group (eds), *Polar peoples: self-determination and development*, London: Minority Rights Publications, 1994; Yulian Konstantinov, 'Field research of reindeer herding on the Kola Peninsula: problems and challenges', *Acta Borealia*, 2, 1996; Yulian Konstantinov, 'Memory of Lenin Ltd: the reindeer-herding brigades of the Kola Peninsula', *Anthropology Today*, 13, 3, 1997; Caroline Humphrey, 'The Domestic Mode of Production in Post-Soviet Siberia?', *Anthropology Today*, 14, 3, 1998; and Yulian Konstantinov, 'Sovkhoz: pre-Soviet pasts of a Soviet concept', *Acta Borealia*, 2, 2000.

Murmansk oblast and the new century

Mumansk Oblast envisions its future as a partner of the Barents Euro-Arctic Region (BEAR). See: O.S. Stokke and O. Tunander, *The Barents region: cooperation in Arctic Europe*, Oslo: International Peace Research Institute, and London: Sage, 1994; Rune Castberg, 'The Kola Peninsula: the restructuring of a regional post-Soviet economy and its foreign trade relations', *International Challenges*, 12, 1992; and J.A. Dellenbrandt and O. Andreyev, 'Russian politics in transition: political parties and organisations in Russia and the Murmansk Region', *Scandinavian Political Studies*, 1994. The reality may be otherwise.

The following articles, which have useful bibliographies, give an invaluable overview of current social conditions: Erik Hansen, *Living conditions on the Kola Peninsula*, Oslo: FAFO-SOTECO Report no. 155, 1993; Yulian Konstantinov, *The Northern Sea Route and local communities in north-west Russia: social impact assessment for Murmansk Region*, International Sea Route Programame (INSROP) working paper 152, Oslo: Fridtjof Nansen Institute, 1999; and Indra Nobl Overland, 'Politics and culture among the Russian Saami: ethnopolitics and legitimacy', Cambridge: Scott Polar Research Institute (PhD thesis), 2000.

A journalistic compilation of views of contemporary life in the eight 'counties' of the four Barents Region countries is Gert Frost and Valery Lemesov (eds), *A time of change: people and life in the Barents Region* (Ostersund: National Rural Development Agency, 1998).

* * *

The Scott Polar Research Institute (SPRI) at Cambridge University and the London Library between them hold much of the above material. SPRI has a dedicated Russia bibliographer.

Acknowledgements

I found Russian Lapland a difficult country to understand but fascinating to explore, both in its towns and in its wild places. I am very aware that my portrayal of the region is a personal one to which some people, including Saami and Russians, will take exception. And foreigners coming after me may find a very different place from that which I have described. The defence I offer to confused or offended parties is that my idiosyncrasies can at least claim to enjoy a certain historical framework, and that I have acquired a genuine affection for the place.

My thanks go first of all to Yevgeniya Yakovlevna Patsiya, historian and curator at the Museum for the Exploration of the Russian European North, Apatity, who turned my innocent adventure into serious historical enquiry, and then shared her knowledge with open and unstinting generosity for several years. The librarians and bibliographers of Murmansk Oblast Library, in particular Yelena Rudolvovna Mikhaylova, Svetlana Alekseyevna Savilova, and Galina Mikhaylovna Suleymanova, left no stone unturned in response to my questions, and worked me harder than I had ever intended. At Murmansk Regional Museum, director Olga Moyseyevna Demidenko, Tatyana Aleksandrovna Timashenko and Irina Vasilyevna Shevchuk must be singled out for their prompt and professional assistance. Igor Viktorovich Pekov at the Faculty of Geology, Moscow State University kindly checked my chapter on the mineralogy of the Khibiny and Lovozero massifs.

I explored much of remote Russian Lapland in the company of Ivan Vasilevich Vdovin, director of the museum at Revda, Murmansk Oblast. Vdovin, an ideal expedition colleague and my favoured travel companion of recent years, helped me unstintingly with almost everything, and over the years I learned much from him and from other colleagues of the Field Research Group for Kola North/Russian Lapland.

Some of the people in Russia who helped me on my way have in effect been thanked within the pages of this book. Unsung angels include: Praskovya Serapiyonovna Artiyeva, Yekaterina Alekseyevna Balakshina, Valeriya Valerevna Bognibova, Edvard Ivanovich Dombay, Antonina Maksimovna Khamyuk, Galina Aleksandrovna Khoreva, Roman Aleksandrovich Kravchenko-Berezhnoy, Zinaida Ivanovna Makarova, Marina Nikolayevna Matskevich, Vlada Nesterova, Anna Olegovna Novoselova, Sergey and Alla Osokin, Aleksandr Nikolayevich Rusinov,

Acknowledgements

Olga Vyacheslavovna Shabalina, Viktor Treferov, and Yevgeny Rubimovich Zagatsky. Certain names, locations and situations have been changed or disguised for legal and security reasons or in order to protect personal sensibilities.

Sergey Sergeyevich Shuvalov, Anzhelika Anatolyevna Pedchenko, Irina Cherkova, Mikhail Mikhaylovich Kalenchenko and Yevgeny Alekseyevich Galchenko assisted most ably and tactfully with interpretation, translation or administration.

Many people outside Russia also helped. They include: Francis Herbert and David McNeill at the Royal Geographical Society Map Room; all the RGS librarians; Helen O'Connor at the Britain-Russia Centre; Librarian Shirley Sawtell and bibliographer Isabella Warren at the Scott Polar Research Institute, Cambridge University; Stephen Sawtell and Olga Tutubalina, both postgraduate students at the same institution; Kirstin Seaver, Stanford University; and Terry Williams, Natural History Museum, London. The Bellona Foundation were characteristically helpful and Thomas Nilsen, co-author of the famous Bellona reports on the Northern Fleet, especially so. Indra Nobl Overland, whose Cambridge University doctoral thesis of the year 2000 is a valuable socio-political study of present-day Russian Saami, was perceptively critical and encouraging during all the later stages of my writing.

Much of this book is the result of field research made possible with the assistance of the Royal Geographical Society, the Rufford Foundation, the Whitley Awards Foundation, WEXAS International, and the RGS Expeditions Office.

I am grateful to the following for reading copy at various stages: Peter Baird, Patricia Cleary (the shrewdest critic of all), Charles Gowlland, Lai Ping Lee, Gerald Lyons, Indra Nobl Overland, Su Snodin, and my brother J.M.E. Took.

Gail Pirkis at John Murray instilled confidence from the start and displayed remarkable powers of incubation throughout the creative process. Antony Wood cast experienced Russianist eyes over my typescript and adeptly undertook the necessary editorial surgery with dedication and affection – life by a million cuts. To both, my thanks.

Roger Took
Baile ui Fhiachain
Chontae Maigh Eo
Eire
May 2002

354

INDEX

Index